UNDERSTANDING
POLITICAL IDEAS
AND MOVEMENTS

MANCHESTER
UNIVERSITY PRESS

UNDERSTANDING POLITICS

Series editor **DUNCAN WATTS**

Following the review of the national curriculum for
16–19 year olds, UK examining boards introduced
new specifications, first used in 2001 and 2002.
A level courses are now divided into A/S level for the
first year of sixth-form studies, and the more difficult
A2 level thereafter. The **Understanding Politics**
series comprehensively covers the politics syllabuses
of all the major examination boards, featuring a
dedicated A/S level textbook and five books
aimed at A2 students. The books are written in an
accessible, user-friendly and jargon-free manner
and will be essential to students sitting these
examinations.

Already published

**Understanding American government and
politics**
Duncan Watts

**Understanding A/S level government and
politics**
Chris Wilson

Understanding
political ideas
and movements

A guide for A2 politics students

KEVIN HARRISON and TONY BOYD

Manchester University Press

Manchester and New York

distributed exclusively in the USA by Palgrave

Published by Manchester University Press
Oxford Road, Manchester M13 9NR, UK
and Room 400, 175 Fifth Avenue, New York, NY 10010, USA
www.manchesteruniversitypress.co.uk

Distributed exclusively in the USA by
Palgrave, 175 Fifth Avenue, New York,
NY 10010, USA

Distribued exclusively in Canada by
UBC Press, University of British Columbia, 2029 West Mall,
Vancouver, BC, Canada V6T 1Z2

British Library Cataloguing-in-Publication Data
A catalogue record for this book is available from the British Library

Library of Congress Cataloging-in-Publication Data applied for

ISBN 0 7190 6151 2   *paperback*

First published 2003

11   10   09   08   07   06   05   04   03   10 9 8 7 6 5 4 3 2 1

Typeset by Northern Phototypesetting Co. Ltd, Bolton
Printed in Great Britain
by Bell & Bain Ltd, Glasgow

Contents

Preface and acknowledgements

The contents of this book, and its general structure, have been very largely governed by the aim of fulfilling the various examining board syllabuses for GCE Government and Politics A2 level. It is particularly relevant to OCR (Module 7), 'UK Politics and Modern Political Ideas: Theory and Practice'; EDEXCEL Route B (Units 4, 5 and 6), 'Political Ideologies'; AQA (Module 7), 'Ideas in Contemporary British Politics'; and AQA (Module 8), 'Government and Politics – Synoptic Module'.

The book should also be relevant to a broad range of Open College Network Level Three Access courses in Political Ideas, Political Studies or Modern Political Movements, and introductory undergraduate courses in Politics.

We hope that people not studying for examinations will find this book of use in helping them understand the political world and the assumptions that shape the clatter and chatter of those who presume to govern us.

We must gratefully acknowledge those who have made a contribution to this book: Erik Olive for his cynical and amusing comments on a number of chapters and Angela Dale, who took on the daunting task of correcting grammar and spelling and untangling the meaning of the more complicated sentences. Our heartfelt thanks to them both. Our sincere thanks to family, friends and colleagues for tolerating us in normal times and even more so as the book moved towards its completion.

Finally, we would like to dedicate this book to Tony Ivers, our late friend and colleague, who is much missed.

Kevin Harrison
Tony Boyd

THE POLITICS ASSOCIATION

is a registered educational charity, committed to the diffusion of political knowledge and understanding. It produces a wide range of resources on government and politics, and on citizenship. Members receive the journal, *Talking Politics*, three times a year.

Further details can be obtained from the Politics Association, Old Hall Lane, Manchester, M13 0XT, Tel./Fax.: 0161 256 3906; email: politic@enablis.co.uk

Introduction

(W)e should try to grasp, in outline at any rate, what the good is, and which science or capacity is concerned with it.

It seems to concern the most controlling science, the one that, more than any other is the master science. And political science apparently has this character. (Aristotle, *Nicomachean Ethics*, Book 1:2)

A good politician is quite as unthinkable as an honest burglar. (H. L. Mencken, *Prejudices*, 1925)

Readers will peruse this book in vain if they seek an outline of the British political system, discussion on comparative government, identification of the structure and roles of parties and pressure groups in modern democracies, or even detailed discussions of the major thinkers and philosophers in the Western political tradition. Neither will they find a guide to the detailed policies of the major political movements in Britain and other liberal democracies.

In liberal democracies there is a belief that citizens ought to take an active interest in what is happening in the political world. It is a view that the authors of this book share. For generations, people have fought and died for the right to put a cross on a piece of paper (or some other means of recording a vote) in countries such as the UK. In far too many countries the sort of views about the government that we regularly express in Britain land people in prison – or worse. We strongly believe that you, as a citizen, should take an interest in politics; after all, even if you don't, you can rest assured that politics will take an interest in you! During your lifetime you will be taxed, observed, regulated and, potentially, conscripted into Her Majesty's armed forces. You are likely to be educated in state schools, colleges and universities, be treated at state-run hospitals by state-trained doctors and nurses when ill, and claim state benefits when unemployed, sick or retired.

Political debate in modern Western democracies is a complex and often rowdy affair. It often gives the impression that it involves little thought and contemplation beyond shouting and opposing whatever the other side proposes as the solution to the ills of society. Indeed, it may have contributed to declining voter turnout in most Western democracies. Some recent studies showed that voter 'apathy' during the record low turnout in the 2001 general election may have little to do with apathy and much to do with voter *disappointment* in politicians and the political process. The 'yah-boo' behaviour of some Westminster politicians does, nevertheless, reflect the intense passions that politics can elicit from its participants. Think about what politicians carry around as their intellectual baggage when they are discussing – shouting about – some of the following questions:

- How much should be spent on health, education, welfare, defence and transport? Should key services and industries be within the public sector, owned by 'the people' or 'the nation' – in fact, by 'the state' – or would these be more efficiently provided by the private sector of the economy?
- Is being motivated by the values of 'public service' likely to produce better value for money in such services than the 'profit motive' of private business?
- What should be the levels of taxation in order to fund these services?
- What is the proper role of the state in society? What are the proper limits on its powers?
- Are there areas of private life, such as religion and conscience, into which the state should not intrude? Or does the survival of the society and the crucial role of the state in ensuring this mean that in times of war and economic crisis the individual and his or her liberty may have to be sacrificed for the greater good? What do 'freedom' and 'equality', 'rights' and 'obligations', in the political community mean?
- Is democracy the best means by which such desirable goals can be achieved? Indeed, what is meant by democracy?
- How 'democratic' are Western democracies?
- Can politics have a moral basis, or is it merely the pursuit of power?

One could go on listing questions that exercise the mind of the active citizen. Indeed, you might believe that this list of questions has already gone too far. If, however, you've ever talked about any of these issues with your friends and family, if you are concerned with what sort of country you want to live in, what sort of future you, your friends, family and future generations might have, then you will have thought about these issues, and will want to pursue your ideas further.

We do not presume to provide answers to these questions. We hope only to provide the *beginnings* of a structure of core ideas and concepts that overtly or covertly influence the political debate in countries such as ours. We believe that much voter disillusionment about politics and politicians stems from the failure of political and educational systems to provide voters with the intellectual tools to analyse the vitally important issues that shape our lives and prospects.

Politics is a messy business, often full of 'grey' areas when one seeks clear answers to the problems of the moment. The complexity of political issues is revealed in most of the chapters of this book. A great deal of politics is, as one ancient philosopher declared, about defining terms and then applying them to society. There is a statement at the beginning of almost every chapter, for example, that warns the reader that this or that concept is 'contested', 'open to considerable debate and argument' or 'a difficult one to grasp'.

Having said so much already about politics as a way of introducing the book, we will look at three fundamental terms – politics, power and justice – and provide an outline of the chapters.

Three fundamental terms: politics, power and justice

There are three fundamental political issues which appear in all the chapters of this book and feature in almost all political discussions and conflicts. These are 'politics', 'power' and 'justice'.

Politics

It may at first sight seem superfluous to define 'politics': the word is in common use and everyone knows what it means. In fact there is more than one way of describing politics and exploration of these different approaches can cast a useful light on the nature of the topic. Supposedly value-free definitions often reveal submerged ideological preconceptions.

Michael Oakeshott, in *Rationalism in Politics* (1962), focuses on the derivation of the word: *politiki* in Greek, *res publicae* in Latin, refers to 'affairs of state'. This superficially straightforward definition implies that there are some things which are *not* 'affairs of state', but belong to the personal, private or civil realm. This is a view that Oakeshott himself held. For Oakeshott, personal and family life was the stuff of existence; ordinary people rightly gave little attention to politics. Liberals, like the traditionalist Oakeshott, identify a private space into which the state has no right to enter. An invasion of this private space by the state appears, to liberals, the essence of tyranny.

In marked contrast, Aristotle famously observed in his *Politics* that 'man is a political animal'; thus, it was entirely appropriate for rational human beings to involve themselves fully in political matters. Totalitarian regimes, like that of the Soviet Union and Nazi Germany, have similarly dismissed all ideas that the individual has a life, with its own value, outside the realm of the political. As the Italian Fascist thinker Giovanni Gentile declared: 'Everything for the state; nothing against the state; nothing outside the state.' Feminist writers also reject distinctions between the political and the personal worlds, as they believe that politics is about power and the most intense power conflicts and greatest oppression lie precisely in the personal relations of men and women.

In private it is not easy to disentangle the political from the non-political. If the state takes an interest in a matter, then it becomes 'political'. The state's interest can vary dramatically from culture to culture and over the centuries. Some states, for example, impose rigid laws governing dress, recreational activities, sexual relationships and the consumption of alcohol. In other societies these are not believed to be the concern of the state to any great degree. At present, the use of recreational drugs is illegal in Britain but in the future it might cease to be so. Thus what is political may be said to expand and contract depending on whether or not the state involves itself in different aspects of social life.

So far we have assumed, without spelling it out, that the essence of politics is something to do with government. But in ordinary speech it is common to refer to 'office politics', 'college politics', 'church politics', usually pejoratively, and implying machinations.

Bernard Crick's in *In Defence of Politics* (1962), approached the matter from another angle by proposing that politics is a process, a means of resolving conflict by peaceful means. Such conflict may well be at the level of the state but need not be so. Politics can refer to international conflict, 'parish pump' disputes in local government, and industrial strife. Crick assumes differences among people – differences of opinion, differences of values, differences of interests. This, for him, is a basic fact of human existence. Politics deals with this fundamental fact by seeking to resolve the resulting conflicts by rational and peaceful means. Politics requires tolerance, rational discourse, preparedness to compromise, democratically accountable institutions and procedures, and, crucially, an acceptance of an authoritative pronouncement of the outcome. 'Politics' in this sense would be clearly evident in a general election, where parties (with their distinctive programmes, principles and interests) compete in a lawful and orderly manner to obtain votes and so gain dominance in the legislature.

The weakness of this position is that it resembles a sophisticated debating society, and has little application to the real world except perhaps as an ideal of what democratic politics is about. It assumes that politics cannot function except in a liberal democratic context. It thus excludes not only dictatorships and other autocracies but also even the political life of actual democracies where strikes, pressures of all kinds, even perhaps including terrorism, influence events as much as dispassionate dialogues. It is difficult, for instance, to fit the politics of Northern Ireland into Crick's framework. Politics there involves a very wide range of democratic and violent elements that clearly influence both the political culture and the processes in the province.

A more robust approach was that of Harold Lasswell. In *Politics: Who Gets What, When, How?* (1931), Lasswell bluntly asserts that politics is about power and is a study of power relationships. It is the task of political scientists to reveal where power really lies, how it is exercised, by whom and for what purposes.

Attractive though this no-nonsense approach may seem, critics have argued that it is two-dimensional. A third dimension is required and that is 'authority'. This point is persuasively put by David Easton in *The Political System* (1953), where he argues that politics is about the 'authoritative allocation of values'. He makes an important distinction between legislative authority and mere force. A dictator may impose his will by the gun or propaganda but this is not a legitimate use of power. Authoritative politics requires legitimate authority.

There may, of course, be dispute as to what constitutes legitimate authority, and what the sources of such authority are. Max Weber, in *Economy and Society* (1922), described three different types of authority: 'rational legal' (the outcome of accepted procedures such as elections, parliaments, constitutions), 'traditional' (the result of history and custom, such as that of tribal elders, kings and other rules), and 'charismatic' (the product of the personal qualities of a leader). Actual political systems involve more than one of these sources.

For Marxists the whole idea of 'legitimate' politics is a sham. Authority is merely a disguise for power, a disguise invented and manipulated by the ruling class the better to dominate and exploit the proletariat. There is, however, a certain ambiguity in the Marxist position. If politics is an instrument of class oppression, it is also an instrument of class liberation, a component in the struggle by which the workers will eventually overthrow the capitalist class and the instruments of their power. This having been achieved, and communism having been successfully established, 'politics' would cease to exist. Pre-communist politics is interpreted as being about class conflict and material scarcity. Such undesirable conditions will be superseded and fade away together with the instruments of state oppression, government, the army, the police and the judiciary. Presumably there will still be some public discussion on the best course of action in the post-capitalist society but it will not be *politics* as we have known it.

There is a persistent tendency in democracies to regard politics as somehow disreputable, unclean, a 'dirty' business. In part this is due to the perceived dishonesty of politicians, who are all 'in it for themselves', manipulating the electorate by mendacious propaganda, making promises that will not be kept, and general skulduggery. Parties are perceived by a cynical electorate as conspiracies against the public good. Such negative views can be heard in every bar-room in the country. Another strand in this anti-politics thesis, though, appears to be distaste for conflict itself. Even quite sophisticated commentators sometimes suggest that important national matters, such as education or defence, should be 'outside' or 'above' politics.

Public opinion polls regularly place politicians below estate agents and double-glazing salesmen in terms of trust, a view radically different from the ancient ideal, as enunciated by Aristotle, which did not mean everyone was naturally interested in politics but that participation in public affairs was appropriate to man's dignity and moral identity – an entirely praiseworthy activity.

In the Middle Ages, Saint Augustine, in *The City of God* (413–27), regarded the state and politics as little more than a regrettable necessity ('the badge of Man's lost innocence') and an instrument of maintaining order. Thomas Aquinas, writing in the thirteenth century, claimed a more positive role for the political activity within the state. That role was the promotion of justice. From this perspective, politics may be regarded as a branch of ethics – the study of what is right.

Focusing on morality in politics has been a feature of political ideologies, government decisions and party campaigners to the present day. Discourse on 'ends' or values, and the morality (not just practicality) of 'means' is a fundamental dimension of politics and is inherent in its very meaning. Descriptions of political systems solely in terms of power relationships and the conflict of interests would, from this perspective, seem quite inadequate.

Niccolo Machiavelli, in *The Prince* (1513), explained how to win and hold power. It was a book that notoriously ignored all moral considerations and was justly condemned, according to many modern political scientists, not because it was wicked or untrue but because it was one-dimensional.

Man is unique in being a social animal. Whereas a colony of baboons exhibits, perhaps embarrassingly, many attributes of human society such as hierarchy, conflict, the emergence of leaders, co-operation, even collective action, it lacks rational debate, discussion, compromise, principle, commitment, analysis and justice. Politics is missing, even if power patently exists in baboon society.

Power

Politics is primarily about the acquisition and maintenance of power. Power is inherent in the relationships between individuals, groups, the state and a wide range of what are known as 'actors' in international politics. Power is the underlying concept in political science, a concept that runs through any discussion on the state, the nation, democracy, freedom, equality and the ideologies and movements that mould history. Like the other major concepts and ideologies discussed in this book, the definition of 'power' remains a source of dispute.

At a fundamental level politics is about who gets power, what they do with it, how legitimate is its exercise, and on whom the power is exercised. All thinkers about politics agree that power involves one actor affecting the actions and attitudes of another. As Denis Healey, a leading British Labour politician, once brutally stated: 'Power is the capacity one has to help one's friends and to harm one's enemies.' The existence and use of power is not confined to the world of politics. Power exists wherever there are social relations: within families, between employer and employee, between friends, in the 'sex war' between men and women, and between racial and ethnic groups. Power is everywhere and affects every political calculation. To ignore it or pretend that it doesn't exist is to invite disaster, or at least guarantee that political goals will not be achieved.

Let us now look at some major thinkers and their ideas about power.

Thomas Hobbes

Living through the turmoil of the civil wars in Britain and the Thirty Years' War in Europe, Hobbes was acutely aware of the importance of power in maintaining a stable political system and the terrible consequences when government lacked sufficient power to enforce order and obedience in society. Power to Hobbes was a relationship of cause and effect, between an 'agent' who has power to produce an effect and a 'patient' who is the passive object of that power. Agents seek to satisfy their desires. Mankind, according to Hobbes in *Leviathan* (1651), is involved in 'a perpetuall and restlesse desire of Power after power that ceaseth onely in Death'. Without government, in a state of nature, such a power struggle would lead to a perpetual state of war. Only by establishing an effective supreme power of the sovereign could the chaotic 'state of nature' be brought to an end and peace be established. The legitimacy, the 'right', of the sovereign to rule is founded on the effectiveness with which such order is established and maintained. If a sovereign fails to maintain sufficient power to ensure order then his legitimacy disappears.

Karl Marx

Marx's voluminous writings may all be described as analysing power. He believes power to be a reflection of class and economic relations in society. Marx makes a distinction between the reality of power, as understood in terms of property ownership and the political power that derives from that ownership, and the representation of power as seen in the 'false consciousness' of individuals, groups or classes who believe their perceived interests are the same as their real interests. The state, the legal system, education, religion and the new media are all tools by which the power of the property owning classes over the working classes is upheld.

Max Weber

In *Economy and Society* (1922) Weber defined power as 'the possibility that one actor in a social relationship . . . will carry out his own will' against others who will be resisting. To Weber, power is something one either possesses or does not. Those who have power use it to further their interests and goals over the objections and resistance of others who do not have power. Power is always organised in a hierarchical structure, Weber observes, and its processes are always clear to see, with some people near the top of the hierarchy giving orders to those below them. This will be the case in government and state bureaucracies, businesses and families, with power being demonstrated in various forms of supervision and control by those in charge. The right to exercise power legitimately rests on the authority and status of individuals at different levels within power structures in society. Legitimacy derives from authority conferred by a job title, such as foreman or manager in a factory, and by religious and social mores, such as those that underpin the position of parents within a family.

Steven Lukes

In his *Power: A Radical View* (1974) Lukes identifies a number of approaches to understanding the nature of power.

The 'one-dimensional view' of Robert Dahl in *Who Governs? Democracy and Power in an American City* (1961) and *Modern Political Analysis* (1963) concentrates on decision-making as the central task of politics and the need to identify 'who prevails in the decision-making process' in order to determine which groups and individuals have power in society.

The 'two-dimensional view' of power is discussed by Peter Bachrach and Martin Baratz in *Power and Poverty: Theory and Practice* (1970), who state that power has two 'Janus-like' faces. One face of power is overt and observable; the other is covert or hidden from view. The lack of challenge to overt power may not mean that there is in fact no challenge, but that covert forms of power may be being used very effectively. Thus two-dimensional power involves decision-making and non-decision-making. Decision-making involves choice among a range of possible actions. Non-decision-making is a 'decision that results in suppression or thwarting of a latent or manifest challenge to the values or interests of the decision-maker'. Both clearly involve power.

Lukes stresses the importance of having a 'three-dimensional view' of power. He believes the previous dimensions of power still concentrate on Weber's ideas that power involves individuals realising their will in the face of resistance from others. The first dimension of power, according to Lukes, involves identifying the group or collective nature of decision-making –

'surface details of power' which can easily be observed and which most people believe is what politics is about. However, Lukes claims that the two other dimensions of power are more important. The second dimension involves 'political agenda-setting' and the degree to which government and groups are able to decide what will be discussed, what will become part of the arena of debate. Power is reflected in the ability of politicians and private groups to get issues on to, or keep them off, the political agenda. The third dimension is what Lukes calls the 'bias of the system', the 'socially structured and culturally patterned ... practices of institutions' that ensure some groups and individuals exercise greater power because they are attuned to these practices, while others find it difficult to succeed against these biases.

Michel Foucault

Foucault argued in many essays during the 1970s, brought together under the title *Power/Knowledge: Selected Interviews and Other Writings* (1980), that power never rests in the possession of one person, or in any obvious willed manner. It permeates all our minds and directs the way we all act. Within institutions, such as government or a business, power not only flows 'top-down', from higher levels in the institution to the lower, but everyone in an institution exercises some degree of power. The extent to which they can do this depends on what people in the institution regard as 'self-evident truths'. Even in an extremely hierarchical structure, such as government or the armed forces, the ability of the most powerful individuals to get their way can be frustrated by much weaker individuals exercising whatever power they have to obstruct the implementation of policies they disagree with. Power is about the achievement of one's own goals or the prevention of others achieving *their* goals. Power, if effective, enables people to collude in their own subjugation. All have some power and all have some choices as to how to use it. We are influenced in our choices by our knowledge of, or belief in, the opportunities and constraints before us. These constitute an indirect form of self-regulation within systems of power.

Power, however defined, has usually been accompanied by claims that it is being used, or should be used, to ensure 'justice'.

Justice

Justice has been upheld by most political theorists as a vitally important feature of a 'good' political system; so important, in fact, that justice has often been identified as the single most important objective of political activity. Revolutionaries often use 'justice' as a rallying cry to overthrow an 'unjust' political system.

Plato's *Republic* was the first and most important attempt to define justice and what constitutes a just society. Most political philosophy over the past 2500 years has involved discussing the issue of justice raised by Plato in his work, which takes the form of a dialogue between Plato's friend and teacher Socrates and a number of other philosophers. Several ideas of justice are identified, outlined, examined and dismissed. For example, Simonides claims that justice consists of ensuring that everyone is given their due, such as doing good to one's friends and harm to one's enemies (a standpoint which might be immoral and unjust if one's enemies are essentially good men). Thrasymachus defines justice as simply whatever the strongest in society claims it to be. The powerful people control the state; they define justice in terms of their own interests and impose this concept on all others in society. Any other basis of an appeal to justice is simply the weak making feeble attempts to persuade the strong to act against their self-interest. Such a view is always attractive to the powerful, but has little to do with the idea of morality that most thinkers believe should underpin justice. In the *Republic* Plato has Socrates identifying justice as residing in the achievement of harmony between each part in society and each carrying out its social role, the creation of a 'balance' of parts being the basis of both justice and social peace. This is a more refined version of Simonides's idea of justice.

What constitutes 'giving everyone his due' is a useful departure point in the search for the concept of justice and includes both rewards and punishments. Just punishment, for example, involves ensuring that only those found guilty of wrong-doing are punished, that any differences in punishment should correspond to the differences in the wrong-doing, and that the degree of punishment should be appropriate to the offence. Simply imposing order on society is not enough to ensure justice is done.

Most people identify a link between law and justice. A just person is a law-abiding person. Morality is a fundamental underpinning of society and the law reflects this in broad rules about social behaviour and the rights and obligations of people. Justice involves demonstrating respect for these rules. Hence, justice derives from fundamental natural or moral law in society.

Associated with this legally defined view of justice is an essentially conservative desire to preserve a particular social order, an order seen as sustaining justice by giving everyone a legally defined status. Such an idea is rather old fashioned today, and would be condemned as having little to do with modern concepts of justice, but it dominated discussions of the meaning of justice until the eighteenth century. Justice involved accepting inequality in society, as long as each person was given what was appropriate to their status.

Some modern thinkers claim that justice should be a straightforward establishment of respect for law and rights with little reference to 'social justice'. Friedrich von Hayek and Robert Nozick, for example, claim that social justice confuses the issue of justice. It merely encourages the expansion of state involvement in society in a misplaced desire to achieve social justice. Justice, so Hayek and Nozick argue, is damaged by a growing state presence in every aspect of life, restricting individual liberty without expanding social justice.

During the nineteenth century, justice became connected with 'social justice'. This involves a belief that it is both proper and realistic to bring the pattern of wealth and income distribution, along with education, health and other desirable social goods, into line with principles of justice. Social justice as a concept involves a belief that one can identify the processes by which society is governed and that one can identify a source of power, usually believed to be the government, to bring about social justice (although neo-liberals, for example, claim that the free market can deliver social justice).

Social justice is usually seen as embodying two major elements: firstly, merit and deserts; secondly, need and equality.

Merit and deserts

In a just society, status and rewards should give recognition to merit. Justice challenges any rewards based on hereditary principles and demands the creation of a society in which people can demonstrate their merit. Conservatives see little problem with privilege and hierarchy, as justice is a consequence of order. In a well-ordered society all are rewarded with peace, a peace that emanates from the order created by a widely accepted social hierarchy. Liberals argue for the free market as the most effective mechanism for distributing rewards in society. Price, which reflects the value placed on an individual's products and services, is itself an instrument of justice in a free-market economy and society. Socialists question the degree of justice implicit in the free market. They believe that success in such an economic system has relatively little to do with merit and the justice of rewards: luck and social class determine most rewards in society.

Need and equality

This element of justice involves the distribution of material rewards among people according to need and is greatly influenced by ideas of equality. The problem here is the great difficulty in distinguishing 'need' from simple 'desire'. The former is an important, even vital, aspect of life (involving food, shelter, clothing and warmth), while the latter consists largely of frivolous non-essentials (there are almost infinite examples of these).

The issue of 'need' is, because of its close association with equality, a strong part of socialist views of justice. Marxism, for example, allows people the full attainment of their needs, while social democracy claims that needs will vary in accordance with the available resources and the existing standards of need in a society. In Western societies this element of justice is identified with the equality of basic needs fulfilled by welfare states.

Other thinkers base claims for social justice on different criteria. Jeremy Bentham and the Utilitarians, for example, claimed that social justice was associated with the distribution of goods and services that generate the greatest degree of happiness. The production of happiness may or may not require egalitarian social policies. John Rawls, in *A Theory of Justice* (1971), argued that social justice does not automatically involve social equality. He argues for everyone having access to an extensive system of equal liberties and opportunities. An unequal distribution of goods and services may be quite compatible with justice if the least well-off in society benefit from it in some way. The provision of incentives to stimulate individual effort, for example, involves unequal rewards but if they help raise the overall wealth in society all, including the very poor, will benefit.

Justice is, along with power, a key underlying theme of our book. Let us now look at the topics covered.

An outline of the chapters

In most of the topics under discussion here we make reference to some of the major political thinkers and writers and to their most important works. We identify some of the basic concepts around which political discourse is structured. This is not an exhaustive compendium, neither are these chapters by any means the last word on key concepts and movements. We hope that there is enough in this book to whet the appetite, to stir the interest, of the reader and to encourage further study of the many excellent books, articles and seminal writing mentioned.

The first few chapters will identify and discuss some key concepts involved in political theory and debate, such as the state, the nation, liberty, equality, democracy, rights, which form the underpinning for the ideologies and movements discussed in the rest of the book.

1 The state and sovereignty

The state is arguably the most important concept in political theory. We introduce you to the main features of the state: territoriality, longevity, a power structure and sovereignty. The second part of the chapter assesses the degree to which the state and state sovereignty are disappearing in the modern world of 'globalised' politics, economics and culture and new international institutions.

2 The nation

Nations dominate many aspects of contemporary politics. The main features of the nation and the problems of defining it are outlined: population, culture, history, language, religion, race. Then the ideas of national identity, how they are formed and their importance are discussed. We make particular reference to the nations of Britain.

3 Democracy

Democracy is not only a very important idea in the modern world but it is also a difficult one to define. Different types of democracy and their most important features are discussed here. The creation of a 'democratic culture', arguments for and against democratic systems of government, and some prospects for the future of liberal democracies are examined.

4 Freedom

'Freedom' is usually claimed to be the prime objective of political activity. Few people are likely to argue that they want less freedom than they already have. The real issue in politics is to discover what is meant by freedom and how it is to be achieved. We discuss the concept in relation to the ideas of some of the major political thinkers on freedom and how it relates to the state and society.

5 Equality

Equality is a major element in modern political discourse. We discuss equality and its value in politics: equality of human rights, distributional equality, equality before the law, the claims for group equality on the grounds of race, gender, class. It is important to be aware of the challenges to equality as a principle, especially when it is seen to conflict with a greater value, liberty.

6 Rights, obligations and citizenship

Rights, obligations and citizenship are closely associated. We look at the nature of rights in society and whether they are natural, innate, created or acquired. Then the issue of political obligations and duties is outlined, especially within the context of a liberal-democratic state. Finally, the issue of citizenship is addressed in relation to these rights and obligations.

7 The role of ideology in politics and society

Ideology is the driving force of political discourse. Politics can be defined as the clash of interests dressed up as ideologies. This chapter examines what is meant by ideology, what forms it takes, how it is transmitted and its impact in both international and domestic British politics.

8 Nationalism

Nationalism is arguably the most important force in modern politics. We discuss nationalism's growth and development over the last two centuries with particular reference to its main features and assumptions. It is an ideology with the chameleon-like quality of adapting to the needs of countries, ideologies and the times. The impact of nationalism in both domestic and international politics is examined.

9 Conservatism

Conservatism is 'a policy of imperfection', based on a pessimistic view of human nature. It argues for a limited style of politics, tradition, organic society, hierarchy, order, authority, private property, the importance of the state and national institutions. We outline the development of conservatism as a political ideology and movement in Britain during the last two centuries.

10 Liberalism

Liberalism can be regarded as the Western world's dominant ideology, stressing ideas of individualism, optimism about society, human nature and its capacity for change, rationality and balance in society, freedom, justice, democracy, human rights, toleration, the minimal state and free-market capitalism. Liberalism is examined to discover how it has changed in order maintain its central position today.

11 Socialism

We investigate the main features and concepts associated with socialism. These include: a class analysis of society, co-operation, fraternity, collectivism, social equality, social justice, an optimistic view of human nature, the role of the state, society and the economy. The development of the British Labour Party will then be studied to reveal the characteristic features of British socialism.

12 Marxism and anarchism

Marxism and anarchism are usually seen as varieties of socialism. Both are critical of capitalist society and both advocate radical and revolutionary change in society. Here we discuss the main features of each movement and the degree of success they have had in improving society. Marxism as a state ideology is studied, as well as anarchism's critique of both capitalism and state socialism.

13 Fascism

Fascism is a reaction to liberalism and socialism, and in many ways it is a truly twentieth-century ideology. We identify some of the many thinkers and ideas associated with fascism and, although concentrating on German Nazism and Italian Fascism, we look at the rise of modern fascism in recent years in both Britain and Western Europe.

14 Environmentalism and ecologism

Environmentalism may be seen as the new political movement of the twenty-first century. The principles of environmental thought are identified and discussed. These include sustainable development, an earth-centred view of the world, the debate between the 'deep greens' and the 'light greens'. The impact of Green thinking on the major political movements will be identified.

15 Feminism

Feminism is an ideology and a movement that tries to explain the reasons for the social, political and economic subjection of women, as well as putting forward proposals for the social, economic and political advancement of women. We look at its origins and development, its major beliefs and approaches to women and their future.

Concluding remarks

It is important to address some areas of concern not covered elsewhere in this book. We look here at some of the new issues involved in politics that might be of significance in the future: politicised religion, disabled rights, gay rights and animal rights. We will also discuss how ideological change occurs and stress the importance of rationality in politics.

Glossary of major figures

This includes the names of most of the major figures mentioned in the text with brief details of their lives, works and contributions to the development of political ideas and movements.

Suggested further reading

Each chapter concludes with some suggested reading on the subject concerned. We include here most sources mentioned in the text and those we have used in the preparation of this volume.

The state and sovereignty

1

This chapter explores the concept of the state, looking at various theories of the state and identifying its major characteristics and then how far real states measure up to these characteristics. Finally, it examines the issue of whether the state is still as fundamental a political institution as it has been over the past four centuries.

POINTS TO CONSIDER

➤ Why are there so many states today?

➤ How does the state differ from the 'government' and the 'nation'?

➤ There are several different analyses of the state. What are the key points of each?

➤ What are the major characteristics of the state? Do all states have them in equal degrees?

➤ Has the state 'had its day'?

The state exists for the sake of a good life, and not for the sake of life only. (Aristotle, *Politics*, 4th century BC)

Free speech, raised in protest, is the life-blood of democracy, yet the freer the speech the more likely it is to inflame its audience to violence. But violence can kill democracy, for if given rein it will destroy the democracy that licensed it; while to curb it freedom itself may have to be restricted, and democracy thus impaled on the horns of a dilemma. Any nation which so orders its affairs as to achieve a maximum of freedom of speech with a maximum of freedom from public disorder may fairly claim a prize among the highest achievements of the human race. In terms of individual happiness it surely ranks higher than a successful landing on the moon. How has the prize been won? Can it be held? (T. A. Crichley, *The Conquest of Violence*, 1970)

The **state** in some form has existed since urbanised and complex societies arose in Egypt, China, India and Mesopotamia over five thousand years ago. Since then, the more 'civilised' members of humanity have never been without the state. States have also always existed in an 'international society' with trade, diplomacy, law, morality and, inevitably, war, shaping their relations.

> **state**
> A political association that establishes sovereign power within a defined territorial area and possesses a monopoly of legitimate violence.

The modern state arose from the break-up of European Christendom during the early sixteenth century. The Reformation instigated a century of religious wars between Catholics and Protestant powers. By the end of the century the modern state had been established in Western Europe: a centralised power with exclusive law-making and law-enforcing authority over a territory. Conventionally, however, the modern state and state system is dated from the Treaty of Westphalia, which ended both the Thirty Years' War (1618–48) and the wars of religion. Westphalia established the key principle of modern statehood: **sovereignty**.

> **sovereignty**
> The distinguishing characteristic of the state. Sovereignty is the right to have absolute and unlimited power, either legal or political, within the territory of a state.

After around 1500, European expansion into the Americas, Asia and Africa spread the concept of the state. European imperialism, itself a product of inter-state competition, encouraged non-Europeans to study the secret of their subjection. Anti-colonial nationalists took European ideas of the 'rights of man', 'liberty', 'equality' and, especially, 'national self-determination', using them against their colonial masters in struggles for independence.

Independence took on the form of Western-style states. The number of states in international society grew dramatically. Only twenty-six states existed in 1914, some tracing their independence from the British and Spanish empires in the eighteenth and early nineteenth centuries. After the Second World War the remaining European empires collapsed, creating over 160 states by 1980. With the end of communist domination in Eastern Europe and the break-up of the USSR the number rose to 192 ten years later.

Although often derided as an outworn concept by its critics, the state continues to have a deep resonance for most people's political aspirations. In the twenty-first century many stateless peoples and nations aspire to statehood as an expression of their national identity. The number of states is, therefore, likely to grow still further.

One problem in discussing the 'state' is that it is much more difficult to define than one might expect. We will first discuss two major misconceptions about what the state is. Then we will identify different 'types' of state in political theory. Characteristics common to all states will then be analysed, the most important of these being sovereignty. Finally, we will discuss the degree to which state sovereignty is being undermined in the modern world.

What the state is not

It is crucial to realise that the 'state' is not the same thing as 'government'. Governments are temporary holders of state office, directing state power. They are the means by which state authority is manifested. Ministers and civil servants make the state 'flesh', so to speak. Indeed, the state is a *theoretical* concept that has no *physical* manifestation. It can be seen as remote and impersonal, above particular regimes, while governments are shaped by often deeply held ideological values and driven by strong personal ambitions.

Neither is the state the same thing as the 'nation', as suggested in the term 'nation-state'. The nation and the state are very different concepts, very different aspects of social and political life. It is rare, very rare, for a nation to correspond exactly to a state. The UK, for example, is not a nation-state. It is a state that comprises several clearly identifiable nations. The Kurds, meanwhile, are a nation spread across parts of the territories of several states. Essentially, the state is a *legal* concept that defines a structure of power. The *nation* on the other hand is composed of a people who share certain characteristics, among which are culture, ethnicity and history.

The state claims the loyalty and support of its population, or at least the vast majority of its population. Many states, while dominated by a particular nation, include national minorities who sometimes feel an affinity to co-national members residing in other states or demand their own state. Such cross-border allegiances can undermine the practical sovereignty of a state and, under certain circumstances, lead to its failure or break-up. The violent end to the Yugoslav Federation and the peaceful break-up of Czechoslovakia in the 1990s are both examples of this.

Nevertheless, the state plays a vital role in 'nation-building' – the creation of a sense of national identity on the part of its population. This can be seen in the USA, where oaths of allegiance, displays of flags and the veneration of the Constitution are closely associated with building up and reinforcing a sense of 'American' national identity.

Theories of the state

The state owes much to political theory. Although not a *tangible* thing, the very *intangible* nature of the state ensures its key political role. The 'state' as a political concept is almost endlessly discussed. Indeed, one might define 'politics' as a distinct human activity – setting it apart from business, trade unions, religion, the family or the local gardening club – as a power struggle that takes place *only* in relation to the state.

All political activity revolves around the state.

- Concepts of rights, liberty, equality, the nation, power, only have practical meaning in relation to the state. It acts as defender or abuser of human rights. It creates national identity. It is the prime structure by which political power is manipulated in a society.

- Conservatism, liberalism, socialism, fascism and ecologism, as models, analyse power in relation to the state. As political parties they seek state power, to use it to implement political, social and cultural programmes. If unable to achieve control of the state, parties will at least try to influence those directing state institutions.

- Some movements do not aim to control the state, but to influence political debate and policy. They are usually described as 'pressure' or 'interest groups'. Here, it does not matter whether they are economic interest groups like trade unions and business associations, essentially defending the pay, conditions and employment of their members, or cause interest groups like Amnesty International or Greenpeace, supporting an issue that their members feel strongly about. Such groups seek to influence holders of state power.

Nevertheless, there are considerable differences in the theoretical approaches to the role and functions of the state. These may be classified as:
  - the liberal-pluralist state;
  - the social-democratic state;
  - the Marxist analysis;
  - the feminist analysis;
  - the self-serving state.

The liberal-pluralist analysis of the state

Liberal-pluralists reject the class analysis of Marxists and the nation-based view of conservatives to stress the central role of individuals and private groups in society.

Liberal-pluralists see society as large numbers of groups and individuals competing, sometimes co-operating, for power to control and/or influence state institutions. The state is neutral, curbing the power of some and bolstering the power of others. Indeed, the state itself is composed of many groups and interests. At times, state institutions and their interests may overlap with the interests of social groups. However, the state is seen to 'stand above' these groups as a 'referee' in their struggle for power.

The state acts for the whole nation. It is a 'servant' of the 'people', set up to defend their natural rights against oppression from home or abroad. Indeed, a 'social contract' exists between people and state, similar to any contract between employer and employee. Officials of the state must, therefore, be accountable for their actions to the people. Should the state abuse its power, and infringe the rights of the people, then state officials can be removed from office – 'sacked' – like any other servant who abused his position of trust. This justification of revolt was one of many reasons why conservatives have seen liberalism as dangerously radical and socially disruptive, and why radicals have found it so attractive.

Early nineteenth-century classical liberal thinkers were so concerned to curb the power of the state that they saw its role in extremely minimal terms. Essentially, the state should ensure the mainte-

> **neo-liberalism**
> A modern version of classical liberalism, sometimes called the 'New Right', which emphasises the central role of individual choice and motivations, free market economics and a minimal role for the state.

nance of internal law and order, defend against external attack, create a structure of laws to protect individual rights, and raise taxes to pay for these three tasks. All else – education, health, welfare, pensions – could, and should, be provided by private organisations. Such views reappeared towards the end of the twentieth century as key elements of **neo-liberalism** in many Western conservative parties.

The social-democratic view of the state

Modern Western states are characterised by features of the social-democratic state. So dominant an ideology is **social democracy** that it is now almost to impossible to imagine that a modern state could be shaped by any other beliefs.

Yet the idea that the state should take upon itself responsibilities for key industries, economic development, health, education, pensions and a wide range of social benefit payments is a new one. In only a few states, such as Germany, did that system exist prior to 1900. The social-democratic state arose during the middle years of the twentieth century in response to economic crises, the rise of socialist and labour movements to greater economic and political power and the demands of war. As a consequence of the effectiveness of state intervention in staving off social

social democracy
A reformist and moderate version of socialism that accepts a significant proportion of market capitalism, rather than seeking its outright abolition.

revolution and prosecuting total war it was increasingly believed that the state could and should have a greater role in society to deal with social problems: want, poverty, unemployment, sickness, ignorance. The state was seen as a tool to achieve social justice, fairness and liberty by setting up institutions to ensure health provision and education. A range of financial benefits provided protection against the consequences of unemployment, sickness, disability and old age. In most Western European countries key industries were taken into public ownership – 'nationalised', as it was known in Britain – and the state became responsible for running railways, coalmines, steelworks, utilities and a growing range of services and businesses.

The apparent economic and social failures of the 1970s discredited social democracy as an ideological direction for the state. In the 1980s and 1990s assaults on the social-democratic state saw state industries in many countries 'privatised', the tax burden on individuals and businesses reduced and state provision of benefits curbed. Nevertheless, many – indeed most – of the core features of the social-democratic state remain in place. The state remains the major provider of healthcare and education, basic welfare and pension payments, and is still seen as a tool of social change in the direction of social justice.

The Marxist analysis of the state

Marxists view the state in terms of **class struggle**. It reflects the economic structures of society and the class struggles that arise out of a particular economic system. As the economy changes through shifts in the means of production, so does the class structure. As the class structure alters so will the power relations and the political struggle between the classes.

class struggle
The conflict between social classes, themselves products of a given economic system which Marx regarded as the driving force of history.

The state is, therefore, not neutral. It is an instrument of power and domination of the ruling class (or classes) in society, the means by which the capitalist class maintains exploitative social structures that benefit them and keep the working class in subjection to them and their interests. Even when the state intervenes to mediate between the capitalist class and the working class, for example in an industrial dispute, the fundamental objective of the state is to ensure the dominance of the capitalist class.

Only when the working class seizes control of the state will the state act in their interests and the interests of the whole people. Indeed, when the working class has created the communist society, free of the capitalist class, the need for the state will disappear and the state, losing its reason for existence, will wither away: thus runs the argument.

The feminist view of the state

Feminists see the state as the most powerful of many social institutions that are instruments of male domination in society. The state is run mainly by men and for the interests of men.

Equal opportunities and equal pay legislation are mere decorations to hide the patriarchal nature of the state and its many sub-institutions. Women are rarely chosen as candidates for parliamentary seats, and, if chosen, are likely to be campaigning in unwinnable seats. The few women who are elected tend to remain out of governmental power. Those tiny numbers that get into government are likely to be ministers in 'low-prestige' or 'women's issues' areas of the government such as health and education rather than high-powered posts such as foreign policy and defence, economic and trade, all 'male' issues.

Women have to work harder than men to achieve political power within the state and generally have less power than men do.

The self-serving state

With the decline of the political power of monarchism in the early nineteenth century the appeal of state power was transferred from the king to the state. The state acquired in the minds of men a degree of powerful, mystic authority. This process helped create the idea of the state as something greater than the people who composed it, and indeed, raised the possibility that people would come to see the state not as their servant but as their master in the service of a greater goal than individual happiness.

The twentieth century gave form to the state as a self-serving power machine, pursuing its own interests and agenda, crushing opposition and bending all other social institutions to its will. It is sometimes called the 'Leviathan state'. Intervening in every aspect of social life, it leaves no room for individual conscience, or for any private institutions existing outside it. All social and political activity serves the state.

Modern fascist, communist, religious and military regimes increasingly have had access to technologies and organisational systems of observation and control, manipulation and oppression that their predecessors could only aspire to. All aspects of human existence were subject to the needs of the state in Stalin's Soviet Union, Mao's China, Pol Pot's Cambodia, Hitler's Germany and, to a considerable degree, Mussolini's Italy. Common ownership of property, or state direction of private property, surveillance techniques and the role of secret police and terror are concomitant with the higher 'good' of the state acting in the interests of the collective and not the individual.

However, critics of the self-serving state do not confine their warnings to states shaped by these regimes. Many liberal thinkers and politicians have argued that even social-democratic states, for the best of intentions, will create bureaucracies and interest groups that will, little by little, tax by tax, create structures of dependency and control that eventually lead to the suppression of freedom. It is not necessarily the intention of policymakers that this should become so, but it is inherent in the logic of increasing state power infiltrating areas that should be firmly outside the remit of politics: family, religion, education. Indeed, this is the consequence of democratic pressures for greater state spending and involvement in solutions to society's ills. Thus this critique of the modern state becomes a critique of some aspects of modern mass democracy.

Major characteristics of the state

Whatever the particular style of the state, its philosophical underpinnings, or the governmental system that directs it, a number of features common to all states can be identified:
- it has the control of an identifiable population;
- It has the control of an identifiable geographical territory;
- it has high degrees of longevity compared to other social institutions;
- it is a structure of law in society;
- it is characterised by sovereignty.

Population

All states have a constituent population that mostly voluntarily, but if necessary by compulsion, will be loyal to their state.

Having said that, there is no maximum or minimum number of people that must exist together to constitute a state. There are enormous differences in the sizes of populations of viable states. Nauru has a population of a few thousand; the UK, France and Italy are all sixty million strong; while Russia, the USA, India and China, with 160, 280, 1,000 and 1,200 million respectively, are clearly in a different population league.

It does not necessarily follow that population size translates automatically into political power for a state. Clearly, population size will determine the human resources upon which a state's power rests: industrial population, the size of armed forces, and so on. Population size does have an impact on the power ranking of a state in world affairs – a large population is needed for great-power status – but technological and industrial prowess and the educational levels of the population are of greater importance in the contemporary world. India, for example, is a large, well-populated country with a strong industrial base, but the USA, with a quarter of its population, has much greater resources to call on than India and is many times more powerful.

Geography

A state has control over an identifiable geographic territory. A state may have enormous territory, such as Russia, Canada and the USA, or may be geographically small, such as the Vatican City State, Fiji and Nauru. There is no maximum or minimum size for statehood. However, what is required is territory, and territory that is recognised as being under the control of a state by the inhabitants of that state and, what is more important, by other states – especially the great powers and the states most closely bordering on it.

State territory is not fixed. A glance at the shifting boundaries of the states of Europe over the last two centuries should demonstrate this most clearly. The Polish state was once geographically very large. During the course of the eighteenth century its territory was nibbled away by Prussia, Russia and Austria until it disappeared altogether. Reappearing as a state under the Versailles Treaty (1919), Polish territory stretched far to the east, taking in lands that had once been part of the Russian Empire, only to disappear in 1940. The post-1945 state lost territories in the east and was compensated by German territories in the west. Even apparently long-established states, such as France and the UK, ended the twentieth century with territory different from a century earlier.

The collapse of the European empires during the twenty years after 1945 and the collapse of Soviet power in 1991 created many new state territories based on national claims for self-government. However, like old states, these new ones often had to resort to war to establish their territorial integrity against other states and internal national minorities. New territorial boundaries, like old ones, require the recognition of other states. Hence, the continued struggles and conflicts over where state boundaries should lie.

Longevity

States claim long lives, because longevity tends to confer legitimacy in the eyes of their populations, and legitimacy invites loyalty. The UK state, for example, can trace its ancestry back to the Anglo-Saxon kingdom of Wessex of over a thousand years ago. The Russian and French states declare their origins to be almost lost in the mists of antiquity. Even modern states, such as those created out of the collapse of Yugoslavia, seek to claim that they are the heirs of long traditions of national statehood.

One can observe, therefore, that the state is something more than the government of the day. Governments come and go with elections. Political parties may change the policies of the government, but not the nature of the state. Sometimes, after a revolution, crisis or war, even the political and constitutional system that characterises a state may be subject to change. But the state goes on. Indeed, its legitimacy depends heavily on its real or supposed age. If necessary, 'age-old' traditions will be invented to strengthen claims of ancient origins.

Nevertheless, most modern states are just that: modern. The vast majority were created during the last fifty years; many are a little older (post-1919); some were in place at the start of the nineteenth century, but very few are above a couple of centuries old and even fewer can trace their present shape beyond 1700. The UK, for example, was founded in 1801, but its present geographical form dates from 1921. Modern Germany was established by Bismarck in 1871; however, the present German state was created in 1949 by the Americans and British, while its contemporary form, which encompasses the former German Democratic Republic, only just pre-dates the 1990s. Even the USA, over two centuries old, acquired its present geographical form only in 1958.

Law and government

The state can be seen as a system of laws. There is no legal authority above it either within its territory or in international society. It is sovereign within its territory, as the only law-making authority, and is bound only by those international treaties – international laws – it has agreed to accept.

A legal tradition shapes the legal order within a state. Order in society must be subject to law and not the other way around. Power must be constrained by law and law must be the basis for the transfer of power. Indeed, appeals to the 'common good', the 'general will' of the people, the needs of 'absolute power' to ensure the 'higher goal' of order without reference to law are arbitrary uses of power which inevitably lead to abuses of power on the part of political holders of office. Legal principles for the basis of the state are essentially a nineteenth-century development in the establishment of the rule of law to check the political whims of monarchs, ministers and the mob.

Domestically, the state can give itself whatever constitutional and political system it likes. The principle assumes that no other state or international organisation has the right under normal circumstances to determine the internal political arrangements of a state. The Treaty of Westphalia established this principle. It is a key element of the legal basis for the modern state. Nevertheless, a major defeat in a foreign war, such as that of Germany after 1945, will involve massive changes in the internal political and legal arrangements of a state.

Over the last few decades the nature of some regimes – South Africa's racist apartheid regime and the religious intolerance of the Taliban regime in Afghanistan – have been subject to considerable international pressure to reform in line with international moral principles. However, such pressure from other governments is likely to occur only when the internal regime affects the interests of other states.

International law is a law created by legally equal, co-ordinated bodies, not subordinated bodies. States *are* subject to law in international society, but are in a system where enforcement is only possible through states. Enforcement depends, therefore, very much on the *power* available to a state and on its calculations of self-interest. But it does not undermine the principle of state sovereignty as applied to law. Most international courts recognise the right of a state to refuse to attend a particular case when issues of national security are involved; and the state itself will decide what constitutes 'national security'.

State sovereignty

Most human associations have many of the above characteristics. A school or college has an identifiable population, a territory, a structure of power, and may have existed for a long time. It may even have a loyal group of students and staff. But there is one defining characteristic that distinguishes a school or any other social organisation or asociation from the state: sovereignty. It is impossible to grasp the concept of the state without reference to this defining feature.

'External sovereignty' is used to describe two elements. Firstly, states have legal equality in international society. Wealthy or poor, strong or weak, every sovereign state is legally equal in international law. The United States and Mauritius are both sovereign states, even though clearly one has a greater range of policy options in domestic and international affairs than the other. This manifests itself in institutions such as the United Nations General Assembly where each state has one vote. Secondly, for a state to achieve full external sovereignty it must be recognised as a fellow sovereign state by 'enough' of the other members of the international system, especially the most powerful states. For example, the apartheid regime in South Africa set up and recognised a number of 'states' within its territory as part of its policy of 'separate development'. Having all the apparent attributes of sovereignty, these 'pseudo-states' were only recognised as sovereign in reality by South Africa and each other. All the other states refused to recognise them as an equal. Hence, they failed to acquire this key attribute of a state.

'Internal sovereignty' is the other vital component of this concept. It consists of two elements: 'legal' and 'practical' sovereignty.

Legal sovereignty encapsulates the right of a state to be the only law-making body for the population inhabiting a given territory. The state has the right to construct and impose laws free of any external involvement by other states or bodies. It must be the *sole* law-making and law-enforcing authority for a territory. Any sharing of sovereignty must, by the very nature of the term, mean that whatever arises out of such an act, the result cannot be called 'sovereign'. Sovereignty does not recognise any superior or equal in the legal right to make laws for a territory.

The citizens and others residing in a state's territory are obliged to obey the laws of only that state. This is a peculiar feature of the state. It existed long before the seventeenth century although it is usually associated with the Treaty of Westphalia that established the legal principle of the duty to conform to the religious and political policies of a state's ruler. As a consequence of the UK's membership of the European Union one hears much of the decline, or even end, of British state sovereignty. However, one might argue that state sovereignty is still intact. Membership of the EU was an act of a sovereign state and continued membership is a demonstration of state decision-making. As long as the state remains the supreme law-making and law-enforcing authority for a territory, it will be sovereign.

However fundamental the concept of legal sovereignty is, one must always remember that it would remain a 'fiction' without the other element of state sovereignty: its practical ability to ensure that the laws of the state are obeyed throughout its territory. This element of the concept of sovereignty raises the issue of a hierarchy of states as a consequence of their power. Clearly, some states are more powerful than others. Generally speaking the more powerful a state the more it will have the practical sovereignty to ensure its writ runs within its territory and that it will be able to defend and advance its interests abroad. A weak state at home and abroad will still retain its external sovereignty and its legal internal sovereignty, but the important element of practical sovereignty will raise issues over its very effectiveness as a state.

State sovereignty, therefore, is not just a legal concept. It must be closely linked to the practical power available to a state. A state defeated in a war will lose, usually temporarily, the right to run its domestic and foreign policy in line with its own principles and interests. That is especially the case if the state is defeated in a major war and is over-run by its enemies (as was the case with Germany and Japan at the end of the Second World War). Peace treaties, however onerous their imposed obligations on a defeated state, do not deprive the defeated state of its legal sovereignty. Indeed, principles of sovereignty can be appealed to by a state to throw off or reduce the burden of such impositions.

Practical state sovereignty can be undermined and even fatally weakened by internal revolt. The consequences for the population of a state when its practical sovereignty fails are usually horrendous. The Lebanese state during the late 1970s and early 1980s, for example, remained the legally sovereign entity for its territory. However, that practical sovereignty was at one time reduced to a few Beirut city blocks while the rest of the country was in the hands of militias and, later, Israeli and Syrian armed forces. Similar problems have been seen in Somalia, Bosnia, Sierra Leone and Afghanistan.

Challenges to state sovereignty

Now nearly four hundred years old, the 'Westphalian state', with sovereignty as its defining characteristic, may be coming to the end of its useful existence, for one reason: its legal sovereignty is undermined by the growing corpus of international treaties that restrict the right of the state to make domestic laws.

The twentieth century raised deep moral questions about the consequences of allowing states under the guise of sovereign independence to have free reign over their citizens. Non-interference in the internal affairs of states ended highly destructive religious wars in the early seventeenth century. However, it is a dangerous policy to pursue today, when some states slaughter ethnic and other minorities, suppress human rights and construct appalling tyrannies.

Practical sovereignty is challenged by the problems facing human society at the dawn of the twenty-first century, problems so great, so complex, that the sovereign state is too small a unit, the concept of sovereignty too archaic, to be of much practical use in solving them. Pollution, environmental degradation, global poverty can be effectively addressed only by new international organisations acting globally, without the intervention of state-based power politics.

These challenges to state sovereignty may sound convincing but are not new. Sovereign states have always placed legal curbs on their own freedom of action by signing and acting in accordance with international treaties. Never, though, have states been bound by so many agreements as today. They accept more international interference in their internal affairs than ever before. One might consider this a matter of degree. States are obliged only to carry out treaties they have signed, the signature being itself an act of state sovereignty. State sovereignty, in legal terms, remains intact.

International organisations designed to deal with international problems are still either state-based, such as the United Nations, or, if non-governmental organisations (NGOs), they have to act through power structures created and maintained by states. State sovereignty remains the *practical* feature of political activity. States remain by far the greatest donors of international aid, the most important actors in international affairs, and, of course, are the major military players in conflicts. The state remains the central feature of the international system. Indeed, alternatives to the state look, on closer examination, to be somewhat larger 'states' with different names.

Nevertheless, there is an issue here about the future of state sovereignty. It is challenged, even if it still is the central feature of the state. While *legal* state sovereignty remains intact, it is the erosion of *practical* state sovereignty that will determine the validity of the concept of the state in the future. We will look here at the major challenges to *practical* state sovereignty in the modern world:

- The structure of international society;
- The impact of **globalisation**;
- the spread of weapons of mass destruction;
- the growth of informal ties;
- the rise of new international actors;
- **neo-colonialism**.

> **globalisation**
> The process by which economic, political and cultural power and influence are transferred to organisations such as multinational corporations and so removed from the control of those most affected by them. This involves the increasing interdependence of states, social and economic organisations and individuals in the modern world

> **neo-colonialism**
> The process by which powerful Western states reassert their dominance over nominally independent states by economically exploiting them through bodies such as the International Monetary Fund and the World Bank, and especially multinational corporations and financial institutions.

The structure of international society

State sovereignty has always been predicated upon political power: the practical ability of the state to defend its sovereignty against internal revolt and external enemies. In international society there have always been considerable differences in practical power among sovereign states; although states are legally equal, the differences mean that some states are more 'equal' than others. However, the modern international system has seen the rise of a whole new class of state, known as the 'superpower'. Superpowers are so powerful that they undermine the practical sovereignty of all other states in the international system.

During the Cold War, so it is argued, the USA and USSR constituted the only superpowers in the international system. They created alliances: structures built around one or other superpower. Junior members of these alliances were subject to interference in their internal affairs by the dominant superpower, so much interference that practical sovereignty was drastically reduced. The present post-Cold War world now has only one superpower, the USA, with enormous economic and military potential to undermine state sovereignty of weaker members of the international system.

This view of the over-riding might of a superpower fails to acknowledge that legal sovereignty, even of smaller states, has a practical validity. Junior states in the international system may use legal sovereignty to ensure a considerable degree of practical sovereignty in the face of superpower pressure. France in 1965 asserted its legal and practical sovereignty by removing NATO and US bases from its territory. The Soviet Union found that its claims of limited sovereignty within the Warsaw Pact were challenged by its member states. Poland and Romania regularly asserted their sovereignty in the face of considerable Soviet pressure. Despite the assertion of Hungarian and Czechoslovakian political sovereignty it was crushed by Soviet military force in 1956 and 1968, respectively, but the desire to restore practical sovereignty remained within those states and contributed to the collapse of the Soviet Empire.

It does not therefore follow that sovereignty is automatically undermined by the existence of superpowers. At times, the sovereignty of small states can be strengthened in the face of superpower pressure. They can be seen as the victims of superpower bullying and can embarrass the superpower accordingly. Perhaps the most obvious element in the continuing importance of states is their sheer number in the international system despite the hierarchical nature of power in international society.

The impact of globalisation

Globalisation is said to undermine practical sovereignty by the rapid spread of technology, ideas, electronic communications and the swift movement of people and capital around the globe. The global economy has created such strong economic ties between states that old concepts of national economic independence are obsolete and, therefore, the economic basis of practical sovereignty has gone.

State sovereignty in the past could be protected by state action to prevent movements of people and ideas across frontiers. However, global technology ensures that states are unable to isolate their people from new ideas. State frontiers and concomitant state sovereignty have become increasingly meaningless as a concept in the modern world.

There is, though, little that is new in this thesis. State sovereignty has always been subject to challenge by communications technology and capital movements around the globe. Even states most integrated into the international economy are ones in which the bulk of economic activity is domestic and only a small part of economic activity is related to foreign trade.

Nevertheless, technological developments ensure that states, for good or ill, increasingly have at their command the means for greater control and surveillance of their populations than ever before. Even the most liberal-democratic state has enlarged its powers to the extent of strengthening its practical sovereignty in the face of challenges to it from within and without.

Weapons of mass destruction

In the centuries before the development of nuclear weapons, it is argued, practical state sovereignty in military affairs was very strong. A foreign power had to destroy the armed forces of an enemy state in order to inflict total destruction on the economic and population resources available to that state. The enterprise was difficult, enormously taxing and prone to failure, and the gains from such actions might be seen to be relatively minor when measured against the inevitable weakening of even the victorious power.

Now the existence of nuclear and other weapons of mass destruction available to states and, potentially, terrorist organisations, means that even the strongest state is vulnerable to devastating military strikes, without warning, which would inflict enormous damage on political, economic and social structures. As a consequence the military basis of sovereignty has been reduced and, possibly, removed. With this key element of sovereignty gone or fatally weakened, the Westphalian state has lost is major characteristic – the monopoly on organised political violence, and its major function, the use of military power to promote the policy aims of the state.

Nevertheless, the state remains the major organiser of military power in the world. Even the most sophisticated terrorist organisations can only compete militarily with the resources available to a very small state. The majority of sovereign states retain considerable military power. Nuclear weapons can strengthen relations between nuclear-armed states by developing concepts of 'nuclear deterrence' to ensure that peace is maintained and caution is a feature of the handling of crises between such armed states. In confrontations between nuclear and non-nuclear armed states, however, one cannot see any evidence that the non-nuclear state is significantly intimidated by the nuclear power and alters its behaviour. Nuclear weapons may not be a credible political tool in crises with non-nuclear-weapons powers. What nuclear-weapons power would threaten, let alone use, nuclear weapons against a small non-nuclear power? The threat would be hollow and would merely isolate the nuclear-weapons state in international society. Hence, the practical sovereignty of states is unlikely to be significantly reduced by developments in weapons technology.

Growing informal ties

The practical sovereign functions of the state are undermined by the growth of informal links between people outside inter-state relations. Subversion, propaganda, ethnic cross-border ties, religious affiliations, the internet, tourism, international media and the creation and spread of a global culture all weaken the power of the state to call automatically upon and expect the loyalty of the people under its legal sovereignty.

For example, religious affiliations place demands for allegiance on co-religionists above the demands of the state in which they reside. Young British Muslims have travelled to Afghanistan to fight for fellow Muslims against the armed forces of their own state, claiming a higher duty than one associated with citizenship. Christian groups challenge their own governments when they violate Christian principles. Indeed, in the struggle against particular state regimes religion plays a very important role. The end of the communist regime in Poland was, in part, connected with the role of the Catholic church led by a Polish pope who could call on the moral and political support of millions of fellow Catholics.

Tourism involves millions of people travelling for leisure to other countries, creating new relationships between peoples that weaken the automatic support of people for their own state. Only over the last thirty-five years or so have millions of people been able to travel to other countries and experience their cultures other than as members of an invading army. Tourism is only a mass phenomenon in relatively rich nations but as with other phenomena it is likely to expand.

The internet and the international media have created the opportunity to spread with ease cultural and political values that challenge and weaken the capacity of a state to control its population free of external and alternative points of view. Indeed, the political messages carried by modern technology may influence the internal political debates and social conditions within other states.

These changes have affected the power of the state to maintain its sovereignty. States may have had to modify their functions in response to tourism and technological change. However, it is doubtful whether practical sovereignty has automatically been undermined. Modern technology is probably more likely to increase the ability of a state to control, track and regulate its population. Cross-border religious affiliations of some members of a population may strengthen the allegiance of the rest of the population to the values of their own state, the former being seen as potential, or real, traitors. Travel and the international media may not broaden the mind. The more people know about foreigners the more they may dislike them and find them a threat. Greater knowledge about other societies and their peculiarities may strengthen xenophobia.

New international actors

State sovereignty is certainly challenged by the growth of a vast range of actors in international affairs. These include Multi-National Corporations (MNCs), environmental and aid pressure groups, terrorist organisations, international capital markets, religious movements and international organisations created by states. Thousands of such groups exist and certainly make the workings of international society more complex than if it had been composed of sovereign states alone.

These new international actors have their own interests and objectives, which will often not coincide with the interests and objectives of states, and may actually be in conflict with them. The very number and diversity of these actors make it difficult for states to assert their practical sovereignty over them. The power of some of these new actors, especially the economic power of MNCs, which is often greater than that of many sovereign states, challenges and undermines the sovereignty of states.

However, it must be acknowledged that most of these new actors are very small and very, very weak compared to states. Furthermore, only a few of these actors perceive themselves as being involved in a challenge to state sovereignty. Although terrorist and guerrilla organisations see themselves challenging state power, usually to create a new state or severely modify a state in line with their own interests, most dissident groups are aware of the need to work through states and to influence state policies if their objectives are to be achieved. MNCs and pressure groups act within a framework that assumes a key role for the state. Many new international actors, such as the European Union, the United Nations or international courts, are created by states themselves and exist to reflect state interests. Indeed, the European Union and the United Nations, among many such bodies, exist only as state-created structures and can only be understood in relation to legal and practical state sovereignty. The state, therefore, remains a major factor in the calculations of most new actors.

Neo-colonialism

Globalisation and international trade in the world economy has, it is argued, undermined the practical sovereignty of states, especially the smaller, ex-colonial states.

Sovereignty is made meaningless by the economic control of foreign-owned MNCs. This is especially true in Africa, Asia, Latin America and parts of the Middle East. Governments may retain legal sovereignty of a state but practical sovereignty is undermined by the influence of MNCs, acting out of self-interest rather than the interests of the state in which they operate. Even powerful states in the developed world find themselves struggling to exert sovereignty in the face of economic pressures from powerful MNCs.

The extent to which such economic processes undermine state sovereignty can be exaggerated. States need the tax revenues, jobs, investment and wealth that MNCs can bring and these, in themselves, can strengthen practical sovereignty. MNCs know they need to tread carefully in dealing with states, as states can assert their control over key national resources by the nationalisation of foreign assets. Many Middle Eastern states nationalised foreign oil companies in the 1960s and used the revenues to develop their countries. However, the success of such a strategy depends on the value of the resources concerned. Oil is a vital commodity for modern industrial societies, being used in products such as petrol, plastics and paint, while bananas, for example, are of major concern only to banana producers. Oil is one thing, bananas are another!

The state is still the major form of political association in the world. It remains the major concentration of political, military and economic power, the major focus of loyalty for people and the one political association for which most people are willing to run the risk of injury and death to create or defend it. Nevertheless, its nature changes over time. For most people the state is no longer 'The Divine Idea as it exists on earth',[1] but it does have a powerful pull on their emotions. It is still the form towards which political nationalists aspire and in recent decades its phenomenal explosion in numbers is further evidence of its attractions.

Sovereignty is not a static concept. It, too, changes as political realities change. The debate in Britain, for example, over the impact of the EU on sovereignty, sometimes sounds as if the idea is an eternal reality and not subject to change. Sovereignty is an attribute of states that is both an idea and a reality of state power. It is one of the means, an important one, by which the government of a state seeks to ensure the best it possibly can for its people. As such, it also changes over time. One might consider the supposed decline in legal sover-eignty resulting from membership of the EU as more than compensated for by the *rise* in the practical sovereignty of enhanced economic and political clout available to the British state in international politics which results from EU membership and the pooling of sovereignty.

One can over-estimate the power of the state. The vast majority of states are poor, weak, with very little practical sovereignty abroad and often precious little at home in the face of powerful economic and sectional interests. Mere sovereign equality does not ensure the ability to exercise real power. The condition of internal chaos in some states poses a threat to their neighbours as well as to the well-being of their own citizens. So great is this problem, and so great the dangers to international stability, that in recent years it has been argued that some form of benign Western 'imperialism', for want of a better word, may be required. Some territories may have to be taken over by powerful states, reconstructed and have order restored.

One may, however, perceive this as demonstrating the *importance* of state power, rather than the declining value of the concept. The state is likely to remain the most important political actor far into the future.

Summary

Although the state can be traced as far back as ancient times, the modern state really emerged in the seventeenth century. The state is not the same thing as 'society', the 'government' or the 'nation' but has its own defining character-istics. Although it is of fundamental importance, in that all political activities revolve around it, there are several interpretations of the state, but certain features are common to them all: the state controls an identifiable population and geographical territory; it has a high degree of longevity; it can be described as a structure of law in society; it is characterised by sovereignty. In recent years, questions have been raised as to the continued significance of the state, which appears to be challenged by such developments as the restruc-turing of international society, globalisation, new forms of warfare, new types of international organisations (such as MNCs) and neo-colonialism. In spite of this the state remains the major form of political association in the world and is likely to remain so.

REFERENCES AND FURTHER READING

1 G. W. F. Hegel, *The Philosophy of Right*, 1821.

D'Agostino, F. 'The State under the Rule of Law', in G. Duprat, N. Parker and A.-M. Rieu (eds.), *WHAT IS EUROPE? Book 3: European Democratic Culture* (The Open University and European Association of Distance Teaching Universities, 1993), pp. 105–31.

Bartleson, J. *A Genealogy of Sovereignty* (Cambridge University Press, 1995).

Cooper, R. 'Dawn Chorus for the New Age of Empire', *The Sunday Times* (28 October, 2001).

Goodwin, G. L. 'The Erosion of External Sovereignty?', *Government and Opposition* 9:1 (1974), pp. 61–78.

Hertz, J. 'Rise and Demise of the Territorial State', in R. I. Matthews *et al.*, *International Conflict and Conflict Management* (Prentice Hall, 1984), pp. 182–93.

Heywood, A. 'Sovereignty, the Nation and Supranationalism', in A. Heywood, *Political Ideas and Concepts: An Introduction* (Macmillan, 1994), pp. 48–56.

Hinsley, F. H. *Sovereignty* (Cambridge University Press, 1986).

James, A. *Sovereign Statehood* (Allen and Unwin, 1986).

Millar, J. D. B. 'The Significance of the Sovereign State', in J. D. B. Millar, *The World of States* (Croom Helm, 1981), pp. 16–32.

Morgenthau, H. J. and. Thompson, K. W 'Sovereignty', in H. J. Morgenthau and K. W. Thompson, *Politics Among Nations* (Alfred A. Knopf, 1985), pp. 328–46.

Puchala, D. J. 'Origins and Characteristics of the Modern State', in R. I. Matthews *et al.*, *International Conflict and Conflict Management* (Prentice Hall, 1984), pp. 177–81.

SAMPLE QUESTIONS

1 What is the state?

2 What should the functions of the state be?

3 Is sovereignty indivisible?

4 How accurate is it to say that sovereignty is the ultimate source of authority in society?

5 'State sovereignty is an outmoded concept.' Discuss.

6 How would you define the concept of a 'failed state' and is the concept a useful one in the contemporary world?

The nation

The powerful but elusive concept of the nation is investigated here. It is distinguished from the 'state' and the relationship between them is examined. Other elements which make the nation are considered, such as religion, language, government, cultural and historical ties, and finally the subjective but still important 'sense of nationhood'. There is also an analysis of contemporary Britain as a nation. Perhaps more accurately the United Kingdom should be considered as a 'state' made up of several 'nations', each of which is discussed in turn. This problem of nation and national identity can be investigated through a study of Northern Ireland, where issues of national and state identity have contributed to the political crisis.

POINTS TO CONSIDER

➤ How do the 'state' and the 'nation' differ?

➤ Are the state and the nation always linked in some way?

➤ To what extent do race, language, religion, government and shared culture and history shape nations? How do these factors vary from nation to nation?

➤ Is a 'sense of nationhood' a purely subjective thing?

➤ How far does a sense of nationhood exist in England, Wales and Scotland? In what ways does this sense, if it exists, manifest itself within modern British society?

➤ Is the sense of nationhood a valuable and useful concept in explaining the politics of Northern Ireland?

A nation is a group of people linked together by a common error about their ancestry and a common dislike of their neighbours. (Karl Deutsch, *Nationalism and Social Communications*, 1953)

The great nations have always acted like gangsters and the small nations like prostitutes. (Stanley Kubrick, 1963)

A nation may be said to consist of its territory, its people, and its laws. The territory is the only part which is of certain durability. (Abraham Lincoln, message to Congress, 1st December 1862)

Many powerful concepts and ideologies have motivated humans. It is difficult to identify a concept more powerful in shaping political activity than the 'nation', or any ideology that motivates people to greater sacrifices or crimes than that of nationalism. Some political movements, such as conservatism and fascism, strongly identify with the nation and are greatly influenced by nationalism. Other movements claim to place the individual at the centre of political activity, as in liberalism, or class, as in socialism, but even these have found that national 'characteristics' greatly influence – indeed, determine – the form in which their ideologies are expressed.

Nevertheless, it is difficult to define the 'nation'. As with the concept of the state, one has an idea as to its meaning that swiftly disintegrates when one attempts to analyse or define it. The state and the nation are not identical, even though the two terms are often used interchangeably by politicians, historians and political scientists. The state is, remember, a legal entity that is directed by a government. The nation, on the other hand, may or may not be closely associated with the state. A nation is composed of a people that share certain characteristics and have a *sense* of belonging to that nation.

So powerful is the concept of nations as fundamental units of human organisation that international organisations rarely talk of them as being made up of states, which is what they are, and they are usually described in such terms as the League of *Nations* and the United *Nations*.

The concept of the 'nation' will be discussed here, first in general terms and then in relation to the nations of the United Kingdom.

The nation

The concept of the nation developed in Western Europe during the post-Reformation struggles of the sixteen and seventeenth centuries, and was further shaped by the industrial and political revolutions of the eighteenth and nineteenth centuries. During the nineteenth century, the development of the political power of the middle classes within capitalist states also refined the concept of the nation. The creation of mass democracies and notions of popular sovereignty during the twentiety century created the notion of nationality being related to **citizenship**. Nations and national identity, in the eyes of some commentators, are artificial formulations:

citizenship
The rights and duties that an individual has as a member of a state. Citizenship can be acquired by birth or by choice, as a consequence of 'naturali-sation' into the citizenship body of state.

> Once you have swallowed the truth that neither our English nor our British identity has their roots in pre-history; once you accept the essential shallowness of nationhood; once you understand that a national identity can be designed in a cynical, professional and calculated way as a life assurance company's corporate personality, you will see why, though our nationhood has fewer certainties, it has fewer shackles too.[1]

Some analysts see 'nations' as modern ideas, largely created by intellectuals and rulers to unite, or fool, the people. Benedict Anderson, in *Imagined Communities: Reflections on the Origins and Spread of Nationalism* (1983), powerfully argues that nations are 'imagined communities', artificially constructed and sustained, and are not deeply rooted in history or some 'natural' cultural identity. Eric Hobsbawm, in *Nations and Nationalism since 1780* (1990), sees nations as constructed around myths of age-old identity and linked to capitalist economic development with the intention of constructing an identity capable of countering the emerging class identity of the proletariat.

Adrian Hastings, in *The Construction of Nationhood: Ethnicity, Religion and Nationalism* (1997), has argued, however, that one can identify the devel-opment of European nations and national identities from the early Middle Ages. Some nations create states as expressions of political nationhood. For Hastings three elements were especially important in the creation of nationhood. War stimulated a sense of national identity and nationalism. The awareness of a wider linguistic sense of identity, rather than dialect, developed as the consequence of writing and the spread of printing. Finally, religion was especially important. The idea of a 'chosen' nation comes from the Old Testament, and kings and national priesthoods used religion to shape national identity.

Friedrich Meinecke, in *Cosmopolitanism and the Nation State* (1907), distin-guished between 'cultural nations' and 'political nations'. Cultural nations are shaped by deep historical, linguistic and ethnic ties that pre-date modern states and may or may not generate demands for political independence. All nations have some elements of 'culture' in their national identity. Examples include the Welsh, the Germans and the Bretons. Political nations, on the other hand, such as the UK and the USA, are bound together by political principles such as 'liberty', 'constitutionalism' and 'the rule of law'. Such principles can come into conflict with other loyalties engendered by 'cultural' national identity. Citizens often find cultural national identity more attractive than political national identity.

Ernest Gellner, in *Nations and Nationalism* (1983), believes that a sense of belonging to a nation, in the cultural sense, is not enough. Nationhood, to have meaning, must be closely associated with the desire for self-government and the creation of state to express that desire.

Thus 'nation' defies a clear definition. Below are some features associated with the nation, identifying both cultural and political aspects of nationhood:
- nation and state;
- race and nation;
- language and the nation;
- religion and national identity;
- government and nation;
- common historical and cultural ties;
- a sense of 'nationhood'.

Nation and state

Although the term 'nation-state' is a popular one in political science it is one which does not easily help define the concept of the nation. It implies that the vast majority of the population of a territory feels itself as part of a nation and recognises the state as the sovereign power. Indeed, since the concept of 'national self-determination' was announced in 1919 at the Versailles Peace Conference the creation of 'nation-states', as an expression of national identity, has been seen as a political ideal and a desirable objective.

In reality very few 'nation-states' can be identified in any clear sense of the term. One might claim Turkey, Thailand, Japan or Sweden, Denmark, Finland and Norway as constituting examples of this species. But even these might be subject to such qualifications as to cast doubt on the validity of the concept. If one talks of Turkey as a nation-state, for example, then one must ignore the presence of Kurdish, Armenian and other 'national' minorities. The same is true of Belgium, Russia, Spain, Sri Lanka, South Africa and India. All these 'nation-states' have 'national' minorities of various sizes that challenge the actuality of the idea. The political reality is far more complicated, especially as national self-determination can generate dangerous political tensions within a state, potentially leading to its demise.

Most states are in fact multi-national. The United Kingdom, for example, is a multi-national state, consisting of four or five identifiable nations. Attempts to create a 'British' nation and national identity since, say, the union of the English and Scottish crowns in 1603, the union of Scottish and English parliaments in 1707, or the union with Ireland in 1801, have at best been only partially successful. Most people within the UK would perceive their national identity as English, Scottish, Welsh, Irish or else some other national or ethnic identity first and British second. Only Loyalists in Northern Ireland define their national identity as solely 'British'.

One needs to distinguish between 'nationality' as an emotional tie with other people of the same 'nation' and 'nationality' as a legal status which may or may not involve a deep emotional identification. Many people have 'British' nationality in the legal sense, but little commitment to British nationality in an emotional sense. The concept of 'citizenship nationality' is often seen as a means by which migrants to the UK can be integrated into national life without giving up their sense of national cultural identity. The concept of legal nationality is often the basis of a strong sense of emotional national identity. For example, the United States has clearly been very successful in encouraging its citizens, many being recent migrants or the children of recent migrants, to develop a strong sense of being 'American' in both legal and emotional terms. At the same time they maintain their sense of ethnic national identity as 'African-Americans', 'Polish-Americans', 'Jewish-Americans', 'Italian-Americans', 'Irish-Americans', and so on.

Many nations, however, are spread over two or more states, as in the case of Koreans, Chinese, Hungarians, Irish, Kurds and Russians. Some of these states may constitute national majorities; in many the nation is a minority, often perceiving itself to be an 'oppressed' national minority. Following the dissolution of the Soviet Union in 1991 an estimated 25 million Russians now live as minorities, often sizeable ones, in new states outside Russia. In some of these states Russians, once associated with the dominant 'imperial' nation, have been subject to discrimination in jobs, education and civil rights. Such national minorities will often appeal to their co-nationals across a state frontier for help, sometimes with dangerous political consequences.

In some cases a nation has no state, not even one which it can share with other nations. Kurds, Armenians, Palestinians all see their national identity as being oppressed, or at least unable to be fully expressed because of the lack of a state. Indeed, it was an article of liberal nationalism in the nineteenth century, and modern nationalism since, that one of the major causes of conflict in the world was the failure of many nations to have a state of their own. Once this was achieved, war, arising from frustrated national identities, would become a thing of the past.

The reality has often been the creation of states that are either too small to be viable economic and political units, or themselves contain disgruntled national minorities that demand further devolution of power, thus weakening the ability of the government to achieve other desirable goals. Oppressive as multi-national states and empires often are, they do 'stop the natives from killing each other' and create a degree of order over large geographical areas.

In some parts of the world there is no relationship between state and nation. This is especially so in Africa, where the great powers in the late nineteenth century drew the borders of their colonies, and where 'spheres of influence' bore no relation to tribal, linguistic or other deeply rooted social groupings. Western-educated local elites, using Western concepts of the nation, agitated for national independence from the former colonial powers, and sought to create modern nations after leaving a colonial empire. However, they faced considerable difficulties in attempting to overlay, or even replace, traditional and age-old social groupings with stronger emotional ties to the population at large than the 'foreign' concept of the nation. In many cases this led to considerable social tension and, in Biafra, Ethiopia, Katanga, Sudan, Chad, Uganda and elsewhere, violent conflict. However, it is worth noting that, in Africa at least, the very weakness of national identities alternative to the 'national identity' associated with the state has ensured that almost all of these states have retained the state frontiers acquired at independence, contrary to widespread fears at the time. One might award much of the credit for this to the role of the state in 'nation-building'.

It is not just in the developing world that the state has played a crucial role in nation-building. A distinction is often made between 'old' nations and 'new' nations. In Europe, or in societies derived from European culture, nations are somehow 'natural' and deeply rooted in ethnic, linguistic or other identity. 'New' nations, usually in Africa and Asia, were 'artificially' created by elites, often somewhat detached from the mass of the population. Here colonial masters imposed the state before a nation existed and the creation of a 'national' identity was, and is, extremely difficult. In Nigeria, for example, there are four main and 245 smaller ethnic groups, and considerable religious, linguistic and regional differences between them.

States thus play a vital role in both old and new nations in creating national identity. 'National' symbols are usually state symbols: flags, anthems, uniforms. The state plays a crucial role in attempting to create a sense of national identity by its educational system, inculcating new generations of citizens with national history, national heroes, national identity and national achievements. It may often identify a national language as the one that all members of the 'nation' should be fluent in. Conscription into the armed forces of the state is often seen as a very important vehicle for encouraging a sense of national identity. This was often used, and still is, as a major justification for the retention of compulsory military service. Indeed, it may even take a civil war to ensure compulsory membership of the nation for disaffected sections of its population (for example, the American Civil War).

Although the state and nation are not the same thing they do play a very important role in shaping one another's identity. Nevertheless, there are many other elements involved in the concept of the nation.

Race and nation

During the nineteenth century 'race' and 'nation' were terms used inter-changeably. 'Races' peopled Europe: the British race, the German race, the Slav race(s), and so on. Race and nation became so intertwined that they were often used to mean the same thing. Indeed, international politics became, as a consequence of the misapplication of the evolutionary theories of Charles Darwin, a struggle for supremacy and survival among nations. Weak nations were doomed, as 'a law of nature', to come under the thrall of the most powerful nations.

However powerful such theories were, especially by the end of the nineteenth century, they are largely discredited today – except on the fringes of right-wing politics. Science and politics have discredited race-based ideas of national identity.

Science, especially genetics, has demonstrated that human beings form one species (*homo sapiens sapiens*) and race consists of a set of superficial biological characteristics, (skin colour, hair-type, eye colour) that bears no relationship to cultural characteristics, which are learnt, such as national identity.

Twentieth-century politics saw many bloody conflicts, both international and civil, fought around racial and ethnic identity. In particular, the racial theories of Nazi Germany contributed to the outbreak of the Second World War and were responsible for the mass murder of ethnic groups identified as racially 'inferior' or a threat to 'superior' races. As a consequence of such theories millions of Gypsies, Slavs and, especially, Jews were killed.

Although patently responsible for the bloody nature of conflicts in Bosnia and Kosovo in the 1990s the link between race and nation cannot be sustained in general. Yes, certain biological characteristics are often associated with particular nations. Most Swedes are blond, Italians tend to have darker skins, most Nigerians are black, but these characteristics are shared with peoples who have different national identity. On the other hand, Americans as a nation present themselves with great diversity without claiming race as a defining feature of American national identity.

Language and the nation

Language is often seized on as being related to national identity. A language expresses the particular experience of a people that constitute a nation. Its words and structure are shaped by and in turn shape the nation. A language carries cultural forms and ideas, expressing national identity. One can hardly imagine English national identity without reference to the impact that the language has had upon it through its literature, especially the works of Shakespeare and Dickens.

Within the British Isles English was spread as the language of social advancement in the nineteenth century to the detriment – and denigration – of Welsh, Scots Gaelic and Irish. Indeed, the survival of Welsh, Scots Gaelic and Irish Gaelic has become a cause championed by nationalists struggling against English imperialism. Even so, English remains the dominant language spoken in those countries and the Welsh, Scottish and Irish have used the English language to great effect to express aspects of their own national identity.

Nevertheless, while language expresses the cultural identity of a nation it cannot be seen as the same thing as the nation. English is spoken by millions of people in many countries. They may share the language, but would not claim their national identity to be English. Indeed, English (and, for that matter, Spanish, Portuguese and other European languages that are now spoken around the globe as a consequence of European colonial expansion) has developed words and expressions that reflect the experience of the populations of the 'new' nations.

Most nations are, in fact, multi-lingual. Belgium is a small nation deeply divided by language and culture, yet Belgians would not see themselves as French or Dutch. The Swiss have a very strong sense of national identity, yet they have three distinct languages in their country. India has dozens of languages, and this is a factor in inter-communal strife, yet there is still a strong sense of Indian national identity.

Religion and national identity

Religion is a factor that has played a very important role in the formation of national identity, but one with a mixed relevance today.

Most modern nations in Europe developed out of the collapse of a united Christendom during the early sixteenth century. Prior to that kings and princes fought to establish a degree of independence against the universalist claims of the church. The Protestant Reformation was seized upon by many princes and kings as a means of reinforcing their sovereignty against the papacy. Catholic monarchs at the same time sought to strengthen their political independence of the papacy. The 'Divine Right of Kings', the right to rule being derived from God and not the people, was a doctrine appealing to both Protestant and Catholic monarchs. In fact, adherence to the religious views of the state became a test of loyalty. Individual conscience may have been claimed as a guide for individual Protestants but Protestant states were no more willing to allow freedom of conscience in practice than the Catholic church and Catholic monarchs were.

All across Europe religious identity became closely allied to national identity and was reinforced by the power of the state. English, Welsh and Scottish nationhood was closely linked to particular forms of Protestantism developed in their countries. Dutch and Scandinavian national identity was linked to various Protestant churches. Catholicism is closely associated with Italian, Spanish, Portuguese, Croatian, French and Polish national identity, while Russian, Serbian and Greek nationhood is still shaped by Orthodox Christianity.

Religious affiliation was also linked to national identity in the 'new' nations born of European colonial empires. Thus Catholicism is the dominant form of Christianity among the nations of Central and South America, the Philippines and the French population of Quebec. Protestantism has played a key role in creating American identity.

However, the growth of the concept of the sovereignty of the people, first effectively aired by the American and French revolutions of the eighteenth century, was strengthened by the rise of nationalism, the love of the nation, as the new secular 'god' for the people. To man's insignificance before God was now added obeisance towards the nation. Nationalism became, for many, a form of secular religion, with its own heroes, martyrs, worship, creed, and so on. The twentieth century was to witness nationalist wars comparable in destructiveness to the wars of religion in the seventeenth century.

Religion is not integral to national identity solely within the Christian world. Japan with Shintoism, India with Hinduism, Israel with Judaism, Pakistan with Islam, and many other nations are closely identified with religions. Religious beliefs are an essential element in shaping a sense of belonging to a nation for many, probably most, peoples on earth.

Modern nations are multi-religious, even if there is a dominant religion, or they are largely secular. While religious affiliation has an impact on nationhood and identity, one must remember that religions are usually shared across national frontiers. Indeed, religions tend to develop national characteristics. Polish Catholicism, for example, is distinctively *Polish*. Irish and Italian Catholicism very much reflect aspects of their respective national cultures.

However, religion is only one feature, albeit an important one, in creating a nation.

Government and nation

Government as an element in influencing national identity is linked to a concept known as 'political nationalism'. National identity, according to political nationalism, is essentially a civic and legal concept that as a consequence does not necessarily stimulate among its citizens deep emotional commitment to the nation concerned. People may choose to join a nation and take on its citizenship without feeling deeply emotionally attached to their new country.

Nations are often created by particular systems of government, not only, as we have seen, in the conscious creation of a sense of national identity, but they also become closely identified with particular systems of government. American national identity is closely associated with the United States Constitution and liberal democracy. The British, when they think about it at all, see parliamentary democracy as an expression of their national development over the centuries. By the twentieth century nationality in such countries was associated with citizenship, regardless of the people's country of origin or any 'blood ties'. Nationality in this sense became a symbol of a new cultural identity which was shared with or replaced other, older, national identities.

In Eastern Europe in the nineteenth century, nationality was linked to communal groups, based on religion or language, identified as such by the government and with legal political and social status. Often these groups enjoyed a considerable degree of self-government, such as the Jews and Finns had in Imperial Russia, but at the same time they were denied equal citizenship rights and equal legal status before the courts.

The experience of history and the effectiveness of particular types of government system affect the sense of national identity. We have already mentioned the American and British experiences. Russian nationhood has been moulded by experience of strong, powerful, autocratic governments under the tsars and, later, communism as a means of defending the nation against powerful external enemies that threaten the long national frontiers.

National existence depends heavily upon the conditions of power, or lack of it, and political circumstances existing both internally and internationally. Strong governments are better able to strengthen the nation at home and defend its interests abroad. The success or otherwise of a government in achieving its domestic and foreign goals will affect its legitimacy and, as a consequence, the strength and effectiveness of the sense of national identity.

Common historical and cultural ties

Often connected with the idea of 'cultural nationalism' is the idea that a nation exists because of a shared historical and cultural experience that is different from that of other nations. Anthony Smith, in *The Ethnic Origins of Nations* (1986), identifies a link between ethnic communities and modern nations, having deep roots in language and history and pre-dating modern political structures. To a great extent this form of nationalism assumes that one can only be born into the nation, and cannot join it. It is often closely associated with the idea that there are deep 'blood ties' between members of an ethnic community.

War has been a major historical element in the creation of modern nations: wars for the expansion of powerful nations, wars for defence, wars to ensure the survival of a nation, wars for national liberation. Indeed, it is difficult to find a nation that has not been, in some sense, created and shaped by its experience of war – either as victor or as defeated contestant. English, and later British, nationhood was forged by centuries of war with the French. American identity was forged in the War of Independence. Israel, India, Bangladesh, Pakistan, Vietnam are just a few modern nations created or shaped by the experience of war.

The cultural concept of the nation can be traced back to the writings of the eighteenth-century German philosopher-poet Johann Gottfried Herder, challenging the **Enlightenment**, rationality, the consequences of the industrial revolution and, especially, the cultural domination of France among the German elite. He conceived the nation in terms of the *Volk*, a term difficult to translate into English. 'People', the usual translation, is too narrow. The *Volk* is a vehicle of culture, language, heritage, historical experience, a *Volksgeist* ('national spirit') shared by a particular people – nation – and develops its special genius. Johann Fichte, writing about the same time as Herder, declared that Germany's unique culture could only be defended and enhanced by the political unification of the German people.

> **Enlightenment**
> An intellectual movement that began in the late seventeenth century and reached its height in the eighteenth. It exalted reason and challenged the religious and political status quo. The Enlightenment is credited with forming the intellectual underpinning of the French Revolution.

This view of nationhood became very influential during the nineteenth century, both in Germany and elsewhere in Europe. In Italy Guiseppe Mazzini adapted the concept to the nationalist cause, and gave it a liberal 'spin'. He believed that once each nation had its own government there would be peace, both internally and internationally. However, this historical and cultural concept is usually associated with the bitter competitive nationalisms of the late nineteenth century and, especially, Nazism in the 1920s and 1930s. There are modern versions of such views, often connected with far-right and extreme nationalist groups who think they are fighting 'globalisation' and the effects of 'globalised' culture, which are undermining 'authentic' national identity.

A 'sense of nationhood'

Although it might seem rather circular, a nation is best defined as a group of people who believe themselves to constitute a nation, have things in common with each other and share a sense of nationhood. The nation can be defined as an 'imagined community' where people believe themselves to have some sort of link, or commitment, to others in the nation, most of whom they will never meet. The imagined community also extends into the past. Members of a nation identify with people who lived centuries before and were of the same nation. These other people 'belong' to each other by having the same birthplace, and having membership of the same national 'family'. Indeed, the very term has its roots in the Latin *nasci*, 'to be born', and can be seen when expressed in the terms 'Motherland' or 'Fatherland'. Germans talk of their 'Fatherland', Russians of their 'Motherland' and the British, cosily and curiously, of their 'Homeland'.

A sense of nationhood is clearly associated with loyalty to the nation, the largest political community from which people will accept a claim over all other forms of social loyalty. Betrayal of one's nation is still regarded as one of the greatest crimes, putting at risk one's fellow national members.

Britain and the 'British' nations

The United Kingdom has great difficulty in being identified as a 'nation-state'. For most of its people there are two competing 'national' identities: 'British', associated with the UK, and 'English', 'Welsh', 'Scottish', and in Northern Ireland 'Loyalist British' and 'Irish'. We will look at these in turn.

Britain

Britain has an image of being an ancient nation, with its national flag, national anthem, and national governing and other institutions, but in recent years it has been under challenge by other identities. The problem with British nationhood, as with all nations, arises out of its history.

British national identity is closely linked with English national identity and the English national experience. 'British' and 'English' are often used inter-changeably by foreigners and by the English themselves (a mistake rarely made by people of the other British nations). This indicates a sense of union of the two national identities in a way that no member of the 'Celtic fringe' (as compared with the English 'centre') would make.

The creation of the United Kingdom is very much the result of England being the dominant power within the British Isles. It has for centuries been the wealthiest country, the most powerful government, and the largest population in these islands. It took centuries of war in Wales and Ireland, and war and economic leverage in Scotland, to establish political union. But it was English power that brought about this union.

After the union of the Scottish and English crowns in 1603, King James I of England (and VI of Scotland) frequently used the term 'British' to describe his new realm. After the union of the English and Scottish parliaments in 1707 the terms 'British' and 'British nation' became increasingly accepted by most people in the Protestant nations of England, Scotland and Wales, and the Protestant 'British' of Ireland; but never so by the Catholic Irish to the same degree. Nevertheless, 'British' and 'Britishness' were useful notions for uniting the peoples of the British Isles, who then directed their aggression overseas and created the British Empire. With the development of 'popular' imperialism, associated with the rise of mass democracy, in the late nineteenth century this British national identity established itself as dominant for the peoples of the UK. The wars of the following century strengthened this British national identity, but this configuration did not remain static.

Twenty years after the Second World War almost all the empire had gone. In 1997 Hong Kong was returned to China and the empire was finally laid to rest. Long before then, the strengthening national identities of the constituent nations of Britain were threatening the UK itself.

Nevertheless, one might say there is much life left in the idea of a British national identity. Citizenship is still 'British'. No 'English', 'Scottish' or 'Welsh' national identity exists in domestic or international law. Many – perhaps a majority of – non-white citizens see 'British' as a valuable form of national identity, along civic national lines. English, Scottish and Welsh still have strong ethnic/cultural national connotations. 'Britishness', for 'Black-Britons', 'Asian-Britons', and 'Chinese-Britons', may be an intermediate stage before their ultimate national integration as English, Welsh or Scottish.

'Britishness' was created by 250 years of near permanent war with other great powers and within the empire. The UK state was a very effective tool for the potential military power of the British nations. The recent conflicts in the Falklands (1982) and the Gulf (1990–91), and the 'war against terrorism' in Afghanistan and elsewhere, may well strengthen the British sense of national identity.

England

The close identification of 'England' and 'Britain' often means that insufficient attention is given to English national identity and its distinctiveness from the other nations that constitute Britain.

English nationhood has been shaped by war. Battles and wars of the fifth and sixth centuries determined the very territory of England. The English–Welsh frontier was established long before King Offa of Mercia built his Dyke in the eighth century. The frontier of Scotland moved backwards and forwards for centuries until Elizabeth I's time. Both the Welsh and Scottish borderlands were for centuries wild and violent frontier zones.

Strong regional identities, having deep roots, still exist in this most centralised of nations. Yet England has had a strong centralised state, and with it a concept of national identity, for well over a thousand years. The Norman Conquest took over a very effective state structure and by the thirteenth century the Normans and Saxons had fused into an English national identity. This national identity survived civil wars and was greatly strengthened by Tudor monarchs during the sixteenth century and the civil wars and political upheavals of the seventeenth century.

England was shaped by many social developments, especially by being the earliest industrialised nation and an old urbanised nation. There are strong strains of political liberalism and social conservatism running through English culture. The Protestantism of the majority of its population, the Catholicism of a large minority of its people, and its religious toleration all have had a profound influence on the development of England. Modern England is, however, a highly **secular society**.

> **secular society**
> A society where religion has no privileged position and is confined to what is presumed to be its rightful non-privileged sphere, as in the United States. Whereas a 'theocratic state' is one in which a particular religion has a special and privileged position, such as Saudi Arabia and Iran.

Immigration and emigration has for centuries moulded English national identity. Empire, economics, politics and overseas colonies encouraged the English to travel and settle widely. These same historical forces were responsible for waves of non- British immigrants over centuries: Jews, Dutch, Germans, Italians, Poles, Ukrainians, Hungarians, Africans, South Asians and Chinese are only some of the major populations that settled in English cities. England is by far the most multi-racial, multi-cultural and multi-religious of the nations of the British Isles.

Some people, especially the English, think there is no such thing as English nationalism. However, many of England's Celtic neighbours think there is, and, moreover, that English nationalism has for centuries oppressed the Welsh, Scots and Irish. Conversely, some English people believe that England actually subsidises Wales and Scotland, for example through over-generous central government grants paid for by English taxpayers.

Scotland

Scottish identity has been shaped by war, especially against the English; deep regional divisions between Highland and Lowland Scots; religious conflicts between Protestant and Catholic, Presbyterian and Anglican; and rivalries between Glasgow and Edinburgh.

Scotland retained its independence as a consequence of the wars of Robert the Bruce at the start of the fourteenth century. Although Scotland was frequently at war with England over the following two centuries, the English and Scottish crowns were united in 1603 with James VI of Scotland succeeding Elizabeth as James I of England. Nevertheless, Scotland saw little of its Stuart kings and, although playing a crucial role in the mid-seventeenth-century civil wars, it retained its own parliament until 1707, when it merged with the Westminster Parliament.

The Act of Union was bitterly resented by many Scots as ending national independence. The accession of the Hanoverians to the British throne in 1714 ended any possibility of peaceful restoration of the Stuart monarchy. The British government, with much Scottish support, crushed Highland rebellions in 1715 and 1745. Emigration from Scotland to England and overseas became a feature of the Scottish national experience. For two hundred years Scots participated in empire-building and the industrial revolution, and in British politics. Scotland retained distinct national institutions: its own legal system, church, local government and education systems; and its banks issued its own paper currency. Few travelling in Scotland for any length of time could be in any doubt that they have entered a country with distinct national characteristics.

By the 1960s the decline of once prosperous Scottish industries – coal, steel, shipbuilding, heavy engineering – and rising unemployment, combined with the discovery of oil, 'Scotland's oil', as nationalists declared it, stimulated demands for greater self-government by the Scottish National Party (SNP).

The SNP, founded in 1934, argued that the major political parties and the Westminster Parliament or the British government did not adequately serve Scotland. Many SNP supporters came from cultural nationalist movements seeking to protect the Gaelic language, Scottish culture and a distinct national identity. The majority, however, came from the Scottish socialist tradition and believed that a progressive, just society could not be created by a Westminster dominated by the English, who often, too often, returned Conservative governments.

The economic crises of the 1970s particularly hit Scotland, with its heavy reliance on declining industries for employment and wealth. The Conservative governments of the 1980s and 1990s, with their electoral roots in England, were regarded as governing Scotland with little legitimacy. Scottish Tories became a very rare political species as national economic policies seemed to be particularly damaging to Scotland. Tory attacks on public housing and public spending particularly hurt Scotland, which had high levels of public-sector employment and was heavily dependent on state support. The introduction of the poll tax in Scotland a year earlier than in England was signally stimulating to Scottish grievances against an 'English' Conservative government.

In the 1990s strong economic growth in Scotland centred on the new IT and service sectors, and the importance of oil to the Scottish economy declined. There was a strong revival of a confident, distinct Scottish cultural identity, as displayed in music, literature and the arts, instead of in the widely derided 'tartan' identity of kilts, bagpipes, Bonnie Prince Charlie, and so on. Demands for a Scottish parliament to reflect this identity grew. The Conservative Party resisted these demands but Labour and the Liberal Democrats support the implementation of devolution for Scotland. The SNP was somewhat dubious about the merits of a devolved parliament when they argued for an independent Scotland.

In 1997 the Labour Party returned to power with a 'landslide' victory, involving the eradication of Scottish Tory MPs and a strong Scottish presence among leading members of the government. Proposals for a devolved parliament with tax-raising powers were approved by a referendum in 1998 and enacted into law. The first Scottish parliament in nearly three hundred years was elected in 1999 and began work with a joint Labour–Liberal Democrat coalition government.

It was clear that the Scottish Parliament would seek to introduce measures reflecting the more left-wing Scottish political culture rather than the Westminster Labour government. Tuition fees were removed for Scottish university students, and higher levels of financial support for the elderly in care homes and greater levels of health and education spending were introduced.

Whether such forms of self-government will for long satisfy Scottish national identity remains to be seen. Pressures are growing for more powers to be trans-ferred to the Scottish Parliament. The SNP continues to argue that only full independence from the UK and membership of the EU will properly allow Scottish nationhood to be fully expressed. This seems unlikely at present. But one may envisage problems with a Labour–Liberal Democrat Scottish government and a Conservative Westminster government at some future time.

Wales

Welsh identity, even more than Scottish, has been influenced by military resistance to English domination. Political disunity and relative weakness in medieval Wales encouraged English monarchs to intervene. Centuries of warfare, celebrated in Welsh literature and evidenced by dozens of castles and strongholds, ultimately ended with political union with England and, with the Tudors, the 'Welsh' acquisition of the monarchy in 1485. Since then Wales and the Welsh have played a major, often crucial, role in 'English' history.

Welsh political independence ended centuries ago. Welsh cultural nation-alism, however, has been at the core of its identity. One element has been its nonconformist Christian tradition. Also important is the Welsh language. This was a language in decline during the nineteenth century and most of the twentieth. English became the language of the Welsh elite. The industriali-sation of South Wales disrupted ancient ways of life and sucked in non-Welsh speakers from England and Scotland. Welsh people emigrated to England and overseas. Finally, there was a systematic attempt by the authorities to destroy Welsh as a language of education and government.

Welsh nationalism finds political expression in Plaid Cymru, which was founded in 1925 and which sought rather to defend Welsh culture than seek Welsh independence. Some Welsh activists believed this programme to be too tame. Some thought radical action was needed to defend the language in order to challenge the growth of English-owned second homes and their impact on Welsh culture and house prices; and to push for economic aid to offset the decline of farming, steel, coal and engineering in Wales. A few planted bombs, burnt English second homes and defaced English on road signs, but the defence of Welsh national identity was overwhelmingly peaceful and parliamentary.

By the end of the twentieth century Welsh was no longer in decline and was officially supported in education, government and the media. New industries had been attracted to Wales by UK regional aid programmes and the EU. Nevertheless, Wales remained a nation divided by language and geography. Transport links tend to run from England into Wales, rather than to connect areas within the country, and Welsh remained largely confined to its heart-lands in the north and west.

Wales, partly as a consequence of long integration into English politics, has been lukewarm about devolution. The 1979 referendum on devolution returned a 'No' vote. Conservative policies in Wales during the 1980s and 1990s combined simultaneously the run-down of traditional industries and considerable regional aid, as well as support for the Welsh language and culture.

In 1997, however, the Conservative Party was eliminated from Wales in the general election, while the Labour, Liberal Democrat and Plaid Cymru parties were all committed to devolution. However, both in the 1998 referendum and the 1999 elections to the Welsh Assembly turnout was low and interest hard to stimulate, especially as the assembly has no tax-raising powers. After some initial teething problems, most notably over the degree of influence the national Labour Party should have over the leadership of the Welsh Party, the assembly is becoming an effective expansion of Welsh national identity within the UK and the EU.

Northern Ireland

Northern Ireland is a very peculiar part of the UK in terms of national identity. One might perceive three 'national identities' here: 'British', 'Irish' and 'Northern Irish'.

'British' is the legal national identity available to all citizens in Northern Ireland. However, for the Protestant population of the province, the descendants of Scottish and English settlers of the early seventeenth century, this is their *sole* national identity. These people were intended as the rulers of Ireland, a distinct minority defined by their religion and political power, in a largely hostile country. Seething resentment and occasional revolt by the Irish encouraged a 'siege' mentality among these British (sometimes identified also as 'Unionists' or 'Loyalists').

Having once dominated the Irish Parliament until its abolition in 1801, Unionists were hostile to Irish Home Rule as a wider franchise would result in a permanent parliamentary majority for the Catholic Irish. By this time the concept of 'Loyalism' was a feature of Northern Irish 'British' identity. This meant loyalty to the British Crown, their British identity, and the Protestant religion, celebrating the Battle of the Boyne (1690) and other landmarks of Protestant ascendancy in Ireland. By 1910, and the Third Irish Home Rule Bill, Loyalists had armed themselves to resist both the Catholic Irish and the British government with the rallying cry, 'Home Rule is Rome Rule'.

The First World War put Home Rule on hold. But by 1919 the issue had reappeared with a vengeance. An Irish revolt in 1916, and its brutal suppression by the British, produced a majority of Irish MPs for Sinn Fein in the post-war election who refused to go to Westminster and promptly declared an Irish Republic. The subsequent Anglo-Irish War lasted until 1921, when the British Government and the Irish 'government' agreed to the **partition** of the island into a twenty-six-county Free State and a six-county Northern Ireland remaining within the UK, but with its own 'devolved' government at Stormont Castle.

> **partition**
> The division of a nation or state into two or more parts, such as Poland in the eighteenth century, and Ireland, Korea and Cyprus in the twentieth.

For sixty years Stormont was an expression of British/Unionist rule in Ireland and Loyalist national identity. Having lost control of Ireland, Loyalists determined not to lose 'Ulster', as they called the province. Vote-rigging, gerrymandering, job and housing discrimination and Loyalist violence were all used to oppress Catholics and ensure their own community was kept voting for Unionist politicians.

By the late 1960s this policy of control was breaking down into sectarian violence arising out of conflicting national identities. By 1972 the situation had reached such a pass that the UK government ended Stormont and introduced Direct Rule. Attempts at a new devolved parliament, involving power-sharing between Catholic and Protestant politicians, broke down in 1974, in the face of Loyalist intransigence, and are at present by no means certain of success as the Northern Ireland Assembly struggles with the competing national identities of the population.

For many Protestants, British governments over the last thirty years have been seeking to accommodate the Irish population in the North and the Republic at their own expense. Every concession to Catholics is perceived by Loyalists as a threat to the British national identity of the majority population. Restrictions on Loyalist marches (a celebration of their identity), changes in the police service (traditionally dominated by Protestants), and Sinn Fein ministers in the Northern Ireland Executive (men associated with Republican terrorism) are seen as part of a long process of pushing the 'British' people of Northern Ireland into some form of Catholic-dominated political system and, thereby, a betrayal of their services to the Crown and Protestantism over the past four centuries.

Irish national identity is largely, but not entirely, Catholic and Celtic, and shaped by centuries of struggle against English, British and 'Loyalist' domination and oppression in Ireland.

English and, later, British imperialism in Ireland began in the late twelfth century with Edward I. The Elizabethan and Cromwellian conquests of the late sixteenth century and the 1650s left bitter memories for Irish nationalists. Revolt in the 1790s, the Fenians in the nineteenth century and the Easter Rising in 1916 are part of a revolutionary tradition in Irish nationalism which believes the British will only leave Ireland when forced out. Only then might Loyalists identify themselves as 'Irishmen'. Failure and defeat only provided another set of nationalist myths and martyrs for the next round of struggle against the British. Running in tandem with this violent struggle for Irish national independence was the parliamentary strain of Land Reform, Home Rule, and cultural renaissance throughout the nineteenth and twentieth centuries.

This struggle did not cease with Partition, but has continued, sometimes violent, sometimes peaceful, but always facing the power of the British state and the 'British' rulers of Northern Ireland. Partition was declared an 'unnatural division of the island'; a united Ireland is the ultimate expression of Irish national identity for both Catholics and Protestants.

One problem with the aspiration to a united Ireland is that the British and Irish identities in Northern Ireland have less and less in common with those of the Republic and Great Britain. Both are active participants in the EU, a project designed in part to reduce national antagonisms and national identities, and both are modern, secular, prosperous liberal democracies, to which the sectarian nationalism of Northern Ireland appears archaic, socially divisive, oppressive, unsuccessful, repulsive and a drag on economic and social development.

One might perceive Northern Ireland as a 'proto-nation', not quite Irish and not quite British but having a national, cultural and political identity of its own deriving from its unique history. Eighty years of the Northern Ireland state have created a social and political environment in which Catholics and Protestants, Irish and British, have more in common with each other and less with the Republic of Ireland and Britain. If this is the case, then Northern Ireland requires unique political and social institutions to reflect this 'proto-nationhood'. Perhaps that is why the Good Friday Agreements have, with all their problems and tensions, come closest to a political settlement in the province which satisfies at least some of the national aspirations of Irish and British.

Some political community corresponding to the nation has existed so long in human history that it is almost impossible to imagine that there might be any alternative to it as a focus of identity and loyalty in the political and cultural world. So strong is nationhood that it is relatively easy to be persuaded how 'natural' the division of the human race into nations is.

Nations and national identity are constantly in flux as social and economic forces work on human societies. However, seemingly strong nations have disappeared during the last century. New nations have appeared, with similar very high levels of identity and emotional resonance for their people. One can see that, however powerful the idea of the nation might be, however likely to continue as a defining feature of human political activity, the particular nation with which people will identify is likely to change considerably during the coming century. Nations in some form are here to stay, although one might question whether the nations of today will exist in their present form by the twenty-second century.

Summary

Perhaps the most powerful of all political concepts to motivate human beings is that of the 'nation'. But the concept is an elusive one. While the 'nation-state' is a term commonly used, many 'nations' do not have states, and there are states comprised of many nations. Important elements in national identity include language, religion, government and common historical and cultural ties. There are enormous differences, however, in the significance of these factors from nation to nation. Perhaps the most useful way of defining a nation is a subjective one. A nation is what its members feel it is, and they are identified by their deep loyalty to it. Britain illustrates the difficulty of identification of the 'nation'. Historically and to a degree culturally it is composed of at least three nations: England, Scotland and Wales. Northern Ireland further complicates matters by being arguably composed of two nations, Irish and British. Moreover, these two nations are themselves not entirely clear about what precisely their individual national identity is.

REFERENCES AND FURTHER READING

1 M. Parris, 'An off-the-peg identity', *The Times* (7 November 1998).

Alter, P. *Nationalism* (Edward Arnold, 1989).

Anderson, B. *Imagined Communities: Reflections on the Origins and Spread of Nationalism* (NLB/Verso, 1983).

Deutsch, K. *Nationalism and Social Communication* (Massachusetts Institute of Technology, 1953).

'Nations and their Past: The Uses and Abuses of History', *Economist* (21 December 1996), pp. 53–6.

Gellner, E. *Nations and Nationalism* (Blackwell, 1983).

Hastings, A. *The Construction of Nationhood: Ethnicity, Religion and Nationalism* (Cambridge University Press, 1997).

Heywood, A. 'Nationalism', in A. Heywood, *Political Ideas and Concepts: An Introduction* (Macmillan, 1994), pp. 152–85.

Heywood, A. 'Nations and Nationalism', in A. Heywood, *POLITICS* (Macmillan, 1997), pp. 103–19.

Hobsbawm, E. *Nations and Nationalism since 1780* (Cambridge University Press, 1990).

Jay, R. 'Nationalism', in Robert Eccleshall *et al.*, *Political Ideologies: An Introduction* (Routledge, 1994), pp. 153–84.

Kedourie, E. *Nationalism* (Hutchinson, 1985).

Purnell, R. 'The Notion of the Nation: Some Images and Myths', in R. Purnell, *The Society of States: An Introduction to International Politics* (Weidenfeld and Nicolson, 1973), pp. 110–27.

Smith, A. *The Ethnic Origins of Nations* (Blackwell, 1986).

SAMPLE QUESTIONS

1 To what extent is the nation the fundamental unit of human organisation?

2 What are the main characteristics of nationhood? Do all nations have all of these characteristics?

3 How recent is the concept of the 'nation'?

4 How far have such developments as globalisation and the creation of supranational entities like the European Union rendered the notion of the nation-state obsolete?

5 Is Britain a nation?

Democracy

3

Here we examine the expression 'democracy', and try to disentangle its value as an objective term of analysis and its misuse as a tool of propaganda. The focus is on 'liberal democracy'. First the various dimensions of democracy and the notion of democracy are considered, and the idea of democracy as 'the sovereign people' governed by consent is closely examined. Then the issue of whether there are particular conditions for the development of democracy is investigated. Arguments for and against democracy are explored and finally there are some reflections on the future of democracy in the twenty-first century.

POINTS TO CONSIDER

➤ Why is democracy a great 'hurrah' word?

➤ Have forms of democracy other than liberal democracy (such as the communist 'people's democracy') any validity?

➤ To what extent does modern Britain fit Aristotle's categories of types of government?

➤ What are the differences between 'defensive' and 'citizen' democracy, and is one preferable to the other?

➤ To what extent are claims that in a democracy 'the sovereign people are governed by consent' merely rhetorical flourishes?

➤ Are claims of the universal applicability of democracy valid?

➤ What would you identify as the main threats to democracy in the modern world?

Democracy substitutes election by the incompetent many for appointment by the corrupt few. (George Bernard Shaw, *Man and Superman*, 1903)

It has been said that Democracy is the worst form of government except all those other forms that have been tried from time to time. (Sir Winston Churchill, *Speech*, House of Commons, November 1947)

The difference between a Democracy and a Dictatorship is that in a Democracy you vote first and take orders later; in a Dictatorship you don't have to waste your time voting. (Charles Bukowski, *Erections, Ejaculations, Exhibitions and Tales of Ordinary Madness*, 1972)

Democracy is a great 'hurrah' word of modern times. From being associated with mob rule at the beginning of the nineteenth century, democracy had become the objective of every 'civilised' nation by its end. A century later, there is hardly a state or regime, no matter how despotic, that does not proclaim its devotion to 'democracy'. Along with 'God, Queen and country' (in Britain), or 'mom and apple pie' (in the USA), 'democracy' is now associated with something good and wholesome, something worth defending and, if necessary, dying (and killing) for.

One can see that there is a problem with the term 'democracy'. If every political system is a 'democracy' then what value can be attached to the word as an analytical tool? One must question, however, Bernard Crick's assertion, in his *In Defence of Politics* (1962), that politics primarily takes place only in democratic systems of government. Politics can take place under any form of governmental system, as it involves a struggle for power. Democratic political systems involve power struggles of a kind very different from those of other political systems, such as dictatorships and one-party states.

We identify here the main features of a democratic form of government. Indeed, as will become apparent, underlying our discussion is an identification of democracy with 'liberal-democratic' forms of government. Liberal democracies are closely associated with particular forms of intellectual, cultural, social and economic development identified and discussed below.

Liberal democracies are among the great creations of the human mind. They establish the conditions for individual freedom and participation in government, for freedom of speech and thought, and, within the **rule of law**, the stability and order required for that freedom to flourish. In the great struggles and fearful wars of the twentieth century liberal democracy met the challenges from authoritarianism and totalitarianism and ultimately triumphed.

> **rule of law**
> The principle that everyone, even the ruler, is under the authority of the law (and those who administer the law in the courts).

Liberal democracies are relatively new, only appearing from the late nineteenth century onwards. They are still in a minority among nations, albeit the wealthiest and most powerful ones. Democratic ideas are worth studying in some detail since they claim universal applicability.

Defining democracy

'Democracy' comes from Ancient Greek: *demos* means 'the people' and *kratein* means 'to rule'. Hence, *demokratia*, 'democracy', means 'rule by the people', as defined in, for example, *The Concise Oxford Dictionary*:

> **democracy 1a.** a system of government by the whole population, usually through elected representatives. **b.** a state so governed. **c.** any organisation governed on democratic principles.

Democracy can refer to popular government, or **representative government**, or participation in government, or republican government, or some overlap between some or all of these. Defining democracy may appear to be easy, but is in fact full of problems.

Many forms of government are described as 'democratic'. For example, Adolf Hitler called the Third Reich 'The German democracy, which is the true democracy'. Benito Mussolini described Italian Fascism as 'the purest form of democracy'. Communist regimes call themselves 'people's democracies'. Most dictatorships in the developing world claim to be 'democratic'. Finally, our own political system is called a 'liberal democracy', combining two political 'hurrah' words. The difference between liberal democracies, established in Western Europe, North America and elsewhere, and other so-called 'democracies' might appear so obvious as not to need defining. Yet define it we must, if we are to have a tool with which to analyse this particular form of government. So, then, what is 'democracy'?

> **representative government**
> A political system in which the government is chosen by the people (for example, by elections), governs on their behalf, is accountable to them and owes its legitimacy to the fact that it is representative of the people in some manner.

One might start by contrasting democracies with other types of government. Democracies have a number of elements by which they might be distinguished from non-democratic systems and 'pseudo-democracies' – systems that claim to be democratic and, indeed, which apparently have some democratic features, but lack certain fundamental elements of 'genuine' democracies.

Elements of democracy

A number of features of democracy can be identified:
- Democracy as a system of government. Here we can discern two forms of democracy: 'defensive democracy' and 'citizen democracy'/'republican democracy';

- democracy and legitimising government;
- majority rule and democracy;
- equality of citizenship rights;
- public opinion in democracies;
- the rule of law and democracy.

Democracy as a system of government

Ancient Greeks, such as Aristotle in *The Politics*, identified three kinds of government, each with a corresponding 'corrupt' form.

- **Monarchy**: rule by one man, usually as the consequence of birth: the corrupt form being *tyranny*.

- **Aristocracy**: rule by a few men, based on education, property ownership, merit or some other quality that distinguished them from most other people: the corrupt form being oligarchy.

- **Democracy**: rule by the whole people – or at least a majority: the corrupt form being mob rule, although 'democracy' and 'mob rule' were seen as the same thing by most thinkers.

All these political systems make decisions accepted as binding on the whole community. Every one has a mixture of decision-making by one person, a few or many people. Monarchs, for example, consult widely about government. Even dictators have to take into account how far they can control the people. Hitler's oratorical powers facilitated his seizure of power in Germany, but also helped him as leader to persuade, cajole and inspire the German people. Ancient Athenian democracy involved the direct participation of all citizens in government and is often seen as the inspiration for modern democracies. Citizenship itself, though, was very restricted. No women, slaves or foreigners could take part, or ever hope to become citizens, in the democracy. In all political systems, ancient and modern, there is a tendency for an 'oligarchy' of professional administrators and politicians to arise. There are also always groups – defending economic interests or advancing particular causes – that influence government without a popular **mandate** to do so.

> **mandate**
>
> This can mean either a general authority to govern conferred on a government by an election or a specific authority (and duty) to implement a policy put before the electorate in a manifesto.

Britain's political system, for example, has elements of: monarchy in the power of the prime minister; aristocracy, or its modern non-corrupt meaning of the form oligarchy, in the domination of the political system by a few political parties and relatively small groups of political leaders; and democracy, in its widespread political debate and regular elections.

Consideration of the term 'democracy' involves identifying the degree to which these three elements exist in a political system. A state may be called 'democratic' because features associated with democracy predominate, while in 'undemocratic' systems they are at a minimum and anti-democratic values predominate. However, this takes us back to the central issue: what is meant by 'democracy'?

One might see a political system defined as democratic by the degree to which people can exercise *effective* influence on government policy. Democracy is not just about voting and voting rights. Most modern political systems have some form of election and legislative assembly. Even in countries that one would never consider democratic – certainly not liberal democratic – we need to consider other factors than **suffrage** and elections as the basis for a democracy.

> **suffrage**
> The right to vote in public elections. It is now usually defined in terms of citizenship and age. In the nineteenth century suffrage was restricted to people on the grounds of gender, education and property ownership

Crucially, popular opinion can influence government decisions in democracies without votes being taken. Governments, political parties and politicians want to win future elections and so will take notice of public opinion.

Oligarchy and monarchy still exist in 'democratic' states, but it is the democratic element that is of greatest value and should be a prominent influence in government. Thus democracy can be interpreted as a *positive* description of the democratic element in government.

In 'non-democratic' states the democratic element may exist but popular influence on government decision-making is kept to a minimum. Here, democracy is interpreted *negatively*.

Support for or against the democratic element among a population depends on many factors. These include emotional, personal, family or class interests, loyalties and traditions; the national historical experience; and cultural support for democratic principles of government. Combinations of these and other factors may lead to a movement in favour of democracy (as in Spain after the death of General Franco in 1975) or against democracy (as in the German Weimar Republic during the 1920s).

Most important are economic conditions. Poor, unemployed, desperate people are, to say the least, likely to be unenthusiastic supporters of a democratic government presiding over their misery. (Alternatively, wealthy societies, too, may be in danger from citizen apathy. Democracy may be viewed as no more than a means by which to remain rich. Plump and prosperous people resent even the time it takes to vote to ensure the survival of their democracy.)

Factors favouring or undermining democracy vary from country to country and from time to time. There is no automatic presumption in favour of democracy or its effortless, inevitable, spread across the globe.

Another way of identifying or classifying democratic systems of government is outlined below.

Defensive democracy

Democracy is the means by which citizens are protected from an oppressive state. It defends the rights of citizens and promotes liberty. Defensive democracy sees a tension between citizens and the state, and a distinction between public and private spheres of life. It has strong roots in liberalism.

Citizens participate in defensive democracies when they fear their rights and freedoms are threatened by the state or a foreign power. Once the threat is removed most citizens will not participate in democracy. In the twentieth century democratic theory extended citizen rights to include full participation in society. State activities expanded into areas of what had once been considered private life, establishing health, education and welfare systems. One might still relate this to defensive democracy. The rights to be defended have expanded to include those of the welfare state. They still have to be advanced and defended by democratic action and most people will only participate when they see threats to these rights. This can be done by either 'direct' or 'representative' democracy. We will concentrate on representative democracy here.

Modern representative democracy includes most of the things that one associates with liberal democracy. It consists of:

> A cluster of rules and obligations permitting the broadest participation by the majority of the citizens in the selection of representatives who alone can make political decisions (that is decisions affecting the whole of the community).

> This cluster includes elected government; free and fair elections in which every citizen's vote has an equal weight; a suffrage which embraces all citizens irrespective of distinctions of race, religion, class, sex, and so on; freedom of conscience, information and expression of all public matters broadly defined; the right of all adults to oppose their government and stand for office; and associational autonomy – the right to form independent associations including social movements, interest groups and political parties.[1]

Representative democracies are closely associated with constitutional arrangements designed to legitimise the state and ensure that citizenship rights are protected. They still assume greater judgement, more political intelligence, among political leaders than among the electorate. Such democracies function as a means of containing the dangers of a direct democracy.

Consent to govern is expressed by regular elections, which also legitimise the actions of the government during the period between elections. Once elected, the government has a mandate from the people to carry out policies outlined in its manifesto. It can take whatever steps it deems necessary, within the bounds of political accountability, to ensure the survival and success of that society and the defence of its citizens.

The vast majority of citizens confine participation in politics to voting. Only a tiny number are likely to join a political party. Even fewer will become party activists, of which a tiny proportion will become a member of the local and national political class. Apathy, or at least non-involvement, is *the* characteristic of modern representative democracies. They are run by **elites**.

> **elite**
> Those regarded (by themselves and those they govern) as superior in some manner to others. In a political sense, those with special access to power.

Robert Michels, in *Political Parties* (1900), formulated an 'iron law of oligarchy' at play in democracies. Small elite groups have a disproportionate role in the running of democratic organisations. Michels and other 'elite theorists', such as Max Weber in his many writings, Gaetano Mosca in *The Ruling Class* (1896), and Mosei Ostrogorski in *Democracy and the Organisation of Political Parties* (1902), stressed the deceptiveness of democracy. They recognised that it was the few at the top of power structures, rather than the many (as in democratic theory), who shaped 'democratic' government. Joseph Schumpeter, in *Capitalism, Socialism and Democracy* (1942), claimed that modern democracy is little more than a power struggle between elites. Voters choose between 'auctions' of public services by oligarchic party elites. Indeed, as others have identified, modern democracy has become so money orientated that it corrupts the democratic process. Politicians and political parties raise vast sums of money to fund campaigns, especially in the USA. All social democracies have large public sectors and elections have become little more than attempts to 'bribe the people with their own money', with scant mature public debate over policies.

The complexity of modern political issues means that political representatives must use their judgement on the basis of the evidence available to decide on the most appropriate policies. It is simply impossible for the majority of voters to understand policy details and reach a rational decision. Ordinary voters have to rely on the experienced judgement of politicians. Edmund Burke, in a speech to the electors of Bristol (1774), drew a significant distinction between a 'delegate' and a 'representative'. Delegates merely reflect the views of their constituents in parliament, while a representative is elected to use his own judgement. Burke clearly states that MPs should be representatives and, indeed, could not be delegates even for the tiny electorates of an eighteenth-century constituency.

This raises the issue of whom the elected politician 'represents'. Modern parliamentary constituencies have tens of thousands of voters, large numbers of whom did not vote for the elected representative. Members of the local party expect their views to be listened to by the person they worked to elect. Local businesses, trade unions, councils and other social organisations all have a right to be represented in the House of Commons by their MP. National pressure groups, trade unions, businesses and the national party all claim and seek representation in the democratic forum of the nation.

Clearly, it is impossible for a politician to represent all these interests equally. Indeed, party discipline, party loyalty and ideological compatibility will reduce the potential for 'representative conflict and stalemate'. The reduction is so great, in the view of many modern democrats and elite theorists, that representation on important issues in modern parliamentary democracies has been replaced by party control and party instructions on how to vote and what to think on issues. Compared with the British system, the US Congress has a weak party system. On the one hand, this offers greater scope for politicians' judgement; but on the other, as critics point out, they are more subject to powerful private interests, especially when these are exacerbated by the demands of almost constant electioneering and fundraising.

Citizen democracy/republican democracy

According to this type of democracy citizens should be active in order to advance their rights. Very importantly, the education and character development of the citizen is encouraged by participation in the political system. It improves the whole of society. Citizen democracy assumes, therefore, greater involvement than merely voting, with citizens taking an active part in the political system. 'Direct democracy' is the means by which this can come about.

Direct democracy describes the citizen's personal involvement in government. It developed in Ancient Athens during the fifth and fourth centuries BC. It worked quite well in a small society, consisting of no more than fifty thousand citizens at most (and probably nearer thirty thousand). Modern states are too large, in terms of both population and geography, for Athenian-style direct democracy to be a feasible means of national government. Direct democracy is limited to school governor boards, trade-union branches, town meetings in New England, some pressure-group activity, and so on. In Switzerland, however, there is a form of direct democracy in central government, its twenty-six cantons and three thousand communities. Referenda can be called for on any national law. In fact, over 450 have been held during the last 150 years and the number is rising to around ten referenda a year.

A society could still have a strong democratic culture in a citizen democracy with representative democratic institutions. Representative democracies often have elements of direct democracy in them. Radicals on the left want more active participation of citizens in decision-making. Some, on both the left and the right, believe citizens should have military training as a means of being integrated into society and learning what their democracy means.

Many democracies allow for referenda on important issues as a form of direct democracy. They can come from the government or be demanded by the populace. The result may or may not be binding on government; it depends on the constitutional rules. Just over half the US states have some form of direct democracy. Referenda are used in Italy, Denmark, France and New Zealand. Australia has had over fifty referenda. The UK has held referenda on political and constitutional issues in Scotland, Wales and Northern Ireland, but only one throughout the UK (concerning continued membership of the European Union, in 1975).

The time for greater direct democracy may have come. People are better educated, have greater access to information, and have more wealth and leisure time than ever before. Representative systems of democracy belong to a less democratic, less educated and less affluent age. Their constitutional systems are increasingly viewed as museum pieces by their electorates, who become frustrated by the lack of effective accountability of the government to the people. Their elected representatives, to put it politely, do not seem to demonstrate a greater level of political judgement than the people they represent.

Democracy and legitimising government

All democracies claim 'popular sovereignty' as providing government legitimacy – 'legitimacy' meaning 'the moral and political right to govern and expect to be obeyed'. Democratic government acts on behalf of the 'people', who are politically 'sovereign'. Democratic governments govern by 'consent'. We need at this stage to define the 'people', 'sovereignty' and 'consent'.

The people

This may describe the whole adult citizen body of the democracy, as it now tends to be the case, or it may merely define a group with special political privileges derived from wealth, class or education. There are many variations on this theme, for example:

- The British consider that the people have shared traditions, shared customs, shared history, and a sense of being part of the nation. The British people exist independently of their state. The state is their servant, carrying out their will as expressed through parliament. Democracy recognises the rights and freedoms of the people and the need to keep government under some form of control and accountability to the elected representatives of the people.

- The French believe the state reflects the 'general will' of the people. The state is closely linked to the identity of the people and reflects their interests. It is part of the people and contributes to national identity. It must not oppress the rights of the people.

- German political tradition maintains that the state reflects the people as the nation. German national identity pre-dates the existence of the state. The state is the machine for the expression of the will of the people. Democracy is one of the means by which the sovereignty of the people in their state is expressed.

Sovereignty

This concept claims that the people have the right to create the government of their choice and to replace it when they see fit. Legitimacy derives from the democratic will of the people, not from the sovereign or a ruling class defined by birth (or some other restrictive attribute). All are subject to government. All should have a say in how it is constructed and, within what is practicable, should be allowed to participate. All democratic governments derive their legitimacy from this concept, a vital element of which is 'consent'.

Consent

In direct democracies citizens give consent to a course of action. In representative democracies consent is the consequence of 'mandates' given to governments by election victories or referenda. Consent is reaffirmed by free and regular elections, with competing political parties putting a programme before the people. Parties that win elections are said to have a 'specific mandate' to govern – a right to carry out those policies they included in their manifesto. A 'general mandate' to govern is also provided by an election victory. A government can take whatever measures are necessary to meet unforeseen problems. Consent for these actions will come from the elected body that seeks, on behalf of the people, to make the government accountable for its actions. Mandates acquired by national governments have superiority over mandates acquired by winners of local government elections.

Majority rule and democracy

Democracy is not the same thing as 'majority rule'. Indeed, many democrats have seen great dangers to individual and minority group freedoms from simple 'majority rule' principles.

One problem is defining 'majority'. No political party in Britain, for example, has won a majority of the turnout in a general election since 1935, although the governing party usually has a majority of the seats in the House of Commons. Many MPs are elected on a minority of the vote in their constituency. Votes are cast for a party and, as a consequence, entail automatically voting for specific policies that one may oppose. Turnouts in local government and European parliamentary elections are low in Britain (averaging 20–40 per cent), and falling in general elections (down to 59 per cent in 2001). To what extent should the views of those who have not voted be considered? One might declare that if one doesn't vote one has forfeited one's say. However, studies in 'voter apathy' in the 2001 general election seem to show not 'apathy' but irritation and disgust at the political class. One might consider the 'democratic' element of public opinion polling as a better reflection of popular opinion than elections. Indeed, we are all in minorities on many issues, and we should be very concerned about the rights of expression of 'minorities'.

In many ways the best criterion for judging a democracy is how it treats its minorities. Minority views of today often become the majority opinion of tomorrow. It is vital, therefore, that there should be a 'free market' of ideas in democracies. Nevertheless, at the end of the day, there has to be some appeal to majority interests and views as the basis of democratic rule after debate and argument has been undertaken. In the last analysis, minority opinion cannot over-rule the views of the majority.

Equality of citizenship rights

Democratic theory argues that all citizens have equal political rights. Citizens (unless disqualified on legal grounds, such as imprisonment or bankruptcy) all have one vote, of equal value, in constituencies of roughly equal size. All citizens have an equal right to run for office. None of these rights can be legally circumscribed by property or by educational or social status.

Such equality is a recent achievement. In the UK, for example, multiple voting rights, based on property and educational attainment, were not abolished until 1948. Fear of the poor and of mass democracy by those with wealth and power has since Plato and Aristotle been the basis of resistance to equal citizenship rights and democracy. Constitutional and other political restraints have ensured that the excesses of mass democracy have been largely contained (although there are those who see a corrupting effect of 'dumbing-down' of political debate in a mass democracy).

In recent decades there has been a challenge to the individual basis of citizenship rights in a democracy by the advocates of group rights, who demand the recognition of social equality by political and institutional means. It is argued that women, the disabled, ethnic minorities, gays and others are disadvantaged by the emphasis on individual rights.

Public opinion in democracies

Democratic systems of government are supposed in some way to reflect 'public opinion'. As we have observed, some form of 'majority rule' is one basic premise of democracy. We have also seen that many democratic theorists have feared mass democracy and the dangers of 'rule by the mob'. One problem arises from differing definitions of 'public opinion'.

Although the term is often used as if it were a single concept, public opinion is rather more complex than one would initially think. There are few issues, if any, on which the public will all have any opinion, let alone the same opinion. In pluralistic democracies there are many groups and individuals with highly diverse views on issues. One can identify three types of public opinion. First, there is 'expert opinion'. Politicians and civil servants will often consult specialists and professionals on policy. Second, one might identify 'informed general opinion' of interested, well-read people, who, without being professional experts, might write to newspapers or MPs, or support particular pressure groups. Finally, we have 'mass uninformed public opinion', with views on the issues of the day, shaped by the mass media and by what appears of immediate concern. Interest is temporary and will pass quickly on to other 'new' issues. Depending on the issue, most of us will belong to one or other of these blocks of public opinion.

Public opinion is cited by politicians as *the* major factor influencing policy formation. There are a number of problems for democracy in this idea. Appeals to 'public opinion' are often used to silence minority or dissenting opinions. The 'will of the people' is a fine phrase, but one which is usually used to over-rule objections from some parts of the public. Powerful groups will often claim that they express 'public opinion' when they are, if fact, advancing their own sectional interests. Some groups, especially business and other economic interests groups, are sufficiently powerful to have many channels of manipulating and shaping public opinion along lines that essentially benefit themselves. If this were the situation one might regard 'public opinion' as without value as a tool for analysing democratic societies. Public opinion arises from the political culture of a society and is only partly influenced by elites manipulating it by using 'spin doctors'.

Public opinion supporting the essentials of democratic values and norms is a vital element in underpinning democratic culture. When it is essentially 'conservative' in its attitudes it might be considered as a useful check on some of the radical and ill-thought out programmes that sometimes appear from reformist groups. Public opinion on important issues can be influenced and changed by democratic action. It is, therefore, of great value in democracies.

The rule of law and democracy

The rule of law is the basis of modern government. There is a logical series of stages in the rule of law for understanding the basis of liberal democracy. Humans have natural rights, based on natural law, which can be discerned by reason. These provide the foundations for the law. Laws are based on universal moral principles, like universal scientific laws. Hence, government could be seen as the rational discovery and application of legal principles to a society with the consent of the governed, accepting the rule of law as the foundation for stable and rational government. Different societies have different legal traditions, but all are shaped by their legal systems. Democratic government, based on the principle of the rule of law, is, therefore, fundamentally different from political systems that claim that the authority to govern, the making of law itself, derives from God, the laws of economics or racial struggle, or some other source.

The above constitutes a 'democratic culture', one that has taken centuries to develop and become established in liberal democracies, a culture that is still some way from being fully developed in most modern societies.

Conditions for the development of democracy

Democracy arises from a peculiar set of historical, social and economic circumstances. One might speculate about the nature of modern society if scientific and humanistic thought had not appeared and if intellectual enquiry had not developed in the form that it did. We can observe this through a resumé of the history of the development of democratic thinking and how modern democracies were founded.

The development of democracies and scientific modes of thought coincided in the Greek world of the sixth and fifth centuries BC. Science sought to understand the structure of the universe, explore its laws, develop intellectual discipline and establish knowledge. Democratic thought entailed similar applications of logic, in this case to the problems facing society. Debate, argument, the testing of theories and experimentation were applied to society to improve the lot of human beings. Greek city-states or *poleis* (singular *polis*) were riven by class conflict. Greek democratic thinkers hoped that argument and debate might reduce such struggle and identify the common causes of the people. Athenian democracy involved the direct participation of all citizens in government. It may or may not have done much to reduce tensions but it did stimulate political thought. Plato, in *Republic*, used reason to identify the principles of the 'best' political system. Aristotle, in *Politics*, classified political systems: democracy, aristocracy, monarchy, tyranny, and so on. However, the decline of Athenian democracy in the fourth century paralleled Greek economic and population decline. Greece eventually became subject, first to Macedon and later to Rome. Its experiment in democracy ended.

The Roman Republican constitution was composed of balanced parts, representing the various social classes of Roman society: patrician, equestrian and plebeian. The Republic built the empire. The Republic destroyed itself in decades of civil wars, giving birth to the imperial system under Augustus (emperor 27BC–AD14). Indeed, it was the Republic that provided many modern constitution-makers, such as the founding fathers of America, with a model to copy. The imperial system claimed to have restored the Republic, but crushed genuine democratic activity beyond the election of low-level officials.

The decline of democracy in the ancient world paralleled the decline of scientific thought. Rome's political and scientific development stagnated. This stagnation continued throughout the Middle Ages, reinforced by the domination and authority of the church. Power struggles between the church and the secular rulers of Europe occurred without reference to the people's views. Intellectual enquiry was overwhelmingly about theological issues which were untestable by scientific method.

Nevertheless, change, though very slow and halting, was underway. It would eventually flower into the **Renaissance** – among whose many achievements, the gradual recovery of scientific and rational forms of thought paved the way for the development of democracy.

> **Renaissance**
> A cultural and intellectual movement in Europe during the fifteenth and sixteenth centuries. In part it involved a revival of classical learning. It brought an understanding of man and the universe which owed little to religious teaching and much to the development and application of scientific methods of thought.

The Renaissance involved new forms of thinking that, although they need not necessarily have led to democratic society, helped develop scientific thought, enquiry and a constant challenge to dictatorship and totalitarianism. Thought would progress by observation, experiment, the application of reason and the challenging of scientific orthodoxy. It was but a step to apply the same principles to society. Like nature, society was subject to enquiry, understanding and the possibility of change and improvement through the application of scientific principles. Established governments and political ideas were also, like the scientific ideas of Aristotle now being challenged by the new science, subject to challenge, reform and, potentially, overthrow.

Machiavelli, in *The Discourses* (1513–17), argued for a mixed constitution, along the lines of Republican Rome, as the most efficient and free system of government. He was highly suspicious of unrestrained government whether democratic, aristocratic or monarchic.

Particularly important was the Renaissance principle of society as the 'stage' on which man shaped his destiny – the basis of modern forms of democratic political thought. Humans were God's perfect creation, fully capable of understanding the world. As part of this understanding, human beings discerned the existence of natural law and natural rights. They also perceived that in a 'state of nature' human beings were essentially equal. Given these assumptions authority was not derived by rulers directly from God, but from the consent of the governed.

By the late seventeenth century new scientific and philosophical ideas, tempered by the horrific religious wars of the first half of the century, had led to the development of new social and political ideas. Men such as Hobbes, Descartes, Pufendorf, Locke, and a host of lesser figures, constructed systems of thought that influenced politics. They placed the individual at the centre of society, along with concepts of citizenship, the state and the law, and, although the term would not be used at this time, 'democracy'. Consent to be governed was not a 'one-off' event. It had to be regularly reaffirmed by some form of consultation – elections, for example. Indeed, some thinkers, later identified as 'liberals', provided the basis for resistance to, and even revolutionary overthrow of, a government that abused the natural rights of its citizens and ruled without consent.

Modern politics, from the mid-eighteenth century, arose from struggles between democrats and anti-democrats. Democrats were associated with modernity and progress, optimism and hope, and the development of balanced constitutions. Anti-democrats were regarded as supporters of out-dated and reactionary institutions and views and the defenders of undeserved privileges of wealth and political power. Rousseau, in *The Social Contract* (1762), was the most influential of many writers who attacked the concept of **absolutist monarchy**. He wanted a new society based on reason, free individuals, and a social contract between government and people. The American and French revolutions (1776 and 1789, respectively) derived their ideological underpinning from English liberals such as Locke, and French rationalists such as Montesquieu and Rousseau. They sought to implement democracy, although it took longer than they imagined.

> **absolutist monarchy**
> A monarchy where the king is above the law and the law is valid only in so far as it is the will of the king. The term is often applied to the monarchs of the seventeenth and eighteenth centuries (for example, Louis XIV of France).

Modern democratic constitutional systems involve universal suffrage, the existence of competing political parties, debate, free media and a highly educated citizenry. Even pro-democrats worried about giving the uneducated and unpropertied too much power before they were ready for democracy's responsibilities. Democratic political systems, to be secure, required a strong democratic political culture.

This culture involves the application of reason to political issues, a belief in reasoned argument, a rejection of violence, an acceptance of the 'rules of the political game' by all parties, and a willingness to compromise in the face of valid evidence. One might argue that democracy requires an underlying political 'myth' of shared political beliefs, not subject to rational and scientific enquiry, to bind people together.

Politics is not just an activity for an elite. The population should feel they can involve themselves in politics. In practical terms this means elite support for democratic systems of government, the existence of a liberal middle class of some size, and working-class identification with, and participation in, democratic culture. All must be willing to make sacrifices to ensure its survival. There should be a high degree of social mobility. People should be able to rise – and fall – in the social structure, depending on ability; and the elite political class should be open to all on the basis of competition and ability and be subject to regular infusions of new people and new ideas.

Such conditions are very hard to acquire and maintain. Democracy demands constant effort and support; it entails the commitment of individuals and groups who might find democracy working against their particular interests and of others who might not want the responsibility of self-government. There are always those who argue that the burdens of democracy are too much for a people to bear.

Let us now look at some of the major arguments *against* and *for* the principle of democracy.

Arguments against and in support of democracy

Democracy has never lost its capacity to stimulate arguments about its desirability. Much recent criticism has been directed at its ineffectiveness in delivering the wishes of the electorate. We shall discuss some fundamental objections to and arguments in support of democracy.

Arguments against democracy

Democracy has always had its critics. The origins of the major arguments against democracy can be traced back, like its origins, to Ancient Greece and the ideas of Socrates, Plato and Aristotle. It should be remembered that the opinions of anti-democrats – usually the rich, the literate, the educated, the aristocratic – have tended to be preserved in the written record.

The anti-democratic argument includes a number of elements

- Government requires a specialised elite. This might be described as a 'conservative' view.

- The majority of the population is incapable of effective self-government. This is an element of 'liberal' concerns about democracy.

- Political democracy tends to ignore the fundamental lack of democracy in economic relations. This is a strong element of the 'Marxist' criticism of democracy.

- Democratic systems reflect gender divisions in society. This is a strong element of the 'feminist' critique.

Government requires a specialised elite: the conservative view

Plato, in *Republic*, put forward one of the most effective attacks on democracy. He argued that any kind of work involves the principle of the 'division of labour'. Thus, specialisation in society – experts in each field refining their art or craft – has led to an overall increase in the wealth and level of civilisation. People choose their work and contribution to society in accordance with their wishes and their abilities. Each function requires the acquisition of specialist knowledge.

The argument runs thus: this principle of specialisation should be applied to government. Why should all people have a say in government, either by voting or in public opinion polls? The work of government is difficult and important, requiring training and specialised knowledge. Most people (however much they flatter themselves) know little of politics, the major issues and how to make important decisions. government should be left to the specialists and those who know best. So, in Plato's *Republic*, the 'Guardians' trained for government on the basis of intelligence and ability. They were committed to government and the administration of society on behalf of the people.

Such an anti-democratic view is rarely stated in such clear terms, outside the ranks of the fascistic right and some on the Marxist left. Yet often reformers and administrators, politicians of both the left and the right, may profess their support for democracy while at the same time expressing the wish to avoid its constraints and frustrations and often evincing a fundamental distrust of the people. For example, an East European Communist official in 1946 stated, 'We could not allow our plans for the betterment of the people of our country to be jeopardised by the votes of a load of ignorant peasants in an election',[2] while Henry Kissenger opined, 'I don't see why we need to stand by and watch a country go Communist due to the irresponsibility of its own people'.[3]

The criteria for membership of Plato's Guardians were ability, training and a commitment to seeking the benefit of the whole community. Later anti-democratic thinkers defended elites based on wealth, race, religion or birth. One would not, modern anti-democrats say, sail a ship with reference to the opinion of its crew, nor, for that matter, choose the captain on the basis of birth or wealth. Captains should be appointed on merit, and *only* merit. So should the ship of state.

In Britain, the upper reaches of the permanent civil service have been likened to Plato's Guardians. They are chosen on merit. One might observe permanent secretaries wielding more expert power and influence than ministers. Yet ministers are specialists in wielding political power. Both in government and parliament leadership groups are chosen by competition and merit, with a very limited role for the populace. Democracy may be a political and ideological tool of government, but one with a very limited reality in modern Western democracies (a fact welcomed by anti-democrats).

The majority of the population are incapable of effective self-government: liberal concerns

Plato associated democracy with passion dominating over reason. Most people lack the intellectual abilities for balanced and sensible participation in government. Hence his argument for government by the philosophically trained. Aristotle declared that democracy polarised the rich against the poor, contributing to political instability. Indeed, most Greek and Roman writers stressed the importance in political systems of having elements of monarchy, aristocracy and democracy in 'mixed', or 'balanced', constitutions; the best features of each would act to counter and restrain their worst.

Nineteenth-century liberals were deeply concerned about the dangers of majority rule by an ill-educated mass of voters. There was a need to restrict democratic rights to those capable of reasoned thought. They also argued for a balanced constitution to contain democracy. Twentieth-century political theorists have been concerned with the complexity of modern societies, which makes issues difficult to understand, about the declining interest in politics, and about the 'dumbing-down' of political debate on complex issues. Supporters of democracy believe that this fear is exaggerated. There is plenty of evidence that voters understand complex issues. Indeed, those who particpate in democracy show considerable knowledge and capacity. Western democracies have high levels of education and information.

Political democracy ignores the lack of democracy in economic relations: the Marxist criticism

Democratic systems do little to mitigate the fundamentally exploitative nature of capitalist economies. Deep social and economic inequalities continue to exist and undermine the democratic system by restricting the real power and influence available to working-class people. Without fundamental reforms of economic inequalities in society the equality of political rights becomes meaningless, democracy is a sham, merely the ideological means by which the many are governed – and exploited – by the few. Only with the transformation of modern society into a socialist, classless one would real democracy occur.

Democratic systems reflect gender divisions in society: the feminist critique

Women are placed at a disadvantage in democracies through the burdens imposed upon them by domestic duties and by their secondary social and economic role in a male-dominated society and political system. Liberal-democratic political systems are dependent on gender divisions and, in that sense, are no different from non-democratic systems. In suppressing the potential contribution of women no society can be truly democratic. This view is not so much against democracy as convinced that there can be *no* democratic society until women are truly free and equal.

Arguments in support of democracy

A democrat might recognise much truth in the foregoing criticisms. All too often supporters of democracy have lacked powerful intellectual champions to publicise its value. The views of ordinary Athenians on democracy, for example, are inferred from their willingness to make great sacrifices to ensure its survival. The relative silence of the poor and their views on democracy – or anything else for that matter – was the norm until the last century and a half or so. Support for democracy has been rare among the wealthy, educated, powerful and literate. Equally rare were cogent arguments on its behalf until the late nineteenth century.

The pro-democratic argument includes a number of elements:
- the democratic view of elites and democracy;
- democracy contributes to social cohesion;
- democracy encourages citizen development;
- a moral claim for participation;
- democracy as an engine of social change.

The democratic view of elites and democracy

The democrat does not believe that the expert element in government should be abolished, but argues that this element should not be trusted with absolute and unchecked power. At the same time, the democrat argues that democracy is of positive value. A strong democratic element in government is important for good government. There are a number of reasons for this.

It is unlikely that an ideal aristocracy or oligarchy, however attractive it may be in anti-democratic theory, could ever be attained in practice. Most kinds of oligarchy would, in practice, be far from ideal. Democracy, for all its weaknesses, would be safer. Any body of people, however carefully chosen, if they were freed from all democratic control and accountability, would become a special class with interests of their own. Elites tend to become self-serving and pursue their interests at the expense of the community. They seek to amass wealth and power for themselves (rather than for the benefit of the community). This corruption would occur no matter how high-minded or how well trained they were. As Lord Acton stated: 'Power tends to corrupt and absolute power corrupts absolutely. Great men are almost invariably bad men.'[4]

Undemocratic elites would become increasingly remote from the people, steadily less capable of understanding popular desires and feelings, and less concerned with the welfare of the people. Eventually, to make the people obey the elite, coercion and repression would be introduced. At the very least, democratic societies tend to reduce corruption, violence and oppression.

A healthy society requires its citizens to think for themselves and to form their own opinions. If citizens are repressed, or discouraged from taking part in government or influencing government decisions, then much useful information becomes unavailable to the government. Ill-informed and wrong decisions are made, damaging society.

As society is made up of a great number of individuals and groups, no elite can know what is best for all. Strong democratic elements in the political system help government make its decisions taking into account the complex nature of society. Dissenting groups should be tolerated as some truth may exist in their arguments and the discussion of many opinions aids the formation of sound policy. Democratic societies are simply better governed than monarchic or oligarchic ones.

Democracy contributes to social cohesion

Governments prefer to govern by consent rather than by force. Creating a sense of membership of a political system, democracy provides the basis for governmental legitimacy and social and political stability. It creates commitment to one's society and, contrary to the views of anti-democrats, it has not led to mob rule, but to a stronger and more balanced society with greater freedom for the vast majority of people.

Democracies are closely associated with liberal capitalism and social welfare. Some democratic theorists believe democracy is possible only in market capitalist societies that allow individual competition to flourish. Others assert that democracy requires social welfare systems to ensure individual freedoms and education for the population. It isn't absolutely proven that these are essential requirements for 'democracy'. There may be other means of establishing it. But there is a close correlation between liberal democracies and capitalist-welfare societies. Such societies do appear to be well governed, prosperous and highly cohesive.

Democracy encourages citizen development

A democratic political system requires that its citizens have knowledge of the major issues of the day. An informed populace is a responsible one, one that takes its role in the political system seriously. Governments and political parties also benefit from a citizen body growing and maturing in its democratic roles and responsibilities, as new people with different experiences and knowledge take part in politics and government at all levels. The dangers of stagnation and of a self-serving elite are reduced.

A moral claim for participation

All citizens have a stake in their society. Whether people will be rich or poor, well or ill educated, free, healthy, even happy and contented, depends largely on politics. Their government affects them all. All have lives to lead, children to raise, friends and family to care for, and taxes to pay. Democrats argue that morality demands the right to participate in one's political system. Indeed, most democrats would argue that there is not only a moral *right* but also a moral *duty* to take an interest in politics, vote and get involved. Not to do so puts existing democracies at risk, perpetuates tyrannical and brutal regimes, and is a moral betrayal of those who fought and died in the past for the right to participate and of those putting their lives at risk for democracy today.

Democracy as an engine of social change

Rational political action – short of violence – has been a vital engine of social change and reform in democracies. Demonstrations, strikes, protests, are often needed to bring issues onto a political agenda. The constitutional system itself may support an unjust society by ensuring the maintenance of a status quo. Britain in the nineteenth century may have been relatively democratic, compared to other European societies, but political and social reform required political agitation. Even in the twentieth century, mass democratic Britain retained a need for extra-parliamentary action to 'improve' society and seek an end to social injustices, such as racial and sexual discrimination.

There is always a danger that deeply committed, ideologically motivated groups that have a grievance, a sense of the 'fraudulent' and 'unjust' nature of the system, will use violence to try to change policy or even overthrow a regime. One might even agree, without supporting violence, that in Northern Ireland political and social reforms have come about as a consequence of Republican and Loyalist violence – the 'bullet and the ballot box'. But in a democracy the legitimacy of violence to secure social and political change is always dubious, except in the minds of its supporters. It lays itself open to such questions as 'Who voted for you?' and 'Who gave you the right to kill in my name?'

The future of democracy

Democracy appeared to be on the march by the end of the twentieth century. It was attractive, successful, adaptable and able to combine freedom with order. The end of the Cold War saw democracies established in Eastern Europe and the former states of the USSR. Elsewhere, too, concepts of citizenship and popular sovereignty appeared to be on the rise. The future of democracy appeared to be rosy. But all is not as well as one might have hoped. There are a number of challenges to democracy that have to be overcome.

Globalisation

The effectiveness of democracy is challenged by 'globalisation'. Capitalism and democracy have often been closely associated, especially in liberal-democratic political theory. However, the power of big businesses, international financial institutions and international money markets challenges both state sovereignty and the ability of democracy to respond to both the demands of the people *and* pressures from the global economy.

Welfare systems have been challenged by global businesses. Demands for lower corporation taxes and reduced health and welfare provision are linked to demands to improve economic competition. There are also pressures for a greater role for 'market solutions' to social problems. Businesses have easy access to government. They have a dominant influence within the media. Indeed, the media are often part of global business empires.

'Rolling back the state', a rallying cry of many on the libertarian right, involves a curtailing of the ability of the state to control corporations and produces a capitulation to the self-interested demands of businesses. It also involves the decline of the people's influence on their political system, a decline reflected by a dwindling interest in politics in most democracies.

Apathy

The greatest danger to democracy is not violence, but apathy. Growing lack of interest in democratic politics can be perceived in several important areas.

Voting is the minimal degree of involvement in a democracy. Turnout in general elections, local elections and referenda is in decline. In the USA, for example, presidential election voter turnout is only around 50 per cent of those eligible and only 39 per cent turnout was achieved in the November

2002 Congressional elections. In Britain's 2001 general election only 59 per cent of those registered voted, and Swiss referenda stimulate around 40 per cent voter participation. This may, of course, not be apathy, but could be taken as evidence of contentment with one's society. However, opinion polls show widespread disillusionment with politics and politicians, and – by implication – democracy. A belief exists in most democracies that voting never changes much, and that participation can have very little influence on events, a view that bolsters cynicism about the democratic process. This can be observed in the declining membership of political parties. Membership has always been a minority interest, but is a shrinking one. Fewer people join political parties than ever before. In the UK, for example, the three main political parties have a combined membership of less than 800,000.

Declining interest and participation in democracy allow political and ideological extremists to have a greater impact on politics than would otherwise be the case.

Anti-democratic and irrational forces

Democracies are not immortal. They have shown considerable resilience to the threats from fascism and communism during the twentieth century and triumphed, but anti-democratic and irrational forces could reappear to challenge them and, perhaps, win. There is evidence of the growth of such forces in Europe: fascism, nationalism, terrorism, religious fundamentalism, and extremism in the cause of animal rights and environmentalism. At present they are on the fringes of politics. However, levels of intolerance of minorities – such as migrants and asylum seekers – have grown among democratic leaderships and among voters.

Nevertheless, despite all these reservations, democratic forms of government continue to show considerable degrees of vigour and reform. The great challenge for democracy in the twenty-first century will be to spread and deepen its roots in those countries from which it has been absent, while finding new democratic systems, reinvigorated democratic cultures, to ensure that it does not wither in its heartlands.

Summary

Democracy claims, and at least in theory is granted, universal applicability. It is such a 'feel-good' word that almost every regime, however tyrannical, describes itself as 'democratic'. In reality, the degree to which a government is democratic can be measured by the extent to which 'the people' influence government. From other perspectives, we need to consider how far the people are protected from an oppressive state ('defensive democracy') or the extent to which they are encouraged to participate in decision-making ('citizen democracy'). Democratic government can be described as governing with the consent of the people. Majority rule, equality of rights and the rule of law are also important dimensions to democracy. Moreover, democracy requires the social underpinning of a democratic culture. Democracy has often been attacked. A conservative view is that governance is best left to a highly-skilled elite; a liberal view is the idea that the masses cannot be entrusted with power. Others, such as Marxists and feminists, argue that 'democracy' is but a façade to hide unjust class rule. Defenders of democracy argue that elites are not to be trusted with power. Besides, democracy promotes social cohesion, encourages citizenship development and enables social change to occur without violence. There is also a claim that, as all have a stake in society, all have a right to participate in its decisions. Democracy's future is bright. It has confronted its fascist and communist enemies during the twentieth century and defeated them. It is quite capable of defeating the threats to it that are apparent in the twenty-first century.

REFERENCES AND FURTHER READING

1 David Held, 'Democracy: From City-states to a Cosmopolitan Order', *Political Studies*, 11 (1992), pp. 10–39.
2 Apocryphal reference.
3 Henry Kissinger, US Secretary of State, on the American policy of destabilising the socialist regime of Salvador Allende in Chile. CIA Official Minutes of 27 June 1970.
4 Lord Acton, Letter to Mandell Creighton (April 5, 1887).

Beetham, D. 'Political Theory and British Politics', in P. Dunleavy *et al.*, *Developments in British Politics 4* (Macmillan, 1993), pp. 353–70.

Coxall, B. and Robins, L. *Contemporary British Politics*, 2nd edn (Macmillan, 1994), pp. 12–17.

Crick, B. *In Defence of Politics* (Penguin, 1994).

Dahl, R. *Democracy and its Critics* (Yale University Press, 1989).

Dunn, J. (ed.) *Democracy: The Unfinished Journey 508BC to AD1993* (Oxford University Press, 1992).

'Survey: FULL DEMOCRACY: Happy 21st century, voters!', *The Economist* (21 December, 1996).

Finer, S. E. 'The Liberal Democratic State', in S. E. Finer, *Comparative government* (Penguin Books, 1974), pp. 62–74.

Goodwin, B. 'Democracy', in B. Goodwin, *Using Political Ideas* (John Wiley and Sons, 2001), pp. 271–303.

Held, D. (ed.) *Models of Democracy* (Polity, 1987).

Held, D. 'Democracy: From City-states to a Cosmopolitan Order', *Political Studies*, 11 (1992), pp. 10–39.

Held, D. *Prospects for Democracy* (Polity, 1996).

Heywood, A. 'Democracy, Representation and the Public Interest', in A. Heywood, *Political Ideas and Concepts: An Introduction* (Macmillan, 1994), pp. 166–94.

Jay, R. 'Democracy', in Robert Eccleshall *et al.*, *Political Ideologies: An Introduction* (Routledge, 1996), pp. 118–52.

Macpherson, C. B. *The Life and Times of Liberal Democracy* (Oxford University Press, 1977).

Renwick, A. and Swinburn, I. 'Democracy', in A. Renwick and I. Swinburn, *Basic Political Concepts* (Stanley Thornes, 1990), pp. 124–49.

Watts, Duncan 'The Growing Attractions of Direct Democracy', *Talking Politics*, 10:1 (1997), pp. 44–9.

SAMPLE QUESTIONS

1 What are the essential characteristics of a 'liberal democracy'?

2 How valid are historical and recent critiques of democracy?

3 'Although democracy has successfully withstood the challenges of the twentieth century, it would be unwise to think it will be equally successful in the twenty-first century.' Discuss this statement.

4 Are there any valid forms of democracy other than 'liberal democracy'?

5 What difficulties are encountered in modern democracies in answering the question 'who governs'?

6 Are there any preconditions for a successful democracy?

Freedom

4

Most people have some idea of what the word 'freedom' means, and most approve of it. In our analysis we examine the term more closely, exploring such themes as freedom of opinion, freedom under the law and economic freedom. To further elucidate the concept we present brief summaries of the ideas of a number of political philosophers on the subject. In particular we analyse the views of John Stuart Mill and Isaiah Berlin on 'negative' and 'positive' freedom. Then we focus on the central issue of freedom and the state, concentrating on three major areas of dispute: conscientious objection, state acquisition of private property, civil disobedience and terrorism. We end with some observations on the cultural environment conducive to freedom and reflect on the problems of freedom in the modern world.

POINTS TO CONSIDER

➤ Why does the term 'freedom' have such a strong emotional appeal?

➤ Is private property essential to human freedom?

➤ To what extent are the writers cited in this chapter agreed as to the meaning of freedom?

➤ Are the concepts of positive and negative freedom mutually exclusive?

➤ What criteria would you suggest as useful in establishing whether a specific restraint on freedom was justifiable?

➤ Does a truly free society demand impossible levels of moral restraint on the part of its citizens?

Forward, you sons of Hellas! Set your country free!
Set free your sons, your wives, tombs of your ancestors,
And temples of your gods. All is at stake: now fight!
        (Aeschylus, *The Persians*, 472BC)

If all mankind minus one were of one opinion, and only one person were of the
contrary opinion, mankind would be no more justified in silencing that one person
than he, if he had the power, would be justified in silencing mankind. (J. S. Mill, *On
Liberty*, 1859)

Liberty does not carry out each of its undertakings with the same perfection as an
intelligent despotism, but in the long run it produces more than the latter. It does
not always and in all circumstances give the peoples a more skilful and faultless
government; but it infuses throughout the body social an activity, a force and an
energy which never exist without it, and which bring forth wonders. (Alexis de
Tocquveille, *Diary*, 25th August 1831)

Everyone is against 'sin' and everyone is in favour of 'freedom', although
neither can be defined so as to ensure agreement on their meaning. From its
origins in the Ancient Greek city-states and their democracies, freedom has
usually been considered a political 'good', good for individuals, organisations
and society. 'Liberty' or 'freedom' has great advantages as a rallying call in
politics arising from its opaqueness in popular usage. Freedom seems to mean
whatever the speaker wants it to be and can be used to gloss over potential
conflicts about a course of policy. Everyone can agree that 'freedom' is worth
defending only because of its vagueness.

People may not know much about political theory, but they know what they
mean by 'liberty'. Usually, people are only aware of liberty when they are
deprived of it in an illegal or unfair manner by the deliberate acts of other
individuals. Thus, freedom concerns human relationships and is clearly
related to power in its many forms: financial, physical and political. Some
people in positions of power will attempt to constrain liberty, usually with
appeals to the 'common good' or a 'higher principle' beneficial to the whole of
society or mankind.

For the last two centuries or so freedom and equality, sometimes allied, often
opposed, have been the two great horses that pull the carriage of modern
politics along. Some critics, usually on the political left, argue that freedom
without a greater degree of economic and social equality between people is
largely meaningless, as the rich and the powerful can exploit their own
freedom to restrict that of the many. Other critics, mainly among classical and
neo-liberals and some members on the modern conservative right, argue that
freedom is such an important value in society that it must always take priority
over equality. One can have freedom, they argue, which might or might not
involve greater equality in society as a consequence. However, if equality is

pursued as a political goal over all else, then liberty is certain to be degraded and damaged (if not extinguished) as a political 'good'. Western politics since the French Revolution has been essentially a discourse between these two fundamental concepts in which freedom has generally prevailed.

Freedom: a starting point

It is worth noting that some thinkers identify a difference between 'liberty' and 'freedom'. 'Liberty' is associated with the type of political system existing in a society, constitutional constraints on state power and guaranteed constitutional liberties. 'Freedom', on the other hand, is a looser term, describing both freedom in relation to the state and freedom for individuals in society. For the sake of simplicity we will use 'freedom' and 'liberty' as interchangeable terms.

There are many ways in which the concept of freedom is expressed in political discourse. A useful starting point in our exploration of the idea is to introduce a number of these elements:
- individual freedom;
- freedom of opinion and expression;
- freedom under the law;
- economic freedom;
- property and freedom;
- national freedom.

Individual freedom

Individual freedom is the central element in Western liberal political thought and has become part of the political discourse in most nations. This aspect of freedom includes freedom of expression, freedom of speech, freedom of religion, freedom to travel. It is linked with the other central element of liberalism (especially in its 'classical' form): the minimal state. The state is seen as a potential threat to freedom and its powers and involvement in society should be kept to the minimum levels possible, concomitant with the requirements of law, order and justice.

Freedom of opinion and expression

Most advocates of liberty believe that academic, religious and political opinions should be allowed to compete freely in order for society to solve its problems, to make progress and to function in a healthy way. Freedom of expression is a central tenet of liberal thought: without it no other freedom can exist. Freedom of opinion is associated with attempting to achieve many other 'good' political and social goals, such as the pursuit by individuals of a better and richer lifestyle, and attempts by governments to stimulate economic growth, reduce crime and eliminate poverty.

Freedom under the law

One of the most important aspects of freedom in the Western political tradition is that there must be some limits if it is to have meaning. These limits may be the consequence of internal restraint and judgements, freeing oneself from, for example, irrational passions and cravings to gain freedom to pursue one's 'true' goals in life. Some limits are what might be called 'normative' constraints. By this is meant the acceptance of social morals, values and customs constraining one's behaviour. However, almost all discussions of freedom sooner or later have to analyse the concept of freedom under the law. Freedom under the law means that there are areas of social life that are not regulated by self-awareness or moral and customary values and thus require the introduction of law to set clearly defined limits on social behaviour with identifiable penalties for their infringement.

Economic freedom

Economic freedom is the right of individuals and businesses to pursue their economic objectives in competition without undue state regulation and inter-ference in the workings both of businesses and the free market. Owners of businesses, in this light, need to be able to run their companies to maximise profits and growth, to employ staff on flexible terms in line with the require-ments of the business. Workers must be able to negotiate contracts related to working conditions and pay, free of government regulations and impositions. Freedom is therefore a vital component in promoting economic efficiency and rationality for the benefit of all in society.

Work and employment form a very important part of most people's conception of liberty. They play a significant role in creating a source of individual identity and self-image that is important if people are to act freely. A larger income and greater wealth tend to give people a greater sense of practical freedom, and more choices in their lives than the poor enjoy. Freedom without some form of economic dimension is likely to remain merely theoretical, and will not survive if its opponents offer better economic rewards. The hungry and starving will readily give up theoretical freedoms if they can instead be fed.

State intervention in economic relations may be necessary to rectify an imbalance between employer and employees, producers and consumers. For instance, employees may be ruthlessly exploited by their employers; unions may use their industrial muscle to force unreasonable concessions on wages and conditions out of employers; businesses sometimes work together to manipulate the market price for goods and exploit consumers. In practice, therefore, the free market may not work to the equal benefit of all and the enhancement of everyone's economic freedom. The concept of the 'greater good' in society may require laws, rules, controls, regulations and taxes to ensure a greater degree of 'freedom' in the 'market'.

Property and freedom

Property is a vital component in most theories of the meaning of freedom. Essentially 'property' can be identified as having two meanings: property in the sense of one's person and property in the conventional sense of goods, wealth and land.

Individuals own property of their person in its body and capacities. This is the foundation on which persons can expand their potential and powers to maximise freedom. Hence, restrictions on freedom of speech are an abuse of a person's 'property' rights to speak one's own views. Similarly, imprisonment without trial is an abuse of freedom of property of one's own body by wrongly restricting the use of it as a means of having freedom of movement. (In **Stoic** tradition, however, one could claim that a person who is wrongly imprisoned could still maintain his property of freedom of thought and ideas, especially if he has access to books.)

> **Stoic**
>
> Zeno of Athens established the Stoic school of philosophy in the late fourth century BC. Stoicism sought virtue as the greatest good and taught that self-control of one's feelings and passions, especially in the face of adversity, was the mark of a good man.

The conventional meaning of the term 'property' is of course tangible material goods and wealth. From a liberal viewpoint, if one's wealth increases, then one's freedom, in terms of exercising practical choices, also increases. Moreover, the ownership of property by groups, organisations and private individuals acts as a check on the power of the state, thus giving society a greater sense of security. Socialists might add a warning that an over-concentration of wealth in private hands is likely to enhance the freedom of the few at the expense of that of the many.

National freedom

National freedom is connected with the concepts of the 'nation' and the 'state'. The doctrine of 'national self-determination', first enshrined in the Versailles Treaty (1919) as a fundamental principle of international society and international law, is the political manifestation of national freedom. According to this doctrine all nations have a right to govern themselves, and for national freedom to have a political reality a nation must be able to govern itself without being dominated or controlled by another nation. This concept of exclusive self-government is the key characteristic of 'sovereignty', the most important attribute of a state. Hence, the creation of its own state becomes a

desirable goal for a nation seeking its freedom, since the state, once established, will exercise exclusive legal and political rights and powers within the
national territory. National freedom, therefore, is expressed and given reality
by the existence of the state.

Some major contributors

Freedom is the most popular political and social aspiration of the modern
world. However, most political thinkers have tended to take the term 'freedom'
for granted and have tended to discuss other political ideas such as order, duty,
good government, sound political leadership, rather than liberty. It is worthwhile examining freedom as discussed by a number of major political thinkers.
A brief survey will give a flavour of the debate.

Plato

Plato's *Republic* is an attempt to establish the meaning of the term 'justice'
and identify the characteristics of the 'good' state. Plato believed that
freedom was bound up with self-discipline and morality. He doubted that the
law was able to establish meaningful moral conditions in society without
there first being a moral impetus from within people themselves. Nevertheless, he had no objection to the principle of morality being enforced by
the law. Without reason and self-discipline, individuals cannot attain
freedom, Plato believed, while doubting whether most people possessed
these requisite qualities. Freedom certainly did not require the existence
of democracy. On the contrary, Plato was keenly aware that the emphasis
placed on 'freedom', so called by the Athenian democracy, created an ill-disci-
plined people who, lacking self-control, generated factions, which degenerated into disorder that, in turn, inevitably gave birth to tyrants and
dictators. Arbitrary and oppressive government, not freedom, is the defining
characteristic of tyrants and dictators and the ultimate consequence of
Athenian-style 'democratic freedoms'.

The Stoics

The Roman Stoic philosophy stressed the possibility of freedom existing within
a person's mind, irrespective of external conditions. Self-discipline and
contemplation of life allow even the slave or the prisoner to be free in a
meaningful sense. The slave could cultivate habits of thought that enabled
him to be free within his mind, whatever his legal status or the physical
constraints placed upon him. In the last resort the slave has the choice
between obedience and death: such a choice is a statement of freedom.

Niccolo Machiavelli

In the *Discourses*, Machiavelli argued for a republic as the embodiment of the positive value of freedom. Self-government was essentially the same thing as freedom, although the people enjoying such freedom would, as in the Roman Republic Machiavelli admired, be constrained in their political influence by a range of political and social factors that confined self-government to the wealthy, powerful and educated. Freedom in the sense of self-government did not mean direct democracy as it did in Ancient Athens. In his other major political work, *The Prince* (1513), Machiavelli glories in the exercise of freedom by the great man, the strong personality, the individual pushing his power and talents to the limit, constrained only by the actions of other men similarly engaged in exercising their freedom to the utmost.

Thomas Hobbes

Hobbes placed 'order' and 'security' as much higher political goals than 'freedom' in his *Leviathan* (1651). Men had 'freedom' in the state of nature, a condition in which government did not exist, but this only led to an appalling state of permanent war of all against all in which only the freedom of the strongest had any reality. Hobbes argued that the creation of the state was a rational response to the excess of freedom previously existing in the state of nature. Freedom was only possible within the order created by the powerful state. Once the state was established, freedom was to be found in the subsequent order and in those areas of life that were not proscribed by the law; this theory is described in modern political thought as 'negative freedom'. To Hobbes the area of private life that should remain outside some state involvement is remarkably small and, in his view, should remain so. Hobbes was highly resistant to the idea that freedom was consequent on self-government and democracy: a democracy would swiftly slide into the violence and chaos of the state of nature and with such a disaster freedom would be extinguished.

John Locke

Locke, in *Two Treatises on Government* (1690), declared that the law is the means by which liberty is defended and enhanced. He believed that government should be regarded as the servant of the people and, as such, an instrument to preserve liberty. The best way to do this is to ensure that government is highly restricted in its functions (essentially to the maintenance of internal law and order, defence against external enemies and the raising of taxes to pay for these two). Freedom in this sense is defined in terms associated with 'negative' freedom: all that is not restricted by law is left over for individuals to enjoy. Locke argued that there should be as large an area of private life as possible over which the state has no right to trespass. Indeed, he declared that the right to the greatest possible degree of freedom was second only to the right to life.

Immanuel Kant

Running through Kant's many works, most notably *Critique of Pure Reason* (1781), *Critique of Practical Reason* (1788), *Critique of Judgement* (1790), is the linking of freedom with making voluntary choices to do good. Kant argues that all men seek to do good and attempt a rational understanding of the universe to discover the goals of life associated with the pursuit of good. Men can call themselves truly free only when their actions are aimed at these goals.

Jean-Jacques Rousseau

Rousseau argues in *The Social Contract* (1762) that true freedom lies in obedience to the laws we have worked out for ourselves. This manifests itself in the social contract, which creates civil and political society, and the subsequent 'General Will' that creates unanimous agreement to obey the law. Laws are valid when they obey the General Will, and freedom consists in obeying these laws. Rousseau even advocated the use of the power of the state to 'force people to be free', if necessary. Rousseau's concept of the General Will and its relationship to freedom has been the subject of considerable attention and controversy since its formulation. On the one hand, the idea of the General Will is condemned as a fundamental threat to freedom, providing the intellectual justification for total-itarian and authoritarian political regimes, as well as providing ready-made excuses for self-appointed guardians of public morals in the non-political and private sphere of life. On the other hand one might claim that the General Will is merely a complex and convoluted way of identifying a popular constraint on the actions of government and making it accountable to the people.

Henri Benjamin Constant

In his many works Constant formulated his views on many aspects of politics as a French liberal. In his important lecture of 1819 Constant identified the considerable differences between what he called the 'liberty of the ancients' and the 'liberty of the moderns'. The liberty of the ancients rested upon slavery and warfare, and was restricted to citizenship and taking part in the delibera-tions of the assembly. Constant claimed that this form of liberty did not guarantee the rights of the individual. Indeed, ancient liberty was essentially a form of privilege of the free man over the slave. In contrast, liberty of the moderns guaranteed individuals equality before the law and also their freedom to pursue their own interests. Constant used this theory to challenge Rousseau's idea of the General Will. In his view the liberty of the moderns was the basis of representative government. The state existed to protect the private interests of the individual.

Karl Marx

Freedom, to Marx and his followers, is not possible under capitalism. The highly exploitative capitalist system reduces both the working class and their capitalist exploiters to a level of servitude to the system. Those who control the means of production may have somewhat greater freedom than those who merely sell their labour to scrape a living, but bourgeoisie and proletariat alike possess a freedom reduced to mere work and consumption. Some modern Marxists claim that capitalism is even more inimical to freedom than it was in the nineteenth century when Marx analysed its workings. Contemporary **capitalism**, so modern Marxists argue, enslaves workers by means of ideological indoctrination, making them compliant to a progressively more exploitative system. Contemporary workers in capitalist societies have been enslaved with 'chains of gold': the material trappings of consumer capitalism have hidden the raw nature of exploitation to some degree, but capitalism is still inimical to the development of human potential in a condition of true freedom.

> **capitalism**
> The economic system in which wealth is privately owned and in which goods and services are produced for profit, as dictated by market forces, which has developed over the last five hundred years to be the economic driving force of the modern global economy.

John Rawls

Defending social democracy in *A Theory of Justice* (1971), John Rawls argued for liberty in an unequal society. He stated that every person has a right to the greatest possible liberty concomitant with the same degree of liberty allowed to others. Liberty is defined in rather narrow terms: freedom of speech and movement, and participation in the democratic system. Rawls also stressed the importance of each person having adequate material resources to enjoy their liberty. He did not argue for material equality, only the existence of suffi-cient material resources for all. To Rawls, freedom, not equality, is the paramount priority in politics. Freedom must not be sacrificed in order to achieve a higher degree of material equality. Nevertheless, Rawls argued for the existence of a welfare state to ensure that the poorest in society have the resources to attempt to achieve their greater freedom.

Mill and Berlin: two key thinkers on liberty

We propose here to discuss some of the issues of liberty in relation to the ideas of John Stuart Mill and Isaiah Berlin. We will offer just a few pointers to their contribution to the debate on the meaning of freedom.

John Stuart Mill

Mill's *On Liberty* (1859) is quite rightly regarded as one of the classical studies of freedom and liberty in society. His ideas are particularly associated with concepts of 'negative freedom'. Mill claimed freedom was the basis for moral improvement of individuals and society, for truth to be discovered and for originality and genius to develop to the full. Freedom of choice allowed men and women to judge what would make them happy, and only individuals, not the state (however enlightened), could know what makes them happy.

Mill, like most nineteenth-century liberals, perceived a considerable threat to freedom from the growth of a mass democracy. Individuals were entitled to a *private sphere* in which they were able to act and think as they saw fit, one which would serve as a great buttress against public opinion and the much-feared 'tyranny of the majority'. Mill made a distinction between actions that affect only oneself, which do not justify restrictions on them, and actions that affect others, which may need to be restrained by other individuals and/or the state:

> the sole end for which mankind are warranted individually or collectively, in inter-fering with the liberty of action of any of their number, is self-protection. That the only purpose for which power can be rightfully exercised over any member of a civilised community, against his will, is to prevent harm to others. His own good, either physical or moral, is not a sufficient warrant. He cannot rightfully be compelled to do so or forbear because it will be better for him to do so, because it will make him happier, because, in the opinion of others, to do so would be wise, or even right. There are good reasons for remonstrating with him, or reasoning with him, or persuading him, or entreating him, but not for compelling him, or visiting him with any evil in case he do otherwise. To justify that, the conduct from which it is desired to defer him must be calculated to produce evil to some one else. The only part of the conduct of anyone, for which he is amenable to society, is that which concerns others. In the part which merely concerns himself, his independence is, of right, absolute. Over himself, over his own mind and body, the individual is sovereign.[1]

This may seem a very clear-cut distinction. But it is extremely rare that one's actions do not have an effect on others. For example, suicide may be thought the ultimate act of individual freedom; whatever other constraints exist on one's freedom one retains the power of deciding to take one's own life; no other individual will be injured. However, family, friends and the social networks in which the individual exists will be deeply affected by a person's suicide. Smoking, to give another example, may damage only one's own health, but does drain health service resources that might be used elsewhere, so smoking cannot be considered in isolation from the social consequences of one's actions.

To Mill, constraints on individuals are only justifiable if they are needed to protect others from harm. What is immediately apparent is the problem of defining the nature of 'harm'. Sometimes the definition of harm is so wide that it can be used to excuse any constraint. Most pornography, blasphemy and film violence for entertainment may not involve harming others directly, but one might claim that long-term harm to individuals and society arises from lack of restraint in these areas. Freedom must, to Mill, involve not infringing the rights and freedoms of other people. Indeed, all Western democracies are founded on this principle, although the problems of its practical application are the stuff of modern political debate.

Although Mill's concept of liberty has been very influential throughout the English-speaking world in particular, and Western democratic societies in general, its universal validity is open to doubt. Severely disciplined societies can also nurture love of truth, integrity and individualism, as witness Ancient Sparta, Medieval Islam and Calvinist Switzerland during the sixteenth century. One must point out that the concept of individual freedom is a rather modern one. Few people before the nineteenth century would have defined freedom in terms used by Mill or modern liberals.

Isaiah Berlin

In *Two Concepts of Liberty* (1958) Isaiah Berlin took up the long-standing ideas of 'positive freedom' (or 'freedom to' act) and 'negative freedom' (or 'freedom from' external restraint).

Positive freedom

This entails people having a choice about their actions. Usually what we *choose* to do is what we *want* to do, but this is not always the case as choices may be determined by internalised attitudes to social duties, what is the right thing to do, linked with freedom of conscience. Hence, a very strong component of positive freedom is the idea of humans being able to strive to reach their full potential. Positive freedom implies individuals' capacity to assert their individuality by means of reason. To enhance their opportunities, education is vital; the state may give poor people financial and other aid towards this end, as late nineteenth-century New Liberals, and modern liberals and socialists have advocated.

Positive freedom reflects the desire of the individual to use his/her own power and reason to assert themselves against the mass of other people, to stand out, to strive to achieve their full potential. Self-discipline is a key element in this view of freedom, involving the suppression of aspects of one's character that might interfere with the achievement of the higher self. Positive freedom involves testing one's own limits and the constraints society places upon one. Successful people in all walks of life see freedom in such terms and not in the rather uninspiring negative form of being simply left alone.

However, positive freedom does have its detractors. Those individuals who are able to achieve their higher self by assertion of positive freedom are often unsympathetic to others who, for whatever reason, are unable or unwilling to pursue a life devoted to self-discovery. All too often positive freedom enables the few to develop iconic status and dominate others. History is littered with oppression and coercion inflicted by people who claimed to have achieved their 'higher self' above those they deemed to be 'inferior'. The positive freedom of the few may involve the extinction of the freedom of the many as the history of nationalism, communism, fascism and religion demonstrates.

> **libertarian**
> One who puts a very high value on freedom of the individual. Extreme libertarians argue for the removal of the state from almost all areas of social and economic life, including health, drug control, education and even policing.

One might argue that the **libertarian** pursuit of power and success, associated with the concept of positive liberty, is fundamentally immoral as it inevitably involves the assertion of the power of some people over others. One might, however, counter that positive freedom does not involve such crude forms of self-assertion. Positive freedom when exercised with reason can liberate people from the pursuit of tawdry baubles to pursue a 'higher self' and goals that do not involve mere pomp and display.

Negative freedom

This is a view of freedom particularly strong among English philosophers. Liberty cannot be unlimited; law and custom set limits to freedom and give it shape and meaning. Negative freedom is usually defined as the absence of restrictions, usually legal, on one's freedom to act. Restrictions on freedom must, in this view, be human restrictions and not the consequence of some natural incapacity or inability to achieve a goal. Under ideas of negative freedom people are free to do whatever they desire so long as there is no law or widely accepted standard of public behaviour forbidding them, but laws and customs must exist to provide some framework within which liberty might be enjoyed. Liberty should be for all and not just for a few.

Negative freedom is not in itself a 'negative' concept in that it is 'bad'; it entails the absence of legal or other restraints on choices of action. Law, for example, enhances the liberty of individuals by protecting them from infringements of their liberties by others. The 'minimal' or 'caretaker' state exists as the main means by which negative freedom is upheld. The state, according to this view, has no business in laying down frameworks of state education and welfare benefits, as they undermine the freedom which all individuals have to decide their own destiny and to make their own choices. Reduction of social disadvantages, as under positive freedom, does not enhance freedom but may undermine it by giving too much potential and actual power to the state.

People, under negative freedom, have the right to choose options. They must have as large an area of private life, free of state control or influence, as is concomitant with public order and this should include freedom of religious views and opinion, freedom of expression and freedom over property. These areas should be as free from state interference as possible, as they constitute what humans cannot give up without offending against the essence of human nature.

Some have argued that negative liberty is rather unsatisfactory as an ideal of freedom. 'Freedom from restraint' lacks the inspiration that positive freedom can offer to the poor and oppressed to expand their human potential. One could argue that even some kinds of tyranny might be compatible with negative liberty: a liberal-minded despot may allow his oppressed people to have large areas of freedom within the private sphere, so long as they obey the state.

The ideas of positive and negative freedom are not mutually exclusive. Their practical application to the affairs of society should ensure that freedom becomes more than a theoretical construct.

Freedom in relation to the state

Freedom is related to the concept of the state. Liberals regard the state as an institution that represents and defends its members. There should not be any essential conflict between a state and its individual members, but liberals are particularly suspicious of state power and its potential threat to the freedom of the individual. They perceive a fundamental tension and possible conflict between the individual and the state.

British liberal Herbert Spencer, in *Man Versus the State* (1884), doubted that there was a universal conflict between the individual and the state. Spencer believed that one can identify *particular* conflicts and that the intensity of conflicts between individuals and the state may vary over time and from country to country. Freedom is associated with the development of a democratic state. The more democratic a state the more opportunities exist for individuals to influence its policy outcomes and, consequently, the greater the freedom existing within society. Democratic states should thus seek to reduce the sources of grievance or hostility within society to ensure good government, while providing the maximum degree of freedom in society. Ultimately, however, the state has coercive power over all other sources of power in society and is in the supreme position to dominate its members and to infringe their liberty.

There will always be points of conflict between the state and the individual which raise issues of freedom. Citizens have recourse to law and the courts to defend freedom in relation to the state and the rule of law. However, political struggle determines the effectiveness of the rule of law in society. Politics creates the kind of political culture in a society, the effectiveness of the rule of law, and the commitment to freedom among its citizens. Anarchists, for example, argue that the state has no right to interfere with individual liberty, while fascists, on the other hand, claim that individuals can only know true freedom when they identify their individual interests with the state. These are two extremes in the debate on individual liberty. Most political debate on this issue falls between these two positions. The greater good of the community may require that some individuals make sacrifices, sacrifices that are imposed by the state. Some such issues associated with freedom and the state can be addressed in the following examples:

- conscription and conscientious objection;
- state acquisition of private property;
- civil disobedience and terrorism.

Conscription and conscientious objection

In wars of national survival the state claims the right to conscript its citizens into the armed forces, train them and expect them to fight and kill for the greater good of the citizens of the state. Many states claim that citizens should be expected to serve some time in the armed forces as a natural obligation of their citizenship. After all, so the argument goes, the liberty of the individual depends on the effective functioning of the state as the defender of its citizens against their external enemies. It is reasonable, therefore, for citizens to be prepared to participate in the defence of the state and undergo military training to do so.

Western states are steadily giving up conscription. Most allow non-participation in the armed forces on conscientious and religious grounds. Citizens who object on principle to training to fight and kill are usually accommodated in some manner, but it does not exempt them from some form of non-military national service. Conscription is in one sense a clear infringement of the principle of individual freedom. It can be argued, however, that freedom involves responsibilities and recognition of obligations to one's society, the society that instils ideas of freedom within us and provides the means by which freedom can be expressed.

State acquisition of private property

Private property, especially among Western liberals, is considered a vital element in advancing and protecting freedom against dangers from state power. However, property is not entirely free from state control or state takeover. The principle of private property does not preclude the state from acquiring private property, by compulsion if necessary. Advocates of freedom argue that four fundamental requirements need to be met for such state action to be acceptable: first, that the property is essential for the achievement of common goals for the good of the whole community, such as the acquisition of land in wartime for air bases and training camps or the state control of vital industries; next, that the desirable goals are achievable only by acquisition of this property; thirdly, that the property acquisition process is clearly enshrined in law for all to see and, if necessary, challenge; finally, that the owner of the property will be compensated for its loss and will have first chance to retrieve the property when it is no longer needed by the state. Nevertheless, there is the fundamental assumption in most ideas of liberty that, all other things being equal, the vast bulk of private property will remain in the hands of private individuals and companies.

Civil disobedience and terrorism

Generally speaking, most theorists on freedom accept that there will be circumstances in which individuals might be justified in challenging the state by recourse to methods that are outside the usual structures of the political process. **Civil disobedience** and terrorism are usually seen as being appropriate only in societies that are not democracies and lack peaceful and deliberative means of changing law and policies.

Even democracies, however, act at times in some way that suppresses the interests of minorities. Civil disobedience is an assertion of the freedom to protest about issues that are being neglected or rights that are being abused. Civil disobedience can involve the refusal to pay taxes, deliberate flouting of the law and other acts designed to demonstrate opposition to a particular policy. As a

> **civil disobedience**
> The deliberate violation of the law, usually in a non-violent manner to advance a political cause. Civil disobedience was used by the Committee of One Hundred in the 1960s to promote nuclear disarmament and in the 1990s by environmentalist groups campaigning against road and airport development in Britain.

political strategy, civil disobedience is intended to raise the public profile of an issue of concern by seeking publicity and highlighting where, in the view of the protesters, the government has gone wrong. Those involved in civil disobedience are aware that they are likely to be breaking the law by their campaign. Indeed, a trial is often sought by campaigners as a platform to gain further publicity. However, governments may choose to ignore the activities of those involved in civil disobedience as of little import, unless the campaigners move towards more violent tactics.

Where civil disobedience has had most impact as a defence of liberty is when it has been attuned to the aims and objectives of large numbers of people. Perhaps the most effective example of campaigning civil disobedience in pursuit of freedom is that organised by Mahatma Gandhi and the Indian Congress Party for national freedom during the 1930s and 1940s. However, one might doubt the effectiveness of such campaigning if civil disobedience had been directed against a regime other than the British Raj. Civil disobedience campaigners in Nazi Germany and Stalin's Russia were somewhat ineffectual in defending freedom against these monstrous regimes. The anti-nuclear campaign in Western Europe during the late 1970s and early 1980s had civil disobedience elements to it. While it failed to stop the deployment of Pershing and Cruise missiles it did contribute to getting governments to explain their nuclear strategy when they would rather have kept it a matter of state secrecy. The Solidarity Movement in Poland used civil disobedience which eventually helped bring down the corrupt and incompetent communist regime and began the unravelling of Soviet and communist domination in Eastern Europe.

Terrorism is a much more controversial political tactic for achieving freedom. Most people would deny it as a valid means of defending and advancing the cause of freedom, especially in democracies. Terrorism uses violence to influence public opinion and state policy in favour of the interests and goals of the terrorist group. Violence might be directed against the forces of state power, such as the police, the armed forces or civil officials, or it might involve attacking civilian targets in order to create public pressure on the government to change policy to the advantage of the terrorist group concerned. Even when terrorism achieves some or all of its political goals, it severely damages ideas of liberty and taints the democratic process by demonstrating that freedom can be achieved by violent means.

> **paramilitary**
> Paramilitary organisations operate on military lines and use force to achieve a political goal – e.g., the Provisional Irish Republican Army (PIRA) in Northern Ireland.

After all, if one can bomb and shoot one's way to the negotiating table with government why should one pursue electoral politics and attempt to persuade voters of the rightness of one's cause?

Paramilitary organisations in Northern Ireland have had an enormous influence on the politics of the Province over the last three decades, arguably more so than democratic political parties. Some, such as **Sinn Fein/PIRA** and some Loyalist paramilitary organisations, have adopted a 'bullet and ballot box' strategy that has paid considerable political dividends in recent years. Both Loyalist and Republican paramilitary organisations claim they are defending the sectarian freedom of 'their' people against oppression. Some violent organisations, such as those on the fringes of the animal rights movement, see no need to be involved in any democratic action to pursue their aims and use violence as a principal means of political action.

> **PIRA/Sinn Fein**
> The PIRA is a terrorist organisation that seeks to achieve a united Ireland by armed force. It is currently (2002) on 'ceasefire'. Sinn Fein is a political party closely associated with the PIRA.

Political theorists have rightly concentrated on threats to freedom from the state. State oppression, because of its potential to be all-embracing, is the major threat that defenders of liberty have concentrated on challenging. State oppression has sometimes led to revolution that overthrows the oppressive state, proclaims freedom, struggles with chaos and, eventually, establishes an even more oppressive system of dominance. One can interpret the progress of the French and Russian revolutions as a warning that liberty does not always follow the end of a particular form of state oppression. Both sought to liberate people and create freedom for the oppressed majority, and both involved terror, violence and dictatorship and the extinction of liberty (as Plato and Hobbes would have predicted).

Freedom and society

Liberty is associated with being 'ourselves', whatever that might be. Ideas of liberty and self-help by citizens derive from their society and from the political culture they have assimilated. If a sense of the importance of freedom is not part of a society's culture, or is not deeply ingrained in the political mores of citizens and leaders alike, then no amount of talk of liberty and the freedom enshrined in a well-balanced constitution will protect it from the enemies of freedom. One can observe this in the Soviet Union, Nazi Germany, Pol Pot's Cambodia and a host of tyrannies, large and small, that litter the pages of twentieth-century history.

Defenders of liberty are usually aware that the state is not the only, or necessarily the most important, threat to freedom. Contrary to the strongly held beliefs of liberals, one might identify elements within most of us in favour of compulsion and against liberty. Psychologists often identify the desire to dominate and the oppressive exercise of power as part of human nature; they note the ease with which some people will identify with a group or a leader, abandoning their own judgement. Men in Nazi extermination squads were often family men and good neighbours, loving fathers and kind to small animals, but they committed appalling crimes with little sense of their immorality or their abuse of the lives and freedom of their victims. The cause of National Socialism was their political god. As Max Stirner, writing in the 1840s, rather chillingly stated: 'Most people are not looking for freedom at all, but for a cause to enslave themselves to.'

Community values and morals may influence the formulation of law, but are not entirely enshrined in law. Normative values such as unpopularity, ostracism and disapproval do have considerable influence over individuals, in some cases a coercive influence. To a considerable degree, such values may be considered important elements in underpinning individual freedom: they establish constraints on individual behaviour that allow other individuals to enjoy their freedom, without recourse to law. However, they can become a source of oppression, imposing restrictions on individual liberty that cannot be challenged in courts of law but are none the less keenly felt. This may be seen in school bullying, the shunning of individuals believed to be somehow 'odd' or 'eccentric' by their 'normal' neighbours, or 'group-think' and pressures to conform to the crowd: all are examples of the fundamental fragility of liberty in social groups.

Restrictions on liberty are needed to avoid licence. Constraints are always required in society to ensure the existence of freedom for all. Licence is not the same thing as liberty. Licence is a lack of restraint, an abuse of freedom, a lack of control and proportion in one's actions. It is a failure to be aware of the ways in which one's actions affect others (however much they may appear initially only to affect oneself), the consequence of which is the erosion of real liberty. For example, there are desirable social restrictions on displays of emotions such as anger, irritation and love – emotions which do not attract legal sanctions themselves but which can infringe the freedom of others by creating fear or embarrassment. While one might question the motives of campaigners for censorship in the arts and information, one might also question the benefits to society of pornography, violence in film and television, or the idea that swearing is some fundamental expression of free speech. In themselves such actions might be regarded as harmless, but they may corrode standards of behaviour and damage the sense of living in a free and balanced society, where respect for others is an important element in social relations.

Moral and political principles directly determine a person's attitudes to liberty. One should not confuse liberty of thinking with liberty of talking. The latter can be legally restrained; the former cannot. As we have seen in relation to the Stoics, the development of a strong set of internal moral values can be the basis of freedom. One might be able to be free in one's own mind even in the most oppressive state and society. However, state and society have many ways in which the private world of the mind can be colonised and ultimately controlled by the values of the oppressor. The neat distinction between the private world of the mind and the public world of society is not today as clear as was once believed. Modern psychology identified the roots of personality, modern totalitarian regimes have demonstrated the political means of control that can be established, and modern advertising techniques mould and manipulate people's thoughts in favour of values that support capitalist businesses.

A future for freedom

One could easily lapse into despair when one contemplates the crimes and disasters committed in the name of political programmes claiming to be defending or advancing the freedom of this or that group, whether they are individuals, the nation, a religion or a race. Nevertheless, freedom has a way of bubbling up through the cracks of even the most oppressive monolith, with the most ruthless systems of terror and mind control. Luckily for the cause of human freedom its enemies fail because of the very strengths of free societies, the ability to question, criticise, challenge and seek out the best options for social change and experiment, the willingness to change when the facts change. The triumph of Western liberal democracy towards the end of the twentieth century has not ended the need to maintain eternal vigilance to defend the cause of freedom. Perhaps the post-Cold War world has made it even more important that freedom survives in our own societies with the trivialisation of politics and the manipulations of the advertising industry, the impact of business interests on government policy and the political 'spin doctors'.

Summary

Freedom is a popular cause, and, at first glance, an easy concept to grasp. However, as soon as we begin to think of whose 'freedom', to do what, matters become more complex. What limits, for example, should there be to freedom of expression? Does personal freedom imply economic freedom? Is private property a precondition of political freedom? A number of political philosophers have been concerned with freedom, among the most important being John Stuart Mill and Isaiah Berlin. Mill propounded a theory of what has become known as 'negative freedom', or freedom from external constraints, centred on the principle of the 'sovereign individual'. In his view the citizen should be completely free to do whatever they want, unrestrained by state or law, with the key proviso that what they do does not harm others. Berlin pointed out that for many people freedom was a mere abstraction, of no relevance to their actual lives. To correct this deficiency, positive freedom has been proposed – that is, the provision by public authorities of the material requirements such as healthcare and education that would enable all citizens to enjoy genuine freedom. Generally speaking, the attitude in the English-speaking world has been to regard the state as the main potential threat to freedom, a viewpoint reinforced by the experience of twentieth-century dictatorships. Left-wing thinkers have usually argued that the state has a more positive role to play in the promotion of freedom.

Freedom remains an issue of contemporary relevance. Areas of controversy include the degree to which the state can legitimately curtail its citizens' rights; how far the citizen can justifiably resist the commands of the state; and to what degree a free society depends not on constitutional arrangements but on widely shared cultural values and moral principles. For some, the twenty-first century has already witnessed the decisive victory of freedom. Others are less sanguine. They question whether in Western culture liberty is confused with licence. They point to the essential triviality of so many of our so-called 'choices'. Others aver that multi-national corporations operate virtually without restraint in a worldwide free-trade environment; it is these corporations, not the state, that now most gravely threaten freedom. Finally, modern techniques of propaganda have become so skilled and subtle that a real tyranny of the mind can exist within a superficially liberal democratic society.

REFERENCES AND FURTHER READING

1 J.S Mill, *On Liberty* (1859).

Barker, E. *Principles of Social and Political Theory* (Oxford University Press, 1961).
Berlin, I. 'Two concepts of liberty', in *Four Essays on Liberty* (Oxford University Press, 1958).
Cranston, M. *Freedom: A New Analysis* (Longmans, 1954).
Friedman, D. *The Machinery of Freedom* (Harper and Row, 1973).
Gray, T. *Freedom* (Macmillan, 1984).
Heywood, A. *Political Ideas and Concepts: An Introduction* (Macmillan, 1994), pp. 195–224.
Raphael, D. D. *Problems of Political Philosophy* (Macmillan, 1990).
Ryan, A. (ed.) *The Idea of Freedom* (Oxford University Press, 1979).

SAMPLE QUESTIONS

1 Which is the most important in modern societies, freedom, equality or democracy?

2 To what extent is the freedom of individuals in conflict with the freedom of groups?

3 Is freedom only really possible within a free-market capitalist economic system?

4 Is liberty unattainable?

5 'Far from inhibiting freedom, state intervention can in fact enhance it.' Discuss.

6 Which is the best guarantee of freedom, a liberal constitution or a liberal culture?

Equality 5

We now explore the term 'equality', defined in two ways: first, that which concerns equality as a starting point to life; second, equality as an outcome. We also consider equality before the law, equal political rights and equal social rights. After that we examine individual and group equality, and equality in terms of the class structure and international relations. Finally, we discuss the present position of 'equality': has its value decreased in general esteem because of the almost universal acceptance of liberal capitalism and its emphasis on 'freedom' as the prime political and social goal?

POINTS TO CONSIDER

➤ Why has equality been valued less than liberty in Western societies?

➤ Do recent advances in genetics give the lie to the statement 'all men are created equal'?

➤ Is absolute equality an unrealisable ideal? If so, is the quest for greater equality of any value?

➤ Equality of opportunity or equality of outcome – which is more desirable?

➤ In what ways, if any, is a society based on 'merit' better than one based on 'privilege'?

When Adam delved, and Eve span, Who was then the gentleman? (John Ball, *Black-heath Sermon*, 1381)

The law in its majestic equality forbids the rich as well as the poor to sleep under bridges, to beg in the streets, and to steal bread. (Anatole France, *The Red Lily*, 1894)

'Equality' has usually been the poor theoretical relation of 'liberty'. The former is usually perceived as less important, less life enhancing and a weaker rallying call to action than liberty. Nevertheless, equality has been a significant element in political theory from its Greek beginnings in the fifth century BC until the present. Plato, for example, denied that men were equal. He observed that they were endowed with unequal talents and virtues. It was unjust to treat men as equal when they were patently not equal. Aristotle agreed with his teacher on the fundamental inequality of men, but he asserted that equality was a major driving force in politics:

> The universal and chief cause of . . . revolutionary feeling . . . (is) the desire of equality, when men think that they are equal to others who have more than themselves; or again the desire of inequality and superiority, when conceiving themselves to be superior they think that they have not more but the same or less than their inferiors . . . Now in oligarchies the masses make revolution under the idea that they are unjustly treated, because as I said before, they are equals, and have not an equal share, and in democracies the notables revolt, because they are not equals, and yet have only an equal share.[1]

Rebellious medieval peasants, the **Levellers** and the **Diggers** during the political ferment of the English Civil Wars, and many other oppressed people all appealed to equality as a fundamental human right and a basis for better treatment by their social and political superiors (who listened to and then suppressed them). The American rebels in 1776 declared that 'all men are created equal', but it was for liberty they fought, not equality. No revolutionary declared, 'Give me *equality* or give me death'.

Equality became an important feature of politics with the growth of liberalism and socialism as ideological movements during the nineteenth century. One forgets today how radical the principle of equality once was and how deeply held were beliefs in a natural hierarchy and human inequality. Liberalism stakes a claim for the fundamental equality of rights possessed by all humans as a birthright. But it was socialism, in its many forms, that positioned equality at the heart of its ideology and its programme for social change. Both

---

Levellers

A faction of Cromwell's army who in the 1640s made remarkably 'modern' political demands, including voting rights for all males who were not servants.

Diggers

A faction in the English Civil Wars of the mid-seventeenth century who set up communes on both common land and the land of wealthy men. They advocated the eventual abolition of private property.

movements linked equality with democracy. *Unequal* societies were declared to be *undemocratic*. Democratic societies had to address fundamental social and economic inequalities if democracy was to have real meaning.

Few modern politicians defend social and political inequality, at least not in their public pronouncements to a mass electorate. Questions are raised, however, as to what form of equality should be pursued. Most people support equality of opportunity, but what does it mean in practice? Is it impossible to achieve? Should there be greater equality in rewards, or 'outcomes', in society? If so, how much? Does greater equality always means erosion of liberty? If it does, should liberty be given the higher priority? Are we right to concentrate on individual equality when people are unequal as a consequence of being a member of a social group? If equality can best be pursued by extending the opportunities available to members of oppressed groups, which groups are to be identified and what are the best ways of creating greater equality for them? All too often such issues have been raised to disguise a fundamental opposition to equality and resist reforms made in favour of greater equality.

One can realise, therefore, that equality is a rather complex political and social issue, one that is worthy of scrutiny.

Equality: a starting point

Complex as the issue of equality is, one can reduce it to two major themes, as Jean-Jacques Rousseau, in *A Discourse on the Origin of Inequality* (1754), attempted:

> I conceive that there are two kinds of inequality among the human species; one, which I shall call natural or physical, because it is established by nature, and consists in a difference of age, health, bodily strength, and the qualities of the mind or of the soul: and another, which may be called moral or political inequality, because it depends on a kind of convention, and is established, or at least authorised, by the consent of men. This latter consists of the different privileges which some men enjoy to the prejudice of others; such as that of being more rich, more honoured, more powerful, or even in a position to exact obedience.[2]

In other words, one can discern inequalities based on *nature* and inequalities that arise out of *social* factors. Egalitarians, as the supporters of the principle of greater equality are known, have taken up this idea and identify two kinds of equality:

- **Foundational, or primary, equality**: all human beings are claimed to be *equal* in some fundamental sense, irrespective of race, creed, class, gender or any other biological or social characteristics. Human beings are equal because they are endowed with 'certain inalienable rights', a proposition that is open to question and is often left rather vague.

- **Distributional, or secondary, equality**: it follows that *if* all humans are equal, as foundational equality claims, one must consider how such equality might be brought about. Society is characterised by a multiplicity of degrees of inequality, as evinced by the present distribution of wealth, power and status among people.

Foundational equality appears to assert a statement of *fact*: all humans *are* equal, while distributional equality may be seen as a statement of political principle: that all people *should* be equal. These two forms of equality, foundational and distributional, are clearly intertwined. If, for instance, human beings are not equal in a foundational sense then there is no need to attempt to reduce social inequalities by distributional means.

If, on the other hand, as liberals and socialists aver, we are all fundamentally equal in some sense, then social inequalities are not 'natural' but come under the realm of politics and raise the prospects of social change. Social inequalities are thus 'unjust'. Some people acquire wealth, power and privilege for no better reasons than the luck of parentage, a win on the National Lottery, or having natural abilities valued in society – so that an ability to sing, for instance, or play football to a high standard, will bring massive financial and other rewards. Egalitarians believe that some inequalities should be removed, such as hereditary peerages in the House of Lords, and that others, such as ownership of wealth, should be greatly reduced.

Let us now study each of the forms of equality in turn.

Foundational, or primary, equality

Here are some anti-egalitarian arguments against the idea of foundational equality and some of the relevant egalitarian retorts.

The major problem with equality as a political principle is that it is very difficult to establish, especially as a starting point from which to develop a political programme. Society is patently unequal and opponents of equality maintain that this is because people are not equal in their innate qualities. Human beings vary considerably in intelligence, height, physical strength, artistic and musical skill, and many other attributes. Anti-egalitarians point out that humans also vary greatly in their capacity for reason and understanding. Indeed, if people were treated *equally* (in whatever manner this might be defined, such as in terms of legal rights and material rewards) when they are so obviously *unequal*, one would not only be ignoring reality but would also be acting unjustly. Injustice would arise because people with 'superior' talent or intelligence, or some other attribute valuable to society, should not be treated as if they were the same as those without these qualities, or possessing inferior versions of them.

Egalitarians point out that modern anti-egalitarians have moved from attacking the principle that people are basically equal in some undefined sense to questioning the idea of equal rewards for people of equal talent. However, egalitarians claim that this is merely a tactic by their opponents, who still believe that people are innately unequal and should be treated as such. Egalitarians argue that fundamental equality remains a very important element in the theoretical discussions about equality, one which has enormous implications for social and welfare policies.

Most egalitarians distinguish between the principle of human equality, which applies to all people in all societies, and the reality of the inequalities of rewards that vary considerably in particular societies, depending on the prevailing economic, social, political and cultural traditions. Very few egalitarians, in fact, support a fundamental equality of rewards. However, they accuse anti-egalitarians of creating a false notion of fundamental equality in order to defeat it as a principle and so undermine the egalitarian hope of greater social equality in health, welfare, education, income and property ownership.

Egalitarians therefore make a strong case for fundamental human equality on the basis of our common humanity. Egalitarians believe that humans resemble each other more than they differ: all people are born, have lives to live as best they can, and all will die. Furthermore, all people have, as Jeremy Bentham and the Utilitarians claimed, an equal capacity to experience pain and pleasure. Finally, all human beings have some basic capacity to act as moral agents, to use reason to discover and follow moral laws, to distinguish right from wrong and to identify their own interest.

From these beliefs derives the principle that all people have equal rights to what might be summed up as 'life, liberty and the pursuit of happiness'. One might dispute what these rights are in practice and one must recognise that they may change over time, but the principle of equal rights is the issue. If this principle is established, then one can use reason to discern what these rights might be. Such equal rights might include freedom of speech, freedom of religion, the right to own property, freedom of association, and so on. (One can see how this concept of equality is closely associated with the issue of 'liberty'.)

The principle of equal rights does not mean the same as equality of rewards or outcomes; as we have mentioned, few egalitarians would endorse that. One might have freedom of speech, for example, but it does not mean that all opinions are of equal validity. Everyone has a right to own property, but the principle does not mean that all should have an equal amount of property. All citizens have the vote, but it does not follow that all can equally influence government policy.

One can discern that the principle of fundamental equality is the basis for a number of principles in modern societies, principles that shape both political culture and political and social institutions:

- equal consideration;
- equal opportunities;
- equal voting and participation rights;
- equality before the law;
- equality of welfare and social rights.

Equal consideration

'Equal consideration' is a vague notion but it links the principle of fundamental equality with the fair treatment of people, unless there is some clear and generally recognised legal or moral reason why they should not be treated equally. In public institutions all citizens have a right to equal consideration, as all pay taxes and all are affected by the decisions of government. In private life everyone is considered to be equally worthy of respect in line with the 'golden rule': 'Treat others as you would yourself wish to be treated.' This assertion of the fundamental equality of all humans acts as a defence against discriminatory and morally wrong policies against innocent individuals and groups, such as existed under the Nazi regime in Germany and apartheid in South Africa.

Equal opportunities

A belief in 'equal opportunities' points to a basic right of an equal chance for people to make the most of their talents. It argues, for example, that equal educational provision is vital if every person is to have such a chance. In practice, some will work harder than others, some have greater abilities, some will take advantage of these chances and others will not. But justice will have been done if such opportunities have been provided. It is important to be clear that, for most egalitarians, equal opportunities do not automatically translate into equal rewards. 'Rewards' are determined by the value placed on a particular skill by the prevailing social system. For example, a schoolteacher and a stockbroker may be equally well educated but the financial rewards for each are significantly different.

Equal voting and participation rights

'Democratic equality' means that all have a fundamental right to participate in political institutions. Rousseau agreed with Aristotle that political communities should be as small as possible, allowing all citizens equal participation in decision-making. In the nineteenth and early twentieth centuries the claims for democratic equality by women and the working classes would be met, they believed, through achieving the right to vote. In Britain the principle of 'one person, one vote, one value' was finally established in 1948 when multiple voting rights were abolished. Supporters of democratic equality doubt that equality of 'value' has in fact been achieved. Parliamentary constituencies are of unequal size, most are 'safe' seats that remain in the hands of one political party, and the voting system ensures that most MPs and all governments are elected on minorities of the popular vote. Democratic equality does not exist in most modern democracies, according to egalitarians, and will not exist until there is greater devolution of political power to institutions which are closer to the people and which offer a greater degree of direct democracy than at present exists.

Equality before the law

'Legal equality' is in modern societies the basis for equality in political, economic and cultural activities. However, this was not always the case. It was once assumed that inequality in social standing should be reflected in the law. **Nonconformists**, Roman Catholics and Jews in Britain did not have the same legal rights as Anglicans until the late 1820s. Slaves had no right to recourse to law until 1772. Members of the House of Lords accused of a serious criminal act could elect to be tried by their fellow peers until 1910. The poor were excluded from the vote until 1918. Women lacked property rights on the same bases as men until 1870 and were excluded from equal voting rights until 1928. Fundamental legal equality is now accepted as a form of strict equality in any democratic society's legal system. Judges should treat all before them equally. Any discrimination in law has to be made on the grounds of relevant elements in the case and all similar cases should be treated alike. Equality before the law as a principle is not, however, balanced by an equal power to exercise legal equality because of the sheer expense of going to law and the very unequal distribution of wealth in society. As Lord Justice Darling said in 1920: 'The law courts of England are open to all men, like the doors of the Ritz Hotel'. Legal aid schemes exist in most modern societies to ensure that the poor get legal advice and some degree of equal access to the law.

> **Nonconformists**
>
> Churches in the Protestant tradition which in the 1660s did not 'conform' to the established church. Non-conformists today include all mainstream Protestant churches outside the Church of England, such as Baptists, Methodists, Quakers and Unitarians.

Equality of welfare and social rights

'Equal welfare and social rights' are viewed as vital elements in fundamental equality. Strictly speaking, one should include these under 'distributional equality' as they involve some degree of equalising wealth and power in society. The egalitarian principle, however, is relevant here and is quite straightforward. All citizens pay taxes to support health, educational and welfare systems provided by the state. All citizens, therefore, whatever their personal wealth, have an equal right to a range of benefits constituting a 'citizenship package'. This package includes child benefit, state pensions, disability benefits, unemployment payments and access to health, education and social services. Citizens may claim other 'means-tested' benefits on the basis of an assessment of their assets. If, however, citizens choose to exercise their freedom and pay for private health and education, for example, it does not entitle them to reduce their contributions to the state scheme, nor does it disqualify them from access to state provision.

Anti-egalitarians have not given up the attack on **egalitarianism** as a principle even though a strong element of egalitarianism has been introduced into modern societies. They doubt the existence of fundamental equality by claiming that modern genetic science provides evidence of innate human inequality. Geneticists have been demonstrating that some human characteristics previously believed to have been social in their origins now lie in a person's genetic make-up. Individual intelligence, for example, may owe a great deal more to genetics than was previously assumed and thus a great deal less to social influences. If genetics are the fundamental determinant of human inequality then, obviously, calls for social engineering to reduce or remove inequalities are doomed to fail.

egalitarianism
The belief that social equality is the main political good.

Egalitarians challenge the implications for morality and fundamental equality of scientific developments that are as yet in their infancy. Genetic differences, they assert, no more justify social inequality than does the long-established genetic basis for hair colour, skin colour or gender, or whether one has blue or brown eyes. People still have fundamental equality irrespective of genetic make-up. Whatever the role of science and technology in advancing genetics and its application to the overcoming of biological inequalities, the fundamental moral equality of people remains unchanged.

In the opinion of anti-egalitarians, foundational equality contributes to the undermining of social order. If people are equal, and are conscious of being so, the authority of those in command will be undermined. Authority requires from the mass of the population the recognition of the basic *inequality* of humans in a hierarchy of social and political power.

Egalitarians challenge the view that good government and social order require fundamental *inequality*, which in their view is little more than a 'political myth' that serves the interests of those who are against greater equality and democracy. Politicians, police and other functionaries of government derive their authority in modern societies, so egalitarians assert, from merit and competitive recruitment rather than from appealing to an underlying inequality of people.

Anti-egalitarians claim that the recognition of natural inequality among people benefits all in society. The moral and religious bases of human equality *might* be acceptable, declare the critics of fundamental equality, but inequality is a powerful engine in the improvement of civilisation, art, culture, science, and so on. The resultant social progress benefits everyone and not just the 'elite', even if the latter get greater rewards. (If they do so, it is because they deserve such rewards for their crucial role in leading and improving society.)

Egalitarians challenge the idea that culture and progress is an inevitable by-product of fundamental inequality. The social inequalities that create 'high' culture and 'progress' do not, they argue, undermine the egalitarian premise that humans are fundamentally equal in their capacity or potential to enjoy high culture or contribute to progress. There are some egalitarians who would deny that some forms of cultural expression are 'better' than others and that 'progress' is to be applauded.

Most egalitarians claim that fundamental equality exists. Some, however, do not think that the existence or not of an innate right to equality is important to the egalitarian case. One must look, they claim, to the social inequalities created by man in a practical analysis of society, rather than merely debating theoretical ones. Many egalitarians doubt that rights of any kind, let alone equality, are inherent in humans by virtue of their common humanity. According to most modern egalitarians equality, or the lack of it, corresponds to the social conditions of real people, in actual social circumstances. In this view, equality is exclusively related to the level of opportunity available in a society. Nobody can reasonably object to a person possessing greater natural abilities than another. However, one can reasonably object to a society where some people acquire opportunities to develop their talents, while other people are denied such opportunities on the grounds of class, gender, race or some other socially determined inequalities. We will now examine how these inequalities might be rectified or moderated.

Distributional, or secondary, equality

If inequality is a consequence of nature, little can be done to alleviate it; if, however, society is responsible, equality can be promoted by changing social conditions and providing the means for people to realise their full potential.

The two major areas governed by distributional equality are equality of opportunity and equality of outcome.

Equality of opportunity

Egalitarians claim that the absence of equal opportunities programmes, or their ineffective implementation, is morally unjust and economically inefficient. It is unjust that people are unable to have the chances to realise what they are capable of and inefficient that talent is wasted while the less able, but more privileged, get access to economic and political power they are incapable of using effectively. Society is damaged by inequality. It is less prosperous than it might be and less united, less cohesive. Political action is required to rectify this undesirable situation: 'Because men are men social institutions . . . should be planned, as far as possible, to emphasise and strengthen, not the . . . differences which divide, but the common humanity which unites, them'.[3]

This principle is generally accepted across the political spectrum. Conservatism (a political stance not usually associated with equality) claims 'equality of opportunity' as a desirable goal of social policy. Conservatives advocate a 'levelling up' rather than a 'levelling down' (as they accuse their leftist opponents of wanting), if for no other reason than claiming to be interested in 'equality' to attract votes. However, they would be opposed to the rise in taxes needed to give all schoolchildren the resources of their counterparts at Eton.

Nevertheless, both Labour and Conservative governments since the Second World War have steadily increased public spending (with concomitant tax rises), providing greater equal opportunities through welfare state policies that originated in the 1940s. Members of all political parties (and none) created the bases for the egalitarian nature of the post-war consensus in welfare, education, employment and health.

William Beveridge (a New Liberal) produced his 1942 report, *Full Employment in a Free Society*, on the provision of 'cradle to grave' welfare protection within a National Insurance scheme and universal benefits for *all* citizens irrespective of wealth or poverty. Conservative politician R. A. Butler's *Education Act* (1944) created an education system based on elitism but with greater equality of educational provision and more opportunities for children than had ever existed. J. M. Keynes (another New Liberal) produced an employment white paper (1944) which committed governments to maintaining full employment using state economic intervention. Finally, the Labour Government introduced the National Health Service Act (1946) to establish a greater equality of health provision in Britain than had ever existed before.

All of these measures, influenced by principles of **collectivism**, were related to increasing equal opportunity in society along distributional lines. All involved creating a united society around common institutions guaranteeing an equality of basic services, available to all on the basis of need.

However admirable these institutions (and their counterparts in other countries) may be, egalitarians realise that people have a different starting point in life. Advantages of income, parental education, social environment and so on, ensure that some individuals have *greater* opportunities for achievement than others do. Equal opportunity ideals might have influenced the welfare state and some aspects of government policy for decades now but massive inequalities of opportunity remain in British society, inequalities that are unlikely to be significantly reduced without unacceptably high levels of state interference in family life and personal liberty.

Equality of outcome

'Merit' may well be the modern basis of rewards and achievement in society but equality of opportunity, even if it were possible, does not justify equality of rewards. As Margaret Thatcher once bluntly stated: 'What is equality of opportunity if it is not the opportunity to be unequal?' Few egalitarians would disagree with her.

It is a matter of equality and justice that people should get paid the same for the same work and for work of equal worth without reference to personal characteristics of age, gender or race. Few egalitarians would support the idea of *equal* rewards for *unequal* work. Such a policy, most believe, would be unnatural and unjust and would remove incentives for effort and ability, incentives vital for the economic and cultural advancement of society. Obviously, most egalitarians would be in favour of a basic wage, a 'minimum wage', to ensure an equal starting point for income and to enable people to fulfil their basic needs of food, clothing, shelter and warmth. Most egalitarians would also favour a 'maximum wage' and taxes to reduce levels of wealth accumulation. As Rousseau declared in *The Social Contract* (1762): 'no citizen shall be rich enough to buy another and none so poor as to be forced to sell himself'.[4] Some egalitarians argue that such policies would *help* the rich by reducing the burden of wealth and the dangers of corruption associated with it.

Greater equality in outcomes, but not *total* equality, does seem to have social benefits. Scandinavian countries have very high levels of taxation on income and wealth and very high levels of distributional equality. Such societies do appear to have lower levels of crime, higher levels of social cohesion and more harmonious social relations than countries with greater social and economic inequalities, such as the USA and the UK. Indeed, there is little evidence to support the anti-egalitarian view that such societies lack incentives for effort or are less free than Britain and the USA. Neither is there much to support the Marxist contention that inequality will only be removed when private property has been abolished. No Scandinavian country has supported the abolition of private property and unequal incomes in pursuit of greater social equality.

Group rights and equality

The discussion so far has concentrated on the essentially liberal doctrine of equal rights as being inherent in *individuals*. This principle was not generally accepted at the beginning of the nineteenth century but had been established in modern societies by the mid-twentieth century. For about 150 years political debate centred on the degree to which individual equality should or *could* be advanced by state intervention in health, education and welfare.

A great deal of equality was achieved by the creation of welfare systems, greater educational opportunities and access to healthcare. However, egalitarians became increasingly dissatisfied as the persistent inequalities in society blunted equality of opportunity for many people who were female, non-white or working class. Many women and many black and working-class people continue to succeed in Western societies, but fundamental inequalities remain for people as members of these and other social groups. Over the last thirty years or so there has developed the concept of 'group rights' to tackle these forms of inequality in society:

- gender equality;
- racial equality;
- class equality.

Gender equality

Feminists perceive debate about equality as being about equality between *males*. They point out that Plato, Aristotle, Locke, Rousseau and most political philosophers, regarded women as fundamentally inferior and not entitled to share equal democratic citizenship with men. Most feminists strongly believe that formal legal and political equality, finally achieved in Britain by the late 1920s, did not remove the remaining deep inequalities for women in income and career opportunities. From the early 1960s feminists campaigned with success for legal measures to advance female equality. In Britain a number of Acts of Parliament established a legal basis for female equality: the Equal Pay Act (1970) and the Sex Discrimination Act (1975) are the most prominent. However, great inequalities remain for women in job security, pay and career advancement. Mere legal reforms do not appear to have advanced women's equality as significantly or swiftly as feminists want. The struggle for gender equality goes on.

Racial equality

Few people outside the fascistic right would today claim that ethnic and racial groups are fundamentally inferior. Nevertheless British society does distribute rewards and penalties in a very unequal manner that results in most black and Asian people having higher levels of unemployment, lower incomes and greater overall poverty that their white neighbours. Black Britons have a higher rate of incarceration in prisons than white Britons and tend to serve longer sentences for the same offences. Legislation, from the Race Relations Act (1968) onwards, has removed most forms of overt discrimination from British society. But covert forms of discrimination continue to exist (usually called 'institutional' racism) and impede the development of non-white people in Britain.

Class equality

Marxists and the political left tend to believe that the fundamental problem of equality in society is the product of social class and the privileges and disadvantages that it confers. Class, rather than gender, race or some other group classification, is the major cause of inequality in society. An Asian businessman or female barrister does not have the same interests as an unskilled Asian textile worker or a part-time woman office cleaner. Address the issue of continuing class inequality in modern society and all the other issues of economic and social discrimination will be alleviated. This type of inequality is particularly related to the distributional equality discussed earlier.

The exercising of group rights and group equality seems to undermine the liberal concept of *individual* rights and *individual* equality as the central concern of political discourse. Group-rights theorists argue for unequal treatment for women and ethnic or racial minorities to overcome their unequal treatment in society. One might have 'quotas' of women and non-whites in education or job appointments to reflect their numbers in society. Such a policy might be combined with 'positive discrimination' to offer opportunities to groups who have suffered past discrimination and disadvantage if other things are equal between candidates.

However, critics argue that the selection of such 'disadvantaged' groups is often rather arbitrary and favours those who can 'shout the loudest'. They also claim that 'equal opportunities' doctrines do little to help those who are disadvantaged but provides many opportunities for those who get jobs in the race relations and equal opportunities 'industry'. Finally, critics believe that equality as a principle is undermined by making some groups more 'equal' than others on the grounds of race or sex. They claim that 'positive discrimination', as this principle is called, causes resentment among those who are not 'privileged' to be members of a 'disadvantaged' group. Group equality will remain as an issue in contemporary political debate.

Equality in international society

We have observed the issue of equality as it pertains to individuals and groups. This principle also applies to international society, where the members of the community are not individuals but nations and sovereign states. We have discussed the issues surrounding national self-determination and state sovereignty elsewhere, but it is worth mentioning them again here.

National self-determination refers to the principle that all nations have an equal right to be independent and self-governing – free, that is, of being ruled by people from another nation within an empire. Nations are notoriously difficult to define, but one might describe them as a body of people having some shared sense of belonging together by dint of language, history, culture, geographical proximity and so on.

National self-determination was a rallying cause of nationalists within the Turkish and Austro-Hungarian empires during the nineteenth century. At the Versailles Peace Treaty (1919) this principle was enshrined in international law (although it only initially applied to nations within the defeated powers, Germany, Austria-Hungary and Turkey). After the Second World War national self-determination was used by nationalists in European colonial empires to demand independence. In the modern world the equality of nations is a principle that contributed to the collapse of the Soviet Union in 1991 and the disintegration of Yugoslavia throughout the 1990s. It remains a major principle in international law and politics.

States are recognised as sovereign legal entities in international society. This is a very important principle on which international law and international institutions, such as the European Union and the United Nations, rest. The UN General Assembly, for example, enshrines this legal equality in the principle of 'one state, one vote'. However, as in domestic society, there are great differences between the *principle* of equality and the notable differences in *power* existing between members of that society. States are unequal in their military capacity, economic power and technological prowess. This guarantees a massive inequality in the ability of states to protect and advance their interests in international society.

The principle of state equality before international law remains. However, states are obliged to obey only those laws that they have agreed to in an international treaty. Even then, a state can give notice if it intends to withdraw from a treaty, or if national security precludes its involvement in a particular court case. States are not subject to a higher authority in international law. The power of strong states has to be recognised by weaker ones. But no legal authority exists over one state by another, unless by an agreed international treaty, unlike in domestic society where the state imposes a legal equality on all individual and group members.

It is to domestic society that we must return to conclude our discussion of equality.

The decline of equality

It is to be hoped that by now you will be aware that equality is an important issue in political discourse. Nevertheless, as we stated right at the start of this chapter, equality remains the 'poor relation' of liberty in political theory. Freedom is always a more appealing concept than equality. If anything, the last quarter of a century or so has seen a decline in the fortunes of equality and a rise in those of liberty in modern political struggle. Why might this be so? We shall suggest a number of reasons, although they are by no means an exhaustive collection.

Western societies are permeated by ideological beliefs and social structures that militate against equality, especially collectivist measures to enhance equality. Individual 'liberty' and 'choice' remain the dominant ideology, and social policies reflect this. Egalitarian policies and institutions have a limited role in comparison. The ideological stress on *freedom* over *equality* ensures that the most powerful economic and social forces are those of the capitalist free market. Public-sector services are perceived as merely a safety net for when the private option is unavailable or too expensive. No British government has been willing to reduce tax and other incentives to, say, private health and educational provision let alone take steps to abolish them. No government has been prepared to raise taxes to the level needed to provide resources sufficient to make state services so attractive that private provision 'withers on the vine'. In fact the trend in recent decades has been to extend the role of the private sector in the provision of health, education and pension provision.

Most politicians and also the public place a greater priority on liberty over equality in their policy preferences. There is no great constituency among voters for extending state provision and raising taxes to pay for it, with the possible exception of the health service. This, of course, may simply be a reflection of the powerful anti-egalitarian ideological elements in Western societies. It may, however, be more the result of the growth of new class and income structures in society that reinforce a commitment to liberty rather than equality. Big industries with large workforces, infused with collectivist and egalitarian beliefs (industries such as coal, steel, shipbuilding, heavy engineering), have largely disappeared, to be replaced by a growing white-collar and professional sector, non-unionised and influenced by individualist ideological assumptions, including the priority of freedom over equality. The 'new' workers in the expanding middle classes do not believe that increasing taxes to pay for greater redistribution in pursuit of greater social equality – taxes they would largely have to find – would be in their interests, and middle-class voters have considerable power to ensure that their interests are protected.

Scepticism among voters about egalitarian policies is reinforced by their awareness that the tax burden to pay for redistributive policies tends to fall on the poor and middle-income groups. In Britain, for example, there is an upper limit on the amount people pay in National Insurance contributions, an amount which remains the same above a prescribed income level. Despite some minor changes in the National Insurance ceiling announced in the 2002 Budget, higher earners pay proportionally less of their income on welfare payments than others, hardly an egalitarian measure. Many studies of the welfare state reveal that middle-income people and the better off benefit disproportionately from the welfare state: they are more likely to stay on in education, demand more from the health services, and draw their state pensions for longer than the poor.

In Britain and most other Western societies there has been little effort to challenge dominant ideological assumptions that militate against equality. Similarly there has been little effort by governments to tackle the *sources* of inequality in society. There has been no sustained challenge to economic and social inequalities, most of which originate in the capitalist and private sectors. In fact, state and welfare systems are viewed as a drain on the productive private sector of the economy and as weakening initiative and effort, especially of the poor (an idea that has changed little since the Poor Law reforms of the early nineteenth century). There has been little attempt to integrate the public and private sectors to increase social equality and little desire to do so.

One can set declining interest in equality in Britain within an international context. The decline and fall of the Soviet Union removed a major force for equality in the West. The USSR was oppressive, bureaucratic and a disaster for its own working class. But it was of great benefit to the Western working classes as their governments created welfare systems to 'tame' capitalism and make it more attractive in comparison to the socialist alternative in the East. The end of the Cold War and the collapse of communism exposed not only the bankruptcy of socialism but also the apparent failure of egalitarian policies as pursued by the Soviet Union. The globalised economy of the post-Cold War world has been dominated by the USA and large corporations. Acting on free-market principles, it has reinforced inequality both within societies and between nations and regions.

There seems little likelihood that equality will move up the political agenda in the foreseeable future, but the problems remain. Social inequality and poverty in Western societies are sources of instability and crime, insecurity and fear that will have to be addressed at some point. Similarly, the increasing inequality between people in different countries is one source of war, disturbance and mass migration that will also have to be alleviated if the hopes of a peaceful and prosperous world stand any chance of being realised in the twenty-first century.

Summary

Equality is a word capable of several different meanings. One can speak of 'primary' equality, which is the claim that, whatever the actual circumstances, all human beings are 'equal' by virtue of being human. However, even if this is conceded, it has little practical consequence unless one accepts a range of other 'equalities' such as equality of consideration, equality before the law, political equality and equal opportunities. These different forms of equality have proved highly contentious. One of the main divisions lies between those who advocate equality of outcome and those who favour equality of opportunity. Equality of opportunity may be a fine thing, but it must include the opportunity for unequal outcomes if liberty is to be respected. Equality as a goal of social policy seems currently to be out of fashion, though in the West there is a general consensus on the desirability of such 'group' equalities as gender equality and race equality which are important elements in achieving greater liberty for disadvantaged groups.

REFERENCES AND FURTHER READING

1 Aristotle, *The Politics* (1236–7).
2 Rousseau, J.-J. *A Discourse on the Origin of Equality* (1754).
3 Tawney, R. H. *Equality* (Allen and Unwin, 1931).
4 Rousseau, J.-J. *The Social Contract* (1792).

Barker, J. *Arguing for Equality* (Verso, 1987).
Heywood, A. 'Equality', in A. Heywood, *Political Ideas and Concept: An Introduction* (Macmillan, 1994), pp. 225–35.
Lucas, J. R. 'Against Equality', in H. A. Bedau (ed.), *Justice and Equality* (Prentice-Hall, 1971).
Rae, D. *Equalities* (Harvard University Press, 1981).
Raphael, D. D. *Problems of Political Philosophy* (Macmillan, 1984).
Rees, J. C. *Equality* (Macmillan, 1972).
Tawney, R. H. *Equality* (Allen and Unwin, 1931).
Wilding, P. 'Equality in British Social Policy Since the War', *Talking Politics*, 2:2 (1989/90), pp. 54–8.
Williams, B. 'The Idea of Equality', in H. A. Bedau (ed.), *Justice and Equality* (Prentice-Hall, 1971).
Williams, B. 'The Idea of Equality', in P. Laslett and W. G. Runciman, *Philosophy, Politics and Society* (Blackwell, 1972).

SAMPLE QUESTIONS

1 To what extent is inequality incompatible with democracy?

2 Is 'equality before the law' a 'fig leaf' concealing the privileges of the rich?

3 To what extent and in what ways do British political parties differ in their commitment to equality?

4 Is it possible to make a serious case for the existence of primary equality? Is this not merely a figment of the imagination of political and social idealists?

5 'The concept of group inequality, and the need to rectify supposed injustices based on this idea, is a dangerous distraction from the essential issue of creating the conditions for greater equality between individuals.' Discuss.

Rights, obligations and citizenship

6

Three related concepts are addressed here: rights, obligations and citizenship. We first consider the development of the concept of 'rights' as being intrinsic to human beings because they are *human*. Different interpretations of the term 'rights' are discussed together with some of the controversies which surround the issue at the present. Next we analyse the idea of 'obligation' or 'duty', notably the obligations the citizen is said to owe to society and to the government. Various theories of such obligation are examined. We look at the currently fashionable idea of 'citizenship', and the various ways in which the term is used. Lastly, we reflect upon the implications of the present British government's promotion of 'citizenship'.

POINTS TO CONSIDER

➤ Is it reasonable to claim that there are universal human rights that should be upheld by all governments?

➤ Should 'positive' rights be included among universal human rights since their observance depends on resources beyond the scope of most governments?

➤ Has the experience of totalitarianism confirmed the traditional liberal view that the main threat to human rights comes from the state?

➤ Does acceptance of 'rights' automatically imply an acceptance of duties?

➤ To whom or what is the citizen's highest duty owed?

➤ Does the term 'citizenship' imply both legal rights and social obligations?

➤ Does the government's emphasis on the duties of citizenship conceal the possibility that it is reneging on its own duties?

Wherever there is a human being, I see God-given rights inherent in that being, whatever may be the sex or complexion. (William Lloyd Garrison, *Life*, 1885–89)

All, too, will bear in mind this sacred principle, that though the will of the majority is in all cases to prevail, that will to be rightful must be reasonable; that the minority possess their equal rights, which equal law must protect, and to violate would be oppression. (Thomas Jefferson, first inaugural address, 4 March 1801)

All human beings are born free and equal in dignity and rights. (Article 1, *Universal Declaration of Human Rights*, 1948)

Rights

The concept of 'rights' is nowadays so familiar, and so intertwined with that of 'democracy', so much part of everyday usage and serious political discourse that it is surprising to discover that 'rights' in the modern sense are very much a creation of the seventeenth and eighteenth centuries.

Although today 'democracy' is universally assumed to presuppose the existence of 'rights', the democracy of the Greek city-states functioned without this concept at all. Certainly, there were some people who had the right to vote, but this was because they were 'citizens'; the franchise was by no means universal, and only male citizens had the vote.

In **feudal** times there was certainly a notion of rights but the word 'right' was closer in meaning to our modern idea of 'property'. Individuals and groups had rights to do various things – to hold markets, to graze animals on specific common lands – but these rights were specific to them as individuals. They did not enjoy them because they were citizens, still less because they were human beings. Medieval society was a complex tapestry of such rights; rights which also often involved duties, such as providing monies or armed forces

> **feudalism**
> A social structure based on strict social differentiation and involving rigid reciprocal rights and obligations. Feudalism was the social structure of medieval Europe.

for their lord or king. As late as the English Civil Wars of 1642–49, Parliament's stand against the king was justified as a defence of 'ancient and undoubted rights and privileges'.

The whole business of rights has in fact been a greater source of controversy than their currently fashionable acceptance would suggest. Eighteenth-century conservative thinkers vigorously contested concepts of the 'rights of man', most notably Edmund Burke. Burke argued that rights did not exist in the abstract as '*human* rights', but only in the concrete and specific world of a political system. One could certainly enjoy rights as an Englishman or a Frenchman, as the subject of a state, but not as 'man' in general. Socialist thinkers were also, at least initially, less than enthusiastic about rights, particularly individual rights. Like Burke they tended to emphasise group rights, in this case the rights of the working class or trade unions. The far left tended to dismiss the whole idea of individual rights as a disguise for the actual exploitation of the working classes, whatever theoretical 'individual' rights they might enjoy. Thus while liberals argued for the individual's right to enter into economic relations, to make bargains and contracts, socialists argued that the possession of such rights ignored the plain fact that the 'playing field' was far from level. In fact, it was tilted steeply against the working class, whose relative social and political weakness made bargaining with employers unequal.

Events in the twentieth century were to modify this belief drastically. Liberals were forced by the inter-war slump to realise that individualism was not enough. The atrocities of the Nazi period forced conservative thinkers to accept that there were real 'human' rights. The experience of Soviet-style communism led the left, even the far left, to a reluctant acquiescence in recognising the importance of upholding individual rights as a defence against the might of totalitarian regimes.

Thus the post-war period was notable for a plethora of proclamations of 'rights'. Human rights were espoused by the Vatican and adopted by the United Nations. Even the British, suspicious of legalistic positive rights, eventually incorporated the European Convention on Human Rights into law. The UK was the first to sign the Convention in 1950 and the last to adopt it as part of its domestic law in 2000. Political demands were often articulated in the language of rights: minority rights, women's rights, gay rights, even animal rights. There were assertions of national 'rights to self-determination' after the First World War, the right to suicide, rights to ingest harmful drugs, the 'right to choose' (to have an abortion), and so on. Ordinary speech soon translated wishes into the language of rights – the right to have children, to various forms of sexual experience, to foreign travel and to self-expression and discovery.

Such language actually tended to debase the whole concept of rights and rob it of meaning.

Moreover, it soon became apparent that simply upholding rights was by no means an uncontentious formula for government action. Rights became highly contentious, as it soon became apparent that there was no universal agreement as to what specific legal or civil rights there should be. Should women, for example, have an exclusive 'right to choose' to have an abortion or not? Such a right would conflict with a child's 'right to life', the right of the father to a say over the welfare of his progeny, and the right of society to ensure sufficient citizens are produced to guarantee its survival. Many other controversial issues spring to mind. Are rights absolute? Does the right to life extend to all persons in all circumstances? If one has a right to life, does one also have the right to end it? Where do the right to freedom of speech end and the right to privacy, and to freedom from racial harassment, begin?

If anything, an appeal to alleged rights does not end controversy; it merely gives it a powerful emotional charge.

Further difficulties have arisen as philosophers have tried to establish the rational basis of human rights. John Locke, for example, argued that human rights are 'God-given', but modern secularisation has lessened the impact of this assertion. Man's claim to special treatment among living things by virtue of his capacity for moral choice, his intellectual pre-eminence and his manifest superiority to the animal kingdom, has been shaken by scientific advances. As a result, some argue for animal rights to be as valid as a human's and that man has a moral obligation to observe them. In fact, animal rights campaigners question the entire legitimacy of a political system based on rights that apply only to humans.

The nature of rights

At this point it might be useful to distinguish between various kinds of rights. Four types can be suggested:
- 'natural' and 'human' rights;
- legal rights;
- civil rights;
- welfare rights.

'Natural' and 'human' rights

Natural or, in today's terminology, human rights are held by people as part of their very humanity. They are a gift from God or nature to every human being. The state is the guardian of such rights, not the creator of them. To deprive human beings of such rights is therefore morally wrong. Governments are obliged to uphold these rights; if a government does not, it acts immorally.

The most articulate early exponent of this view was John Locke, writing in the late seventeenth century. In his *Two Treatises on Government* (1690) he itemised these rights as 'Life, Liberty and Property'. Eighty-six years later, Thomas Jefferson wrote this principle into the American *Declaration of Independence* as 'Life, Liberty and the pursuit of Happiness'. This proclamation of the centrality of rights in the system of government implied that government was 'good' in so far as it observed these rights, a doctrine which had important consequences for the institutions of government, and for the principles of which they were the expression. One such principle is the 'separation of powers' in the US Constitution which has separate bodies for the legislature (Congress), executive (President), and judiciary (Supreme Court). The framers of the American Constitution further assumed that *limited* government would be in practice essential if rights were to be preserved. Moreover, the whole legitimacy of the American War of Independence itself was predicated on the assumption that 'rights' are essential to decent human existence – so essential, in fact, that there was in nature itself another 'right', the right to rebel: 'whenever any Form of Government becomes destructive of these Ends it is the Right of the People to alter or abolish it, and to initiate new government' (*Declaration of Independence*, 1776).

Legal rights

Legal rights are those which are enforceable in courts of law. These may derive from natural rights but are not identical to them. Thus, for example, a child might be said to have the human right to life, but not the *legal* right to vote or dispose of property.

Civil rights

The term civil rights is sometimes applied to legal rights but more often refers to rights which do not actually exist in law but which in some sense ought to exist, or to rights which may exist on paper but not in reality. Civil rights are held to be essential for the satisfactory functioning of society. Thus the civil rights movement in America in the 1960s campaigned for non-discrimination towards African-Americans in education, transport and restaurant facilities. In Northern Ireland the civil rights movement of the late 1960s campaigned for a wide measure of social justice in housing and jobs, as well as in 'genuine' democratic institutions and non-sectarian policing.

Welfare rights

Welfare rights include the right to employment, education and adequate healthcare. Such rights are, it is claimed, 'positive' rights, as opposed to the 'negative' rights that protect the individual from the actions of a tyrannical state. As has been suggested, the liberal approach to rights, exemplified by Locke and, later, J. S. Mill, assumes that the greatest potential threat to rights is the state – the state whose prime function ought to be the very protection of these rights.

By the late nineteenth and early twentieth centuries, though, many thinkers had come to regard this fear of the state as misplaced. The real threat to vast numbers of people, they argued, is not the state but powerful institutions and ingrained economic and social forces before which the ordinary citizen is powerless. This understanding implied a positive role for the state as the guarantor and even provider of welfare rights.

This new conception of rights has had a major influence on the European Union. In 1989 the Commission proposed a draft 'Charter of Fundamental Social Rights', concerned with conditions of work, minimum wage rates, equal opportunities and so on. That charter was eventually incorporated into the Treaty of Maastricht (1992) as the 'Social Chapter'.

The reappraisal of rights and the role of the state in providing them have not been without controversy. Some have argued that these are not 'rights' in the usual sense at all, since they are contingent on the state's actually being able to supply them. If they are rights at all, they are better described as 'aspirational rights'; in other words, they are *desirable* objectives but not necessarily ones that are possible to implement *practically*.

Obligations

Although much attention has been paid to 'rights' in recent years, some consideration is now being given to 'duties' (or, as it has become more usual to call them, 'obligations'). The implicit assumption is that rights need to be balanced by duties. Historically, the left has been more anxious to stress rights; nowadays even the liberal left has focused on duties. In part this is a consequence of the development of the belief in 'civil society', the network of family, voluntary and informal groups and activities that underpin a decent society. This belief derives partly from a reaction to the rampant individualism of the Thatcher years. Another source of this belief is an analysis of the weaknesses of the former communist regimes of Eastern Europe, regimes in which there were no intermediate stages, no buffer, between the state and the individual.

Since 2000 both the Labour and Conservative parties in Britain have stressed the need for people to recognise their public duties and to act upon this recognition.

The nature of obligations

As with rights, the terms duties and obligations cover a number of rather different concepts, which may be summarised as follows:
- moral obligations;
- legal obligations;
- civic obligations;
- social obligations.

Moral obligations

Moral obligations are the things people ought to do because in some sense they owe such actions to God, to others or to themselves. Thus there is a moral obligation to speak the truth, to help others in need, to refrain from adultery, and so on. These obligations are not enforceable by law in Britain (although in some countries they are: adultery is illegal in Saudi Arabia; failing to assist an injured person is illegal in Spain). Moral obligations do, however, often become the basis of legal obligations, as the foregoing examples illustrate.

Legal obligations

Legal obligations are things one has to do which are enforceable in the courts, such as paying one's taxes and driving only when in possession of a valid driving licence. Such obligations are closely linked to state sovereignty. Citizens and other individuals resident in the territory of a state are under an obligation to obey the laws of that state.

Civic obligations

Civic obligations are actions we should perform as a tribute to the rights we enjoy as part of a political community. We may be said to have the right to vote and also the civic obligation to do so. (In some countries, such as Australia, this is a legal obligation which incurs a fine if breached.)

Social obligations

Social obligations are an extension of civic obligations. They involve a broadly similar concept but have wider application. They include those obligations we owe to society that contribute to the general good. Such duties are only tangentially linked to specific rights. For example, one might claim the right to have children and decide on their education. The concomitant obligation would be to bring them up properly, as good citizens, introduce them into the culture of their society, and teach them right from wrong. Such obligations can be discharged on a personal and an individual basis. The present British government encourages people to fulfil their obligations by operating within groups and organisations of all kinds; for example, the obligation of childcare can include the care of other children besides one's own, by such means as working in the Guide or Scout movements.

The sources of obligations

By and large, obligations have proved less contentious than rights. Many supposed obligations seem little more than pious aspirations with which no one would quarrel. There are few campaigns, violent or otherwise, in defence of an extension of obligations. This is not, however, to say that there are no areas of dispute. One question concerns the source of such obligations. If they are to be taken seriously they need a firmer grounding than just decent feelings.

The earliest basis for asserting the binding nature of obligation is the idea of contract. In a sense this can be traced back to the biblical notion of the covenant of God with His people, who keep His laws in exchange for His protection.

Of greater importance to our deliberations here, though, are the theories concerning the notion of a social contract which were devised in the seventeenth century by Thomas Hobbes and John Locke. Both men sought to explain the origins of government by reference to a **state of nature**, a situation of primal chaos caused by the absence of established authority. Having logically discerned what such a condition would be Hobbes and Locke used logic to establish the basis for government and the obligation of the citizen to obey. In such situations, they argued, human

> **state of nature**
> Human society as it was before the establishment of government characterised by total freedom and the absence of law or authority.

beings established a 'contract' between the governed and the governors. This formed the basis for both rights and obligations of both parties. Neither writer regarded the 'state of nature' and the subsequent creation of a contract as historically based; they both saw it as a sort of metaphor, an 'explanatory myth'.

Hobbes, in *Leviathan* (1651), argued that in order to escape the barbarism of the 'state of nature', where every man was pitted against every other in an endless cycle of violence and distrust, human beings voluntarily surrendered their unbridled freedom to an authority, a government, which subsequently had absolute claims on their obedience. As long as such a government provided security for those people they were obliged to support it. However, should the government fail in this crucial duty then the citizenry were released from their obligation to obey and were, in fact, obliged to obey any new government able to offer them security.

A less totalitarian interpretation of the social contract was that of Locke. His state of nature was not one of instability and violence. Human beings could maintain order and peace without government, but government was necessary to provide a stronger framework for the protection of their natural rights. In his *Two Treatises of Government* (1690), Locke argued that there were in effect two contracts. The first was one in which individuals agreed to impose limits on themselves to form 'society'. The second was a contract between society and government by which government would be obeyed in exchange for its protection of natural rights. Both contracts form the basis of liberal ideas of politics and government.

Conservatives have not been impressed by Locke's thesis, particularly by its dependence on a belief in 'natural rights'. Instead, they have suggested that every individual owes a natural loyalty to his society, in much the same way as he bears a loyalty to his own family: 'We begin our public affections in our families. No cold relation is a zealous citizen.'[1] Society and the family are natural rather than artificially contrived institutions and can therefore rightly lay claim to a natural obligation.

A more pragmatic argument is one based on the value to the individual of fulfilling his obligations to society and, by extension, to the government. A 'good' government will, in the words of Jeremy Bentham, pursue 'the greatest happiness of the greatest number'. This principle is called **utilitarianism**.

Questions necessarily arise. Are obligations to society the same as obligations to the state? If not, what if there is a clash between the two? If we equate 'state' with 'nation' then much conflict might well occur. For example, Germany defeated France in 1940. The French government surrendered and ordered its armed forces to cease hostilities. Some Frenchmen, such as Charles de Gaulle, felt this as a betrayal of the French nation by the French state. In his view this betrayal absolved him of all loyalty to the (admittedly legal) government of Marshal Philippe Pétain that emerged after the fall of France. Indeed, de Gaulle and his followers believed that they had not only the right to continue the war, but a positive obligation to do so.

> **utilitarianism**
> A political philosophy that sees the highest political goal as promoting the 'greatest happiness of the greatest number'.

Yet another question arises. Can the 'nation' be equated with 'society'? Or is there a global society that has an equal, if not superior, claim on loyalty? Other claimants to loyalty may also be considered: conscience, race, class, church, religious community, the environment, even the human race itself. All of these may, in certain circumstances, appear to have a greater claim than the state or nation.

Even if it is admitted that the state has valid claims to obedience (and Marxists and anarchists explicitly reject such claims), what is the nature of that obedience? Is it simply observing the law or does it go beyond that to a positive and enthusiastic support of the regime? **Totalitarian** states, like Nazi Germany, clearly demanded unconditional obedience to the state (regarded by them as the ultimate representation of the *Volk* or 'people').

> **totalitarianism**
> A political system in which the government controls all areas of political, economic, social and cultural life. It allows no opposition and effectively eliminates 'private' life. Examples of such totalitarian societies include Nazi Germany and the Soviet Union.

Liberal theorists have argued that there are limits to the obligations which the state can impose on people. They have proposed specific constitutional arrangements to give effect to these limitations. Liberals assume that the state's role in society is very largely to safeguard natural or human rights.

A problem arises if the state does not, in fact, guarantee such rights. At what point does the bond of obedience dissolve? Is there a right of the citizen to rebel against, and even overthrow, such a state by force? This question has, of course, been of acute interest in the twentieth and early twenty-first centuries, but originally arose in the seventeenth and eighteenth centuries. Locke argued that there was such a right and the argument was made explicit in the American *Declaration of Independence* (1776), which boldly asserted that when government degenerated into despotism 'it is the right of the people to alter or abolish it, and to institute a new government'.

Even if it is accepted that there is such a right to revolt, difficult questions arise as to precisely what circumstances justify such a rebellion and whether there should be any constraints on the methods of the revolutionaries. These questions, of course, are points not simply of academic interest, but of urgent contemporary political importance. As early as the thirteenth century Thomas Aquinas had laid down certain conditions for justified rebellion that were subsequently absorbed into the writings of other theorists. The Latin American bishop Oscar Romero of San Salvador has in the twentieth century reiterated this view: 'When a dictatorship seriously violates human rights . . ., when it becomes unbearable and closes channels of dialogue . . ., the church speaks of the legitimate right of insurrectional violence.'[2] The main criteria were that oppression was intolerable, that no other means were available, that the good done would exceed the harm, that there was a reasonable chance of success and that the struggle be conducted by 'just means'. Many of these principles were also associated with those of the just war, for example avoiding deliberate injury to the innocent. In practice such conditions are necessarily highly subjective.

Citizenship

'Citizenship' appears to be enjoying something of a vogue. It has been incorporated into the lexicon of the major parties and the present British government (2002) intends making classes in 'citizenship' part of the National Curriculum. The general impression given is that a 'good citizen' more or less equates with a 'good person', and what is 'good' appears to be what is held to be so in contemporary society. Hence, much emphasis is apparently to be placed on 'tolerance' as a value to be promoted in citizenship classes.

The nature of citizenship

There is more to the term 'citizenship' than simply pious do-gooding. It is a word capable of multiple meanings:
- legal citizenship;
- sociological citizenship;
- participatory citizenship.

Legal citizenship

Legal citizenship can simply mean 'having legal status'. A citizen of a country enjoys certain legal rights (for example, to live and work there) in contrast to 'aliens' who may be admitted and may enjoy some of the rights of citizenship, but not all. Legal citizenship may well involve political rights, such as the right to vote, campaign and stand for public office.

Sociological citizenship

This category, 'sociological', means that a person may be a 'citizen' of a country (or of a larger unit, such as the European Union) as well as holding other identities such as race, class, religious affiliation and so on. One can, of course, also be a citizen of a city (indeed, 'city' is the root origin of the word), and proud of it. Cicero, the Roman writer and politician, was proud of being a Roman citizen: *civis Romanus sum* ('I am a Roman citizen').

Cicero's pride in his Roman identity suggests that there is something more to citizenship than just legal status or sociological classification. It indicates an emotional tie with that identity. In most understandings of citizenship there is a sense not only of the right, but also of the privilege of participation in society as a matter of pride, even of honour and duty.

Participatory citizenship

The idea of 'participation' as an important feature of citizenship has raised the issue of what in reality (as aside from formal legal provision) makes such participation possible. Obvious factors include the opportunity to work and to contribute to society, a reasonable level of income, access to public authorities and channels for the expression of views.

There are many in society to whom these desiderata do not in fact apply: 'second-class citizens', the 'excluded', the 'underclass'. Recently government attention has been given to regeneration schemes, skills training, social welfare benefits, so as to bring these people within the normal functioning of society – in short, to make them citizens. This necessitates the empowerment of the socially excluded by means ranging from consultation mechanisms to advocacy schemes (whereby a trusted person acts as 'advocate' for the less articulate and educated members of society).

One problem with this approach is its open-endedness. Just what constitutes *normal* participation in society – being able to afford Christmas and birthday presents, holidays abroad, tickets for football matches? There is also the practical difficulty of the cost to the state (or really to its taxpayers) of such initiatives. A further criticism is that state intervention in this area is counter-productive. Far from being empowered, the subjects of this intervention are in fact made dependent on the state. A 'dependency culture' emerges in which the poor, ethnic minorities and other under-privileged citizens have their self-reliance undermined. They may eventually come to expect the local council or the state to do everything for them, with disastrous consequences for themselves and the wider society.

In reaction, therefore, to the notion of 'social citizenship', in which the state intervenes to ensure a measure of social equality, right-wing commentators have redefined citizenship in terms of not being a burden, of contributing to society positively by hard work and engagement in various voluntary activities. These activities create what the Conservatives have recently called a 'neighbourly society'.

A similar concept of citizenship seems also to have informed New Labour's approach to the matter. One aspect of Tony Blair's 'Third Way' is a fruitful partnership of the public, private and, crucially, voluntary sectors in improving the community. In this vision the state would aid charities by funding assistance, expertise, 'charity friendly' regulations, and so on. Such a project would rely heavily on volunteers, on 'active' citizens.

For both the Labour and Conservative parties these versions of citizenship represent a considerable divergence from previously held positions. The Conservatives under John Major introduced a 'Citizen's Charter' which provided quality benchmarks for public services such as hospitals and railways. By doing so, they redefined the citizen as essentially a consumer of services rather than as an active participant in the workings of political society.

At one level 'active citizenship' is unexceptionable. One can hardly advocate 'bad neighbourliness'. On the other hand, there are problems. Who, for example, sets the agenda of 'socially beneficial' initiatives – voluntary bodies or the state? The very association of voluntary bodies with the state may deprive their members and clients of 'ownership' of those bodies. The vital role of voluntary associations as potential critics of government policy is also blunted if their criticism leads to a withdrawal of state funding, or, even more seriously, of access to the locus of power.

Moreover, imposing citizenship on the school curriculum can be criticised as producing a bland and conformist citizenry, 'voluntarily' doing the government's bidding while being rendered intellectually and emotionally incapable of critical analysis and evaluation of the effects. It is worth noting that all the totalitarian regimes of the twentieth century have been keen to promote such 'voluntary' activity by their citizens.

Finally, one could argue that the government is shifting responsibility for what is properly its own function on to the shoulders of its people. These functions include, for instance, care of the elderly, reduction of street crime and preservation of the environment.

Summary

Rights in some sense existed in the Middle Ages, although the idea of 'human rights' dates from the eighteenth century. Historically, there has been some debate on what exactly these rights consist of, while conservatives and socialists have, from different directions, supported the liberal commitment to universal human rights. By the end of the nineteenth century it was widely agreed that a focus on 'individual' and 'negative rights' was inadequate to meet the social needs of the time. This led to the development of 'group' and 'social' rights, such as those accorded to groups like trade unions and to individuals in the form of welfare benefits. Critics have questioned whether social rights are properly so described; the expression 'aspirations' might be more appropriate. Obligations, or duties, to society and the state have received considerable attention in recent years, partly in an attempt to give them a sound philosophical underpinning and partly to establish what are the limits to the individual's duty to the state. Governments, especially 'New Labour', have been anxious to incorporate the idea of obligations as well as rights into the political consensus. Citizenship has been subject to some reappraisal in recent years. It is a reappraisal that moves away from a purely legal definition to a concept that includes full participation of citizens in the democratic process.

REFERENCES AND FURTHER READING

1 Edmund Burke, *Reflections on the Revolution in France* (1790).
2 Archbishop Oscar Romero, quoted in Anthony Jay (ed.), *Oxford Dictionary of Political Quotations* (Oxford University Press, 1999), p. 308.

Barbalet, J. M. *Citizenship* (Open University Press, 1988).
Cranston, M. *What are Human Rights?* (The Bodley Head, 1973).
Dworkin, R. *Taking Rights Seriously* (Duckworth, 1979).
Heywood, A. 'Rights, Obligations and Citizenship', ch. 6 in A. Haywood, *Political Ideas and Concepts: An Introduction* (Macmillan, 1994), pp. 137–65.
Finnis, J. *Natural Law and Natural Rights* (Clarendon Press, 1980).
Flathman, R. *Political Obligation* (Atheneum, 1972).
Heater, D. *Citizenship: The Civil Ideal in World History, Politics and Education* (Longman, 1990).
Meldon, A. (ed.) *Human Rights* (Wadsworth, 1970).
Pateman, C. *The Problem of Political Obligation* (Wiley, 1979).
Raphael, D. D. (ed.) *Political Theory and the Rights of Man* (Macmillan, 1967).
Waldren, J. *The Problems of Rights* (Oxford University Press, 1984).

SAMPLE QUESTIONS

1 Compare and contrast the liberal, socialist and conservative concepts of rights.

2 To what extent is belief in human rights founded on reason?

3 What is the basis of political obligation in a democracy?

4 Is rebellion against the state ever justified?

5 Are there fundamental differences between the democratic and totalitarian concepts of citizenship?

6 'All too often modern concepts of citizenship tend to over-emphasise the rights a citizen has and to ignore the corresponding duties associated with citizenship.' Discuss.

The role of ideology in politics and society

7

We attempt here to clarify ideas about ideology – what it is, how it is transmitted, how useful it is in making sense of society. We also examine its relevance to recent modern history both in Britain and in other parts of the world. Then we analyse the situation in contemporary Britain and consider whether it can be reasonably asserted that there is an ideological consensus in Britain or whether we are now 'beyond ideology'.

POINTS TO CONSIDER

➤ Do ideologies help or hinder us in our understanding of society?

➤ Is there any sense in which ideologies (or any specific ideology) are 'true'?

➤ How might one distinguish between 'dominant ideologies' and 'ideologies of resistance', and also between 'restrictive' and 'relaxed' ideologies?

➤ Are the terms 'left' 'right', and 'centre' still useful ways of categorising ideological positions?

➤ What do some writers mean by the 'end of ideology'?

➤ British political parties nowadays often claim to be 'non-ideological' – are they right to do so?

Our lives may be more boring than those who lived in apocalyptic times, but being bored is greatly preferable to being prematurely dead because of some ideological fantasy. (Michael Burleigh, *The Third Reich: A New History*, 2000)

We are now again in an epoch of wars of religion, but a religion is now called an 'ideology'. (Bertrand Russell, 'Philosophy and Politics', *Unpopular Essays*, 1950)

Ideology is . . . a system of definite views, ideas, conceptions, and notions adhered to by some class or political party. [Ideology] is always a reflection of the economic system predominant at any given time. (*Soviet Philosophical Dictionary*, 1954)

Political debate is widespread in society. Whether we are aware of it or not, most of us are, at a very simple level, political philosophers. In democratic societies like the UK and the USA citizens are expected to have opinions on a wide range of issues that either directly as individuals or collectively as citizens affect their lives.

Even at a simple, unsophisticated level we have views on the 'correct' form of government, freedom, equality and equal rights, the 'proper' role of government in society, how 'democratic' one's own political system is, the right levels of public spending, and so on. How we think about these and many other subjects will be influenced by the kinds of ideological beliefs we carry around in our heads, the product of our social conditioning, our life experiences and our reflections on them, the nation we live in, our educational level and our social class.

We regularly draw on this store of ideological beliefs when we try to make sense of the world. They may not be logical, well structured or even consistent (tortured are those who try to force their experiences into an ideological strait-jacket; and, given enough power, they will often similarly torture others into wearing the same garment), but one's opinions and actions will make reference to those beliefs. Ideologies can be seen as a form of intellectual 'map' to help us find our way about the world, understand our place in it, analyse the political and social events going on around us. Maps vary in their degree of accuracy. One can assess their value by comparison with objective reality and debate with others.

Ideologies are associated with power structures. Politicians seek power. Their ideology and the social, economic and political circumstances of the time influence what they do with that power when they have achieved it. Indeed, it is impossible to separate the two. This applies even to those who deny having an ideology. The use of power always takes place in a framework of ideology. Modern politics can only be properly understood by reference to the great ideological movements: conservatism, liberalism, socialism, fascism, and so on.

Ideologies tend to have a bad press. They are often dismissed as 'errors' or 'untruths'. If ideology is 'a window on the world' it is a window with glass that distorts the vision. The viewer has difficulty thinking beyond these distortions and assumes what he or she believes to be the 'truth'. Ideology often distorts 'reality' and encourages conflict: 'One man's ideology is another man's falsehood.' Nevertheless, one must not fall into the trap of assuming that all ideologies are of equal validity. They should be respected as important ways of understanding the world. One should also attempt to examine one's own ideological beliefs, to better understand the role of ideology in politics and society.

The meaning of the term 'ideology'

So, given that ideology is very important in politics, what *is* 'ideology'? Is there something about ideological thought that is distinct from other forms of thinking? David Joravsky provides a useful starting point:

> When we call a belief ideological, we are saying at least three things about it: although it is unverified or unverifiable, it is accepted as verified by a particular group, because it performs social functions for that group.[1]

In other words, holders of beliefs do not need to have had them 'proved' by some rational, scientific form of testing. To the believers they are the 'truth', the 'reality'. All political ideologies claim 'true' definitions of liberty, equality, justice, rights and the 'best' society. The 'particular group' mentioned above might be any social group: class, nation, profession, religious organisation, party or pressure group. All will have sets of ideological assumptions that are unquestioningly accepted as 'proper'. The 'social functions' ideologies perform are numerous. They will include the creation of a sense of group solidarity and cohesion for members of that group through shared ideological values; an explanation of the past, an analysis of the present, and, usually, a vision of the future with some description of how a better future will come about.

There has always been a widely held view in politics and political philosophy that 'ideology' merely provides a cloak for the struggle for power, the real stuff of politics. To justify their power and to persuade the people to obey, follow and support them, rulers use ideologies of various kinds. Machiavelli advised, in *The Prince* (1513), that religion was a very useful tool for the ruler. To Machiavelli the real objective of politics was the getting and keeping of power. Appeals to the welfare of the people were merely part of what we would call the ideological window-dressing, hiding the raw struggle for power.

Machiavelli put his finger on one of the most important roles of ideological belief systems (if we may include religion as one of these, for the moment). Until the last couple of centuries, in most societies the dominant form of belief was religion. During the seventeenth and eighteenth centuries rational and scientific forms of thought provided a growing challenge to religion. By the eighteenth century there were sharp and bitter tensions between religious and secular attitudes. One of the features of the Enlightenment was a strong, rational critique of religious beliefs and the perceived baleful influence of religion on politics. It was hoped that one could use reason to discover the laws governing the organisation and functioning of society as the laws of science were being used to discover the workings of nature. Once religion and other forms of irrational thought were removed from political discourse, it was believed, rational programmes would enable human society to improve dramatically.

These 'rational' forms of thought contributed to the criticism of the **ancien régime** in France, the French Revolution, and the development of what we now call 'political ideologies' that dominated political debate in Europe and the world during the following two centuries. Far from introducing new forms of rationality into politics, ideological forms of thinking tended to create new forms of 'irrational' thinking, stirring up and releasing deep political passions that in many ways resembled the emotional commitment to religion. Indeed, political ideologies for many became 'pseudo-religious' belief systems that had many of the hallmarks of religious commitment: 'heretics' were persecuted, 'true' interpretations of the creed formulated, ideological 'prophets' identified and definitive texts written to direct the 'faithful' into 'correct' ways of thought.

> **ancien régime**
> The political and social order that existed in France before the Revolution of 1789

Marxism and economic/class factors

By the middle years of the nineteenth century industrialisation was transforming the economies, societies and the belief systems of the Western world. A new way of thinking about society was required. Many writers at the time contributed to the development of what came to be called a science of society: 'sociology'. The most influential were Karl Marx and Friedrich Engels, who had a striking influence on the study of ideology. In fact, they claimed to have created a 'science' of ideology.

In their studies of early industrial society Marx and Engels, especially in *The German Ideology* (1846), argued that there was a close link between the material conditions of society, the ways in which wealth was produced (the 'substructure'), and the resultant class structure and belief systems (the 'superstructure'). As the economic system changed so would the ideological system that sustained it, as would the class system that arose from the economic 'relations of production' associated with it. Class interests, in their view, shape ideologies. Take liberalism, for example.

Liberalism is an ideology. It claims, like all ideologies, to be a universal set of 'true' values that are appropriate for all people in all societies, and not just in a **liberal society**. Marxists believe that this is not the case. They argue that liberalism is of considerable use as an ideological tool to protect and reinforce the class interests of the property-owning classes (the 'bourgeoisie') and help them to exploit the working classes (the **proletariat**). Liberalism may make eminent sense to the bourgeoisie, Marxists argue, and it may even convince members of the proletariat, but it essentially serves the interests of the former and helps the exploitation of the latter.

liberal society

A society characterised by freedom of thought, expression and political activity.

proletariat

In Marxist terminology the proletariat is the class that lives by selling its labour for a wage. Often, but not strictly accurately, identified with the working class.

As ideology is associated with class interests, once society has become a one-class society as a consequence of the inevitable 'proletarian revolution', these 'false' bourgeois ideologies will disappear.

It is worthwhile identifying the interests behind ideological statements of principle by politicians. There is much that is of value in the Marxist analysis of ideology, despite the failure of political systems that described themselves as 'Marxist', such as the Soviet Union. However, there was a tendency for Marx and Engels and their ideological descendants to claim that their analysis of society is the one most in line with objective reality – the 'truth'.

V. I. Lenin, the Russian revolutionary, refined this doctrine of ideology further. In *What is to be Done?* (1902) Lenin not only worked out a strategy for a revolutionary party but saw socialist ideology as the ideology of the proletariat, a tool which they could use in their struggle for power with the ruling classes. This is a key development in the study of ideology. Henceforth, all Marxist analysis of ideology would treat it as a tool of class interests, whether working-class or ruling-class. Thus the Soviet Union, created by Lenin and built around his revolutionary party, was governed by people using a socialist ideology as the justification for their rule. The 'exploitation of man by man' under capitalism was replaced by the 'exploitation of man by man' under Soviet socialism.

'Dominant ideologies' and 'ideologies of resistance'

One can understand that ideologies may be perceived as a tool used by dominant social groups to maintain and enhance their established power position in a struggle of ideas. Antonio Gramsci, in *Selections from the Prison Notebooks* (1921–35), stressed the important role of dominant, or 'hegemonic', ideologies in capitalist societies as the means by which the dominant capitalist classes maintain their rule. Dominant ideologies permeate all aspects of society, from popular culture to the education system, from religious institutions to sports. Such ideologies legitimise the political system and the established social system in the minds of the working classes and ensure that the 'slave is persuaded that he is free': 'The proletariat wear their chains willingly. Condemned to perceive reality through the conceptual spectacles of the ruling class they are unable to recognise the nature or extent of their own servitude.'[2]

However, dominant ideologies do not have the field all to themselves. Social and political groups in subservient power positions do not always accept the legitimacy of the system in which they live. Ideologies of resistance, or 'counter-ideologies', develop to give purpose and meaning to the social and political struggles of those wishing to reform or overthrow a given social and political structure.

An ideology may shift from being a counter-ideology to a dominant ideology by means of political success: Lenin's Bolshevik Party, for example, took over the Russian state and created the Soviet Union. Or an ideology might be one of both domination *and* resistance. Nationalism, for example, can be used by dominant nations as 'imperialist nationalism' or by subject nations as 'anti-colonial nationalism', the former to support their power, the latter to challenge the status quo.

'Restrictive' and 'relaxed' ideologies

It would be wrong to assume that, although ideological thinking forms a part of all our waking thoughts, the experience of it and degree or intensity of commitment to a set of ideological beliefs are the same for all people. One can make a distinction between what might be called 'restrictive' ideological thought and 'relaxed' ideological thought.

'Restrictive ideologies' are a tightly argued body of ideas that logically hang together in a well-constructed framework, as can be seen in the 'great texts' of the ideological traditions that have shaped modern political life. Liberalism, conservatism, socialism, Marxism, fascism and the other ideological traditions and movements all have a recognised body of literature expounding the main tenets of their ideological belief systems. So, for example, the writings of John Locke, Adam Smith, David Ricardo and John Stuart Mill have considerably influenced the development of liberalism. No study of conservatism in Britain would be complete without reference to the speeches and writings of Edmund Burke, in particular his *Reflections of the Revolution in France* (1790). Marxism, and its class analysis of capitalist society, is, of course, honoured by its eponymous core thinker and voluminous writer, Karl Marx. Hitler and Nazism, Stalin and Stalinism, Mao and Maoism. In all these cases it is impossible to think of the movement without also thinking of the ideological tracts that shaped its image along lines formulated by the leader.

The term 'restrictive ideologies' conjures up the image of rigidity, narrowness and bigotry in the ideological cause. It does not necessarily describe some of the great texts associated with political movements. They provide a reference point for thought and action, a sense of identity with, and commitment to, the movement, and often demonstrate a degree of flexibility in practical use that enables ideologies to keep in touch with the world around us and so remain relevant to contemporary concerns. Indeed, democratic politicians sometimes clearly state their political programme in terms of a struggle of ideologies

> Paradoxically unless we stake out our ideological boundaries and defend them against external assault and internal subversion we will not attract to our cause the millions of non-ideological supporters who are necessary for our victory. A clear statement of our philosophy is essential to our success and perhaps our survival as a major political force.[3]

However, all too often restrictive ideologies can become mere excuses for lack of rationality on the part of the ideologically committed. Ideology becomes a source of narrow-mindedness and unthinking conformity that crushes the originality of the individual adherent. The lives of millions can be oppressed, distorted or lost by political movements driven to impose an ideological 'truth' on their society.

'Relaxed ideologies', on the other hand, are sets of ideological assumptions shared by a social group. Such beliefs are often not clearly thought out or logical or coherent. They may be indirect and accidental connections of ideology and power. We are all creatures of ideology, even though our ideologies are not necessarily well thought out or logical. The holders of relaxed ideological beliefs may not even be aware that their opinions are ideological; they seem to be just 'common sense'.

'Left', 'Right', and 'Centre'

These terms are a common shorthand in discussions of politics – so common, in fact, that one often uses them without a real grasp of what they mean. The application of 'left' and 'right' to politics derives from the French **Estates General** (1789), chaired by King Louis XVI. Delegates were divided into aristocratic members, who sat at the right hand of the king, and the revolutionary and populist members, who sat to the left.

Estates General
The body which in pre-Revolutionary France represented the three 'Estates' or legal and social classifications. The First Estate was the nobility, the Second the clergy, and the Third was the rest of society.

Those on the political right stress patriotism, order, social discipline, traditional values, suspicion of over-powerful governments, and freedom and individuality as a higher political 'good' than equality. The centre has somewhat different political values, involving less inequality, a greater role for the state in helping individuals, a greater stress on freedom, and optimism about the possibilities for improving human nature and society. To the left of the centre the emphasis on the role of the state in creating greater social equality grows, including collective ownership of the means of production, greater emphasis on class rights and a class analysis of society. One might imagine a political 'spectrum', a *horizontal axis*, with these ideas and principles shading into one another, rather than distinctive 'boxes' with sharp dividing lines between them on principles of social and economic policy.

Political scientists also identify a *vertical axis* of degrees of 'authoritarian' or 'democratic' inclinations of ideological supporters. Another vertical axis might be identified as leaning towards the 'status quo', or 'conservative', view of resisting change as compared with the 'revolutionary' or 'radical change' wings of an ideological movement.

In recent years the political 'spectrum' has been largely replaced as a conceptual tool by a 'political horseshoe', in which the far left and far right bend round to be so close as to have much in common in terms of authoritarianism and totalitarianism. It is relatively easy for some voters to shift their support from communist to fascist parties and vice versa.

The nature of modern domestic and international politics has raised questions about the continuing validity of the spectrum model of political values and ideologies, which originated in the nineteenth century, for the early twenty-first century. Green politics, environmentalism, feminism, gay politics and animal rights, as well as religious politics, do not fit very easily into such a conceptual framework.

The end of ideology?

It might seem strange, given our view that ideological thought is a permanent feature of politics, to claim that ideology is in decline or even 'dead'. Yet several writers have argued this, most notably Daniel Bell and Francis Fukuyama.

Daniel Bell, in *The End of Ideology* (1960) and later in an article in *Government and Opposition* (1988), argued that ideological debate was in decline as a means of understanding society. Societies have changed so much that 'old ideological' forms of analysing those societies, especially Marxism, are virtually useless. Modern societies are concerned with non-ideological problem solving. They have become more moral, more liberal and only distantly connected with a class analysis of society. Bell's analysis was greatly influenced by the Cold War struggle and the need to show that Marxism was defunct both as a conceptual tool and for political action.

Francis Fukuyama, in *The End of History and the Last Man* (1992), elaborated ideas he had previously published to argue that the end of the Cold War had shown the triumph of liberalism and liberal democracy to be the ideologies of modern scientific and technological societies. Liberal democracy was of universal application and represented the ultimate objective of mankind. Ideological conflicts arising out of feminism, nationalism, environmentalism and anti-racism are merely representations of the fundamental worth of liberal-democratic values. Indeed, they take place within a framework of liberal-democratic ideological assumptions.

Bell and Fukuyama and other 'end of ideology' writers have been very influential. But they have been attacked for being propagandists for American economic and political domination of the planet. They have also been attacked for having ideas that are in fact highly ideological in themselves and for systematically ignoring evidence that challenges their thesis. There are many peoples, such as those in the Islamic world, who adhere to ideological systems that do not assume that the 'American' way is best, or that liberal democracy is the answer to their social and economic problems.

The transmission of ideologies

We have observed that ideologies arise out of particular social circumstances and reflect the structures of power in society. An ideology, however, is customarily presented as a natural and rational analysis of society. It will carry with it the assumption, overt or covert, that opposing ideologies are somehow unnatural and irrational. Ideologies claim they are universally applicable to all peoples in all societies and are not the product of a particular time and place. They create a particular language of meaning and explanation to encourage the individual to develop a sense of being a full member of a major movement for social reform. Certain words and images will act as 'triggers' to stimulate a chain of ideas associated with a particular ideology, to encourage solidarity among its supporters and stress the divisions among the supporters of counter-ideologies. As part of this, criticism of the ideology will be associated with negativity and can be dismissed as such by its supporters.

These points may give the impression that one is talking about the restrictive ideological forms of ideology, but they also apply to the relaxed forms of ideology in society. A study of newspapers, television programmes and advertisements reveals many subtle, and not so subtle, conscious or unconscious, 'tricks' of the ideological transmission trade.

Ideological assumptions thus affect all aspects of society: family, political parties and pressure groups, local and national politics, and international politics. One must not, however, think that ideologies emerge as part of a conspiracy by a Machiavellian elite to brainwash the public. This would be far too simplistic a view of how ideology develops. Members of the elite in any society rise from that society and generally share the ideological and cultural values of most of its members. There is an ideological element to most aspects of culture. The elite themselves may not realise they are acting selfishly. They may genuinely believe that their views are in the interests of all in society. Marxists, however, would claim such a view of the elite's awareness of their interests and ideology to be naive.

There are many vehicles by which ideological values are transmitted to society: they include family, work, friends, the mass media, political parties and other political and social institutions. The family plays a crucial role in the socialisation of new citizens into the ideological values of their society. There are power relations between men and women, parents and children, all of whom are influenced by ideological concepts, often unthinkingly acted upon by the members of that family. A child's first experiences of power in society and the ideological values it acquires occur, almost literally, with their mother's milk in the context of the family.

Families have an enormous effect on the life chances of their members. Especially important are their occupational and social-class positions, which will play a major role in influencing the educational level of the children, their future occupations, their religious and moral values and their choice of friends. All of these factors will have ideological messages that influence the political values of the individuals concerned. Most such ideological values will be of the relaxed kind, but some people will seek a more restrictive ideological expression of their political views and will join a political party.

Political parties are clearly ideological vehicles, designed to fight elections by appealing to the electorate with a manifesto containing policy proposals that are shaped by ideological values. They must appeal to the electorate with some resonance with the electorate's own ideological values, garnering enough support to win seats in parliament and, possibly, control of the local or national government. Appointments to cabinet posts by, say, the British prime minister, will be made with reference to a range of factors, which will include experience, competence, intelligence, loyalty; but one of the most important will be ideological compatibility and conformity with the prime minister's outlook and the broad ideological and policy aims and objectives of the party.

The importance of ideology in modern history

By now the importance of ideologies in political discourse should be clear. But if there are any lingering doubts, the importance of ideology can be observed in the shaping of world history.

The musings of thinkers have ideological content which, in a myriad of direct and indirect ways, influences the thoughts, policies and actions of politicians and people alike. There is not some 'real' world where people act in a pragmatic manner. We can only understand the world by reference to ideological points of view, while at the same time being aware of the limitations and distortions of our own deeply held ideological beliefs. One can, therefore, gain some idea of the importance of this key link between ideology, thinkers, power and society by studying examples from history.

Ideological debate was an important feature of political life before the twentieth century, but it has influenced politics during the twentieth century in ways that are different from previous times. To begin with, governments and politicians seek clear ideological justifications for their actions and consciously attempt to carry out policies in line with an ideological agenda. Next, modern communications technology ensures that ideological debate and competition is now global in scope. Furthermore, modern states buttress their power by manipulating public opinion along ideological lines by appealing to ideological principles shared by voters and rulers alike. Third, the role of genuine public opinion (formed as a result of people's own experiences) in influencing policy is reduced. Ideological 'spin doctors' manipulate public opinion to such an extent that there is little ideological debate that does not originate from within the political elites. Finally, sections of the intellectual classes in liberal societies adopt the ideological views and positions of extreme political parties and provide political and economic elites with powerful ideological tools for manipulation of the citizenry.

Political ideology now, more than ever before, is very closely linked to state power whatever the political system. The twentieth century, and one sees little hope that this will change in the twenty-first, was one in which ideological falsification, exaggeration and simplification held sway. Ideologies have often taken on the guise of 'political religions', pursuing some form of human perfection, the elimination of all social conflicts, and making claims of being the only vehicles for the 'truth'. It seems as if this form of ideological politics is a natural product of the mobilisation of millions of voters in a mass democracy.

If one accepts Eric Hobsbawm's thesis, in *The Age of Uncertainty* (1994), that the twentieth century makes historical coherence by being considered as lasting from 1914 to 1991, then it was dominated by ideological struggles for dominance among liberal democracy, fascism and communism.

Societies shaped by liberalism dominated the international system at the start of the twentieth century, although a strain of pessimism seemed to be in the ideological and intellectual air, despite a previous century of great economic, social, political, technological and cultural progress. A belief that the onward march of liberal civilisation would not last was a theme among many thinkers as 1900 dawned.

The First World War was a greater shock than people could possibly have imagined. It badly disrupted the global economic system that had been created by Britain in the nineteenth century and wrecked the liberal assumption of inevitable progress. During the two decades after 1918 pessimism deepened as liberalism appeared discredited and out-dated to millions of Europeans. Many therefore turned to fascism and communism, which they envisaged as offering youthful, optimistic and more effective ideologies of renewal and progress.

One could hardly say that ideology does not matter when one considers its impact on the domestic politics of Italy, Germany and the USSR under Mussolini, Hitler and Stalin, respectively. Fascism and communism contained the most extreme elements of ideology found among the many forms of twentieth-century ideological thought. Complex realities were simplified into one fundamental truth of a struggle of good and evil, right and wrong, with a chosen group based on class, race or belief leading the way to a better world. Political opponents, 'undesirable' racial groups and whole social classes were subject to stereotyping, oppression, incarceration and extermination in line with ideological considerations. Common also to both fascist and communist movements was the hatred and contempt for liberal values and parliamentary democracy, which supposedly betrayed the nation or the class.

The consequences for the international balance of power were very great. Nazi foreign policy was formed by an aggressive ideology of expansion. Western liberal democratic suspicions of communist Russia (suspicions that were recip-rocated by Stalin) dogged attempts to create a united diplomatic front in the face of the Nazi threat and contributed to the slide into war in the late 1930s. The Nazi–Soviet Pact of August 1939 was shocking not only in terms of its strategic implications, but also in the breathtaking implausibility of two ideological enemies making a non-aggression treaty. Equally implausible was the alliance between liberal democracy and communism that arose during the war that followed.

The Second World War was an ideological struggle with several military dimensions. Fascism and Nazism fought a war against liberal democracies in the West, which their leaderships hoped could be ended by a negotiated peace, despite the Allied declared policy of 'unconditional surrender'. Nazism fought another war against Soviet communism in the East, a war in which there could be no ideological compromise, no end other than the total defeat of side or the other, a war of incredible levels of ferocity and brutality. Nazi ideology defined whole groups as 'sub-human' and the extermination of millions of Jews, Gypsies and Slavs followed. A third ideological conflict, that between the liberal West and Soviet communism, was suspended while Nazi Germany still posed a threat. But even before fighting in Europe had ended, the conflict that was to lead to the Cold War was well under way, with growing suspicion and hostility between the Anglo-Americans on one side of a divided Europe and the Soviets on the other.

The Cold War was the second great ideological struggle of the century. The planet divided into a bi-polar world of liberal-democratic nations under the leadership of the USA and a communist world under Soviet leadership. A 'Third World' between the two, neither communist nor capitalist, progressively became the battleground for the ideological and military conflicts of the Cold War. Only the possession of massive conventional forces and nuclear weapons by both the USA and the USSR prevented the deep ideological animosity between the two superpowers from erupting into war during the many crises that punctuated their struggle. By the mid-1980s the Cold War was coming to an end and the ideological conflict was winding down. However, nothing prepared the world for the dramatic end of the Soviet Union and the communist regimes in Eastern Europe between 1989 and 1991.

The post-Cold War world seemed to be one in which the ideological struggles of the previous seventy years had come to an end. Liberal democracy appeared triumphant, with the last of its totalitarian enemies gone. However, the end of communism did not mean the end of ideology. Virulent nationalism erupted in Yugoslavia, tearing the state apart, and again in Chechnya, Georgia and other parts of the former Soviet Union. Fascism began to march again in many of the previously communist nations of the East and gained new supporters in the West. Finally, as the new century dawned, virulent Islamic fundamentalism offered a massive challenge to the smug ideological assumptions of the West of a decade earlier.

Ideology was not dead. It had never been absent even in the supremely pragmatic politics of Britain.

The role of ideology in British politics during the age of consensus

It is often stated that the British are 'pragmatic' in their political and social arrangements and not greatly influenced by ideological considerations. Implied in this is an assumption, itself ideological (related to nationalism), that British politics is a superior way of doing things compared to the consciously ideological 'European' politics. Yet ideological values greatly influenced the development of British politics during the twentieth century, as one can see from a quick resumé of British political thought.

Adam Smith, in *The Wealth of Nations* (1776), and David Ricardo, in *Principles of Political Economy* (1817), have had great influence on the development of free-market economics in Britain during the last two hundred years. Liberal ideas about the minimal state and free trade as the best means towards economic growth and the generation of wealth owe much to their works. Indeed, it is impossible to follow an economic debate today without hearing people, often unconsciously, using the ideas of these long-dead liberal economists. John Locke, writing almost a century before Smith, expressed key liberal elements of the importance of property and individual conscience in economic and political discourse in his *Two Treatises of Government* (1690). John Stuart Mill, in *On Liberty* (1859), drew together widespread liberal beliefs of his day to create a powerful statement on behalf of individual freedom. Late nineteenth-century New Liberals reinterpreted liberalism to encourage a greater role for the state in society so as to enhance individual potential in ways that the minimal state would not do. These thinkers and their ideas have had a considerable influence on the development of the post-war **consensus**, and will no doubt continue to influence twenty-first century politics and economics.

> **consensus**
> A general agreement on basic principles, disagreement being confined to details. Government in Britain from 1945 to 1979 is often said to have been 'consensual' since most main parties accepted a mixed economy with a substantial public sector, welfare state provision and a measure of social equality.

The modern British political debate over the welfare state, the NHS, education, employment and taxation levels makes reference to ideological values. Modern Neo-Liberals (who make a strong case for a return to nineteenth-century classical liberalism) face an uphill battle against the dominance of social-democratic ideology in the debate. So strong is the ideological consensus, so deeply entrenched in the social and political values of modern Britain, that it is almost impossible for us to imagine life in a society without these values and the institutions created to bring them into existence.

This may be true in the case of the restrictive view of ideology. There is, apart from the political extremes, very little reference to liberalism, socialism, conservatism, and so on, in the debates that occur in British politics. Even at election time, so it is argued, there is little that might be called ideological, only a pragmatic reference to, for example, what level of taxes to pay for public services.

However, that is not the case with relaxed ideologies. Some writers, such as Samuel Beer, in *Modern British Politics* (1965) and *Britain Against Itself* (1982), and Peter Jenkins, *Mrs Thatcher's Revolution* (1987), have argued that British politics is *very* ideological; so ideological, in fact, that it has damaged the country's economic performance as incoming governments abruptly changed policies in line with their ideological commitments: nationalisation and privatisation, high taxes or low taxes, high public spending or spending cuts, and so on.

The post-war consensus and ideology

Even if the arguments of Beer and Jenkins are not completely accepted there are grounds for claiming that British politics has been very ideological in the relaxed sense of the term, even if not in the restricted sense.

The post-war era since 1945 has been dominated by an ideological 'consensus', whatever the pragmatic claims made for it. Policy considerations, while acquiring the label 'pragmatic' or even 'common-sense', can be ideological in their underlying assumptions, in a sense that is associated with social democracy. From the wartime coalition government until the early 1980s all the major parties, both in and out of government, largely agreed on the basics of government policy. These included the following:

- a commitment to full employment by the use, if necessary, of Keynesian Demand Management techniques;
- the creation of a welfare state with extensive social benefits in terms of health (the NHS), pensions, childcare and benefits, unemployment and sickness payments and expanding educational opportunities;
- the encouragement of economic growth to ensure full employment and the means to pay for welfare state provision;
- a 'mixed economy' of state-owned ('nationalised') key industries, such as coal, steel, railways, working within an economy that largely remained in private hands;
- a 'corporatist' (sometimes called 'tri-partist') approach to economic planning that involved the co-operation of government, business and organised labour;
- the dissolution of the empire (largely completed within twenty years of 1945);
- a commitment in defence and foreign policy to the Atlantic Alliance with the USA, the acquisition and maintenance of a nuclear deterrence, and, from the late 1950s, closer political and economic links with the states of Western Europe.

There was often little difference between Labour and Conservative governments. Their **pragmatism** was based on the acceptance of similar policy goals in order to win elections. Yet this is clearly an example of ideology. It assumes a significant role for the state in the economy and society. There is a strong belief in state intervention to improve social and economic conditions, a belief based on a very clear set of ideological assumptions that can be identified as being 'centre-left' or 'social-democratic' in their orientation.

However, even during the high point of this consensus, from, say, 1945 to the early 1970s, there were those in both major parties who were

> **pragmatism**
> An approach to decision-making that is focused on desirable outcomes to solving social and economic problems, rather than ideological principles.

opposed to the consensus policies of their respective leaderships. The left of the Labour Party wanted greater state intervention and control in society and the economy, while the right of the Conservative Party wanted a massive withdrawal of the state from any areas of social and economic activity and a significant reduction in the levels of taxation. They had little actual effect on the policies of their parties, as consensus politics appeared to be what the majority of the electorate wanted. Political debate and electoral competition revolved around who could manage the system best, who could deliver the greatest level of economic growth, public services and social improvement for least cost and effort.

This social-democratic consensus was successful in establishing an ideological grip on British politics for a number of reasons. The mass unemployment, poverty and failure of the 1930s discredited the minimal state policies of the governments of the day. The Second World War involved massive state intervention in the form of 'War Socialism' that led to victory. If such methods could defeat the Nazis why, it was widely demanded, should state planning not defeat poverty and unemployment afterwards? At last, the long economic boom of the 1950s and 1960s appeared to show that Keynesian economics worked and governments did not have to make difficult choices about state spending and private income levels. Economic growth would enable Britain to have both excellent public services and high individual standards of living.

Challenges in the 1970s

The 1970s challenged the post-war consensus. There were a number of reasons for this. The post-war economic boom came to an end with growing economic difficulties, especially rising inflation and unemployment. Economic decline became more obvious as mining, shipbuilding, steelmaking, textiles and heavy engineering went into apparently terminal decline. With that decline came the shrinking of trade-union membership. By the 1970s the post-war generation that grew up with the welfare state and social democracy were a majority of the electorate. At the same time economic prosperity was growing in the new service sector and white-collar areas of the economy. With that came a new individualism, a new impatience at the inefficient and collectivist provision of state-run services and industries.

In both the Labour and the Conservative parties the anti-consensus elements recognised their opportunities for power. The Labour *Party* moved to the left, thereby losing both members and a close connection with the Labour *Government* (1974–79). In 1981 it split over ideological issues, with many of its right wing going on to form the Social Democratic Party (before ending up after its demise a few years later in the Liberal Democrat Party). The Conservatives moved to the right, slowly at first, but gathering pace under the leadership of Mrs Thatcher after 1975. These ideological changes were of significance in the following decade. The Labour Party was condemned by voters as extreme, and it subsequently lost four elections in a row. The Conservative Party, in power (1979–97), was able to pursue policies that challenged many aspects of the post-war consensus.

A new consensus?

The Thatcher and Major governments attempted to create a new right-of-centre ideological consensus for British politics, heavily influenced by neo-liberalism, and to bring about a fundamental shift away from the social-democratic consensus. The features included the following:

- The concept of the mixed economy was to be challenged by the transfer of state-owned industries to the private sector, a process known as 'privatisation'.

- Corporatism was to be rejected and the role for trade unions and business in formal government economic planning was to be ended.

- There was a strong commitment to market economics as the best means of ensuring economic efficiency and high levels of economic growth.

- Keynesian economic management was to be abandoned, along with the commitment to maintaining full employment. Inflation was to be the major economic 'dragon' for the government to slay, by the adoption of free-market and 'monetarist' policies.

- The welfare state was to be challenged with cuts in benefits and entitlements, the introduction of more means testing for claimants, and the introduction of market solutions into the health and education services.

- The level of taxation on both individuals and businesses was to be steadily reduced as incentives for both to work harder, and take risks and succeed. There were clearly strong elements of liberalism at work here in the economic policies and in the stress on individualism and individual choice and effort. Conservatism raised the role of the family, traditional values, patriotism, discipline and hierarchy. It was even possible to see elements of Marxism in the emphasis on the role of economics in building society.

The new consensus can be recognised in the Labour Party's shift to a right-of-centre programme under Neil Kinnock, John Smith and, especially, Tony Blair. There was no significant reversal of Conservative policies after Labour came to power in 1997. Welfare spending was kept under tight control, helped by high levels of economic growth and low unemployment. Attacks were made on benefit fraudsters and the automatic nature of some benefits. There was considerable support for free-market capitalism, no return to corporatism and no great changes to the tough trade-union legislation of the 1980s. No nationalisation occurred, although Conservatives claimed that the end of RailTrack in 2001, during Labour's second term, was the thin end of the wedge leading to renationalisation. Even policies such as the minimum wage and family income-tax credits were designed to encourage people into work rather than rely on state benefits. Pragmatic policies, yes, but with ideological under-pinnings familiar to the post-war consensus and its successor.

Summary

People have ideological beliefs, even if these beliefs are not very coherent. Ideological beliefs are beyond rational or scientific testing, whatever the claims of their proponents. Such beliefs perform a social role for those who hold them. Some critics argue that ideologies are simply instruments of power, wielded by the dominant groups in society. Another hostile opinion is that ideologies, especially 'restrictive' ones, mentally enslave those who believe in them. Some modern thinkers have argued that 'ideology is dead', that no one believes in any ideology, and that conflicts no longer have an ideological basis. Opponents of such views can point to abundant evidence that liberal capitalism is deeply influenced by ideology. Ideological beliefs were of profound influence in twentieth-century history. New forms of ideology, such as militant Islamism, seem likely to be important in the twenty-first century. While it may be true that ideology in the 'restrictive' sense is largely absent from British politics, this is certainly not the case with 'relaxed' ideology. From 1945 to 1979 there was a clear consensus between the major parties which constituted such an ideology. A consensus exists today, though it is far more influenced by neo-liberalism than was the case in the period before 1979.

REFERENCES AND FURTHER READING

1 D. Joravsky, 'Soviet Ideology', *Soviet Studies*, 18 (1966).
2 J. Femia, *Gramsci's Political Thought* (Oxford University Press, 1981).
3 R. Hattersley, *Choose Freedom* (Michael Joseph, 1987).

Barry, N. 'Ideology', in P. Dunleavy *et al.*, *Developments in British Politics 3* (Macmillan, 1990), pp. 17–41.

Dutton, D. *British Politics Since 1945: The Rise and Fall of Consensus* (Blackwell, 1991).

Eagleton, T. *Ideology: An Introduction* (Verso, 1991).

Eatwell, R. 'Ideologies: Approaches and Trends', in R. Eatwell and A. Wright (eds.), *Contemporary Political Ideologies* (Pinter, 1993), pp. 1–22.

Goodwin, B. 'Ideology', in B. Goodwin, *Using Political Ideas* (John Wiley and Sons, 2001), pp. 17–31.

Heywood, A. 'Introduction: Understanding Ideology', in A. Heywood, *Political Ideologies: An Introduction* (Macmillan, 1992), pp. 1–23.

Leach, R. *British Political Ideologies* (Philip Allen, 1991).

MacKenzie, I. 'Introduction: The Arena of Ideology', in R. Eccleshall *et al.*, *Political Ideologies: An Introduction* (Routledge, 1994), pp. 1–27.

McLellan, D. *Ideology* (Open University Press, 1986).

Plamenatz, J. *Ideology* (Macmillan, 1972).

Plant, R. 'The Resurgence of Ideology', in H. Drucker *et al.*, *Developments in British Politics* (Macmillan, 1984), pp. 7–29.

Plant, R. 'Ideology', in H. Drucker *et al.*, *Developments in British Politics 2* (Macmillan, 1988), pp. 8–33.

Seliger, M. *Ideology and Politics* (Allen and Unwin, 1976).

Thomas, G. P. 'British Politics 1945 to Date: The Postwar Consensus', *Taking Politics*, 7:2 (1995), pp. 117–24.

Vincent, A. 'The Nature of Ideology', in A. Vincent, *Modern Political Ideologies* (Blackwell, 1996), pp. 1–21.

SAMPLE QUESTIONS

1 Are ideologies simply a cloak for the pursuit of power?

2 Are ideologies developed in the nineteenth and twentieth centuries of any value in the twenty-first?

3 'While ideology shaped the twentieth century, we have now come to the end of ideology.' Do you think this is true, and if so is it a cause for rejoicing?

4 Why do you think 'ideological' is seen as such a term of abuse in modern Western democracies?

5 To what extent would you agree with the opinion that politics has become less ideological?

6 'In Britain at least, the old ideological divisions between the parties are obsolete.' Is this true?

Nationalism

8

Nationalism is perhaps the most powerful ideology of the last couple of centuries. We attempt here to distinguish a number of varieties of nationalism – liberal, reactionary and radical. There follows a brief history of nationalism from the pre-Renaissance period to the twentieth century, after which we consider whether nationalism as an ideology serves particular political interests. Then the psychological appeal of nationalism is examined, as is its impact on international politics, and on empires and multi-national states. Finally, we offer a critique of nationalism and some reflections on its possible future.

POINTS TO CONSIDER

➤ Is nationalism anything more than extreme patriotism?

➤ How would you define a 'nation'?

➤ Is nationalism an ideology of the left or the right?

➤ To what extent is the nation a 'natural' social organisation and to what extent an artificial construct?

➤ Is the principle of 'national self-determination' still a viable one? Was it ever a viable political principle in international affairs?

➤ Why does nationalism still seem to be a powerful influence in the twenty-first century?

➤ What is the future of 'identity politics' and 'regional nationalism' in a 'globalised' world?

> Nationalism has two fatal charms for its devotees: it presupposes local self-suffi-
> ciency, which is a pleasant and desirable condition, and it suggests, very subtly,
> one's belonging to a place which is definable and familiar, as against a place which
> is strange and remote. (E. B. White, 'Intimations', *One Man's Meat*, 1944)

> Nationalism is primarily a political principle, which holds that the political unit and
> the national unit should be congruent ... Nationalist *sentiment* is the feeling of
> anger aroused by the violation of the principle, or the feeling of satisfaction aroused
> by its fulfilment. A nationalist *movement* is one actuated by a sentiment of this kind.
> (Ernst Gellner, *Nations and Nationalism*, 1983)

Nationalism has proved to be one of the most powerful of all political ideologies over the last two centuries and seems likely to remain a potent force well into the present century. Often presented as an ancient, even primal, political ideology, nationalism in the modern sense of the word is arguably a creation of the nineteenth century. As the word itself suggests, it is often seen as somehow 'natural' for people to be members of a readily identifiable 'nation' and to have deep emotional ties to it. In fact, nationalism is much more complex.

It is certainly possible to trace a sense of belonging to a particular group of people, beyond family, clan or tribe, to classical times. By the Middle Ages love of country, 'patriotism', was widespread in Europe. Nationalism, however, goes beyond patriotism. It is, for example, perfectly possible to be a Welsh patriot and cheer one's rugby team without being a nationalist. Nationalism has political implications; patriotism does not necessarily do so. A nation, in nationalist theory, requires some form of political expression, with appropriate institutions. This may involve full independence or devolved political institutions within a larger state.

Nationalism as an ideology

As an ideology, nationalism involves creating a 'world view' – a *Weltanschauung* – a set of coherent ideas and values that gives meaning to the past for a social group, explains the present, and offers a programme for possible future action. Nationalism is the least intellectual of the major ideologies while being the most irrational and emotional, tapping into deep passions.

Uniquely among ideologies, nationalism has no theory of human nature. It may, of course, have theories as to the particular nature of specific peoples, such as the unique 'soul' of the Russians or the commitment to fairness of the English. However, there is a sense in which nationalism entails a view of human nature. Nationalists claim that each nation is a 'natural' unit, and the bonds that bind a nation are both natural and good. For the individual, therefore, the welfare of the nation is a supreme good.

Nationalism places loyalty to the nation above all other forms of political and *social* loyalties. One may place one's moral or religious beliefs above national identity, but nationalism assumes that these must give way to loyalty to the nation if there is a clash. Nationalism not only makes the nation the focus of political loyalty but also insists that the nation is the only proper basis for the organisation of any political activity. Thus the nation, made up of all the people who belong to it, can legitimately claim property, lives and any other sacrifice from its members to ensure the survival of the collective.

One of the big questions of nationalism is just how 'natural' a nation is. It can be plausibly argued that nations are 'invented' either by the literary endeavours of poets or the processes of state power. Nationalism nevertheless assumes that the 'people' or 'the nation' is an entity with sovereign rights and a fundamental unity of 'blood', 'culture' or 'citizenship'. We shall now consider these elements of nationalism: sovereignty of the people; Ethnic nationalism and Civic nationalism.

Sovereignty of the people

From this viewpoint the 'nation' is essentially the same as the 'people', involving the idea that people are bound together into a group united in common patriotic identification with the nation. Popular sovereignty is a very important basis for loyalty to the state or for struggles by a subordinate nation to create a state. Conservatives regard popular sovereignty as an appeal to national unity over class, religion and other social divisions. Radicals use it to rally popular support against an unjust government. Appeals to popular sovereignty can be seen in revolutionary documents such as the American *Declaration of Independence* (1776) and the French *Declaration of the Rights of Man* (1789).

Ethnic nationalism and Civic nationalism

Ethnic nationalism identifies a close connection between national members linked by race, language or other cultural attributes that persist over centuries. One is a member of the nation by birth and bloodline, by genetics, and bears an identity that cannot be sloughed off by becoming a citizen of another nation or acquired by choice and filling in an application form. So, for example, ethnic Germans, who for centuries had lived in what had become Russia, could apply to rejoin their nation and return to German soil. They were, until recently, able to stake a better claim to German citizenship than Turkish 'guest workers' and even the latter's German-born descendants.

Civic nationalism is the basis of American, French or British nationalism. It identifies the common historical ties that exist between the people in the nation, ties that can easily be extended to other people through citizenship and the loyalties and obligations associated with acquiring that citizenship.

There is no ethnic limitation on who can potentially be a member of the nation. However, one should not forget the difficulty of attaining this form of nationalism in practice. Existing members of the nation may have very strong objections to large-scale additions of people to the nation by acquisition of citizenship.

Nationalism is, therefore, not a straightforward ideology. It can wear many faces, display many forms. It can be conservative, fascist, liberal, socialist, even Marxist. All political ideologies have used nationalism for their ends. Even anarchism, probably the least influenced by nationalism, is affected by national identity and the national experience of anarchists, bringing different theoretical contributions to the movement. Nevertheless, nationalism is characterised at a fundamental level by the belief, demand even, that each nation should be governed by its own sovereign state.

We can usefully sub-divide nationalism into three categories:
- liberal nationalism;
- reactionary nationalism;
- radical nationalism.

Liberal nationalism

According to this school of thought, mankind is naturally divided into nations, all of which have certain territorial limits to which they are equally entitled. Each should be sovereign, self-governing, with its own political institutions. National rights are analogous to human rights and are also universal. This form of nationalism sits easily with the more internationalist, pacifist and idealist elements within liberalism. A world of sovereign nations would respect each other's national rights and co-operate readily within international institutions. Certainly this was the hope of liberal nationalists such as Giuseppe Mazzini in Italy. The revolutions that swept across Europe in 1848 were greatly influenced by liberals and were almost always successfully crushed by the threatened states.

It is taken for granted that such nationalism would involve respect for minority rights, whether ethnic, religious or linguistic. This 'acceptable' form of nationalism was popular among liberals and some socialists during the early nineteenth century. After the First World War it was resurrected in the institution of the League of Nations, founded on the principles of national self-determination and collective security. After the Second World War this form of nationalism was embodied in the United Nations and other liberal international bodies set up to regulate human rights and the free-trade international economy.

Liberal nationalists under-estimate the problems of identifying natural national units in terms of population, geography and economic viability. They disregard nationalism's potential for evil, and over-estimate its positive elements. Nevertheless, liberal nationalism was and still remains a very strong element in many modern nationalist movements.

Reactionary nationalism

With the failure of the liberal-nationalist revolutions of 1848, nationalism in many European countries became increasingly associated with the conservative and reactionary forces involved in creating and preserving the nation and its institutions, which were threatened by revolution and socialism. Nationalism became a means by which the national identity of some citizens was crushed or suppressed to ensure the unity of the larger nation. This was especially the case in the sprawling multi-national Austro-Hungarian and Russian empires, both struggling with rising nationalism and both trying to assert imperial nationalism and unity over the demands for greater self-government and independence of restless subservient nations.

After 1870 with the setting up of the Third French Republic and the unification of Germany, reactionary nationalism became ever more powerful in Europe. It was linked with an organic national identity as expressed in religion, social order, traditional hierarchies, language, culture and customs. Overseas, it involved **imperialism**, racism, and claims of the right to rule over 'inferior' nations, along with vigorous political and military competition with other nations. Such nationalism repudiated socialism and liberalism and instilled itself as an ideological alternative in the minds of the newly enfranchised masses.

> **imperialism**
> The process of creating an empire. An empire is a type of political system where one nation by dint of its superior power dominates and controls other nations. In Lenin's view, imperialism was a phase of capitalist expansion involving the subjugation and economic exploitation of the less developed part of the world.

By the twentieth century, this model of nationalism became allied with conservatism, so closely that the radical and socialist left worked hard in most Western democracies to distance themselves from the nationalism of their political opponents and, hence, from nationalism altogether. Reactionary nationalism may stress patriotism and the unique nature of the nation but it is not necessarily imperialistic, even if it was associated with late nineteenth-century 'popular imperialism'. It is often indifferent to events outside the nation, so long as the rest of the world leaves it alone.

Radical nationalism

This emerged after the First World War, though arguably it could be traced back to the French revolutionaries. Radical nationalism was (and is) connected with a desire to change the domestic and/or international order, an order that seemed to need changing in favour of one's own nation. It took two major forms. One form of radical nationalism was an essentially rightist form of politics; the other was the mainstay of anti-colonialism.

Radical-right nationalism despised the old order, the privileged classes and out-dated institutions, all of which were condemned as having betrayed the nation. Often it required energetic and dramatic social, economic and political reform, intended to renew the nation. It sought to offer the working classes an alternative to the internationalism of communism and socialism after the Russian Revolution.

Defeat in war was a stimulus to this form of nationalism in Germany and Turkey, but it also emerged in Italy and France, where formal victory had been purchased at a terrible cost. This form of radical nationalism tended to be intolerant of minorities that were not regarded as authentically part of the nation, and vociferous in its claims against neighbouring states. In its extreme form it sets the superiority of the nation above other nations and may be used to justify wars of territorial aggrandisement. Such nationalism merges easily into fascism.

Radical nationalism may, however, take an almost entirely opposite path: anti-colonial struggle against reactionary or imperialist radical nationalism. In this form it uses the values of nationalism to make a case for independence from a political structure that is seen as oppressive of the members of the nation. It appeals to the doctrine of national self-determination and the logic of national independence. Nationalism played a significant role in the ending of the European empires during the decades after the Second World War.

In the same period this form of nationalism often contained a strong socialist element as it was linked to the communal values of indigenous societies as well as the overthrow of the colonial ruling class. After independence, this form of nationalism involved resistance to Western economic, cultural and political domination (condemned as 'neo-colonialism') and led many developing world states to nationalise the assets of foreign-owned multi-national corporations based in their countries.

Nationalism: the history of an ideology

One might assert that modern history has been directed by the rise, development and spread of nationalism. We can identify a number of stages in the development of nationalism:

- proto-nationalism;
- early modern nationalism;
- nationalism in the age of revolutions;
- twentieth-century nationalism;
- post-**Cold War** nationalism.

Cold War
A term which refers to the struggle between the West and the Soviet Union from just after the Second World War to the late 1980s. It was a conflict that stopped short of a full-scale 'hot war'.

Proto-nationalism

Before the European Renaissance there was among Europeans some sense of national differences and identification with kings, princes, languages and cultures. The context was the universalist claim of loyalty to **Christendom** in the shape of the Pope and the **Holy Roman Emperor** in the face of the threat from the Muslim world.

> **Christendom**
>
> Essentially an alternative name for Europe during the Middle Ages which described the domination of Christianity and its claim to create a degree of unity among Christians in the face of the threat from Islam.

Early modern nationalism

The break-up of Christendom during the later Renaissance helped to create a sense of national identity. Shared language, increasingly explicit 'national' culture, 'national' religion, constant wars all helped strengthen the sense of national differences, national identity and support for strong centralised states that increasingly had the ability to create national loyalty among their populations.

> **Holy Roman Empire**
>
> The Western part of the Roman Empire was revived by Charlemagne in 800 when he was crowned Emperor. The title Holy Roman Empire was established in 962 and endured until 1806 when it was abolished by Napoleon who dismissed it as neither Holy, Roman nor an Empire.

Nationalism in the age of revolutions

Nationalism, however ancient its roots, is a relatively modern phenomenon. Agricultural and industrial revolutions in the eighteenth and nineteenth centuries broke down many older, lesser loyalties without initially replacing them with new ones. The nation would become that replacement.

The American Revolution and, especially, the French Revolutionary and Napoleonic wars played a vital role in the development of modern nationalism. Before these conflicts an individual's loyalty was essentially to another individual (the monarch, for example). Most aspects of Europe's *ancien régime* were overthrown during the French Wars and a sense of nationhood was stimulated in most nations across Europe, from Spain and Portugal to Russia. The highest form of political loyalty shifted from the monarch to the 'nation', or the 'people', from an individual who embodied the nation to a group. Indeed, so powerful did the concept become that most nationalists argue that the nation is a *natural* social organisation.

Although nationalism today is often related to the political right, during the nineteenth century it was usually a liberal and revolutionary ideology, certainly up to the revolutions of 1848. It played a vital role in the unification of Italy (1861) and Germany (1871), and the struggles for national liberation of oppressed nations such as the Irish, the Czechs and the Poles throughout the nineteenth century.

In some ways the concept of the nation became more tangible as people identified the nation as consisting of their fellow citizens, rather than some remote monarch. During the nineteenth century centralised and powerful states increasingly legitimised their actions by claiming to represent 'the people'. Nationalism legitimised a state's actions and was often used as a means to suppress opposition to the state's policies and rule – hence the development of the vague but powerful concept of the 'national interest'.

By the end of the century nationalism had spread with European power across the globe. Embryonic nationalist movements grew up within the colonial empires to press for greater self-government and, eventually, independence.

Twentieth-century nationalism

The twentieth century was an era of total warfare that strengthened nationalism at the time. It was also a century during which the viability, and value, of nations as political units was questioned with increasing urgency. Nationalism as a valid ideology for human affairs was also challenged. Twentieth-century wars were too destructive, the loss of life too great for nationalism to be free of blame for its contribution to the horrors. A considerable degree of hostility to nationalism grew during the century, especially after the world wars.

There were attempts to distinguish between imperialist nationalism ('bad') and anti-colonialist nationalism ('good'). After the Second World War national liberation movements were boosted by the nature of the struggle against fascist nationalism. The British, for instance, could hardly fight a war against imperialism and racism and then go back to governing an empire built on imperialism and racism. Whatever the form it took, nationalism remained widely perceived as a dangerous and destructive force, open to little rational explanation and unleashing extreme violence and intolerance into politics.

Nationalism was used as a reinforcement of other political ideologies. Fascism obviously had nationalism at the core of its values. However, the concept of socialist internationalism also gave way to nationalism. Communist regimes, such as the Soviet Union and Communist China, created 'socialism in one country' and quarrelled over the 'proper' interpretation of the meaning of socialism along national lines while pursuing traditional national foreign-policy goals.

Nationalism remained the most powerful and widespread ideology in the world, influencing, challenging and defeating other ideologies. As has already been pointed out revolutionary communism, which stressed the common interests of the working class, evolved into 'national' socialism in most countries – especially when those movements took over the state.

Post-Cold War nationalism

The end of the Cold War and the collapse of the Soviet Union coincided with the rise of 'globalisation' as a driving force for change in world society. There were also increasing attempts to strengthen international institutions as alternatives to states in international politics. Nationalism appeared to be an idea that had had its day; but it refused to die.

Decades of suppression among the nations of the USSR and Yugoslavia culminated in the demise of communism and the uprising of virulent nationalism in those societies. Wars broke out in Yugoslavia and several states of the former Soviet Union, resulting in massacres and widespread destruction. Nationalism remains a powerful force in many countries in Europe and in the developing world. If anything nationalism has had a new lease of life after the Cold War.

There are great movements of people taking place in the modern world, migration on a scale not seen since the late nineteenth century. Some historians have characterised it as comparable to the great *Volkswanderung* – people movements – of the fourth and fifth centuries AD that ended the classical world and gave birth to modern European nations. The USA is a nation of recent immigrants, and is still a major magnet for people seeking a better life. Nationalists often feel threatened by large-scale migration into their country. They feel that immigrants threaten their national identity. This is especially true of nationalists in European nations who are not influenced by the concept of the 'melting pot' of peoples that exists in the USA.

Nationalism and the serving of political interests

In any study of politics one sooner or later comes across the issue of who gains from a political programme and who loses. In the case of nationalism, there is a considerable debate among political scientists as to who benefits from nationalism as an ideology.

Nationalism can be seen as being intimately linked to the interests of the society as a whole. It is a product of the development of modern statehood and industrialisation. Over the last two centuries there has been massive social and technological change, involving scientific enquiry, greater rationality, the development of a more centralised state, greater social mobility and the prospect of social reform. These enormous changes created a modern sense of history and also an understanding of the processes of social change. Pre-industrial society and its deep emotional ties to traditional national identity was the major casualty of this vast social and intellectual change. Nationalism, as Ernest Gellner argues in *Nations and Nationalism* (1983), became an ideological tool of elites to mobilise people to welcome change. The nation was claimed to have deep historical roots, compensating people for the loss of their strong pre-industrial social ties.

Critics who oppose these social and economic changes also use nationalism as a support, appealing to some ancient ethnic past in their attacks on modernisation. This may manifest itself as an ethnic nationalism fighting the nationalism of a dominant national group within a state or against other competing national groups. For example, during the nineteenth century the subject nations of the Austro-Hungarian Empire resisted Austrian and Hungarian domination and also asserted their national identity against each other and, especially, Jews. The empire was a seething pot of nationalism, ethnic rivalries and anti-Semitism.

The political uses of nationalist ideology depend on how one sees it in relation to other major ideological traditions.

Conservatives, for example, assert that nationalism creates social cohesion and social order. All people have a place and a valued role in the nation. The organic nature of the nation must be upheld, as being a natural social unit. Conservatives do not accept that patriotism and nationalism must lead to aggression and imperialism. Nevertheless, nationalism in late nineteenth-century Britain was used by the Conservatives as part of 'popular imperialism' to encourage political support for themselves and to support overseas expansion.

Liberals sometimes claim nationalism is closely linked to 'freedom', both national and individual. It is a means by which the common interests required to enable a society to function can be balanced against the necessary individualism of a free-market economy and a free society. Indeed, the idea of national self-determination and free trade is one of the major means by which world peace can be established.

Social democrats have a similar view to the liberals. They make more of a class analysis of nationalism, but many social democrats will stress the importance of the nation over the individual. In practice, social-democratic governments in modern democracies have shown themselves to be as nationalistic as governments of other ideological hues.

Marxists declare that nationalism is an ideological tool of the ruling capitalist classes and, as such, has developed out of industrialisation. Traditional Marxists claim that capitalists use nationalism to divert the working class from their 'true' predicament by encouraging a sense of commitment to 'national' identity: imperialism is one of the many unacceptable uses to which nationalism is put in the service of the interests of the capitalist class. Modern Marxists have argued that nationalism can have legitimacy when it is identified with the struggle for national independence of an oppressed nation, or when it is used as the means of challenging class power within a nation.

This holds true during both the anti-colonial struggles of the twentieth century and the liberation struggles against neo-colonialism today. Nationalism, often with a Marxist dimension, will sometimes be associated with demands for greater democracy in oppressed nations. This kind of 'revolutionary nationalism' will claim to be more democratic and liberating than 'old nationalism'.

The impact of nationalism

If, as it appears, nationalism is the most powerful ideology in modern politics, one needs to identify and discuss the ways in which it has transformed the modern world. In this section we will discuss the following areas:
- the psychological appeal of nationalism;
- national self-determination;
- nationalism and international politics;
- nationalism and the end of empires and multi-national states.

The psychological appeal of nationalism

Nationalism forms a vital focus of identification for citizens. Membership of a nation is emotional and intangible. The nation can satisfy people's basic psychological needs to identify with and belong to a group, to be part of something greater than oneself, to take part in something that lifts one out of the ordinary. People often complain that their lives are subject to uncomfortable pressures and control. Employers, social customs, lack of money all regularly stress, in a myriad ways, the essential powerlessness of most people. Identification with the nation, that 'super-individual' made of a collective 'we', can give individuals a sense of power, control, glory, success, greatness that they rarely, if ever, achieve in mundane, everyday life.

Membership of a nation is bound up with notions of collective consciousness. Increased contact with other national groups can stimulate consciousness of national differences, cultivate a feeling of 'us and them' divisions, and create and reinforce an impression of superiority over peoples of other nations. Regular conflicts between nations over centuries reinforce that sense of national identity. Irish nationalism was forged during the struggle against English power. English and French, Turk and Greek, Serb and Bosnian Muslim, Indian and Pakistani, all are nationalities wrought by centuries-old conflicts and wars, the cheering of victories, the brooding on defeats. History, or mythologised history, is therefore a crucial feature of nationalism.

National identification is stimulated by such myths, but also by flags, national anthems, martial music, founding fathers of the nation, images of the country – usually rural, rather than urban – and the national stereotyping of the members of other nations.

However, nationalism is only one of a number of ideologies competing for the attention and allegiance of an individual. Other ideologies, such as socialism or Marxism, may challenge nationalism. There may be competing nationalisms, such as 'British' and 'Scottish', or even a growing sense of 'European' identity. One can understand in these circumstances that a certain degree of psychological turmoil may affect a person.

National self-determination

Nationalism not only creates a sense of national identity. It presents the state as the most important form of political organisation for a people. Nationalism encourages the view that 'nations' should be governed by a 'state' made up of members of that nation. National self-determination really strengthens the validity of the state as an expression of 'nationhood'. This is not a new idea: 'All nations and reasonable men prefer to be governed by men of their own country and nation, who share the same language as them . . . rather than by strangers.'[1] If this desirable state could not be achieved peacefully then it was to be prosecuted by war, if necessary.

Nationalism seemed to offer freedom, wealth and power. Nineteenth-century Europe was characterised by the rise of nationalism as an ideology and the nationalisms of its many peoples. Indeed, the rise of nations was allied to the acquisition of statehood. Italy existed as a nation before its political unification into a state in 1860, as did Germany before Prussia created the Reich in 1871, but both were forged into nation-states by war. Both countries became steadily wealthier after they were unified. The national struggles of the Balkan nations against Turkish rule are further examples of the success of this new powerful ideology. For some nationalists in India and elsewhere if nationalism could be used by Europeans to overthrow an Asian empire in Europe, such as Turkey, perhaps it could be used by Asians to overthrow European empires in Asia. If sacrifice was required to achieve this, then nationalism provided the justifications for the struggle.

Nationalism acquired a considerable degree of legitimacy after the First World War through the concept of 'national-self determination'. President Woodrow Wilson had, at the Paris Peace Conference (1919), used American power and prestige to establish the principle of 'national self-determination' (although there was no clear formula as to what constituted a 'nation' to be 'self-determined'). This principle stated that 'all peoples are equal in their right to govern themselves as a nation' and was incorporated into both the Covenant of the League of Nations (1920) and the Charter of the United Nations (1945). The preamble to the UN Charter claims that its members '. . . reaffirm faith in fundamental human rights, in the dignity and worth of the human person, in the equal rights of men and women and of nations large and small'.

Originally seen as an ideological and policy basis for the break-up of the German and Austro-Hungarian empires in Europe, this principle also contained the seed for dismantling the vast European empires in Africa and Asia. However, it took another world war and the fundamental weakening of the European colonial powers for this stage of imperial disintegration to take effect.

The logical consequence of the principle is the creation of ever-smaller states. The great majority would be poor, small, unstable, and, in a fundamental political and economic sense, unviable. This effect can be seen in the fragmented 'successor' states that appeared across Eastern Europe after the Versailles Treaty. Their existence between Germany and the USSR, weak states between powerful ones, helped to make war inevitable. The post-war break-up of the European empires created similar problems that have still not faded from the international system.

The problem with national self-determination as a major political principle is that few nations exactly correspond to the image of the nation-state. Most have national minorities within their borders. Sometimes this has led to the loss of territory to another state as a response to the vociferous demands of the minority (the Sudetenland Germans in Czechoslovakia during the 1930s, for example). Sometimes such minorities are expelled. In 1945–46 over 8 million Germans were expelled from Poland when its western frontiers were moved further west into formerly German territory. On the partition of British India into India and Pakistan in 1947 millions of Muslims and Hindus moved, forcibly or peacefully, across the new international boundaries about to be created. It is estimated that over 2 million died. In Cyprus, Burma and Rwanda, Palestine, Northern Ireland, Bosnia, Croatia and Serbia, national identity has been a source of violent expulsion of national and other ethnic minorities from a particular territory in the desire to create a 'pure' ethnic national identity.

European expansion spread the concept of the nation and nationalism right across the globe. Some form of national identification existed in most parts of the world, but that was often confined to ruling elites and often had little popular support. But it was the experience of European power and, usually, colonisation that stimulated the development of non-European nationalism.

Nationalism and international politics

Nationalism, as we have seen, developed in its modern form during the French Revolutionary and Napoleonic Wars. First in France and then among the enemies of France, nationalism mobilised the powerful emotions of loyalty and fighting for a cause. By 1815 almost all the nations of Europe had become carriers of ideological nationalism. Evidently, the nineteenth century was the major formative era of modern nationalism. By the end of the century it was a powerful political force in the politics of the emerging European democracies, the German and Austro-Hungarian empires, and the autocracy of the Russian Empire. All governments appealed to national images and national identity as means of building political legitimacy for their governments.

However, nationalism also contributed to increasing rivalry and suspicion between the Great Powers during the years before 1914. It promoted conflict by stressing the differences between nations, and stimulated arms races and the building of alliances. It also made peaceful resolution of differences by diplomacy increasingly difficult. Nationalism did not make war inevitable, but it made war more difficult to avoid, less easy to contain once begun, more violent and destructive as it progressed and extremely difficult to end. War became a struggle for whole nations, for national self-determination, even national survival. Thus war was intensified by becoming an ideological struggle of peoples, of popular passions, of national pride. Any questioning of the motives for which the war was fought, any demand for peace, was likely to be suppressed as potential or actual 'treason'. The greater the national sacrifices, the greater the demands for the war to go on until final victory for the nation was achieved.

Even more destructive was the Second World War. Fascists and Nazis used nationalism to strengthen their idea of the world being made up of nations struggling for survival. The 1930s experienced the world steady drifting towards conflict, and after 1939, the Second World War was on a scale of destruction unimaginable even after the 1914–18 War.

The defeat of the Axis powers by 1945 was not the end of nationalism as a powerful motivating ideology. The ideological conflicts of the Cold War, the struggles between Western democracy and communism, were given an edge by nationalism. Anti-communism in the USA became associated with 'Americanism', a set of ideological and national ideals that led to the creation of an 'Un-American Activities Committee' in the House of Representatives and the attempted suppression of any dissent characterised as 'unpatriotic'. The Soviet Union, Communist China and North Vietnam may all have claimed to be socialist states, but their rivalries with each other were deeply influenced by nationalism. Indeed, at times it is difficult to see where the 'socialism' lay in their exchange of vitriolic statements, while their 'nationalism' is clear. Almost all of the many wars and conflicts in the developing world during the Cold War and afterwards were impelled by nationalism and national aspirations.

Nationalism and the end of empires and multinational states

Nationalism played a crucial role in the overthrow of the European empires. Canada, the USA, Australia, New Zealand, all nurtured a sense of national identity even when they were part of the British Empire, eventually leading to their independence. In Africa and Asia, Western-educated nationalist elites sought the creation of new nations, but there was usually the lack of a strong sense of 'national' identity in these European colonies, compared with religious, ethnic, linguistic or other identities.

This is because the borders of most African and Middle Eastern states were established by European Great Powers mainly concerned with the international balance of power and showing little or no consideration for ethnic, linguistic or cultural affinities. The European withdrawal from the continent left 'nations' with little or no sense of nationalist identity and affinity among the bulk of the population: civil wars and political upheavals were too often the consequence. Middle Eastern states are also the result of balance of power politics following the collapse of the Ottoman Empire after the First World War. The claims of Iraq to Kuwait and Syrian interest in Lebanon are just two of the modern tensions in the region arising from a weak sense of nationalism among the members of the local states.

Elites, especially in Africa, tried to create a sense of national, racial or even continental identity but were themselves seen as somewhat 'alien'. They had often spent much time outside the country, usually in the colonial power, and were often thought to be connected with a particular ethnic group. Appeals to these broad identities were an attempt to skate over the very real differences between people who had little in common with the new 'national' identity. Many of the new nations were, in turn, riven by the demands of other competing divisions, often impelled by nationalism or at least ethnicity presented as nationalism. The stability of these countries often remains tentative: nationalist movements frequently grew up within the newly independent 'nations', creating forces for further disintegration. Biafra in Nigeria, India and Kashmir, Sikhs in India, Tamils in Sri Lanka all have involved and are still beset by levels of conflict that threaten the unity of the modern state.

In some societies, such as China, India and the Arab world, nationalists could appeal to 'real' national identities of ancient origin in their struggle with the Europeans. Nevertheless, colonial powers and their colonial boundaries moulded even their national identity. Appeals were made by some African and Arab politicians to identities that cut across nations, such as *Pan-Africanism*, *Pan-Arabism* and *Pan-Islamism*, often with little, or at most temporary, success. Usually 'traditional' nationalism was too powerful a force for such broad identities to have much popular appeal.

Anti-colonialism was especially linked to Marxism and socialism. Nationalism when seen as serving the interests of a colonial or capitalist elite was attacked, but 'revolutionary' nationalism was a challenge to the capitalist exploitation of the world's poor. Only 'national' control of 'national' resources and the establishment of a new level of international justice could overcome the backwardness of the developing world.

The end of the Cold War was not the end of nationalism as a powerful force in world affairs. It has, in fact, become stronger in many countries. The collapse of the Soviet Union, the heir of the Russian Empire ('the prisonhouse of the nations', as Marx called it), was partly due to the failure to create a sense of Soviet nationalism as distinct from Russian nationalism. With the weakening of totalitarian controls under Gorbachev the suppressed nationalisms within the USSR helped break it up into nation-states. This process of disintegration has not ended there. National conflicts have exploded in Georgia, Armenia and the Chechnya region of Russia. Nationalist tensions were already present in the new nations of the post-Soviet states, where large Russian minorities lived within the boundaries of the 'new' nation. It is estimated that 25 million Russians live in the former states of the USSR outside the Russian Republic. Many ex-communist politicians reinvented themselves as nationalists in order to retain power as the Soviet state collapsed. Nationalism played a violent role in the break-up of Yugoslavia during the 1990s and the peaceful dismemberment of Czechoslovakia in 1992.

These forces of disintegration and re-creation can be seen in nations such as Canada and Britain, countries far more stable and well established than the communist regimes of Eastern Europe and the USSR. Canada's future is questionable because of the continuing conflicts between its English and French-speaking peoples. The UK, even, may disintegrate as a consequence of the various nationalisms within its multi-national state territory

The unification of Germany, on the other hand, seems to have stimulated nationalism in that country, especially in the former communist eastern part of the republic. In Western Europe the expansion of the European Union, both geographically and in its powers, appears to have stimulated a nationalist reaction to this 'usurpation' of many of the roles of the state. This has occurred both at the level of the formal state members of the EU and at sub-state, regional, levels with demands for 'national' recognition of the political aspirations of many nations: Welsh, Scots, Basques, Bretons, Corsicans. Most of this nationalist argument, one must recognise, pre-dates the European Union and the modern force of globalisation.

Critique of nationalism

Nationalism is out of favour in the West. Even the alleged ideological benefits of the nationalist tradition, such as its potential for social cohesion, are looked on askance. It has been subject to much criticism over the last fifty years.

Up to the mid-twentieth century, socialists believed that nationalism was a liberating ideology because of its support for national self-determination and anti-imperialism. However, they usually saw nationalism as, at best, a distraction from the class struggle and, more often, as a means of manipulating the working class, to divert it from the reality of its exploitation by the bourgeoisie. For most of the twentieth century nationalism, especially in the opinion of liberals and socialists, became identified with reaction, aggression, intolerance, war, religious bigotry and atrocity. It is certainly possible to make a case against it with reference to the Second World War, to the recent wars in the former Yugoslav and post-Soviet states, to the nationalist conflicts in the developing world, and the activities of various fascist movements in Europe and elsewhere.

Based on the nation, itself a concept with multifarious interpretations, and on an irrational, emotional response, nationalism remains a force for division and aggression. Assumptions that nations occupy distinct areas that they legitimately call 'theirs', and which are hallowed by history and validated by geography, are simply misguided. Minority groups, perceived as outside the larger national community, are frequently threatened by nationalist fervour. Nationalism may have arisen out of the eighteenth century, but it represents the dark alternative to the rationalism of the Enlightenment.

Nationalism is irrelevant to internationalists in a world where problems transcend national boundaries and must be addressed on a global basis. Liberals see it as an impediment to greater international co-operation and integration. From a conservative standpoint, competing nationalisms disrupt the social order. A socialist, like a Marxist, believes nationalism is at best a diversion from the class struggle, at worst a weapon used by exploiters to divide the international working classes.

The future of nationalism

After the Second World War nationalism was thought by many in Europe to be out of date and discredited, confined to the 'backward' parts of Europe – conservative, poor, often Catholic. By the 1960s and 1970s nationalism was back in fashion in many parts of Europe. It was used by many as the basis for resisting dominant nationalist and cultural values linked to the most powerful nations on earth, especially the USA. By the 1990s, 'globalisation' was used to describe a range of social and economic processes, long in existence but 'maturing' in the post-Cold War world. Nationalism and national identity were taken up by many on both the left and the right as ideological instruments to resist globalisation and assert the positive claims of cultural diversity in an increasingly homogenised world.

Within the UK nationalism was linked to the economic crises of the 1970s and 1980s and the growth of regional and national disparities of wealth. This can be observed in the violent conflict in Northern Ireland, the rise of Scottish and Welsh nationalism and their demands for better treatment from the British Government. Northern England has not been able to make a coherent 'national' claim, but shares a degree of resentment with the Celtic nations of the UK towards the economic, political and cultural dominance of London and the South-East of England.

Nationalism is still a major force in world affairs. Nevertheless, there are powerful economic and cultural forces undermining nationalism, usually described as 'globalisation', developing around multi-national corporations, banks, insurance companies, global communications, the dominance of the English language.

Globalisation creates new identities and new loyalties by its cultural and economic processes, but it also creates a potential 'backlash' of resistance to the 'threats' to national identity that it produces by its international, Westernised, homogenised character. Many people appeal to nationalist senti- ments for an ideological basis to resist the 'McDonaldisation' of their culture.

Nationalism is used in a very broad sense to support the claims of 'identity' politics. Political claims are asserted by groups acutely aware of their identity – but an identity that falls short of being a nation as measured by the usual criteria. African-Americans constitute a fairly clearly delineated group with identifiable political goals. Louis Farrakhan, the leader of the 'Nation of Islam', has called for a separate state for black people in America. The Unionists in Northern Ireland might also be said to constitute a similar group, as do the Inuit in Canada. Northern Irish nationalists might aspire to a unification of Ireland but will settle, at least temporarily, for power-sharing with the Unionists. Flemish groups in Belgium focus on equal rights with the Walloon (French-speaking) population. Such groups may polarise around language, race and religion.

'Regional nationalism' is another sub-species of nationalism. It refers to a claim for regional autonomy, which nevertheless stops short of outright independence. A good example would be Catalan nationalism in Spain or the Northern League in Italy. In practice regionalism and nationalism often converge because nationalist parties perceive tactical political advantage in seeking the minimum goal of autonomy rather than full independence.

From a Western liberal perspective it is difficult not to be uneasy about nation alism. It is evidently still a powerful force. Even in Europe some forms (nationalism are clearly alive and well. It may be argued that it is possibly countervailing force to the insidious processes of economic and cultuı globalisation, and in the confused and atomised societies undergoing profound changes it is a source of dignity, security and social cohesion. It is not likely to fade away in this century. Growing competition for water, oil, food, land and clear air is likely to be a feature of international and domestic political life during the twenty-first century, so war between nations is likely to continue.

Summary

Nationalism in some sense of the word can be traced back to pre-Renaissance times. In its modern sense, of having political implications, it is a relatively recent phenomenon. We can distinguish between 'ethnic nationalism', which links nation with race and language and birth, and 'civic nationalism', which links nation with citizenship, with no ethnic limitation on who is potentially a member of the nation. We can also distinguish between liberal, reactionary and radical nationalism. Furthermore, nationalism can fulfil a number of political functions such as promoting social change, creating social cohesion, or strengthening the hold of the ruling class. Nationalism has had an immense impact in the nineteenth and twentieth centuries, especially in undermining empires and multi-national states. To critics, this process has not necessarily been beneficial; witness the atrocities committed in its name in, for example, Yugoslavia. Nevertheless, even in the 'global' society of the twenty-first century it remains a powerful force.

REFERENCES AND FURTHER READING

Claude de Seyssel, bishop and chancellor of France (1510).

ter, P. *Nationalism* (Edward Arnold, 1989).

derson, B. *Imagined Communities: Reflections on the Origins and Spread of Nationalism* (NLB/Verso, 1983).

clough, G. *An Introduction to Contemporary History* (Penguin, 67).

s and their Past: The Uses and Abuses of History', *The Economist* (21 mber, 1996), pp. 53–6.

. *Nations and Nationalism* (Blackwell, 1983).

B. 'Beyond Nationalism', in B. Goodwin, *Using Political Ideas* (John Wiley and 001), pp. 249–67.

ationalism', in R. Eatwell and A. Wright (eds.), *Contemporary Political* (Pinter, 1993), pp. 147–68.

The Nation', in A. Heywood, *Political Ideas and Concepts: An Introduction* 1994), pp. 56–66.

ations and Nationalism', in A. Heywood, *POLITICS* (Macmillan, 1997),

Heywood, A. *Political Ideologies: An Introduction* (Macmillan, 1998).

Hobsbawm, E. *Nations and Nationalism since 1780* (Cambridge University Press, 1990).

Jay, R. 'Nationalism', in R. Eccleshall *et al.*, *Political Ideas: An Introduction* (Routledge, 1994), pp. 153–84.

Kedourie, E. *Nationalism* (Hutchinson, 1985).

Morgenthau, H. J. and Thompson, K. W. 'Roots of Modern Nationalism', in H. J. Morgenthau and K. W. Thompson, *Politics Among Nations* (Alfred A. Knopf, 1985), pp. 120–6.

Purnell, R. 'The Notion of the Nation: Some Images and Myths', in R. Purnell, *The Society of States: An Introduction to International Politics* (Weidenfeld and Nicolson, 1973).

Smith, A. *The Ethnic Origins of Nations* (Blackwell, 1986).

Vincent, A. 'Nationalism', in A. Vincent, *Modern Political Ideologies* (Blackwell, 1996), pp. 238–77.

SAMPLE QUESTIONS

1 Is it possible to argue a rational case for nationalism?

2 How useful is it to distinguish between liberal nationalism, reactionary nationalism and radical nationalism?

3 'Nationalism has a very bad press today, one which is undeserved when one considers the contribution nationalism has made to the progress of human culture.' Why might you agree or disagree with this statement?

4 Which form of nationalism characterises contemporary nationalist movements?

5 Can we expect an increase or decrease in nationalist sentiment in the twenty-first century?

Conservatism

9

Conservatism is one of the major intellectual and political strains of thought in Western culture over the last two centuries. Originating as something of a 'reaction' to the radical, liberal and, later, socialist movements during the early period of industrialisation in Britain and Europe, conservatism remains a powerful ideological force in Western societies today. We explore conservatism from its intellectual and cultural roots in the eighteenth century to current developments in the early twenty-first century. Considerable attention is given to the historical experiences of conservative parties, especially in Britain, in the nineteenth and twentieth centuries, experiences that have been at least as significant in the development of conservative ideology as particular individual thinkers.

TO CONSIDER

e conservative reaction to the Enlightenment and the French Revolution less han that of other ideological and political movements?

events in the last hundred years tended to support conservative attitudes re, society, the economy, and the importance of law and tradition?

e has the British Conservative Party reflected the conservative intellectual

onservatism as an ideology bound up with the future of the nation-state?

Society is indeed a contract ... but it is not a partnership in things ... of a temporary and perishable nature. It is a partnership in all science, a partnership in all art; a partnership in every virtue, and in all perfection ... As the ends of such a partnership cannot be obtained in many generations, it becomes a partnership between ... those who are living, those who are dead, and those who are yet to be born. (Edmund Burke, *Reflections on the Revolution in France*, 1790)

Conservatism is less a political doctrine than a habit of mind, a mode of feeling, a way of living. (R. J. White, *The Conservative Tradition*, 1964)

A conservative is a man with two perfectly good legs who, however, has never learnt to walk forward. (Franklin D. Roosevelt, radio talk, October 1939)

There are a number of caveats to be made before we explore the nature of conservative thought. In Britain the connection between the Conservative Party and conservative thinkers is tenuous. Edmund Burke, who is generally regarded as the greatest early conservative thinker, was a 'Whig'. Many modern 'conservative' thinkers have little or no connection with the Conservative Party. Moreover, the meaning of 'conservatism' has shifted over time. European or American conservatism is not the same as British. To add to our difficulties, some conservatives have argued that the British Conservative Party has a distinctive way of thought, including its 'common-sense', realist and non-ideological or pragmatic nature. As the former Conservative leader, William Hague, once said in a *Today* (Radio 4) interview: 'We're not claiming to have an ideology; the Conservative Party is not based on ideology, it is based on doing what is best.'

Cynics point to the electoral success of the British Conservative Party during the nineteenth and twentieth centuries as evidence that it is simply the political instrument of the 'haves' against the 'have nots', a fact that it has successfully obscured. Or that it simply defends the status quo (whatever that happens to be) against change (whatever that happens to be). This is the sense in which journalists and political commentators often use it. Thus we get the paradoxical situation where in extreme Marxist or Islamic regimes those who oppose 'liberal' reforms are often condemned as 'conservatives'.

Like socialism, and to a lesser extent liberalism, conservative thought comes in many varieties and there is considerable tension between rival schools, and, of course, within contemporary 'conservative' parties. Even if it lacks the universal scope and intellectual coherence of other ideologies, it has characteristic ideas and values. In Britain these ideas and values continue to have an impact on modern conservative thought and the contemporary Conservative Party.

Given the emphasis on tradition and the historical roots of society it is especially important to look at the historical roots of conservative thought.

The historical origins and later evolution of Conservative thought

As with most political philosophies, it is difficult to establish a particular starting point for conservatism. Some commentators look to Plato, others to the Middle Ages, still others, especially in England, pinpoint the seventeenth century. This latter starting point has its merits. The crises that led to the civil wars produced defenders of royal power and of order, such writers as Thomas Hobbes (who is claimed by both liberals and Marxists as one of their ideological forebears) and Sir Robert Filmer (a defender of the traditional rights of kings). The loosely organised political groupings later to be known as the Tories are the direct ancestor of the modern Conservative Party.

However, systematic forms of conservative thought can be attributed to fear of domestic political radicalism, as for instance developed in reaction to the American and French revolutions. The revolutionary consequences to British society (and its later manifestations in Western Europe) of the agricultural and industrial revolutions also called for some sort of conservative analysis of resistance and accommodation.

Conservatism arose and developed as an ideology in response to the claims of other, *radical*, movements: liberalism, at first, then nationalism, socialism, fascism, feminism, environmentalism, all of which sought *change*, massive social 'improvement', reform and the removal of 'old', 'discredited', social orders, institutions and ways of life. Conservatism sought, and still seeks, to resist such change, to retard change, arguing for reflection, reassessment, and a willingness to consider the possibility that reformers might be mistaken. They believe that one should be very cautious about removing or radically changing old and long-lasting institutions and ways of life.

This was the argument of Edmund Burke, especially his *Reflections on the Revolution in France* (1790). Burke, almost the 'founding father' of British conservatism, was a distinguished parliamentarian and fully involved in the controversies of his day. He was not a reactionary thinker; for example, he showed considerable sympathy for the American rebels. Burke's ideas fed into existing traditions and political debate, to have a profound and enduring impact.

He realised that the crucial trigger for the revolutionary changes of his own time was the cultural and intellectual movements (known as the 'Enlightenment') which swept Europe and the American colonies in the late eighteenth century and culminated in the French Revolution (1789). Burke's political philosophy was based on a critique of the Enlightenment and its consequences. The intellectual basis of the Enlightenment and subsequent revolutions was the assumption, founded on a particular understanding of Newtonian physics, that human society was like a machine, and that this machine could be rationally understood. It was composed of discrete elements and could be dismantled, reassembled and radically improved by men in the light of reason.

Burke's understanding, and that of later conservative theorists, was based on a quite different analogy. Human society was 'organic'. It was like a living being, highly complex, with a distinctive history and nature. In fact, although all human societies had similarities, their differences were more significant than what they had in common. Thus arbitrary interference in the natural course of social development would be, metaphorically speaking, 'fatal' to that society. Moreover, the intellect of any one man, or even the knowledge of any particular epoch, is inadequate to grasp the complexities of a society. The accumulated wisdom of the centuries (what Burke called 'prejudice'), experience, tradition, custom should be brought to bear and any adjustment should be made with the greatest caution: 'The individual is foolish, the multitude, for the moment, is foolish when they act without deliberation, but the species is wise, and when time is given to it, as a species, it always acts right.'[1] 'Prejudice' in fact was a better guide in human affairs than the short-term intellectual fashions of any particular age. Attempts to base society on abstract principles, such as the French Revolution's 'Liberty, Equality, Fraternity', were particularly dangerous and would have, as the Revolution clearly demonstrated, calamitous results.

During the nineteenth century, while conservative thinkers in Europe tended to stress monarchy and authoritarian government, bolstered by strong conservative nationalism, British conservatism followed its pragmatic approach to social and political affairs. Sir Robert Peel sought new links between the landed gentry and the rising manufacturing classes around principles of free-market economics, principles of which conservatives were deeply suspicious during the early part of the century. Benjamin Disraeli dealt with the political consequences of the growth of a skilled industrial working class and demands for extension of the franchise to include them. In particular, he stressed in his speeches and, especially, his novels, such as *Coningsby* and *Sybil*, the need for social improvement to integrate the working class into the **one nation** he believed Britain should become.

one-nation conservatism
A strand in conservative thought going back to the nineteenth-century Conservative politician Benjamin Disraeli, which emphasises reform as an instrument of preventing social conflict and uniting the nation.

Popular imperialism was one means of encouraging the working classes to identify with the Conservatives and not be seduced by the appeals of socialism. Conservatives were also committed to educational and social reforms.

Post-1945 Conservative leaders came to terms with the social-democratic welfare state by both accepting and extending it. Harold Macmillan, R. A. Butler and other modernisers within the Conservative Party ensured its post-war electoral successes. In the 1980s Mrs Thatcher struggled with what she perceived as the hegemony of socialist and social-democratic doctrine permeating all levels of British society. Her conservatism sought to link the prosperous and ambitious sections of the working classes with her ideas of popular capitalism and 'traditional' values. The ideas of 'liberal' thinkers such as Karl Popper and F. A. von Hayek were brought in to provide intellectual weight for her brand of conservatism. These responses to social and political change are typical of the pragmatism that is a special feature of British conservatism.

Major conservative themes

Conservatism adjusted, with some difficulty at times, to two hundred years of unprecedented social and political change. Claims to being 'non-ideological' by some conservatives are, in essence, claims to superiority over the 'nonsense' of other perspectives. The main themes varied in importance at different times, but they had a number of things in common, to create a body of ideas, an ideology, that could be called *conservative*:

- a pessimistic view of human nature;
- an organic view of society;
- a view of politics as a limited activity;
- a belief in patriotism;
- a valuing of tradition;
- a commitment to strong national institutions;
- a high regard for property and the economy;
- an emphasis on law, freedom and authority.

A pessimistic view of human nature

From Burke onwards, conservatives have had a pessimistic view of human nature. For some, this view is rooted in the Christian doctrine of 'the Fall of Man' (or St Augustine's understanding of it). As a consequence of disobedience to divine command, human nature is flawed: greedy, irrational, selfish and power hungry. Improvements to human behaviour and hence to society as a whole require religious references and God's grace rather than philosophy and rational action. Imperfect individuals in imperfect societies produce imperfect human nature, even if some conservatives do not accept the religious basis of the assumption, and this means that radical social improvement is impossible.

Using human virtue, individually and especially collectively, to create a **Utopia** by political action will make things worse, not better. Belief in, and attempts to create, human perfectibility is one of

Utopia

A word that literally means 'Nowhere'. It is an imaginary perfect society and is usually used dismissively by those who disapprove of plans for social improvement. The word derives from the book of the same name by Sir Thomas More.

the great causes of human misery. The best a government can do is to hold society together while awaiting the heavenly 'Jerusalem'. Indeed, one must see the very severely limited scope of politics in society as far as 'social improvements' are concerned. Any social improvement can come only though morals and faith, not through government or newly invented social institutions. It is not that people are bad. Most people most of the time are kind, considerate and law-abiding and are concerned with the well-being of their neighbours. Nevertheless, flawed human nature needs to be constrained so as not to damage society.

An organic view of society

Society or, perhaps more accurately, the 'nation' is essentially organic in its nature, a kind of living creature, developing according to its own laws and to specific historical and cultural circumstances. Individuals are the 'cells' that make up the nation, each having a vital role to play in its well-being. This analogy of society with a living organism has proved to be of fundamental importance to conservatives. As a living thing has structure and hierarchy, with various parts contributing to the overall functioning and well-being of the whole, so it is with human society. The organism analogy also allows for adaptation and change. This view can, however, lead to a dislike and suspicion of foreigners and immigrants (*xenophobia*) who are seen as 'alien' bodies 'infecting' the national organism and undermining social cohesion and homogeneity. While most conservatives would reject racism they would also reject 'multi-culturalism' as divisive and stress the need for immigrants to 'assimilate' into national culture

It would be a mistake to assume that conservatism implies total opposition to change. Change should be gradual, natural and appropriate – evolutionary, not revolutionary. Social and economic change should be incorporated within the body politic. Disraeli, for example, defended both the Trade Union Act (1871), which gave the unions legal recognition, and the extension of the franchise (1867) in order to accommodate the social realities within the nation and to ensure its long-term survival by making limited compromises with rising political and social forces that might become revolutionary if endlessly frustrated.

Structure implies order, direction and hierarchy. Conservatives may vary on the precise nature of this order, and how a hierarchy develops and is sustained, but all are agreed on their necessity. Conservatives stress their importance to ensure the maintenance of a sound and well-governed society. Authority derives from tradition and the legitimacy that attaches to those individuals who hold positions in the nation's institutions. Hierarchy, both within national institutions and in society, is vital for the well-organised society, for the

instilling of habits of social discipline, obedience and obligation. Conservatives see nothing wrong in a hierarchy based on birth, wealth, authority, so
long as that hierarchy and its authority are founded on tradition and the rule
of law. Indeed, some conservatives have been suspicious of meritocracy as the
basis for social hierarchy as it creates stresses and competition in society that
put its harmony at risk.

Conservatives see, therefore, a natural inequality among people in society,
caused by the wide and unequal distribution of talents among people. Elites
are the foundation for successful organisation, for the development of higher
elements of culture and for the establishment and defence of property. These
factors benefit everyone in society, and not just the elite, so long as the elite
recognises and carries out its social obligations to lead. Attempts to create
egalitarian societies fail, but they create misery and oppression, often death
and destruction, before they are abandoned.

The basic and most important institution in society is the *family*. It educates
children into the values of the nation and binds them into a set of strong social
ties. Strong families create strong societies and family breakdown weakens the
bedrock on which society and the nation are built. Family life is not just a
private matter. Government should pursue policies that encourage successful
family life.

A view of politics as a limited activity

Conservatives claim that politics is a limited activity. As Lord Hailsham
observed in *The Case for Conservatism* (1947): 'Conservatives do not believe
that the political struggle is the most important thing in life . . . The simplest
of them prefer foxhunting.' Belief in the limitation, the *desirable* limitation, of
state power is a recurrent conservative theme from Burke to Thatcher's 'rolling
back' the frontiers of the state and contemporary conservatives looking to the
voluntary sector to redress society's ills. Politics is a *practical* pursuit, not a
theoretical or *technical* one. Living society cannot be deliberately planned,
organised or controlled according to some technical blueprint, some master
plan. If politicians fail to recognise this, then they will attempt to force society
and people to conform to theory with resulting misery and, ultimately, failure.

The main object of politics is the survival of the nation, even, if necessary, at
the expense of individuals. Some twentieth-century conservatives, such as the
poet T. S. Eliot, have maintained a religious element in their resistance to an
over-optimistic view of the effectiveness of politics in bringing happiness,
while others, like the political philosopher Michael Oakeshott, have dispensed
with the religious underpinning to a conservative society. The latter argued
that simply observing the catastrophes arising from attempts to construct new
societies, such as the Soviet Union and Nazi Germany, provides evidence

enough of man's imperfectibility and the dangers of attempting to create a 'perfect' society.

Conservatism raises questions as to how 'democratic' it is, or should be. Early conservatives, like Burke, rejected the notion outright. (He famously called the voters of Bristol 'The swinish multitude'.) Democracy would rapidly degenerate into mob rule, violence and, ultimately, dictatorship and the end of liberty. Later conservatives sought to hold democratic pressures in check by emphasising hierarchy (based on an aristocracy, property ownership or merit). Traditional constitutional barriers to democracy are often emphasised, such as, in Britain, the monarchy, and the (unreformed, now partially reformed) House of Lords. The rule of law, the independence of the judiciary, and constitutional checks and balances are also emphasised by conservatives.

Indeed, it is the erosion of constitutional balances that many conservatives see as the basis of the Britain's **elected dictatorship**, the government's domination over parliament. Conservatives have not, however, been keen to support the idea of a written constitution. This is presumably because it would lead to a Bill of Rights, itself the product of that whole line of reasoning about 'natural rights' which Burke, among others, deplored as being both nonsense and a stimulus to revolution.

> **elected dictatorship**
>
> A term used to describe the British system of government by the Conservative politician Lord Hailsham. It implies that, except at elections, the executive has almost total domination over the legislature and society in general.

Conservatism, unlike some ideologies, does not place politics at the centre of human concerns. Prime Minister Harold Macmillan, for example, once famously advised those who needed to find meaning in their lives to look to the bishops rather than to politicians. In terms of party politics, this has meant an emphasis on self-help, and on private education, private property, privacy, and the family. Politicians, it is assumed, can do much evil, but little good.

A belief in patriotism

Conservatives stress their love of country, implying that they are more patriotic than their opponents. The nation, with its distinctive culture, history and identity, is second only to the family as the natural unit of human society and having a similar emotional tie, can demand huge sacrifice from its members. Often, explicitly or not, conservatives doubt the patriotism of their opponents and deride the 'foreignness' of their ideas.

Conservative politicians are often strident about promoting the 'national interest', the touchstone of right action in foreign and defence policy. Much is made of national institutions: flag, armed forces and the constitution. The Conservative Party identified itself closely with the empire and the UK state. Patriotism, however, has caused problems for British conservatism. The empire has gone and, with Welsh and Scottish devolution, the new administration in Northern Ireland, and the advance of European integration, the UK is not what it was. Immigration, especially from the 'New Commonwealth', has raised difficult questions of national identity. The Conservative Party has many internal tensions over its policy towards the European Union.

British 'Euro-sceptics' regularly make references to Britain's glorious and independent past and the dangers of becoming subject to 'Europe', 'Brussels', or, even, the Germans. A senior Conservative minister once described the EU as 'a German racket'. A Tory backbencher once summed up the danger to British sovereignty from the EU:

> Here is a country that has defended its sovereignty for a thousand years against Philip II of Spain, Louis XIV of France, Napoleon, Kaiser Bill and Adolf Hitler. It is now expected to give up its sovereignty to Jacques Delors [the then EU president] with the squiggle of a pen.

Also troublesome is the question of the object of one's patriotism. In multinational states, or states with ethnic and linguistic diversity, a problem arises for conservative patriots. For example, are Conservatives patriotic to Britain as a whole or, – as the party's support in Wales and Scotland weakened in the 1990s – specifically, England? Is *English* nationalism emerging as the hallmark of modern *British* conservatism? Time will tell.

A valuing of tradition

Tradition is very important to conservatives. Tradition, that collection of values, myths, attitudes of mind and beliefs that make up the common 'mental baggage', is what gives a nation its 'character', its resources to act in the face of adversity, its courage to face and shape the future. Past glories, great military victories and even defeats, heroes and villains all play their part. Tradition binds the people together creating that sense of an organic identity linking individuals to the nation. Where ancient traditions do not exist, conservatives will invent them and invest them with archaic language, ceremony and architecture so that the nation will readily accept them.

Conservatives' reverence for tradition is not to be interpreted as slavish adherence to the notions, values and institutions of the past but as the bringing to bear on contemporary problems the accumulated wisdom of the past, especially the national past. This wisdom is a better guide to policy than the fickle fashions of the present. National history, particularly its more glorious moments, is therefore rightly venerated, as are the institutions, customs and values associated with it. Tradition also places the individual in a wider context than his own selfish and limited perspective. It gives meaning and dignity to all members of society, however humble, and binds the society together in a shared community of experience. By extension, 'tradition' may even include the seemingly trivial, with imperial weights and measures being British as against the foreign metric ones, Sterling against the Euro, British English spelling against American English.

A commitment to strong national institutions

Conservatives lay great stress on the institutions that embody the nation and unite it. Indeed, ancient institutions, with the blood of tradition pumping through their veins, play a vital role in the organic notion of the nation. Monarchy, the constitution, churches, ancient universities, old regiments, all have or claim to have ancient roots that ensure, as Burke said, that the national contact between generations long gone, those alive today and generations yet to be born is constantly renewed. The revolutionary overthrow of ancient institutions and their traditions is disastrous to the psychological as well as the physical well-being of the nation and its people.

A high regard for property and the economy

Property, to conservatives, has particular significance. The ownership of property gives independence and dignity to the individual, relieving him of complete dependence on the state. It also acts as another 'check and balance' in society on the power of the state. The desire to acquire property encourages initiative and a constant replenishing of social elites. Inheritance and the passing on of wealth link both individuals and societies with their past and future, underpin order and emphasise the continuity of society. Most conservatives emphasise the 'sanctity of property', but this is not necessarily incompatible with a degree of redistribution if that is what is needed to ensure social stability. It is, however, incompatible with state ownership except for the most cautious, modest and pragmatic of measures.

One of the fundamental bases of law and liberty in conservatism is the right to private property, a right guaranteed by the law, traditions and values of a nation. Conservatives nevertheless believe that great wealth and ownership of property, whether inherited or the result of hard work and enterprise, carries obligations towards those less fortunate. The wealthy and powerful have a duty to lead society, provide models of high standards of personal behaviour, and take action to alleviate the sufferings of the poor (although not necessarily by governmental action).

Conservative attachment to private property raises the issue of the link between conservative thought and the market economy. Since the late nineteenth century, the British Conservative Party, for example, has drawn support from 'big business'. It generally opposed the extension of public ownership in the 1950s and 1970s and, under Thatcher's governments of the 1980s, privatised huge swathes of state-owned industry. Nevertheless, the party's position on untrammelled free enterprise has been more complex than that of uncritical enthusiasm.

The principle of **free trade**, for example, has had varying fortunes among British Conservatives. In the nineteenth century they were usually opposed to it. By the end of the century substantial sections of the party supported protection or **imperial preference**. Now they are generally strongly in favour of it. The Conservatives tolerated state ownership of substantial sections of industry in the 1950s and 1960s. In the early 1970s the Heath Government imposed state controls on prices and incomes in the face of serious inflation problems, and nationalised Rolls Royce. Even at the height of the commitment to privatisation and a liberal-economic ideology during the 1980s there were Conservative politicians like Ian Gilmour and conservative philosophers like Roger Scruton who challenged the idea that all could be reduced to the market.

> **free trade**
> Trade within and between nations with little or no restraints imposed by the state, particularly tariffs on imported goods.

> **imperial preference**
> The practice of allowing goods to be imported into Britain from the empire without being subject to the same duty as that imposed on goods from outside the empire.

Continental parties generally regarded as conservative, such as the German Christian Democrats, found themselves theoretically and practically at odds with the British Conservative Party because of the former's commitment to the 'social market'. This term describes a basically market economy, substantially complemented by detailed regulation by the state and generous social welfare provision.

Wholehearted conservative commitment to the free market has been evident only since 1979, with the phenomenon known as 'Thatcherism', the intellectual foundation of which was laid by reference to philosophers such as Hayek, economists like Milton Friedman, social commentators such as Charles Murray and politicians such as Sir Keith Joseph.

The essence of their message was the economic and social excellence of the free market. For Hayek, it was the indispensable prerequisite of the free society. For Milton Friedman even such modest state intervention as advocated by Keynes (and practised by all Western governments since the 1940s) was ultimately futile in reducing unemployment; it produced inflation, undermined competitiveness and ultimately corrupted the economic order. Murray argued that a large welfare state actually exacerbated social problems by creating a socially irresponsible and dependent underclass.

Some philosophers, such as Michael Oakeshott, and politicians such as Enoch Powell sought to reconcile traditional conservative values with a vigorous championing of the free market. Others, mainly on the left of the party, have been very unhappy at the way some neo-liberal enthusiasts have tried to apply the free market to social as well as economic issues, for example by advocating a free market in hard drugs. Critics have raised doubts as to whether such 'libertarianism' is really conservative at all.

An emphasis on law, freedom and authority

Their opponents accuse Conservatives of favouring a highly controlled society, one with human rights and freedoms drastically curtailed. It is a charge they vehemently rebut. Actually, contemporary conservatives have tended to support economic liberalism and the free market precisely because economic freedom is an essential prerequisite for other freedoms. For conservatives, freedom is both possible and desirable, but only 'under the law'. As Lord Hailsham said in 1975:

> I believe there is a golden thread which alone gives meaning to the political history of the West, from Marathon to Alamein, from Solon to Winston Churchill and after. This I dare to call the doctrine of liberty under the law.[2]

Law, the rule of law, and its effective enforcement are key elements in establishing and maintaining order and, thereby, freedom. In their absence anarchy would reign: only the strong would be free (and then only so long as they remained strong) and the majority would be terrorised and oppressed. Thomas Hobbes made clear the consequences of weak government and a breakdown of law and order:

> In such a condition, there is no place for industry; . . . no culture of the earth; no navigation, . . . no commodious building; . . . no knowledge of the face of the earth; no account of time; no arts; no letters; no society; and which is worst of all, continual fear, and danger of violent death; and the life of man, solitary, poor, nasty, brutish, and short.[3]

Human rights are less the inherent properties of human beings than the result of a particular social and historical context. Much conservative unease with the incorporation of the European Convention of Human Rights into British, and especially English, law in 2000 sprang from this view. The ECHR is seen by many conservatives in Britain as undermining English common law and parliamentary sovereignty by importing European legal systems and principles from the European Union or, as in the case of the ECHR, from other European organisations.

Law presupposes an authoritative legislature. Historically, in Britain this has been the 'sovereign in Parliament' (often designated as 'parliamentary sovereignty') – the single source of legislative power in the United Kingdom. Conservatives tend to venerate the British Constitution, a constitution that still exists in the twenty-first century after centuries of steady evolutionary development, gradually adapting to massive social change. This veneration underlay the strong conservative opposition to Labour's proposed constitutional changes after 1997, especially devolution and the reform (albeit partial) of the House of Lords.

Conservatives profess devotion to freedom and a commitment to law and order. However, this may give rise to practical and philosophical contradictions. One strand, the *libertarian*, emphasises freedom as the highest social and political good (the Federation of Conservative Students in the 1980s, for example, caused embarrassment to the government by proposing the legalisation of hard drugs and abortion on demand). The other strand, the *authoritarian* (sometimes described as the 'New Right'), on the other hand, places emphasis on order and the institutions and values associated with order: the moral pluralism of contending ethical positions, which liberals applaud, is viewed with intense suspicion as a threat to order.

British Conservatism in the nineteenth and twentieth centuries: adaptation to change

British conservatives stress constitutional limits on government, pragmatism, scepticism and flexibility. They, more than their European and American counterparts, are very suspicious of 'grand plans' for social reform, emphasising the importance of social organisations outside the state. Indeed, British conservatives have absorbed liberalism's belief in minimal state involvement in health, education and welfare. Nevertheless, pragmatism has enabled the Conservative Party to adapt successfully to change and remain a major force in politics – almost the 'natural party of government'. It is worth considering the career of Europe's most successful conservative political movement.

The nineteenth and early twentieth centuries

The early emphasis on Burke's ideas and theories, which can be discerned running through conservative thought, obscures the factors that have enabled conservatism to sustain itself and even thrive though the cataclysmic changes of the nineteenth and twentieth centuries. There are a number of reasons for this. Conservatism adjusted to new social realities and brought new classes and groups within the Conservative 'broad church' and garnered support for Tory policies. Conservative beliefs were able to adapt to some of the intellectual current of the last two centuries. Finally, in their vigorous desire to take and keep power, they moderated their ideological stance to gain electoral support.

These factors are apparent throughout the period. The early nineteenth century was rocked by the French Revolution, war and the agricultural and industrial revolutions and their consequences. The Conservative prime minister, Robert Peel, tried to reconcile the party to the 1832 extension of the franchise to the new manufacturing classes. This involved the attempted but abortive conversion of the party to free trade and the scrapping of the Corn Laws (1846) that, to some extent, damaged landed interests and so split the party. It was around this time that the term 'Conservative Party' began to be generally used.

Later in the century Disraeli was to attempt to adjust the party to new realities once more, notably the 1867 Reform Act, which enfranchised some of the skilled working class, the continued growth of industry and towns, and the emergence of trade unionism. At the practical level Disraeli sought to construct an alliance of the old ruling class, the new middle classes and the emerging skilled working class (the 'respectable working class') for the Conservative Party. At the intellectual level he sought to construct 'one nation' in which the upper classes, animated by a sense of social obligation, would pursue a paternalistic approach towards the needy and try to incorporate the authentic interests of the trade unions into the body politic.

Disraeli, in his novels *Coningsby* (1845) and *Sybil* (1844), identified the emergence of 'Two Nations – the Rich and the Poor', an idea much more dramatic in theory than in practice. There were some practical reforms in the legalisation of trade unions, and in health and housing. Most significantly, Disraeli envisaged a more routine role for public institutions, notably at local level in the field of health and social welfare. These ideas were taken up in the 1890s by figures such as Joseph Chamberlain, who tried to convert the party to 'fair trade' (as opposed to 'free trade' espoused by Peel). This involved a tariff on imports, the proceeds of which would be used by the state to fund social-welfare benefits such as old-age pensions. Chamberlain failed to carry the party with him. Notions of tariffs and state welfare only became orthodox Conservative doctrine after the First World War.

By the end of the nineteenth century the Conservative Party was increasingly identified with business interests in resisting organised labour, while its support for farming interests was reduced but not eliminated. At the same time the party was very successful in mobilising working class support. This was particularly so under 'one-nation conservatism', attracting a third of the working-class vote, and ensuring long periods in power during the twentieth century.

Conservatism in the inter-war years

Once again British conservatism had to redefine itself in reaction to events. Near full democracy arrived in 1918 with the extension of the franchise to virtually all men over 21 and all women over 30. (Women finally got the vote on the same age basis as men in 1928 – under a Conservative Government.) The 'threat' from socialism grew with the Russian Revolution in 1917, and, more immediately, the rise of the Labour Party which formed its first (minority) government in 1924.

Conservatism adapted to new conditions. A prime minister could no longer sit in the House of Lords (as had often been the case until Lord Salisbury left office in 1902). Conservative leaders had to project an image of being 'one of the people'. High levels of unemployment, upheavals like the General Strike (1926) and the perceived threat from international communism pushed the party into emphasising law and order, but also social reform (albeit very limited and of no threat to the established order).

During the 1930s the rise of the fascist and Nazi threat led conservatives to emphasise traditional national institutions, such as the monarchy and the empire, and the politics of moderation. Stanley Baldwin, the Conservative leader who dominated the inter-war years, was no intellectual. Within the party there was little attempt to underpin Conservative policy by ideological means. There were, however, *some* contributions. Harold Macmillan, in *The Middle Way* (1938), advocated mixed state/private ownership and 'planned capitalism'. In 1936 he claimed: 'Toryism has always been a form of paternal socialism.' This approach looked back to Disraeli and the combination of a hierarchical social structure with state intervention to benefit the under-privileged and also to preserve the social order. Not all conservatives were as accommodating towards the lower orders. T. S. Eliot, for example, defended conservatism as a bulwark against the barbarism of mass democracy.

Conservatism after 1945

After the Second World War the Conservative Party was once again confronted by major changes in society, and once again it chose the path of accommodation. Some conservatives condemned its new policies as 'domestic appeasement' of the working classes, just as it was associated with 'international appeasement' of the fascist dictators – with similar potential for disaster. But most supported them as a necessary adjustment to new realities.

The Labour landslide victory in 1945 led to the acceptance of a consensus in British politics by most Conservatives. The consensus included the creation of the modern welfare state, a mixed economy and a commitment to full employment, all of which involved a substantial role for the state in society. The end of empire and the Cold War struggle with the USSR also involved a commitment to a strong state. The victory in the world war apparently vindicated such a strong state. This capitulation to the spirit of the times could be justified ideologically by politicians, such as Iain Macleod and R. A. Butler, as being in substantial harmony with 'one-nation' conservatism and the tradition of Conservative **paternalism** traceable back to the nineteenth century.

paternalism
A mode of conservative thought in which the relationship of governors to the governed is compared to that of father and children. The governors provide the needs of the governed but maintain their authority and superiority.

The adaptation to new realities proved politically astute. The Conservatives won a succession of elections in the 1950s. In many ways conservatism at the time resembled the 'revisionist' socialism of leading contemporary Labour figures such as Anthony Crosland and Hugh Gaitskell. From the outset, however, Conservatives had their own particular understanding of 'consensus', an understanding which held that it was fully in harmony with traditional conservative beliefs; for example, the belief in the merits of private property (an emphasis that was very apparent in the ideas of a 'property-owning democracy' in the 1980s).

From their inception consensus policies had their critics from within and outside the party. Pressure groups and think tanks, such as the Institute for Economic Affairs and Aims of Industry, and politicians such as Enoch Powell from the late 1950s and Sir Keith Joseph in the 1970s, began to question the intellectual bases of the post-war consensus and whether conservatives should share it. Drawing on the works of philosophers such as Hayek and Oakeshott they emphasised free-market economics as being more economically viable, more socially effective and morally preferable to the semi-socialism of welfare-statism.

In 1970 the Conservative victory of Edward Heath suggested that a commitment to a more robust free market would be more evident in government. Two years earlier he had made a number of speeches at the Selsdon Hotel in London, proposing a reversal of British economic decline by a vigorous promotion of private business, a reduction of trade-union power and a major rethinking about the welfare state. However, domestic problems such as industrial unrest, rising unemployment and high inflation led to a reversal of such policies in 1972; massive oil price rises in 1973–74 and their impact on the weakening British economy also contributed to a return to the consensus within the Conservative Party.

This, however, proved to be a brief aberration. The two humiliating Conservative election defeats in 1974 and Labour's seemingly inexorable march to the left, as well as the continuing failures of the consensus to stop Britain's decline as an economic power, rising unemployment and near hyper-inflation, encouraged a movement in the Conservative Party towards those who challenged the consensus. Although not clearly offering a reversal of such policies at the time, the political beneficiary of these crises was Margaret Thatcher, who was elected Tory leader in 1975. It soon became apparent that she was determined to follow a different political course from her post-war Conservative predecessors.

Thatcherism

'Thatcherism', as the constellation of attitudes identified with Margaret Thatcher (Conservative prime minister 1979–90) came to be called, was a reaction against the collectivist drift of post-war Britain and the crisis of the 1970s. This drift, in her view, had led to economic failure, social problems, national decline, moral decay and a general undermining of freedom and individual self-respect. Conservative Party leaders had shamefully colluded in this consensus.

Herself no intellectual, Margaret Thatcher nevertheless had an ability to take the ideas of others and was adept at combining them with populist attitudes into a formidable political project. Mrs Thatcher's political astuteness, personal charisma, toughness of character and luck in the weakness of her opponents both within and outside the party produced a period of radical transformation of the British political and ideological landscape in favour of 'New Right' or 'neo-liberal' ideas with her electoral successes in 1979, 1983 and 1987.

Thatcherism involved a wholehearted commitment to the market economy. This was combined with a drastic reduction in state economic management, 'monetarist' policies to tackle inflation by control of the money supply, an attack on economic vested interests, an extension of property ownership and the privatisation of state assets, including even utilities such as electricity, gas and water. There was a rhetorical commitment to cutting taxation, although, in practice, taxes tended to rise during the 1980s.

There was to be a reduced role for the 'nanny' state in providing welfare, in line with liberal elements of Thatcherism. This would be associated with a move towards private provision of healthcare, education and pensions. The aim of these policies was both to reduce the tax burden on society and to encourage greater self-reliance in individuals and their families.

Paradoxically, although the functions of the state were to be reduced, its strength was to be increased in areas of social control and governance, in line with authoritarian elements of Thatcherism. The police acquired both higher pay and greater powers. There was a corresponding reduction in the power of those viewed with suspicion, notably the trade unions. The end of the miners' strike (1984–85) finally dispelled any doubts as to the ability of British governments to govern, a common theme of the 1970s.

Conservative themes such as patriotism, freedom under the law, order, hierarchy, discipline, inequality and traditional institutions were emphasised. The final element of this ragbag of liberal and conservative ideas was a moral crusade that emphasised individualism rather than collectivism and self-reliance rather than state support.

The practical outcomes of these positions, notably the huge increase in unemployment, an increase in the gap between rich and poor and a general sense of deepening social division, caused great unease among 'one-nation'

Conservatives. Indeed, for some, at least, the question was raised as to whether Thatcherism was an authentic expression of Conservatism (and conservatism) at all, or some form of neo-liberalism.

There was also an inherent problem that only fully emerged under Thatcher's successors, John Major and William Hague. How far was an emphasis on a rapidly changing competitive society, the minimal state and the central value of economic freedom, compatible with other conservative values, such as the organic community, the obligations of the privileged towards the needy and the value of hallowed institutions, customs and values?

Post-Thatcher conservatism

John Major's values, in rhetoric at least, were far less ideological in character than those of his predecessor. As prime minister (1990–97), however, he continued with privatisation. Coal and the railways were moved into private ownership. His commitment to the creation of a 'classless society' proved on closer examination to be a commitment to 'equality of opportunity', a belief quite compatible with Thatcherism. A public image of a more humane and compassionate conservatism was promoted, 'Thatcherism with a human face', but this had little of intellectual or practical substance. Some attempt was made to extend market economics into public services. The 'Citizen's Charter', which set down standards for the services to meet, redefined citizenship in consumer terms, placing the citizen's relationship to the public services on a footing somewhat akin to the same person's relationship with private businesses.

Major's disinclination to develop a distinctive intellectual contribution to conservatism lay with his own pragmatic personality, and with the government's political difficulties caused by its small and ever-shrinking parliamentary majority (only twenty-one in 1992). Its internal divisions over Europe, and the growth of a much more right-wing and ideologically motivated body of MPs and party members, also contributed to party difficulties and the subsequent crushing defeat of the Conservatives in 1997. There was, however, another factor. Conservatism had historically defined itself as being 'against' something, such as the French Revolution, early manufacturing, the rise of socialism, the labour movement, communism. Now there was little left to be against. Internationally, the Soviet Empire and the communist threat had collapsed. Domestically, the Labour Party had adopted the quasi-Conservative economic and social policies, as the whole area of political discourse in Britain had moved from left of centre to right of centre.

The dilemma of what to react to was even more acute under Major's successor, William Hague (party leader 1997–2001). His initial thinking was to see the problem as one of adaptation. As previous leaders had adapted the party to new social and economic circumstances, so Hague would adapt to new realities. The new realties he at first confronted were changing patterns of sexual morality, a decline in marriage, more single parents, a growing acceptance of homosexuality. Here, a morally neutral position was advanced, emphasising 'tolerance' and 'compassion'. Michael Portillo, a leading shadow cabinet member, admitted to homosexual behaviour in his youth and received support from Hague for his honesty. A general policy of 'inclusion' of groups not historically associated with the Conservative Party, such as ethnic minorities, was announced. A more relaxed attitude to the new moral climate, especially among younger voters, had emerged and had to be responded to by the party.

This libertarian strand of conservatism was, however, soon abandoned. Ordinary party members rejected this shift to permissiveness as Hague adopted a strategy of 'listening' to the party. Even Hague's choice of Steven Norris as Conservative candidate for Mayor of London provoked grass-roots unease because of Norris's social liberalism and his reputation as a womaniser. However, Hague later appointed him as the party's vice-chairman. As Conservative Party membership shrank it became increasingly elderly, right-wing, 'Euro-phobic' and intolerant of social permissiveness among some of its leaders. Indeed, Tory MPs were, as their numbers dwindled after the 1997 electoral debacle, more ideologically right-wing, more 'Thatcherite' as a body, than ever before.

This reaction, and the internal party realities, soon led to a change of direction. A party document, *The Commonsense Revolution*, reaffirmed 'traditional' Conservative positions, 'traditional' now meaning much more right-wing than previously. By 1999 the Conservatives were loudly denouncing the repeal of Section 28 of the 1988 Local Government Act that forbade the 'promotion' of homosexuality in schools. At the 2000 Party Conference Ann Widdecombe, the shadow home secretary, proclaimed a policy of instant fines for the possession of cannabis. This was soon abandoned when a number of shadow cabinet members admitted to trying cannabis when young. Increasingly, the party sought to align itself with the churches and a (presumed) religious right. By 2001 the party was advocating the delivery of some social welfare services by the churches and other religious organisations.

The British Conservative Party suffered a repeat defeat at the 2001 general election. William Hague resigned as leader and was succeeded by Iain Duncan Smith. Party membership continued to shrink and to become more elderly and right-wing, more ideological and intolerant. It seemed that the Conservatives were doomed to be out of government for a long time. The relatively weak upturn in the Conservative position in the May 2002 local government elections, at a time of growing popular disenchantment with the Labour Government, seemed to offer little hope of a renaissance in Conservative political fortunes.

Conservatism has been successful because of its willingness to adapt to social change – and even initiate it. Its pragmatism, lack of ideological constraints and an ability to tap into deep-seated strains of popular emotion and beliefs have ensured its importance in Western democracies as a major political force. British conservatism has been the most successful of the species, both in terms of mobilising support for electoral victories and adapting to social and political realities, even over the last century and a quarter of mass democracy. It is unlikely, whatever problems face British Toryism at the start of the twenty-first century, that it will disappear.

Nevertheless a Labour Party that has successfully positioned itself as the 'caring conservative' party, adopting many of the elements of traditional conservatism into its policies, leaves the Conservative Party with a major problem. It needs to offer an alternative programme to the Labour Party, but that might involve becoming more ideological and right-wing and less likely to get elected.

Summary

Conservatism cannot be simply identified with the Conservative Party in Britain (or elsewhere). Moreover, although conservatism is less universal in scope or intellectually coherent than other political theories, there are nonetheless clearly defined conservative attitudes, values and assumptions. Conservatism, for our purposes, may be traced back to a reaction to the eighteenth-century Enlightenment and the French Revolution. Although there are different nuances within conservatism some broad themes are common to all. These are a pessimistic view of human nature; a reverence for each society as organic and unique; a belief that politics is of limited relevance to human affairs; a high value on patriotism, tradition, strong national institutions; a belief in private property, authority and liberty under the law. British conservatism has essentially been the adaptation of these values and beliefs to the realities of the nineteenth, twentieth and now twenty-first centuries. Different strands of conservative thought have been stressed at different times – for example, under Thatcher there was greater emphasis on the market economy. Although in the 1997 and 2001 general elections the British Conservative Party did badly, conservatism as a philosophy has proved adaptable and resilient and a revival in Britain is by no means impossible.

REFERENCES AND FURTHER READING

1 Edmund Burke, speech on the reform of representation in the House of Commons (1782).
2 Lord Hailsham, quoted in Anthony Sampson, *The Changing Anatomy of Britain* (Hodder and Stoughton, 1982).
3 Thomas Hobbes, *Leviathan*, ch. XIII (1651).

Eccleshall, R. 'Conservatism', in R. Eccleshall *et al.*, *Political Ideas: An Introduction* (Routledge, 1994), pp. 66–102.
Goodwin, B. 'Conservatism', in B. Goodwin, *Using Political Ideas* (John Wiley and Sons, 2001), pp. 147–67.
Green, D. G. *The New Right* (Wheatsheaf Books, 1987).
Heywood, A. 'Conservatism', in A. Heywood, *Political Ideologies: An Introduction* (Macmillan, 1998), pp. 66–102.
Leach, R. 'Conservatism', in R. Leach, *British Political Ideologies* (Philip Allen, 1991), pp. 88–116.
O'Sullivan, N. *Conservatism* (Dent, 1976).
O'Sullivan, N. 'Conservatism', in R. Eatwell and A. Wright (eds.), *Contemporary Political Ideologies* (Pinter, 1993), pp. 50–77.
Scruton, R. *The Meaning of Conservatism* (Macmillan, 1984).
Vincent, A. 'Conservatism', in A. Vincent, *Modern Political Ideologies* (Blackwell, 1996), pp. 55–83.
White, R. J. *The Conservative Tradition* (Adam and Unwin, 1964).

SAMPLE QUESTIONS

1 'Conservatism is anything that enables the ruling class to carry on ruling.' Do you agree?

2 Is conservatism anything more than a 'rag-bag of prejudices'?

3 To what extent does conservatism go with the grain of human nature?

4 Are the views of the 'New Right' a repudiation of traditional conservatism?

5 Why has the Conservative Party been so spectacularly successful in winning political power in Britain during most of the time since a mass democracy has existed?

Liberalism

10

Liberalism has become the dominant ideology at the start of the third millennium. Like conservatism it cannot be easily identified with one particular political party. We trace the origins of liberalism back to the late seventeenth century and the political turmoil in England that followed the civil wars of the middle of the century. After this, liberalism's 'golden age' during the nineteenth century is studied and the main themes of 'classical' and 'New' liberalism are outlined and discussed. The limitations of British liberalism began to become evident just before the First World War and it was almost eclipsed during the inter-war period. We discuss the apparent renaissance of liberalism that followed the collapse of Soviet communism during the late 1980s and the apparent triumph of liberal capitalist democracy on a global scale. Some of the inadequacies of contemporary liberalism are discussed and an estimate is made of the future that lies in store for liberalism.

POINTS TO CONSIDER

➤ Is liberalism culturally specific to Westernisation or is it of universal value?

➤ To what extent is the liberal focus on the individual based on a misunderstanding of human nature?

➤ At what point does liberalism end and socialism begin?

➤ Why were nineteenth-century liberals so uncomfortable with democracy and why don't modern liberals appear to share the doubts?

➤ In the twenty-first century is the state still the main threat to the individual?

➤ How far is it true to say that the triumph of liberal ideology has been at the price of the eclipse of liberal political parties?

A rich man told me recently that a liberal is a man who tells other people what to do with their money. (Le Roi Jones, *Home*, 1966)

If all mankind minus one, were of one opinion, and only one person were of the contrary opinion, mankind would be no more justified in silencing that one person, than he, if he had the power, would be justified in silencing mankind. (John Stuart Mill, *On Liberty*, 1859)

Liberalism . . . it is well to record this today – is the supreme form of generosity; it is the right by which the majority concedes to minorities and hence it is the noblest cry that has ever resounded on this planet. (José Ortega y Gasset, *The Revolt of the Masses*, 1930)

In many ways liberalism is the dominant ideology of Western society. It could be claimed that it is not just *an* ideology but is *the* ideology for all mankind, a fundamental truth that is not culturally specific to the West but is of global value. Indeed, with the collapse of the Soviet Union in 1991 and the adoption of elements of liberal capitalism in most countries, some liberals were moved to declare that liberalism and liberal values were now the only future for mankind's development.

However, although liberalism has in many ways been the defining political ideology of the Western world for nearly three centuries, this very ubiquity makes it difficult to separate out from Western culture a distinctive 'liberal' identity. Many values once regarded as characteristically 'liberal', such as freedom of speech and religious toleration, have become so much part of the mainstream of Western life that only the most extreme dare challenge them. While there is no universally agreed corpus of writings that is specific to the liberal creed, several key writers appear in all lists of the liberal canon.

Nor can liberalism be simply identified with a particular political party, such as the Liberal/Liberal Democrat Party. In the 1980s and 1990s one could plausibly argue that the Conservative Party was in some respects closer to the tenets of classical liberalism than were the Liberal or Liberal Democratic parties. Moreover, the term 'liberal' has non-political connotations, such as generous, or broadly or humanistically educated, or, in religious terms, opposed to a rigid orthodoxy. In contrast to such a positive perspective, for many on the political right in the USA today 'liberal' is a term of abuse, with accusations of naive or semi-socialist values that supposedly threaten 'natural' conservative American ones.

The origins of liberalism

Forewarned by these caveats, we may reasonably locate the origins of liberalism in the seventeenth and eighteenth centuries. It arose with the early development of capitalism and became particularly strong with the development of an industrial middle class from the 1750s onwards. Locke, Voltaire, Montesquieu and Adam Smith were all regarded by nineteenth-century liberals seeking intellectual ancestors as being early liberals, although they themselves would never have used such a term. Before, during and to a degree after the English Civil Wars there was turmoil in political speculation and debate from which a number of theories emerged that entered into liberalism. Among these was the idea, eloquently articulated by John Locke in *Two Treatises on Government* (1690), that society was based on a 'social contract'. Authority was conferred on government by the consent of the governed 'to maintain order and justice and to uphold essential rights' such as those of property. It followed that citizens have a right to rebel if the state abuses the rights of the citizen as included in the social contract. Another liberal value put forward by Locke, in his *Letter Concerning Toleration* (1689), was that of religious toleration. Indeed, many seventeenth-century writers and thinkers, such as the Englishmen Thomas Hobbes and John Milton, and Baruch Spinoza in Holland, all called for a debate on religious principles and the granting of a degree of toleration concomitant with social order and loyalty to the state.

In so far as these ideas found practical expression, they did so through the Whig Party that emerged as the dominant political force in the eighteenth century. For the Whigs, 'rights' were applicable to all freeborn Englishmen. These rights were embodied in the Act of Settlement (1688) and the Bill of Rights (1689) that established a monarchy constrained by the rights and privileges of Parliament. This was the outcome of the 'Glorious Revolution' (1688), an outcome that the Whigs regarded as a definite conclusion to the political struggles of the seventeenth century. Dominated by a few wealthy aristocratic families, the Whigs were actually less than radical.

Many of the more radical elements of the struggle emigrated, physically and intellectually, to the American colonies. Further fortified by the influx of ideas from the European Enlightenment and by further waves of the disgruntled from Britain, they provided the intellectual bases for the American Revolution and its subsequent constitution (1787). The *Declaration of Independence* (1776) is a classic statement of the liberal contract theory of government.

> We hold these truths to be self-evident, that all men are created equal, that they are endowed by their Creator with certain inalienable Rights, that among these are Life, Liberty and the pursuit of Happiness. That to secure these rights, Governments are instituted among Men, deriving their just powers from the consent of the governed. That whenever any Form of Government becomes destructive of these ends, it is the Right of the People to alter or to abolish it, and to institute new Government, laying its foundation on such principles and organising its powers in such form, as to them shall seem most likely to effect their safety and Happiness.

Fundamental was a belief in the right to representation (though not necessarily on a 'one-man, one-vote' basis) and a national government that incorporated the notion of 'balance' between the various branches of government (legislature, executive and judiciary). This fitted well with the concept, derived from the physics of Isaac Newton, that identified a natural equilibrium of forces in the universe. Liberalism similarly identified a number of political laws of nature: a 'balanced' society, the universalism of political laws and the consistency and predictability of human nature. Social harmony and social cohesion could, liberals averred, be achieved if individuals established their fundamentally common interest in holding society together.

The French Revolution (1789) was to have an impact on the development of liberalism by injecting into its mainstream a sharper, more radical element. Thomas Paine, in *The Rights of Man* (1791–92) and *The Age of Reason* (1794), proclaimed a radical liberal programme. Paine, having taken part in the American Revolution, took up the cause of the French Revolution. His passionate belief in human reason, his optimistic view of human nature and his robust atheism were much influenced by, and in turn influenced, continental liberalism. He also attacked monarchical and hereditary government, and insisted on popular sovereignty, republicanism and human rights. He offended virtually everyone, including the British Government, the French Revolutionaries and American Radicals, but provided the basis for many liberal and socialist ideas of the nineteenth century.

The nineteenth century and 'classical liberalism'

The nineteenth century was the heyday of what can be termed 'classical liberalism'. Indeed, Britain can be seen as the society which took liberalism most to its heart in shaping its development during that century, as the USA was to do in the twentieth. By the 1840s a recognisable set of ideas generally described as 'liberalism' had emerged but it wasn't until 1868, and William E. Gladstone's first ministry, that a distinct 'Liberal' government rather than a simply relabelled Whig Party came to power in Britain.

'Utilitarianism' provided a further moral basis for liberalism in the early nineteenth century. As advanced by Jeremy Bentham and James Mill, Utilitarianism argued that reason could be used to discover human rights and organise human institutions. Utilitarianism measured the rightness of any act by the degree to which it contributed to happiness. People sought to maximise pleasure and minimise pain in the rational pursuit of their own interests. Only individuals could know what was considered best for them, not the state. Utilitarians declared that democracy was the best means of securing 'the greatest happiness for the greatest number' in society. This doctrine substantially influenced liberal thought and practical measures, although it was open to the criticism that it subordinated individual human rights to the perceived good of society.

Although Adam Smith lived in the eighteenth century his ideas triumphed in the nineteenth with the progress of the industrial revolution. In *The Wealth of Nations* (1776) Smith laid the theoretical foundation in economics for what became known as 'classical' liberalism. He argued that free markets, and trade unhampered by government interference, were fundamental to successful economic development. Free markets were efficient, in that they led to the most productive use of resources and everyone got what economic rewards they deserved. They were 'free' in that economic decisions, agreements and commitments were freely made by individuals and ultimately beneficial to the whole society as **market** economies provided the social dynamic that ensured ever-greater prosperity for all.

> **market**
> A system of exchange between buyers and sellers in which prices are established by the interplay of 'supply' and 'demand', in other words by 'market forces'.

John Stuart Mill's particular contribution was to systematise nineteenth-century political liberalism. In his numerous writings, chiefly *On Liberty* (1859) and *Considerations on Representative Government* (1861), Mill argued for democracy, tempered by a 'balanced' constitution with enshrined rights; firstly, rights to freedom of thought and belief, and freedom of expression, because of his conviction that individual opinion and belief were the highest good in society; and secondly, a franchise weighted to strengthen the voting power of the better-educated, so as to prevent the smothering of informed opinion by the uneducated majority. He feared that demagogues might mislead the masses and thus destroy the very foundations of a free society in the name of equality. They might stifle the unorthodox by making public opinion the touchstone of 'right', as the French liberal writer Alexis de Tocqueville had previously suggested in his influential *Democracy in America* (1835–40).

However, in other writings, such as his *Principles of Political Economy* (1848), Mill was more sympathetic towards some degree of state intervention in society to deal with social evils, such as poverty, than were most mid-nineteenth-century liberals. He also supported trade unions and even ideas later seen as socialist, such as worker co-operatives. The improvement of social conditions would enable the working class to get better educated, become 'rational human beings' and so be intellectually equipped to take part in democracy.

By the late nineteenth century, however, reality had begun to present a serious challenge to classical liberalism and the *laissez-faire* policies of government associated with it. Poverty, disease and ignorance remained brutal facts of existence for most people. The scale of the catastrophe of the Irish Famine (1845–48) was partly due to these economic doctrines and the belief that the state should not intervene to alleviate social problems. Practical politicians and liberal philosophers began to revise their views of the role of the state although they faced opposition from the 'Social Darwinian' wing of liberalism.

Although 'Social Darwinists', such as Herbert Spencer and Samuel Smiles, are sometimes described as 'liberal', on the grounds that they emphasised rigorous **laissez-faire** policies, the harshness of their conclusions was usually too far removed from the humanitarian impulses of liberalism to be acceptable to most liberals. Spencer, in *The Man Versus the State* (1884), claimed to have based his theories on Charles Darwin's ideas of evolution and the idea that a species evolves and 'ascends' by conflict between members of that species for survival. Social Darwinists proposed applying these principles to human society. Society was seen as a struggle for survival among individuals, the weakest being trampled underfoot by the

> **laissez-faire**
> 'let it be' or 'leave it alone'. A term used to describe the political and ideological belief dominant in Britain during the nineteenth century that the state has no active role in running the economy or solving social problems.

strongest. Smiles, in *Self-Help* (1859), proclaimed vigorous self-reliance as the means by which the individual and society might be improved. This became something of a gospel for *laissez-faire* liberalism during the second half of the nineteenth century. It was claimed that this was not only how things *are* but also how things *should* be. State intervention on behalf of the weakest was thus counter-productive and should be rejected.

Late nineteenth-century and early twentieth-century 'New Liberalism'

Most liberals, however, were moving in the direction of *more* rather than less state intervention. It was not only a matter of principle. It was a recognition of the need for liberalism to respond to the rise of organised labour if it was to survive as a political force, attracting the vote of the newly enfranchised working classes. T. H. Green was the leading exponent of what came to be known as 'New Liberalism'.

Green, in his *Lectures on the Principles of Political Obligation* (1879–80), emphasised a more tender understanding of human nature. Man was not simply an asocial individual leading a life of rationally calculating self-interest, but was from the start immersed in society, from which his rights derived. The market economy and the policy of *laissez-faire* capitalism thwarted the values which liberals expounded so well. Classical liberalism had advocated a 'negative freedom' in which the external restraints to freedom, such as law, were reduced. Green argued that in reality the impoverished masses were effectively denied such freedom by factors of social inequality such as ill health, poverty and ignorance. Only collective, rather than individual, action could remove these obstacles, empower the poor, and create a genuinely free society:

> Only through the possession of rights can the power of the individual freely to make a common good of his own have reality given to it ... The idea of true freedom is the maximum of power for all members of human society to make the best of themselves.[1]

These rights were similar to the ones associated with classical liberalism; but New Liberalism offered working-class people the chance to acquire 'positive' freedoms, to achieve property rights and levels of health, liberty and happiness similar to those enjoyed by the better-off in society.

Other New Liberals, such as L. T. Hobhouse, *Liberalism* (1911), and John Hobson, in *Crisis of Liberalism* (1909), went even further. They did not believe that the free market alone could solve social problems and create social justice. They emphasised co-operation rather than competition. Hobson even argued that capitalism was not the best mechanism for producing and distributing goods but tended, in fact, to concentrate wealth in the hands of the few at the expense of the many. Extensive state ownership, welfare provision and redistributive taxation should counter this undesirable social trend. Wealth was the product of social conditions, not just of individual effort. However, most New Liberals were against extensive state ownership of industries.

So radical a departure was this from classical liberalism that some doubted if it could be still called 'liberalism' at all. Defenders of the New Liberalism (or 'social liberalism' as it is sometimes called) argued that the ends of a liberal society remained unchanged. Such a liberal society would be based on individual liberty, but classical liberalism had been found to be inadequate for the task; it had become the ideology of the powerful, the only individuals who were fully able to take advantage of individual liberty.

New Liberalism had a powerful influence on the Liberal Party in Britain throughout the twentieth century. In Lloyd George's 'People's Budget' (1909) a National Insurance scheme was introduced to cover sickness, unemployment and pensions. Moreover, it was very largely absorbed into the other main parties so that, although the Liberal Party's political fortunes languished, New Liberal ideals lived on. It is no accident that the basis of the post-1945 social-democratic consensus originated with two New Liberals: William Beveridge, the architect of the welfare state (1942 White Paper), and John Maynard Keynes, the apostle of state management of demand in the economy to ensure full employment (1944 White Paper). These and other elements of the welfare state have been accepted by the Labour and Conservative parties, both in and out of government, until the present day.

We have touched upon some of the key ideas associated with liberalism. It is time to take stock of these in greater detail.

Liberal themes

To liberals, society is underpinned by a morality of self-interest and mutual support and respect. While the driving force of the liberal society is enlightened self-interest, this becomes a balance of interests, institutions and, ultimately, political power in society. Thus both chaos *and* tyranny are avoided. Liberalism has a number of key themes:

- the individual and his/her rights;
- an optimistic view of human nature;
- a belief in progress;
- a commitment to freedom;
- limited government;
- the economy and liberalism;
- a commitment to internationalism.

The individual and his/her rights

At the heart of liberalism is the individual. Each human being is unique. Every individual is endowed with innate rights of equal value. Each person is capable of understanding what is best for him or her. This is the rationale for the liberal idea of equality as the basis of justice for everyone. For some this takes the form of claiming that, as a matter of fact, individuals act rationally and choose what they need to be happy in their own interests. For classical liberals this has the effect of benefiting society as a whole. In a famous passage Mill made the case for the defence of individual rights:

> The only purpose for which power can be rightly exercised over any member of a civilised community, against his will, is to prevent harm to others. His own good, either physical or moral, is not a sufficient warrant. He cannot rightfully be compelled to do or forbear because it will be better for him to do so, because it will make him happier, because, in the opinion of others, to do so would be wise, or even right. These are good reasons for remonstrating with him, or reasoning with him, or persuading him, or entreating him, but not for compelling him, or visiting him with any evil in case he do otherwise. Over himself, over his own body and mind, the individual is sovereign.[2]

Others approach the individual from a more ethical direction: that the individual's welfare is the highest good and that this principle should be the basis of society. Along with positive attitudes to the individual comes the value placed on tolerance for individuals and **pluralism** for society as a whole.

Eighteenth- and nineteenth-century British liberals vigorously defended religious freedom and opposed the accordance of privileged status to particular creeds such as the church of England. Liberals championed the rights of slaves in the nineteenth century. In the twentieth century liberals have promoted homosexual rights, gender and racial equality, rights for the disabled and civil rights in general. Some have even sought to extend some form of rights to animals, especially the higher primates (such as gorillas and chimpanzees).

pluralism
A belief in the diversity of opinion, freedom of choice and the value of a society made up of many competing and co-operating groups. In a pluralist society the state exists to act as a referee between these competing groups and individuals.

To liberals, rights are innate, inherited as a consequence of being born human. The state exists to support these rights, to defend them. Human rights, which liberals regard as inalienable (i.e. they cannot be transferred to someone else), are derived from God (or Nature) and it should therefore be the first duty of government to defend them. The state cannot take away these rights. It may abuse them, it may claim that they do not exist, but they are not the state's property to dispose of. In practice, liberals have historically promoted the inclusion of such rights in constitutions such as the American in the eighteenth century and, recently, the British in the form of the Human Rights Act (2000).

Towards groups, liberals favour toleration. Pluralism in which different beliefs, values and interests freely compete is regarded as good, indeed essential. Liberals have a tendency to be anti-censorship and strongly in favour of the maximum degree of freedom of speech (although most would place limits on this in line with laws of slander, libel and incitement to racial hatred). This is in contrast to conservatives, who are uneasy with pluralism, which they regard as potentially socially divisive. Tolerance was apparent in liberal attitudes to the emancipation of Catholics, Jews and nonconformists in the early nineteenth century and acceptance (or even welcoming) of a multi-cultural society in the late twentieth. Religion was a matter for individual consciences and not for the state.

It is, of course, easy to tolerate views we agree with. The real test of a liberal is allowing the right of people to hold and propagate views one disagrees with – even views that are fundamentally intolerant: fascism, racism, religious bigotry, sexism. People have a right to hold and express such views, but they can expect – should expect – such views to be vigorously challenged. All liberals have a duty to defend liberal values and challenge illiberal ones. Tolerance does not mean that one should be unquestioningly open-minded. Nor should all views be seen as morally of the same value.

Linked with this theme of tolerance is a general disposition to 'humane' approaches to such issues as the treatment of prisoners and animal welfare. Tolerance, however, has difficulties for those liberals who regard some groups as illiberal (such as the Catholic church on abortion or some Islamic views on women's rights). This dilemma was thrown into sharp relief by the Salman Rushdie affair, when his book *The Satanic Verses* (1988) enraged Muslims because of its alleged blasphemy. Iranian clerics issued a **fatwa**, condemning Rushdie to death. Most

> **fatwa**
> A term used in Islam to denote an authoritative judgement by a religious institution or dignitary.

liberals sprang to Rushdie's defence on the grounds of freedom of speech. Some, however, were uneasy that this book used freedom to affront a religious group.

An optimistic view of human nature

Liberalism tends to an optimistic view of human nature, which is perceived as 'individual human nature', with apparently little influence from society, history or culture. There is an underlying assumption that liberal principles about human nature are of universal value, applicable to all societies at all levels and types of social and economic development. This inclines liberals to support human rights movements throughout the world. They dislike justifications for the denial of human rights by reference to cultural, economic, developmental or historical circumstances. Thus the extension of liberty contributes towards 'progress', moral, educational and material.

Human beings will act and think rationally, provided they have the freedom to do so. Rationality is the key element in liberal views about human nature. Human beings have the capacity to decide what is best for themselves when considering the advantages and disadvantages of various courses of action. Reason will ensure that individuals and society progress in an essentially beneficial manner. Debate, not violence, is the means by which differences should be resolved.

A belief in progress

The optimism that liberals evince towards human nature is also apparent in their attitudes towards the past. They are much less inclined than conservatives to perceive the past as a source of wisdom, or regard the antiquity of institutions as any guarantee of their worth. Historically, liberals have been friendly towards science and evolutionary theory in particular (though the misapplication of science in war and environmental destruction in the twentieth century have caused distress to liberals). Generally, liberals look to the future with optimism, believing that social improvement is not only possible and desirable, but is likely to take place over the long term.

A commitment to freedom

Liberal attitudes to human nature, progress and the individual all come together in the very high value placed on freedom. Mill, as we saw above, talked of the 'sovereignty of the individual'. This freedom includes freedom from restraint on the (adult and rational) individual and freedom of nations and groups from oppression, freedom of economic activity, and freedom of thought and expression. Freedom, though, it is conceded, cannot be an absolute – there must be some restraint on those who in exercising their own liberty, infringe that of others. Without such restraint freedom becomes licence. Liberals hold to the general assumption that restraint should be mild, but they have little in the way of logical principles to define just how mild.

Restraint should be imposed by a clear set of rules under the law. Indeed, most liberals think of liberty as only being possible within a framework of law to settle potential disputes between individuals. As John Locke stated: 'where there is no law, there is no Freedom. For Liberty is to be free from restraint and violence from others which cannot be, where there is no law'.[3] Human reason and human energy, stimulated by living in a free society, ensure the self-regulation and progress of society. The moral underpinning of these relationships is natural law and natural rights that ensure that individuals live in a high degree of harmony with one another. Government should, therefore, create the conditions in which moral life is possible and the widest possible degree of freedom can be maintained. A repressive society would be inefficient, immoral and unstable. Thus, to liberals, a free society is a stable society and a stable society is one in which freedom can flourish.

In the eighteenth and nineteenth centuries liberals focused on the state as the most serious threat to freedom and therefore in need of most restraint. Later liberals realised that poverty, and the unjust distribution of private property and the political power that went with that, were the main limitations on the freedom of the common man. This has led to some tension between twentieth-century liberals. Friedrich von Hayek, in *The Road to Serfdom* (1944), *The Constitution of Liberty* (1960) and *Law, Legislation and Liberty* (1973–9), argued for the rule of law, under which individuals exercise choices, as the key principle of justice. John Rawls, in *A Theory of Justice* (1970), argues that inequality is permissible only if it contributes to the advantage of the 'least favoured'. He believes in civil liberties for all as the basis for a principle of justice. He claims that in practice inequalities in wealth can ultimately benefit even the poorest citizens. However, there is an important role for the welfare state to ensure a degree of equality and fairness.

Limited government

As a general rule, liberals have been inclined to view the state with suspicion, as a threat to the rights of the individual. It is a necessary 'servant' employed to ensure order and efficiency, and the protection of individual rights, but it is a servant that should be kept under close restraint, and one that can be dismissed if it breaks its 'contract of employment'.

Institutions of government should be so arranged as to minimise this risk – hence the principle of the 'separation of powers' in which the legislative, executive and judicial functions of government were kept separate. Montesquieu crystallised this theory in *The Spirit of the Laws* (1748). He believed that, as every man invested with power is apt to abuse it, to prevent such abuse 'power should be a check to power'. Recognition of this is the foundation of entrenched rights and written constitutions in political systems, structured around the rule of law. This strand in liberal thought has continued into the twenty-first century, with liberals showing enthusiasm for constitutional reform in Britain and Europe.

It might appear that democracy is the natural partner of liberalism, but that is not so. Liberals have been almost as afraid of the mob and its ignorance and envy as they have been of the state and the aristocracy – hence the emphasis on 'balancing' the institutions of government in the American Constitution. Even J. S. Mill advocated a system of 'weighted' votes to favour the propertied classes as a bulwark of a liberal society against the mob, misled by demagogues. De Tocqueville also feared the 'tyranny of the majority'. Modern British liberals have been in the forefront of constitutional reform, advocating such restraints on the state as a written constitution, a bill of rights and dispersal of power to devolved authorities. Although no modern liberal would support differential voting patterns, based on property or educational level, all would support democratic systems of government and are inclined to support the devolution of power.

Government must be based on the consent of the governed. Consent is the basis for its legitimacy, its right to rule. Government agents should be accountable to the elected representatives of the people. Thus government must represent the interests of *all* the people, not just of interest groups. Indeed, liberals see the state as a sort of 'referee' between the competing groups and individuals. It should not become merely one among other interest groups, which is the danger if the state gets too involved itself in the providing of goods and services. Therefore the state – the 'minimal state' – should for classical liberals be confined to three essential roles: the maintenance of defence against external enemies, the ensuring of internal law and order, and the raising of taxes to fund these two roles.

The economy and liberalism

Both in theory and in practice liberals have favoured private property and the market economy as efficient, just and essential to the underpinning of liberal political institutions and a free society. Choice is seen as a positive good, an end in itself and a key element of freedom in a liberal society. Individuals should be rewarded in line with the 'market value' of their talents: the market acts as an incentive to individual effort and realisation of human potential.

Free trade and the self-regulating, balanced working of the free market for goods, services and labour are also seen as positive goods in encouraging economic efficiency and well-being. These beliefs were particularly associated with Adam Smith and, later, the nineteenth-century 'Manchester School' of economists, dominated by the Anti-Corn Law activists John Bright and Richard Cobden, and were reiterated in the twentieth century by the 'Chicago School' and the ideas of Milton Friedman, von Hayek and Robert Nozick.

However, the limitations of this approach led to the emergence of New Liberalism at the end of the nineteenth century. New Liberals sought the management of the market economy by the state in a manner advocated later by J. M. Keynes and his followers in the twentieth. For modern liberals there is something of a dilemma over how far to go in regulating a market economy. No obvious answer is forthcoming, but in general liberals have been inclined to support the principles of the welfare state, this being justified as promoting 'positive rights', as opposed to the classical liberal insistence on negative rights, that is rights which depend on the withdrawal of state power. Modern liberals tend to see a major – and proper – role for the state in economic management and the provision of goods and services. In fact, in America, the term 'liberal' can be applied to those who support an extension of state action in the area of welfare and human rights.

The chief British intellectual contributor to the development of liberal economic thought was J. M. Keynes. Classical liberals, like Adam Smith, had regarded a free economy as 'self-regulating' through the operation of a 'hidden hand' (i.e. the personal self-interested choices of producers and consumers). Keynes, in *The General Theory of Employment, Interest and Money* (1936), argued that the capitalist system could work efficiently only if the government managed 'demand'. Put crudely, this meant that when there was high unemployment the government should increase demand in the economy by pumping money into it, cutting taxes and/or increasing public spending on housing, roads and services. When inflation was a problem the state should raise interest rates, cut public spending and increase taxes to reduce demand in the economy.

Highly controversial in the 1930s, these views became established orthodoxy after the Second World War throughout Western liberal capitalist economies. By the 1970s, however, severe and persistent inflation *and* high levels of unemployment led to a formidable challenge to the apparently failing Keynesian 'demand management' by economists known as 'monetarists', such as Milton Friedman. They claimed as their intellectual ancestors classical liberal economists of an earlier era. To some extent, Margaret Thatcher's governments in the 1980s adopted their values, with mixed results, but by the end of the twentieth century Keynesian demand management was back in fashion, up to a point.

A commitment to internationalism

This is an oft-neglected theme of liberalism, but it is important. Its practical application found expression in the liberal emphasis on 'free trade' in the mid-nineteenth century as a means of ensuring peace and the universalist nature of morality and human rights that should be defended when threatened by oppressive governments in other countries.

Many liberals were against British imperialism in the nineteenth century on the grounds that it was not necessary for trade and economic development and that it infringed the rights of those over whom Britain ruled. Some Liberals strongly opposed Britain's involvement in the First World War – even though it was a Liberal Government that declared war on Germany. Still others, Keynes for example, were highly critical of the Versailles Treaty (1919) that ended the war and imposed punitive financial reparations on Germany. Nevertheless, most liberals were highly supportive of the League of Nations, which was established by the Treaty, during the inter-War period. They believed that it, and 'collective security' (whereby states would unite to resist an aggressor), offered an alternative to the balance of power in organising international relations, creating a law- and custom-based society in international affairs similar to that which prevailed in domestic society.

The failure of the League and collective security with the outbreak of the Second World War did not destroy liberal support for internationalism. Liberals have been vigorous in their support for the United Nations since its foundation in 1945. They are the most enthusiastic supporters of wholehearted commitment by Britain to the European Union and its project for European integration.

This internationalism springs from the liberal belief in free trade and from the assumption that human nature is everywhere essentially the same and that human beings enjoy rights by virtue of their humanity rather than of the particular society or culture into which they are born. These rights are universal, indivisible and inalienable. The Universal Declaration of Human Rights, attached to the United Nations Charter, is a classic statement of liberal principles on this issue.

Liberal attitudes in this field, however, do not necessarily translate easily into specific political choices. For example, in the 1930s liberals were divided on 'appeasement' as the mainspring of British foreign policy, and in recent years they have been divided on Western intervention in the Gulf, the Balkans, Africa and, recently, Afghanistan, and Iraq.

Liberalism in the twentieth century

The twentieth century began with liberalism triumphant, being a major element of the dominant states that ruled the world by means of their empires and committed themselves to the continuation of the social, economic, political and cultural progress that liberal societies had undergone in the previous century.

However, liberalism suffered a severe shock to its ideas of progress during the horrors of the First World War. After the war, liberalism not only produced the disastrous Versailles Treaty, but the ineffectual League of Nations. Liberalism failed to ensure a prosperous world economy in the inter-War era. It failed to deal with the tide of fascism and communism and slid into war again in 1939. Indeed, fascism and communism appeared as young, vibrant alternatives to what had become the apparently old, tired and worn out ideology of liberalism.

Nevertheless, liberalism prevailed in the twentieth century's ideological wars. On a world scale its greatest enemies, fascism and communism, had been destroyed: fascism by the Second World War and communism by the end of the Cold War. Liberal values, a global free-trade system, moderate welfarism and the onward march of technology seemed to be universally accepted. Western military, economic, technological and cultural domination of the world at the end of the century ensured that essentially liberal economic systems, political institutions and moral values were extensively imposed on Africa, Asia and Latin America and the states of the former Soviet Empire. This has, of course, stimulated resistance to the 'globalisation' of Western liberal values and Western power.

Ideologically, liberalism flourished as never before. As the Soviet Empire collapsed in the early 1990s and Marxism withered on the vine, liberalism was refreshed by a plethora of writers such as Karl Popper, Friedrich von Hayek, Isaiah Berlin, Ronald Dworkin, Milton Friedman, Robert Nozick, John Rawls and Michael Walzer. A number of right-wing 'think-tanks' such as the Adam Smith Institute, the Institute of Directors and the Freedom Association contributed policy ideas to the neo-liberal assault on the social-democratic state. Thinkers such as these, arguing for a much reduced state and a greater role for private initiative and the rigours of the free market, were very attractive to Western conservative politicians seeking a way out of the low growth and 'stagflation' (a term coined to describe simultaneous inflation and zero economic growth) of the 1970s and long-term American and British economic decline.

In the 1980s most Western societies had apparently adopted classical liberal economic theories, usually now known as 'neo-liberalism'. In the USA it was known as 'Reaganomics', after President Reagan, and in Britain as 'Thatcherism', but in different forms it appeared in France, Germany, Spain, Italy and other countries and with governments of both the political left and right. Privatisation of state-owned assets, reductions in income tax, the weakening of organised labour and attempts to reduce the role of the state in welfare provision were all tried in these countries, with varying degrees of success. The British 'New' Labour Party converted to this and the rest of the liberal credo (devolution, civil rights and communitarianism) in the 1990s. Liberal attitudes to divorce, abortion and homosexuality all seemed to be generally accepted across the political spectrum.

This very achievement created problems for liberal parties, such as the British Liberal/Liberal Democrat Party, as they seemed to have worked their way out of a job. The British Liberals had been perceived by the electorate as a party of the middle ground during the post-war era. By 2001 the Liberal Democrats were beginning to position themselves somewhere to the left of New Labour on taxation, asylum seekers and immigration, public spending, constitutional reform, and many other issues. Serious questions have been raised within the Liberal Democrat party about the strategy, pursued since 1997, of a 'critical alliance' with the Labour Party. Nevertheless, the strategy appeared to work in the 1997 and 2001 elections when it helped establish a strong Liberal Democrat presence in the House of Commons.

Internationally, challenges to liberalism emerged in various guises. In the United States, the election of George W. Bush in 2000 signalled a new attitude to welfare, abortion, crime and internationalism which was clearly a sharp move to the right. More alarming was the upsurge of religious fundamentalism especially in, but not confined to, the Islamic world, the flare-up of intense nationalism in the Balkans and the Middle East, and the rise of racist and fascist movements in Europe. Liberalism, closely associated with globalisation, was clearly subject to challenges to its values and to the globalising process.

There were also more profound intellectual challenges. Reappraisals of human nature from a neo-Darwinist perspective, based on scientific study of animal behaviour, cast doubt on liberalism's optimistic perception of human nature. From another angle environmentalists pointed to the inadequacy of liberal theory to deal with the environmental destruction being perpetrated as much by liberal capitalist regimes as by totalitarian ones. Finally, there was a growing unease that a society based on the absolute primacy of the individual as the source of all moral values was simply unsustainable: it would degenerate into licence and anarchy, to be replaced by dangerous and reactionary fanaticisms, or some form of popular authoritarianism.

In practical terms this has caused problems for liberals over deciding which side of the barricades to stand. Was British intervention in Kosovo in 1998 a 'humanitarian war' (and thus to be supported) or 'imperialism' by another name (and thus to be opposed)? Liberals were often to be found campaigning for non-intervention in crises that involved massive abuse of human rights and loss of life.

After the end of the Cold War it had seemed as though liberalism had conquered the last of the great totalitarian ideologies that had challenged and warped twentieth-century history. There appeared to be no realistic alternative to liberal-capitalist democracy as the most effective form of creating and maintaining freedom, progress and social and intellectual achievement and improving the material standards of living of the majority of mankind. However, this confidence was to be succeeded by some loss of faith.

The stubborn problems of the past, like crime, ignorance and poverty, seemed ineradicable, and new problems, such as illegal drugs and environmental degradation, did not seem remediable by either classical or social liberalism. Indeed, liberal ideas of 'liberty' appeared to be increasingly taken by many people to mean 'licence', a lack of restraint, a lack of moderation and self-respect, as well as lacking the central liberal value of respect for the rights of others.

Liberalism, as a distinct ideological movement, continued to be squeezed by both conservatism and social democracy. Politicians of both the right and the left plundered liberalism for ideas and made them their own, leaving a prominent question mark over what modern liberalism was meant to represent: what did it stand for? Some liberals lapse into an almost conservative dependence on the past in their hope of the survival of liberalism. Others pursue radical policies of state intervention and higher taxation that make it difficult for the observer to distinguish them from socialists.

Nevertheless, such doubts and worries over the nature and future of liberalism are to be expected. Liberalism has always had a capacity for self-analysis and adaptability. One can assume that liberalism will continue to be a major influence on the future development of human society on a global scale: 'In the West, by and large, we are all liberals now. Instead of ignoring or affecting to deplore this, we should be recognising and reaffirming it. Or else, you never know, it might one day no longer be true.'[4]

Summary

Liberalism now appears to be the universal ideology, its assumptions being almost automatically accepted – certainly in the West. Liberalism had its origins in the seventeenth century, developed in the eighteenth and flowered in the nineteenth, when 'classical liberalism' emerged. By the early twentieth century liberal doctrines were subject to considerable revision and 'new liberalism' emerged. There are several themes of central importance to the individual and his/her rights. The prime duty of government is to defend these rights. Liberals have an optimistic view of human nature, the future and the possibility of progress. Freedom is highly esteemed, while the state is viewed with some suspicion as a potential threat to individual freedom. Institutional arrangements to restrain the state are therefore necessary; and the rule of the mob is as dangerous a threat as any tyrant. Private property and a market economy are efficient from an economic perspective, although at the same time may undermine other liberties. Furthermore, while national independence is generally 'good', liberals favour an international approach to foreign affairs and reject imperialism. Although liberalism may be said to have vanquished its main opponents, fascism and communism, in the twentieth century, it has not been without its critics. A market economy does not necessarily produce social justice. Liberalism has not so far provided very satisfactory answers to problems such as crime, poverty, terrorism and environmental destruction. Nevertheless, liberalism has, more than any other ideology, a built-in capacity for self-criticism and change that augurs well for its future.

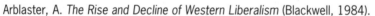

REFERENCES AND FURTHER READING

1 T. H. Green, *Lectures on the Principles of Political Obligation* (1879–80).
2 J. S. Mill, *On Liberty* (1859).
3 J. Locke, *The Second Treatise of Government* (1690).
4 'Liberalism Defined: The Perils of Complacency', *The Economist* (21 December 1996), pp. 19–21.

Arblaster, A. *The Rise and Decline of Western Liberalism* (Blackwell, 1984).
Beer, S. 'The Roots of New Labour: Liberalism Rediscovered', *Economist* (7 February 1998), pp. 23–5.
Bellamy, R. *Liberalism and Modern Society: An Historical Argument* (Polity Press, 1992).
Bellamy, R. 'Liberalism', in R. Eatwell and A. Wright (eds.), *Contemporary Political Ideologies* (Pinter, 1993), pp. 23–49.
Eccleshall, R. *British Liberalism: Liberal Thought from the 1640s to 1980* (Longman, 1986).
Eccleshall, R. 'Liberalism', in R. Eccleshall *et al.*, *Political Ideologies: An Introduction* (Routledge, 1996), pp. 28–59.
'Liberalism Defined: The Perils of Complacency', *The Economist* (21 December 1996), pp. 19–21.
Goodwin, B. 'Liberalism', in B. Goodwin, *Using Political Ideas* (John Wiley and Sons, 2001), pp. 35–63.
Gray, J. *Liberalism* (Open University Press, 1995).
Heywood, A. 'Liberalism', in A. Heywood, *Political Ideologies: An Introduction* (Macmillan, 1992), pp. 24–65.
Leach, R. 'Liberalism', in R. Leach, *British Political Ideologies* (Philip Allen, 1991), pp. 54–87.
Manning, D. J. *Modern Ideologies: Liberalism* (Dent, 1976).
Vincent, A. 'Liberalism', in A. Vincent, *Modern Political Ideologies* (Blackwell, 1996), pp. 22–54.

SAMPLE QUESTIONS

1 How would you characterise the role of the state in liberalism? Is it always perceived as the enemy of freedom?

2 Is liberalism fundamentally mistaken in allocating a central role to the individual in its social and political theory?

3 How true is it to say that liberalism is now the 'dominant ideology' in the Western world and globally?

4 'The liberal obsession has been the fear of the all-powerful state; but the real threat to freedom is now elsewhere.' Do you agree?

5 'Once used to defend individual liberties, liberalism has become the ideology of powerful business interests that most threaten individual freedom in a capitalist society.' Discuss.

Socialism   11

Here we explore socialism – an ideology that, uniquely, sprang from the industrial revolution and the experience of the class that was its product, the working class. Though a more coherent ideology than conservatism, socialism has several markedly different strands. In order to appreciate these, and the roots of socialism in a concrete historical experience, we explore its origins and development in the last two centuries in some depth, giving particular attention to the British Labour Party. We conclude with some reflections on 'Blairism' and the 'Third Way', and the possible future of socialism as an ideology.

POINTS TO CONSIDER

➤ Does the assertion that socialism is the product of specific historical circumstances cast doubt on its claims to universal validity?

➤ Is utopian socialism mere daydreaming?

➤ Which is the more important of socialism's claims: justice or efficiency?

➤ Does common ownership equate with state ownership?

➤ Do socialists mean more by equality than liberals do?

➤ Is socialism in Britain simply what the Labour Party does?

➤ Is there a future for socialism?

The general diffusion of manufacturers throughout a country generates a new character in its inhabitants; and as this character is formed upon a principle quite unfavourable to individual or general happiness, it will produce the most lamentable and permanent evils, unless the tendency be counteracted by legislative interference and direction. (Robert Owen, *Observations on the Effects of the Manufacturing System*, 1815)

(T)he difference is that the enemy is more subtle and stealthy than before. Capitalism remains the oppressor it has always been, but the inequality and humiliation which used to stare out at you at every street corner is now harder to see, even possible to miss altogether. (A delegate at the Labour Party Annual Conference, 1973)

Like liberalism and conservatism, socialism was a nineteenth-century development with its roots in the eighteenth century and even earlier. It grew up with **industrialisation** and urbanisation, a process that was under way in Britain by the 1750s and spread to Western Europe during the early part of the 1800s. This process created the modern factory system (which is only now beginning to disappear in the industrialised West) and generated new industrial and manufacturing classes and elites, and, most important for socialism, the modern industrial working class. Out of this working class arose trade unions, building societies, co-operatives, all influenced by socialism, the ideology of the working classes.

> **industrialisation**
> The process of developing increased output of manufactured goods by the application of technology and capital resources. It involves a massive reform of all social, economic, cultural and ideological structures in society.

Any political movement or ideology requires a group in society to which it can appeal. Socialism without industrialisation, without a working class, was essentially a utopian or idealistic movement. Without a collectivist or class doctrine it would have essentially been an ideological wing of radical liberalism. To reiterate: it was nineteenth-century capitalist industrialisation that created the working class and socialism.

From its very beginnings socialism was a many-faceted ideology, one that can be roughly divided into four main types, all of which have been influenced by idealist or 'utopian' socialism:
- social reformism or social democracy;
- Marxism or Marxism–Leninism;
- anarchism;
- Third World socialism.

All these movements would call themselves 'socialist'; all criticise liberal capitalism; all desire social change to improve the lot of the mass of the population. However, they are often involved in bitter ideological argument with each other. Socialism is the most self-consciously *ideological* of the major political movements. Theory and ideas are essential to an analysis of capitalist society and how it might be replaced or at least reformed. As a consequence it has a tendency to fragment into competing ideological groups, each claiming the 'truth', each based on the 'correct' interpretations of key texts.

The experience of these socialist strains in changing society is varied. In most Western societies socialism or social reformism has rarely held political power for long. However, it has greatly influenced Western European political culture and may be considered a major element of the dominant ideologies in those societies, as it is closely associated with welfare states, Keynesian economic management and a culture of social and political rights. While it constitutes a class analysis of society social reformism offers high levels of personal freedom aided by state action and state institutions.

Socialism of the Marxist strain was connected with the communist states of Eastern Europe, the USSR and the People's Republic of China (PRC). It stressed egalitarian values more than individual freedom. State power was used to strengthen these values as a stage towards the achievement of communism. All too often state socialism tended to stress the 'state', rather than 'socialism', and oppressed the working classes more than the capitalism it replaced. The opponents of social democracy in the West tended to envisage Marxist socialism as the kind that social-democratic parties were planning to introduce.

Anarchism is confined to the fringes of politics and socialist movements. It is dismissed as largely an irrelevance in complex Western societies, confined to 'eccentrics', 'drop outs', and the like. However, it offers an often-powerful critique of state power.

Third World socialist states have attempted to create a form of socialism without a working class or the industrialism that goes with it. Such states have usually become associated with poverty, backwardness and failure. There is a strong current of nationalism and anti-colonialism in this form of socialism.

We concentrate here on social reformism, also known as 'revisionist socialism', 'social democracy' and 'democratic socialism'. In particular, we look at the British version of socialism in the form of the Labour Party. Marxist and anarchist contributions to socialism will be discussed in Chapter 12. Third World socialism is usually a variation of one of the three other versions adapted, with varying degrees of commitment and success, to non-industrialised societies.

Defining socialism

Perhaps more than most political philosophies, socialism resists easy definitione, chiefly because of the wide range of theorists, writers and activists who have claimed (or have been accorded) the title 'socialist'. Confusion has been compounded by the eagerness with which many 'socialists' have denounced the beliefs and actions of other 'socialists' as a betrayal of the faith.

It could, however, be argued that there are at least two fundamental points on which all socialists agree, and which distinguish all the many varieties of socialism from other ideologies. First is their attitude to property. For socialists the structure of property ownership in a capitalist society at any given time is radically unsatisfactory. Property, at least *productive* property rather than personal possessions, should be redistributed, not to individuals but rather to some form of communal or collective ownership.

The second feature is that socialism offers a *class analysis* of society arising out of the relationships between social groups as a consequence of the unequal distribution of property ownership. Financial inequality and the unequal opportunities open to people as a consequence of their position in the capitalist class structure are seen as fundamentally unjust and should be reformed in favour of greater social equality.

Admittedly, even this definition does not entirely suffice to cover the extensive rethinking of socialism in very recent times, but it forms a useful starting point.

Divisions within socialism

From the outset there were major divisions within socialism. One obvious source of division concerned the end product: what sort of society ought to replace the existing system? While this might seem an obvious question, in fact the main dispute within socialism, the basic faultline, was the issue of *how* a new society might be brought about.

Utopian and revolutionary socialism

Early nineteenth-century socialists may be divided into 'utopian' and 'revolutionary' socialists.

Utopians believed that moral argument, reason and action *within* the existing order constituted the way forward. They spoke in the name of reason and natural rights, but they still had a mystical belief in change. Hence, for example, the visionary schemes of Charles Fourier in France, who argued for the creation of associations and planned co-operatives; and as another instance, the founding of 'communes' by Robert Owen in Britain and America as an alternative to capitalist systems of production and ways of living.

Revolutionary socialists, such as Karl Marx, dismissed these schemes as pipe dreams. Only the violent overthrow of the state, the tool of the capitalist class to oppress the workers, would make possible the creation of a socialist society.

While revolutionary attitudes dominated the middle part of the nineteenth century the slow evolution of at least a degree of democracy through the extension of the franchise, and slow but steadily rising living standards for the workers, led to the emergence of 'revisionism'.

Revisionist and revolutionary socialism

The revisionist view of socialism was that the state was more or less neutral and that socialists could gain control of it by peaceful, constitutional means by contesting elections and ultimately being voted into power. Once in government they would enact socialism via the normal legal processes. These ideas developed out of the German Social Democratic Party from the middle of the century.

An important figure here was Eduard Bernstein, who joined the SDP in 1872 and soon became one of its leading journalists. In *Evolutionary Socialism* (1898) he argued for reform through parliamentary action, rather than by revolution, as the basis for a socialist party. He believed that Marx's predictions of revolution were simply wrong. Working-class movements, such as trade unions, offered a means to achieve real gains for workers without revolution or some form of 'proletarian dictatorship'. Despite Bismarck's anti-socialist laws the SDP's vote continued to grow, thus showing that a democratic means to socialism had developed. Revolution was redundant.

The socialist Second International (1889–1914) was dominated by rows between supporters of revolutionary and revisionist roads to socialism. Marx and Engels opposed Bernstein's revisionist views of socialism and called for his resignation from the SDP and the Second International. They disliked intensely his claims that Marxism was irrelevant and a nuisance to socialist development. To revolutionary socialists revisionism – or 'reformism' – failed to grasp the essentially exploitative nature of capitalism and the capitalist state. They believed that capitalism could not be reformed. At best it would only make sufficient concessions to ensure the continuation of capitalist power.

While during the nineteenth and much of the twentieth century the main conflicts were over alternative 'roads to socialism', by the late twentieth century socialists were increasingly questioning what the ultimate destination should be. Revisionism, first applied to the means of gaining power, was now applied to what should be done with that power once it was achieved.

Continental and British socialism

Socialists have historically been anxious to stress the international nature of the movement and the universal applicability of its principles. In fact, though, the various strands of socialist thought have been powerfully influenced by the historical and cultural setting in which they developed. Continental socialism evolved in a markedly different context from that of British socialism. Of particular significance were the powerful traditions of despotism, revolution and **anti-clericalism** in many European countries. British socialism, by contrast, had its own indigenous roots, its own political and economic environment

> **anti-clericalism**
>
> A feature of most leftist politics in Catholic European countries. Anti-clericalism claims that the Roman Catholic Church has too much say in politics and its role should be resisted and, eventually, eliminated.

and its own distinctive qualities. Of major importance were the traditions of constitutional government and political continuity.

British socialism has rejected Marxism as a major trend. It has been greatly influenced by revisionism and the Fabian movement of Sydney and Beatrice Webb, who regarded Owen as the founder of British socialism and preached human brotherhood rather than class war. A class analysis is certainly part of British socialism but class war is regarded as irrelevant to the solving of practical social problems. Indeed, parliamentary roads to socialism can be more effective than revolutionary means. British socialism has always considered, for example, the European socialist stress on the political general strike or activity outside the lawful political system to be illegitimate and actually counter-productive.

The close links between the Labour Party and the trade unions have undermined the role of extra-parliamentary movements for socialism. Only in recent years, under New Labour, have these links been weakened.

The Labour Party as the dominant form of socialism in Britain has close cultural links with the natural conservatism and moderate values of British society. Early nineteenth-century near-revolutionary conditions abated with mid-nineteenth-century prosperity. Marx, who believed the **Chartist** campaign for parliamentary reform had the potential for a mass revolutionary movement in the 1830s and 1840s, eventually came to see little potential for revolution in Britain. He once famously described Britain as having 'a bourgeois aristocracy, a bourgeois middle class and a bourgeois working class'.

The Labour Party steadily emerged as the major anti-Conservative party during the 1920s and 1930s. The 'safe' nature of the Labour Party was underlined by two short periods in government and, especially, by its role as a partner in the National Government during the Second World War. No charges of unpatriotic 'shirking' could be made against it when it came to power in 1945.

> **Chartism**
>
> A mass working-class movement for political reform in Britain during the 1830s and 1840s. It called for six reforms, among which were universal adult male suffrage, annual parliaments and wages for MPs.

Scientific and romantic socialism

Another tension within the socialist tradition might be identified as that between 'scientific' and 'romantic' socialism.

Scientific socialism harks back to the Enlightenment, the idea of human perfectibility and the application of human reason to the understanding and appropriate modification of human society. For this school, socialism was right because it was more *rational* and more *efficient* a means of organising society than the free market. A variant of this approach was that of the later writings of Karl Marx, where he claimed that the ultimate triumph of socialism was built into laws governing the development of human society. These laws could be uncovered by the application of scientific method and once discovered could be applied to improving society, 'nudging' historical events along to bring inevitable change forward.

Romantic socialists based their approach on a moral vision of humanity. The existing capitalist order crushed the human spirit, blighted creativity, caused poverty, misery, degradation and crime. It was deemed a fundamentally unjust system, based on selfishness, cruelty, exploitation and greed. These evils could and should be removed or mitigated. Romantic socialism, therefore, was essentially moral, its inspiration revolutionary and its appeal emotional.

Socialist themes

There are, in addition to the common views of socialists already identified, a number of major themes around which socialists build their creed, even if they do not agree on the relative importance or priority of their realisation:
  • an optimistic view of human nature;
  • a belief in some form of common ownership;
  • a commitment to equality;
  • freedom as a goal of socialism;
  • socialism and the state.

An optimistic view of human nature

Socialists of all persuasions have generally held an optimistic view of human nature. They themselves would call it *realistic*. Most people have a natural desire to help others, to be part of a common project, to be valued members of society. Man is perfectible by his own efforts. A good society is possible. Such a society will come about by greatly modifying the existing capitalist society or replacing it with one based on socialist values, however they might be defined.

The evils of war, crime, ignorance, unemployment, poverty and even disease are regarded as largely the product of capitalist economic and social arrangements.

Remove these and all would be improved. Scientific socialists can, in this sense, be regarded as heirs to the Enlightenment tradition. Romantic socialists, with their preoccupation with the soul of man, may have had a post-Enlightenment starting point but their conclusions were much the same.

Such a socialist vision has a strong ethical component, even when, in the case of scientific socialism, it purports to be based on scientifically proven fact. This moral drive comes from a belief in the essentially social nature of humanity. As we attain our 'true' humanity through social interaction, and this interaction occurs in a specific context, it is crucial that the structures in which the interaction takes place be designed to maximise human co-operation and community. Given the appropriate structures, man's instinct to co-operate will flourish and the individual will achieve his full potential. Co-operation, therefore, rather than competition, is the hallmark of a socialist society. This applies with particular force to *economic* competition.

A belief in some form of common ownership

Since co-operation is essential to human well-being, and humans are naturally co-operative, social animals, it follows that economic co-operation is crucial. Socialists criticise capitalism and the institution of private property for promoting *conflict* rather than *co-operation*. Moreover, the private ownership of productive wealth is unjust since the owner of such wealth derives personal profit from the product of the *community's* work.

Classical socialists, therefore, argue that private ownership be replaced by *collective* ownership. More moderate or revisionist socialists propose various means by which private ownership should be subject to the common good. These involve either *state* ownership of certain key industries on behalf of the whole people, or some form of worker joint ownership, or joint ownership by means of a co-operative community working together to earn a living and raise children.

A commitment to equality

It might seem from the above that socialists are committed to *full equality*, or *egalitarianism*, as one might define it. In a sense they are, but this commitment is often misrepresented. Only the most extreme versions of socialism propose that everyone should have exactly the same amount of material wealth. Most socialists assume some variations in wealth among people and, in practice, are inclined to favour *less inequality* rather than mathematically exact equality.

While they share with liberals a belief in the equal value of human beings (who should all be accorded equal rights and consideration), socialists

attribute most inequality not to differences in inherent talent, effort or responsibility, but to social factors, such as access to education, wealth and social
class. Thus unequal outcomes in education or health are due to inequalities in
starting points. Such unequal outcomes are both *unjust* and *inefficient*, since
much human capital is thereby squandered. Moreover, only in a society
founded on equality can the liberal goal of liberty be achieved.

As private property is the root cause of social inequality, socialists say that it
must be tackled as an issue. Revolutionary socialists see a need to *control* most
private property for the public good and social improvement. Revisionist
socialists, on the other hand, seek not the abolition of private property but the
application of measures, most notably by the tax system and public spending,
to *redistribute* wealth in society along more equitable lines.

Freedom as a goal of socialism

Liberals defend the freedom of the individual to pursue his or her own
interests, trusting in the 'hidden hand' for the overall amelioration of society.
Socialists, however, believe that the deep inequality and poverty created by
capitalism mean that society cannot be free until the economic system is transformed. To them such a society will have a 'hidden elbow' as the poor, the
weak and the working classes are pushed to one side. Their freedom will be
infringed, if not removed altogether, by untrammelled capitalism and the
minimal state.

Hence, to ensure increased *real* freedom for the majority of the people, the
freedom of the few may need to be curbed and institutions set in place to help
people realise their potential as individuals. This may involve the outright
removal of capitalism or its reform, including state-provided education, health
services and benefit systems.

Socialism and the state

It is a widespread misconception that socialism's commitment to the
collective ownership of property equates with *state* ownership, and that the
state therefore plays a very positive role in
socialist thinking. In fact, there have historically
been many attitudes towards the state within
the socialist tradition. The equation of state
ownership and collectivism was dominant only
from the late nineteenth to the late twentieth
century and even then it was never complete.
For example, many early twentieth-century
British socialists thought **nationalisation** would
just replace oppressive private capitalists with

nationalisation
The taking into state ownership
of major industries to be
managed for the public good
rather than private profit. In
Britain during the late 1940s
this involved the nationalisation
of the coal, steel, railway,
water, electricity and gas
industries.

even more powerful oppressive state employers. Indeed, it could be argued that in the twenty-first century Western social democrats are moving away from state ownership as rapidly as conservatives are. Nevertheless, it is true that some versions of socialism present state ownership as the absolute and defining truth, denouncing all deviation from this as a gross betrayal of fundamentals.

Broadly speaking, socialists have held three contrasting attitudes to the state. One is that the state is essentially irrelevant. The people, especially the working class, must construct socialism. Another view is that the state is an enemy, the tool of the oppressing classes that must be smashed by force for any real socialist advance to be made. Thirdly, there is the belief that the state can be captured and turned to the positive benefit of the people.

During the early nineteenth century, prior to the existence of states with universal suffrage and respect for civil rights, and when the working class was but a small minority of the population, revolutionary socialism aiming at the overthrow of the state predominated. The dismal failure of revolutionary action throughout Europe during 1848–9, the widening of the franchise and extensive social reform in countries such as Britain, even state provision of welfare benefits like pensions as in Germany, led many socialists to a fundamental reappraisal of the role of the state. Some, such as Bernstein in Germany and the Fabians in Britain, concluded that the state could be adapted to a very positive role if socialist parties acquired power by constitutional means.

This belief reached its apogee in Britain during and just after the Second World War. State planning helped to defeat Britain's enemies and could, it was believed, win the war against ignorance, poverty and want at home. Social reformism was the dominant ideology throughout most of the post-war era. Recently, though, socialist thought in Britain and in the Western world has lost confidence in state ownership as a panacea.

The early history of socialism

Although most critics have argued that the term 'socialist' can be applied only to critiques of capitalist society, some have seen the genesis of socialism in Plato and even Moses. Others have seen radical socialism in the declarations made by the leaders of peasant revolts in England in the 1380s or Germany in the 1520s. There may even be a plausible case for the origins of British socialism to be found in Thomas More's *Utopia* (1516) or in the activities of Gerrard Winstanley and the Diggers in the mid-seventeenth century. For our purposes, however, modern socialism can be said to have originated in the early nineteenth century as a response to two major historical events, the French Revolution (1789) and the industrial revolution from the mid-eighteenth century onwards.

The French Revolution overturned the existing political order and thrust such concepts as the rights of man and values such as equality and fraternity to the forefront of political discourse. Such was the perceived threat to the established order from British radicalism that it was ruthlessly suppressed by the authorities during and after the Revolutionary and Napoleonic Wars (1792–1815). However, radical ideas remained to fertilise the development of socialism in Britain.

The industrial revolution produced, as we have observed, new economic and social structures – a new class system – based on capitalism. These structures nullified in practice the values espoused by the French Revolution. Industrialisation was characterised by injustice, inequality, suffering and degradation for the vast majority of the population. It was this state of affairs that early socialists tried to confront and turn to good.

Socialism before the Labour Party

We have already seen some ways in which British socialism differs from its European counterparts. We will now study its development in somewhat more detail.

Utopian socialism

Utopian socialism (so-called by Marx to distinguish it from his own scientific socialism) emerged in the backwash of the French Revolutionary and Napoleonic Wars and the steady spread of the industrial revolution in Europe. In continental Europe the most notable figures were Charles Fourier and his schemes for new associations, and Claude, Comte de Saint-Simon, who believed industrialisation could be harnessed by engineers and technicians to modernise society for the benefit of all.

In Britain it was Robert Owen who played a crucial role. Owen's socialist career began with his development of the New Lanark cotton mill in Scotland into a model factory and community (after 1800). He believed that people could be changed if society was changed. Owen subsequently developed ideas for other ideal communities based on the co-operative principle and when these received little support in Britain he set one up at New Harmony in America (1824–29). Later in Britain he promoted a wide range of organisations, such as trade unions, co-operative societies and friendly societies. Crucially, Owen's socialism depended not on the state but on voluntary action. Most of these initiatives proved stillborn and, apart from the Christian Socialists, who urged moral revival rather than institutional reform, the utopian socialist movement in Britain faded. The nascent trade-union movement, which Owen once thought would play an important role in socialist development, concentrated on improving working conditions *within* the existing capitalist framework, rather than on changing the whole of society.

British Marxism and William Morris

Marx spent much of his time in England. His ideas were largely based on an analysis of the capitalist system in England and he borrowed many of his concepts from British economists, such as Adam Smith and David Ricardo. However, Marx's ideas had little impact in Britain until the worsening economic circumstances of the 1880s led to the creation by the wealthy eccentric H. M. Hyndman of the Social Democratic Federation (1884), a tiny and unorthodox Marxist faction which came to nothing.

A more significant figure was William Morris, who was much influenced by the art critic John Ruskin. Ruskin argued that the 'bad' art which he thought characteristic of the nineteenth century was the product of a bad society. Morris, himself an artist, craftsman and poet, further refined these notions, believing that all human beings were essentially creative. The exploitative capitalist system and its associated industrial production methods stifled this creative urge. Originally a member of Hyndman's SDF, Morris soon left to found the Socialist League (1884). In his extensive writings, such as *News from Nowhere* (1891), Morris tried to propagate his beliefs, though without any discernible impact on the politics of the day.

Ethical socialism

Another tributary flowing into the broader current of British socialism was 'ethical socialism'. In part derived from an interpretation of Christianity, in part a quasi-religion in its own right, ethical socialism had considerable influence on the New Trade Unionism, which was developing in the 1890s, and subsequently on the Labour Party, founded in 1900. Important figures were the pioneer Labour leader, Keir Hardie, and Robert Blatchford and John Bruce-Glasier. Although ethical socialism had little intellectual content it nevertheless combined romantic socialism with Fabian gradualness and legality.

Ethical socialism stressed a strong commitment to social justice and the better distribution of economic and other rewards in society – to reduce inequality, not actually to create equality. There is little here about abolishing capitalism, only reforming it. Justice and freedom are as important in this strain of British socialism as in any other. Indeed, British socialism derives its inspiration from some of the New Liberal thinkers of the late nineteenth and early twentieth centuries, while shading into Fabian socialism.

Fabianism

Perhaps the most distinctively British contribution to socialist thought was that of the Fabians. The Fabians took their name from the Roman general Fabius Maximus Cunctator who fought Hannibal with what today would be described as guerrilla tactics. Founded in 1884, the Fabian Society was essentially a group of intellectuals with a keen interest in social reform.

Sidney and Beatrice Webb, Graham Wallas and George Bernard Shaw elaborated Fabian ideas. They argued that there was an identity in class interest between the middle classes and the working classes, both of which were exploited by the few 'idle rich' who lived off the rent on land or capital. Moreover, socialism was seen to be emerging as a reality, with the steady advance of collectivist institutions, notably local government bodies. Socialism would be advanced not by the setting up of a socialist party, still less a working-class socialist party, but by permeating society in general with socialist arguments founded on irrefutable, factual and, especially, statistical evidence. The Fabians envisaged that in a future socialist society a major role would be played by an enlightened, uncorrupted and highly efficient civil service. The Fabians could claim to be the 'wave of the future', as such a civil service was already emerging. Simultaneously, even the Liberal Party was moving towards state provision of pensions, while local authorities were increasingly providing utilities like gas and electricity, public transport, and amenities like parks, swimming baths and libraries.

> **pacifism**
> The belief that violence in any cause is morally wrong and should not be resorted to in order to pursue political goals in domestic or foreign policy. Pacifism is particularly associated with religious movements such as the Quakers.

The Labour Party: a very British socialism

Utopian socialism, Marxism, nonconformist Christianity, class struggle, trade unionism, Fabianism, vegetarianism, **pacifism** and New Liberalism all contributed to the development of British socialism in the form of the Labour Party. The Labour Party is one of the least ideological socialist parties in Europe but, arguably, one that has changed its society the most.

The formation of the Labour Party

The formation of the Labour Representation Committee in 1900 led to the creation of the Labour Party in 1901, which was to prove of the utmost importance for the development of British socialism. Its initial inspiration was not, however, socialism but 'labourism' – that is, the promotion of the interests of the working class, especially the male, skilled working class, by vigorous trade-union action.

Although the trade unions were developing rapidly at the end of the nineteenth century, with the emergence of large unions composed of unskilled workers, they were badly hit by an adverse court decision in the Taff Vale Case (1901). A railway company sued a union for damages caused to its business when its employees went on strike. The court's decision in favour of the company undermined the entire legal basis on which trade unionism had operated for decades, so the unions were anxious for legislation to redefine their legal position. Moreover, while the unions had tended to support the Liberal Party, even sponsoring some Liberal parliamentary candidates in working-class areas, the intellectual baggage and social composition of the Liberal Party were not unambiguously on the side of the unions.

The initial aim of the Labour Party was to secure the return of working-class and trade-union men to the House of Commons. The party's name and its complex structure, which incorporated trade unions and socialist societies, like the Fabians, clearly proclaimed its identity.

Before the First World War the Labour Party enjoyed some electoral success – by 1914 it had forty-two MPs. By 1918 the situation had been transformed. The Liberals had split in 1916 over the formation of a wartime coalition government with the Conservatives. In 1918 the franchise had been extended to include most men and women. Finally, the party adopted a new constitution whose famous Clause IV committed it:

> To secure for the worker by hand or brain the full fruits of their industry and the most equitable distribution thereof that may be possible upon the basis of common ownership of the means of production, distribution and exchange and the best obtainable system of popular administration and control of each industry or service.

This could only mean socialism, but the exact form of socialism remained unclear.

Labour in office: the 1920s and 1930s

Labour came to office in 1924 and again in 1929–31. In both cases it was a minority government. The first term, on the face of it, achieved nothing. The second ended in apparent disaster when Labour Party leader Ramsay Macdonald split the party by joining a **coalition government** dominated by the Conservatives in response to the world economic slump and financial crisis.

coalition government
A government made up of two or more different political parties or groups. The National governments of 1931–35 and 1940–45 were coalition governments.

These two periods of office were, however, not as futile as might first appear. Under Macdonald the party established that it had the capacity to govern, moved further away from Marxism, and decisively committed itself to the 'parliamentary road' to socialism, especially after the abortive General Strike (1926).

Intellectually, there was considerable activity. 'Syndicalism', the doctrine that the working class could and should seize power by a 'general strike' prompted by the unions, was increasingly attractive as an industrial road to socialism. Syndicalism had been popular on the fringes of the movement but was decisively rejected.

Ramsay Macdonald made some contribution to socialist thought, arguing, for example, in *The Socialist Movement* (1911), that socialism was in a sense a *conservative* creed in that it aimed at moving society back to its natural path of evolutionary social integration, a path temporarily blocked by capitalism.

G. D. H. Cole advocated 'guild socialism', in which each individual industry would be run by the workers in a co-operative system, the whole being co-ordinated by the state. In *Guild Socialism Restated* (1920) Cole helped guild socialism to become a major element in socialist theory in the early twentieth century. He believed that it would strengthen democracy and resist the capitalist treatment of workers as a commodity.

The most significant thinker, however, was R. H. Tawney. Tawney based his socialism on Christian ethics. In *The Acquisitive Society* (1921) and *Equality* (1931), as well as in many public lectures, he emphasised community, co-operation, service, duties – rather than rights – in a way that has interesting echoes in attitudes displayed by Tony Blair in recent years.

Nevertheless, advocates were still to be heard for the radical transformation of society, one of the most important of whom was Harold Laski. In *Democracy in Crisis* (1933) Laski argued that capitalism still controlled the state and would prevent the realisation of democracy and socialism unless a radical Labour Government used whatever methods were necessary to overcome capitalist resistance and to introduce socialism. Such methods might include emergency powers and a radical departure from traditional constitutional means.

Labour in power: 1945–51

In 1945 Labour swept to power with an unprecedented majority. It was in a position for the first time to embark on a genuinely democratic socialist programme. Events during the war had had a profound influence on Labour. Labour was part of the wartime coalition government. Its leader, Clement Attlee, was deputy prime minister. Other senior Labour figures held important Cabinet posts and dealt with real and pressing problems, demonstrating judgement and competence.

The war effort had involved state control and planning on a huge scale, establishing a general consensus that state wartime planning could successfully be applied to peacetime problems. Once more, the general sense of optimism and of 'no turning back' to the evils of the twenties and thirties boosted Labour's confidence. Already before the war, the National Government had introduced a number of welfare reforms, which culminated in the Beveridge Report (1942) on which Labour based its 'welfare state', a 'cradle to grave' protection of the citizen by the state. Keynesian theories of Demand Management to regulate levels of employment in the economy were now part of the conventional wisdom of both government and governed.

The government was also determined to 'nationalise' major industries and utilities. These would be organised into state-owned public corporations, run in the 'national interest' as a hard-headed, practical form of socialism, as distinct from the unrealistic dreams of syndicalists and guild socialists.

In many ways the government was extraordinarily successful. Unemployment did not recur, as it had after the First World War. A National Health Service was established. Major industries, coal, steel, shipbuilding and railways, were taken into public ownership. A host of social reforms accompanied these remarkable achievements, all accomplished in spite of the material and financial devastation created by war and the perceived threat from Soviet communism.

Paradoxically, though, Labour's style of socialism was beginning to decline in the moment of its apparent triumph. Planning proved inefficient, over-bureaucratic and less appropriate for the goals of peace than it had been in wartime. Added to the acute economic problems of the post-war world were rationing, shortages and a general feeling of overbearing officialdom. Nationalisation became less and less popular, even among workers in the state corporations, and the welfare state became steadily more expensive, with the bulk of the tax burden to pay for it resting on working-class people.

By 1951 Labour was widely perceived as an exhausted government. Many of its ministers had been in government for ten years through war and post-war reconstruction. Nevertheless, the Conservatives only just won the election. They were to stay in power for thirteen years.

Labour in opposition and in government: 1951–79

During these years Labour was riven by tensions between the 'democratic socialists' who wanted to press on along the road Labour had taken in 1945, and the 'social democrats' who hoped Labour's goals might be achieved by another route. This was no mere intellectual debate. At all points, electoral considerations were fundamental.

Anthony Crosland made an important contribution to the debate. In *The Future of Socialism* (1956) his revisionist thesis stressed that the essence of socialism was the ends not the means. Crosland argued that capitalism had changed radically. Ownership was irrelevant since the typical business enterprise was now a corporation run by managers concerned with the long-term success of the company. Owners were essentially passive share-holders. Such firms were a positive benefit to socialism. Their profits were ploughed back into businesses, improving efficiency and raising living standards. Full employment would eliminate the exploitation of the workforce since workers could choose whom to work for and competition would eliminate the exploitation of consumers. Such wealth-producing enterprises could contribute to social improvement by making possible the provision of welfare benefits and the reduction of inequality by redistribution and progressive taxation.

These ideas had a seismic impact on the Labour Party. The right-wing 'social democrats' seized on them enthusiastically, while the left wing rejected them. Rows over the direction for the Labour Party were to contribute to Labour's successive electoral defeats in the 1950s.

In spite of these tensions Labour was returned to power in 1964 (and again in 1966) under Harold Wilson. Intellectually, these proved sterile years. Wilson and several Labour leaders were later to produce memoirs, diaries and analyses of their Labour Government, although they rarely discussed the nature of British socialism. Indeed, many Labour supporters were deeply disillusioned by Labour's failures to manage the economy successfully or extend socialism in society.

Labour returned to power in 1974 with a considerably more left-wing agenda, but with very little in the way of a mandate from the voters to carry it out and almost no commitment to it by the Labour leadership. It did increase welfare spending and take over some failing industries, notably British Leyland in 1975, but it was soon overwhelmed by the world economic recession that gathered pace after 1973. Inflation and unemployment rose. The Labour Government cut public spending; social conflicts, especially strikes, multiplied. The social-democratic approach appeared bankrupt. Keynesian economic management techniques no longer worked and the inherent conflict between high taxation (for welfare and wealth redistribution) and economic efficiency became clearly evident.

Labour in opposition again: 1979–97

After losing power to the Conservatives in 1979 Labour had once again to face internal sectional conflicts. The result was the defection of a substantial part of the right wing of the party to the newly formed Social Democrats in 1981; and on the left there was a revival of 'classical socialism', tinged with Marxism. The ideological civil war in the Labour Party, which was to contribute to its being out of power for eighteen years, was exacerbated by rows over nuclear disarmament and Europe.

The re-emergence of classical socialism was already under way during the 1970s. It became closely identified with Tony Benn, who campaigned energetically for it in the Labour Party. Benn's ideas were propounded in *Arguments for Socialism* (1980) and *Arguments for Democracy* (1981). For Benn, socialism and democracy were two sides of the same coin. He argued for full-blooded Clause IV socialism, a radical foreign and defence policy, wealth distribution and democratisation, especially of the Labour Party itself. This last was implemented in the new arrangements for the election of the leader in 1981. The Labour manifesto for the 1983 general election was so radically socialist that one senior Labour politician described it as 'the longest suicide note in history'.

After the crushing defeat that followed, the party leader, Michael Foot, resigned and was replaced by Neil Kinnock. Despite his leftist reputation, Kinnock began the process of reform by purging Militant supporters. Although the party was mindful of electoral considerations (but still defeated in 1987 and 1992) there was a strong ideological rethink under Kinnock and his immediate successor John Smith, and at an accelerated pace under Tony Blair (who became leader in 1994 on Smith's death).

Symbolic of these reforms was the abolition of Clause IV at the 1995 party conference. The new Clause IV was considerably longer than the 1918 version, and less dignified in its language. It described the Labour Party as a 'democratic socialist party', but its essence was to commit the party to:

> work for a dynamic economy, serving the public interest, in which the enterprise of the market and the rigour of competition are joined with the forces of partnership and co-operation to produce the wealth the nation needs and the opportunity for all to work and prosper, with a thriving private sector and high quality public services, where those undertakings essential to the public good are either owned by the public or accountable to them.

'New Labour', as it liked to be called, had clearly moved a long way from classical socialism. The question remained, where was it moving to? Politically, New Labour was far more a party of the centre than of the left. Beyond that it was difficult to tell.

To make sense of New Labour, it needs to be set in both a global and a domestic context. On the global stage, the collapse of Soviet communism in the late 1980s and early 1990s sounded the death-knell of the command economy as a viable alternative to capitalism. The term 'globalisation' suggests that the nation-state no longer had a sufficient power base to control its own economy or even effectively to influence global economic forces. There were important consequences for all forms of state regulation, but especially taxation, interest rates, exchange rates, subsidies and, ultimately, welfare benefits. The power of international markets was clearly illustrated by Britain's forced withdrawal from the European Exchange Rate Mechanism in

September 1992 (membership of which had been a key plank of the government's economic policy) – a policy debacle from which, politically, the Conservative Government never really recovered. Globalisation was reinforced at an institutional level by such bodies as the World Trade Organisation, the International Monetary Fund and the World Bank, all of which are designed to ensure the effective running of the global capitalist economy. Socialist parties were thus confronted by acute social problems. Most have been forced into some sort of accommodation with the global market system, dominated by the arch capitalist power, the USA.

Domestically, British society has been transformed over the last twenty years. Old industries, coal, steel, shipbuilding, heavy industry, large factories, the bedrock of Labour's traditional voting strength, have largely disappeared. As a result, the power of trade unions has declined, especially after they suffered a number of spectacular defeats during the early 1980s at the hands of the Thatcher Government. New industries arose, especially in new technology areas and the service sector, with little unionisation and very little sense of class solidarity among the workers. Indeed, the class system was radically altered and with it the nation's voting patterns. Most of the population could be described as 'middle class' by the 1990s. Property ownership had grown: houses, cars, shares, private pensions were all more widespread than previously. Voters increasingly perceived their lives in personal terms, rather than as members of a group. Individual choice, responsibility and advancement became the prevailing aspirations of a majority of the population. An appeal to simple class resentment or class solidarity would not garner the votes Labour needed to win power again.

It was these changes that Tony Blair sought to address. Perhaps the most surprising influence on him was Margaret Thatcher. She astutely exploited the changes in society that were weakening the skilled working class's traditional commitment to Labour. Labour was associated with high taxes and apparent over-generous support for the work-shy, and Mrs Thatcher persuaded enough workers to vote Conservative to win several elections. Blair admired her challenge to entrenched vested interests and encouragement of an enterprising and dynamic society. For Blair, though, Thatcherism was inadequate. There were still powerful interests to curb – hence his commitment to 'modernisation' in the face of the 'forces of conservatism', few of which seemed to be in the Conservative Party itself. Mrs Thatcher's antipathy to the state led her to under-estimate its positive economic value in promoting, for example, 'education, education, education' (Blair's three top priorities as identified during the 1997 general election). Worst of all, Thatcher had ignored the social and cultural impact of globalisation and competition and the consequent destruction of communities, families, social stability and moral values.

'Blairism' and the 'Third Way'

Unless one accepts Herbert Morrison's definition, 'Socialism is whatever a Labour Government does', one might argue that under the leadership of Tony Blair the Labour Party has finally cut its bonds with the form of socialism established in 1918, and has become more of a social liberal party. One could claim that there is no distinctive New Labour or 'Blairite' ideology at all, merely an intellectual black hole attracting any passing fad. Is it merely 'conservatism with a human face', a 'nice' form of Thatcherism, which is electorally highly successful but intellectually and ideologically completely barren?

Alternately a more positive interpretation can be maintained. While Blair is in no way an 'old Clause IV' socialist, his 'Third Way' is genuinely based on socialist tradition and enriched by contemporary socialist thought.

Blair certainly accepts the economic and social changes of the last two decades. He even welcomes them. What he does not accept are the ethics of selfishness and greed associated with them. In this, Blair consciously reaches back to the Christian and ethical socialism of the nineteenth century, later expounded by R. H. Tawney and others. The focus is on community – the world, the nation, the local area and the family. These naturally co-operative entities should be strengthened by a sympathetic state. This 'communitarian' approach is clearly evident in Blair's rhetoric. It emphasises duties rather than rights, a 'stakeholder capitalism' in which all have an interest in a successful market economy, 'one-nation socialism', where economic efficiency is married to 'fairness', the sovereignty of the people, and the benefit of the many rather than the few.

In so far as these slogans translate into policy, there has been a number of radical measures, for example a general toughening up on tackling crime. Welfare has moved towards 'handups', rather than 'handouts'. 'Prudence' has characterised economic management, with a very cautious approach to public spending (now redefined as 'public investment'). More specifically, there has been a policy of partnership of the state with private capital in, for example, Education Action Zones and the Public–Private Partnership to finance hospital building, the London Underground and air traffic control. In 2001 there was much talk of expanding the role of 'faith communities' (churches and religious groups) in education and welfare, with state backing. At the same time the participation by the people has been enhanced by constitutional reform, especially devolution in Wales, Scotland and Northern Ireland.

The question arises, is this in any meaningful sense, other than Morrison's, 'socialism'? Certainly, there is a role for the state as regulator, enabler and deliverer of social guidance, but not as *owner*. Equality is proclaimed but it is the equality of the 'level playing field': that is, equality of opportunity rather than equality of outcome. Redistribution of wealth via the tax and welfare system has had only modest support. The emphasis has been on bettering the lot of the poor by full employment, a dynamic economy and compulsory training rather than state handouts. There has been occasional reference to the 'stakeholder' society, though this has been interpreted as to do with promoting private pension schemes rather than retaining the meaning first given to the term by Will Hutton in his book *The State We're In* (1995). In his view, it was not merely the shareholders who had a 'stake' in a business, but employees, customers and the wider national community. This reality, therefore, should have 'institutional recognition'.

If this is socialism, it is socialism of a highly modified variety. Critics of Blairism (who are not confined to the left of Labour) assert that this simply isn't socialism, and whatever its merits, it shouldn't pretend to be so.

Blair has spoken much of citizenship and the value of a caring and responsible community. Not surprisingly Robert Putnam, whose book *Bowling Alone: The Collapse and Revival of American Community* (2001), deplores the decline of community in the USA, was rewarded with a personal audience with Tony Blair.

Socialism outside the Labour Party

Labour has not always been avowedly a socialist party. Some critics have disputed its claim to the title and many more would dispute its socialist credentials today. For socialism this may be an advantage. It can be argued that socialism has been released from the constraints of its association with the Labour Party, in much the same way as the demise of the Soviet Union has liberated Marxism. For example, some, like the Socialist Philosophers Group, have tried to reconcile socialism with the market economy. Others, such as Alisdair MacIntyre and Michael Sandel, have stressed the over-arching importance of the 'public good'. The difficulty here is that such concepts might logically be aligned with the liberal or conservative tradition; or else they might be reduced to mere platitudes so anodyne that virtually no one could disagree with them.

More positively, it could be maintained that socialist ideas and values have migrated elsewhere, possibly to the Green Party and the ecology movement, or even outside conventional politics. Here, suitably modified, they may yet prove fruitful sources of intellectual and moral challenge and political action.

A socialist future?

The end of the Soviet Union and the apparent triumph of liberal capitalism appear to have marked the end of socialism as an experiment in state power and pose a major challenge to social democracy in the West. Conservatives have pronounced socialism discredited and capitalism vindicated, but one might reflect that such announcements are premature.

Western voters appear deeply committed to the main planks of the welfare state as they have been described over the past half-century or so. The state institutions created to deliver social-democratic priorities such as health, welfare, education and benefit payment are stubbornly popular. Opinion polls regularly show people's willingness to pay higher taxes to improve public services. Globalisation and free markets are not automatically seen as the boon to mankind that they claim to be.

According to many opinion polls in the West, voters are strongly in favour of state planning and state ownership of key services such as electricity, water, the railways, gas, and so on. Continuing of global poverty and growing inequalities at home and abroad demonstrate that all is not well in the new liberal capitalist world.

Capitalism may, once again, be dominant in the world, but there are many people willing to challenge its moral validity and efficiency. Socialism, married to other movements such as ecologism and feminism, may yet prove an effective challenge to the dominance of the market and offer a rallying call for opponents of capitalism.

Summary

Socialism is very much a product of the industrial revolution and the class to which it gave birth, the industrial working class. While socialism has many competing branches, all agree that the existing structure of property ownership is unsatisfactory. Furthermore, socialism presents a 'class analysis' of society based on property ownership. Socialism contains many divisions – the main area of dispute being how a socialist society could be achieved. Utopian socialists believed that society could be transformed by peaceful processes. Revolutionary socialists advocated the violent overthrow of the state by the working class. Revisionist socialists declared that social change was possible by working within the existing political order. The values espoused by socialists include common ownership and social equality. Human nature is regarded as moulded by social structures. Attitudes to the state vary from outright hostility to the more positive view of the revisionist school, which believed the state could be turned to good. This latter view powerfully influenced the British Labour Party, drawing on an indigenous socialist tradition. Labour held office for a number of periods during the twentieth century and broadly implemented a socialist programme. By the 1990s, and after a long period out of office, the Labour Party reinvented itself as 'New Labour' with a more centrist and less socialist programme for government.

FURTHER READING

Berki, R. N. *Modern Ideology: SOCIALISM* (J. M. Dent, 1975).

Callaghan, J. *Socialism in Britain since 1884* (Blackwell, 1990).

Geoghegan, V. 'Socialism', in R. Eccleshall *et al.*, *Political Ideologies: An introduction* (Routledge, 1994), pp. 91–117.

Goodwin, B. 'Socialism', in B. Goodwin, *Using Political Ideas* (John Wiley and Sons, 2001), pp. 97–119.

Heywood, A. 'Socialism', in A. Heywood, *Political Ideologies: An Introduction* (Macmillan, 1998), pp. 103–51.

Leach, R. 'Labourism and Socialism', in R. Leach, *British Political Ideologies* (Philip Allan, 1991), pp. 117–49.

Lichtheim, G. *A Short History of Socialism* (Fontana/Collins, 1977).

Sassoon, D. *One Hundred Years of Socialism* (Fontana, 1997).

Vincent, A. 'Socialism', in A. Vincent, *Modern Political Ideologies* (Blackwell, 1996), pp. 84–113.

Wright, A. *British Socialism* (Longman, 1983).

Wright, A. *Socialisms: Theories and Practices* (Oxford University Press, 1987).

Wright, A. 'Social Democracy and Democratic Socialism', in R. Eatwell and A. Wright (eds.), *Contemporary Political Ideologies* (Pinter, 1993), pp. 78–99.

SAMPLE QUESTIONS

1 In what sense is socialism uniquely a class ideology?

2 Are the differences between revolutionary and revisionist socialism greater than the factors which unite them?

3 What does it mean to say socialism is about 'equality'?

4 How socialist is 'Blairism'?

5 'Revolutionary socialism does not achieve liberty; revisionist socialism does not achieve equality.' Discuss.

Marxism and anarchism

12

Although Marxism and even anarchism are sometimes treated as if they are simply varieties of socialism, we consider that they have sufficiently distinctive characteristics to warrant separate treatment. Starting with Marxism, we examine Marx's theories of history, economics and politics before discussing the controversies within Marx-inspired political organisations in the nineteenth century, particularly the challenge mounted to orthodox Marxism by the 'revisionist' school.

We then analyse twentieth-century attempts to establish concrete political systems claiming 'Marxist' legitimacy, with particular attention to the rise and fall of the Soviet Union. Finally we examine attempts to reinterpret Marxism to make it relevant to twenty-first-century social and economic conditions. Turning to the wide-ranging form of political thought known as anarchism, we discuss anarchist views of human nature, the state, liberty and equality, and economic life. The chapter ends with a critique of anarchism and some thoughts as to its relevance to modern politics.

POINTS TO CONSIDER

➤ Is Marxism correct in identifying class as the most important form of social identity and 'class struggle' as the driving force of history?

➤ Does the importance of theory in Marxism undermine its potential for political action against capitalism by stimulating intra-Marxist strife and the proliferation of Marxist movements?

➤ Has Marxism's association with oppressive communist regimes in, say, the Soviet Union been damaging to its professed role as a liberating movement for the working classes? Or is Marxism inherently oppressive?

➤ Are we too precipitate in dismissing anarchism's analysis of the oppressive nature of the state?

➤ Has anarchism's importance as a political movement been undermined by its over-concentration on theory and its neglect of practical measures for reforming society?

The history of all hitherto existing society is the history of class struggles.

Freeman and slave, patrician and plebeian, lord and serf, guild master and journeyman, in a word, oppressor and oppressed, stood in constant opposition to one another, carried on an uninterrupted, now hidden, now open fight, a fight that each time ended either in a revolutionary reconstitution of society at large or in the common ruin of the contending classes. (Karl Marx and Friedrich Engels, *The Communist Manifesto*, 1848)

No conception of anarchism is further from the truth than that which regards it as an extreme form of democracy. Democracy advocates the sovereignty of the people. anarchism advocates the sovereignty of the person. (George Woodcock, *Anarchism*, 1962)

Revolutions have never lightened the burden of tyranny, they have only shifted it to another shoulder. (George Bernard Shaw, *Man and Superman*, 1903)

Marxism and anarchism are very important parts of the socialist tradition but they differ so significantly from democratic socialism and social democracy as to be worth studying as distinct ideological movements.

The collapse of the USSR and its empire in Eastern Europe during 1989–91 is often hailed by Western conservatives as vindicating their belief that Marxism is a failed ideological system, unrealistic and of no value as a political movement or an ideological tool. However, for many Western Marxists the demise of the USSR removed an oppressive and corrupt form of Marxism that held back its potential as an anti-capitalist movement. They claim that Marxism remains a perceptive critique of capitalism and its class system – a critique that has, they believe, increasing value in the modern 'globalised' economy of multi-national businesses and international financial markets.

Anarchism in Northern Europe and the USA has always been a minor strain of socialism, though in Spain, Italy and France it has been very influential within both trade unions and socialist politics. Anarchism's anti-state analysis has much value. Particularly interesting and important is anarchism's critique of capitalism, social democracy and Marxism as state-oriented ideologies doomed to create and maintain political and economic systems that are fundamentally oppressive of the human spirit and its potential.

Marxism

It is usual to regard 'Marxism' as a branch of socialism, but we have chosen to deal with it separately for a number of reasons:

- Marxism constitutes by far the most internally consistent of socialist theories and forms an all-embracing ideology.

- Although Marxists have sometimes suggested that their brand of socialism is uniquely valuable and authentic, there is, in fact, much more to the socialist tradition, especially in England.
- The major divide in socialist thought is between evolutionary and revolutionary socialism: Marxism is the obvious example of the latter.
- Marxism has had, for good or ill, a greater impact on human history than other strands of socialism, notably in the emergence in the twentieth century of the self-styled 'socialist' states of the Soviet Union, China, Cuba and Eastern Europe.
- Karl Marx, who after all gave his name to the ideology, rather disliked the term 'socialism', which he associated with daydreaming and impracticality. From *The Communist Manifesto* (1848) to his final writings, Marx preferred the word 'communist' with its unambiguously revolutionary connotations.

As the term suggests, it is customary to regard Karl Marx as the only begetter of Marxism. It is worth mentioning, though, that most Marxists attribute a major influence on the development of his theory to his friend, patron and collaborator, Friedrich Engels. Some have even detected nuances of difference between the views of Marx and Engels, especially concerning the alleged 'scientific' basis of Marxism. Some argue that much of what we now describe as 'Marxism' was largely created by Engels's writings *after* the death of his friend.

Although German, Marx spent most of his life in exile in England, after having been identified by the authorities in his homeland, denounced as a threat to public order and forced to flee. He devoted himself full-time to writing, revolutionary agitation and political organisation. Marx's ideas made a substantial impact on nineteenth-century European political thought and in the twentieth century they profoundly influenced the course of world history.

By then, however, the processes of systematisation and reinterpretation by professed followers, such as Karl Kautsky and Georg Plekhanov, had arguably led to much distortion of the original message. Further distortions of Marxism were made by Lenin, Stalin, Mao and other Marxist revolutionaries during the twentieth century. The emergence of powerful totalitarian regimes, such as the Soviet Union and Communist China, which claimed Marxist legitimacy on the grounds that they were more authentic, exacerbated the process of reinterpretation.

Marx himself revised his ideas considerably over time. His earlier writings, for example, reveal a more humane, even liberal, Marx than the narrow determinist of his later years. Moreover, the prestige accorded to Marx by some of his followers led to his words being accorded the status of sacred scripture, rather than debatable propositions. Thus Marxism's claim to be a 'scientific' analysis of society was somewhat weakened, to Marx's irritation. He once famously asserted that if some of the latest ideas being described as 'Marxist' were indeed such, 'I am not a Marxist'.

Marx's ideas on historical development

It has been observed that Marxism is essentially a mixture of German Hegelian philosophy, English liberal political economy and French revolutionary politics. Marx emphasised the practical functions of his theories when, in his *Theses on Feuerbach* (1845), he said: 'The philosophers have only *interpreted* the world in various ways; the point, however, is to *change* it.'[1]

Marx believed he had uncovered the laws governing human society by empirical, scientific investigation. The modern capitalist industrial society was emerging in Britain (especially in Manchester) during his lifetime. Britain was by far the most advanced capitalist society on earth. Industrialisation and the class system it spawned were the most developed in Europe. These economic and social trends would, Marx argued, be repeated in other industrialising countries in Europe and in the USA.

Marx's starting point was the German idealist philosopher G. W. F. Hegel. According to Hegel, history was a process of self-realisation and unfolding by the 'World Spirit'. It proceeded through conflict ('dialectic') between a given state of affairs ('thesis'), which produced its opposite ('anti-thesis'), a conflict resolved in a higher state ('synthesis'), which in turn becomes another 'thesis', and so on. This mode of thinking is particularly alien to the Anglo-Saxon mind, to which Marx's drastic remoulding of Hegel's theory is somewhat more congenial, if still rather too theoretical and revolutionary for most Britons and Americans.

History was Marx's preoccupation as well as Hegel's but Marx held to a materialist theory in which the material conditions of human existence were fundamental, and which determined all other facets of life, such as philosophy, religion, art, culture and politics.

In Marx's scheme of things each successive stage of history rested on economic foundations, called the 'substructure'. Marx asserted that all humans must first earn a living and that all societies must therefore rest upon some system of wealth production. Thus the 'mode of production' played a key role. The mode of production was not just the type of technology prevalent at each stage but the associated economic system with its attendant social and cultural 'superstructure'. Art, culture, ideology, politics, family structure and the rest all belong to the superstructure and change with the economic sub-structure.

The dynamic that drove human history onwards was the disfunction, or 'contradiction', within each mode of production. Each mode had its own definitive stage, which Marx identified in *The German Ideology* (1846) as 'primitive communism', 'slavery', 'feudalism' and 'capitalism'. Each, apart from primitive communism, had a characteristic class system. As each mode developed, antagonism between the classes grew. In political terms, this class war always culminated in violent revolution. Thus the French Revolution (1789) was essentially a class struggle between serf and landowner in which the feudal system, established in the Middle Ages, was challenged and overthrown by the emerging capitalist system. In class terms, the **bourgeoisie** (the capitalist owners of the new means of production) emerged as the new ruling class who were soon engaged in class war with the *proletariat* (the newly created industrial working class).

> **bourgeoisie**
>
> Originally the French word for 'town dweller' it has come to mean 'middle class'. In Marxist terminology it refers to the owners of productive wealth, the ruling class in capitalist society.

It is important to realise that by 'class' Marx meant not social status as conferred by occupation, education or culture, but relationship to the means of production (specifically, the ownership or non-ownership of productive property). At the time Marx was writing, the bourgeoisie owned all the means of production – factories, banks, shops. The proletariat owned nothing. Conflict between the two classes was growing, driving history forward, and, Marx believed, would culminate in the violent overthrow of the capitalist class by the working class (the 'grave-digger' of capitalism) and the emergence of 'socialism'.

Under socialism, property would be collectively owned, class would disappear and with it class conflict and the state, which was a crucial actor in this struggle. Socialism would then evolve peacefully into 'communism', a barely imaginable utopia, characterised by material and cultural abundance and an end to conflict, war, crime and all the miseries of the ages. Even if suffering, sickness and death remained, humanity would be equipped, scientifically, economically and politically, to at least ameliorate the worst of these afflictions of mankind.

Marxist economics

Much of the plausibility of Marxism derives from its economic theories which, supported by considerable statistical data, gave an apparently solid, down-to-earth basis to its more abstruse philosophical dimensions. The most impressive manifestation of his work is Marx's multi-volume *Capital* (Volume I: 1867, Volume II: 1885, Volume III: 1893–94), a magnificent, if now largely unread, early example of social science research.

Marx held to the 'labour theory of value'. That is, the value of goods or services was not based on the interplay of *supply* and *demand* in a free market but on the amount of labour, physical and intellectual, invested in their production. The proletariat provided this investment, but they did not receive the full value of their labour, because capitalists creamed off a substantial part of the profits (known as 'surplus value'). In effect, the workers were robbed by their employers.

Factory conditions further dehumanised the proletariat, who were oppressed not only physically but even spiritually by being *alienated* from the objects of their labour (which they did not own and whose production brought them no creative satisfaction) and from the society which created these conditions.

Even worse, the position of the proletariat would deteriorate, if not absolutely then relatively, since the capitalist system was inherently very unstable. Competition between capitalists increased the exploitation of the proletariat as it drove down wages and extended working hours to maintain profits. Alternatively, capitalists would combine in monopolies that pushed up prices. Society would be *polarised* into rich and poor, with growing class conflict.

The worst aspect of the capitalist system was its inevitable tendency to produce more than could be sold in an economic boom ('a crisis of overproduction'), causing regular slumps of ever-increasing severity, length and unpredictability. The polarisation of society would intensify, the misery of the proletariat would grow and class conflict would become ever more intense.

Eventually, the proletariat would shed its illusions (which Marx described as 'false consciousness'). Those illusions were political, moral, religious and cultural beliefs and values held by the working class but benefiting only the capitalists. Perceiving, at last, its own real interests the proletariat would organise itself and fight back through militant trade unionism. Finally, the proletariat would overthrow its oppressors by violent revolution. Towards the end of his life, however, Marx modified his position somewhat to allow for the possibility of a *peaceful* revolution.

Marxist politics

Marxist politics followed logically from Marxist historical theory and economics. The aim was to promote a proletarian revolution, which would overthrow the bourgeois state (run in the interests of the capitalist class) and usher in socialism (and a state run by and for the workers). For Marx, the contemporary liberal state was a class instrument, the means by which the bourgeoisie maintained its privileges and oppressed the proletariat. In strictly limited circumstances, as in the France of Emperor Napoleon III (1848–71), a balance of social forces could allow the state to develop something of a life of its own and hold the ring between conflicting classes. However, to Marx the state rarely maintained a role as a 'referee'. The slightest challenge from the proletariat would cause the mask of neutrality to slip from the face of the bourgeois state, revealing the ugly reality of class power underpinning it.

Marx believed that the capitalist system would undergo a series of revolutionary crises that would create a revolutionary situation and cause the overthrow of the bourgeois state. A temporary 'dictatorship of the proletariat' would establish itself to secure the revolution and govern in the interests of all the people. This proletarian state would soon 'wither away' as the new society, having no class conflicts, had no need for state instruments of bourgeois class repression, such as the army, the judiciary and the police. The new society would be communist, a society of harmony, prosperity and peace.

Marxism in the nineteenth century

Many commentators have pointed out that Marx was quintessentially a figure of the nineteenth century. Critics have claimed that Marx's relevance to later historical periods is seriously limited, as his analysis is specific to mid-nineteenth-century industrialisation.

Clearly, Marxism owed much of its impact to its effective blending of many elements of nineteenth-century culture: science, the belief in progress, the revolutionary and romantic traditions and a powerful moral critique of the industrial revolution and the civilisation derived from it. Moreover, Marxism was a *European* creed and strongly influenced socialist movements and thinkers across that continent. It provided the framework of language and ideas within which most socialist thought developed from the 1870s onward. It is important to realise that there was, and is, no one united Marxist party. There were many parties, groups and factions among which ferocious quarrels of interpretation and reinterpretation soon began. The German Social Democratic Party (SDP), the largest and most significant socialist party in Europe by the 1870s, was divided over 'revisionism', which was a reworking of Marxism associated with Eduard Bernstein. He argued that a socialist society could be brought about without violent revolution by political action within the existing framework of the Imperial German Constitution, a policy formally adopted by the SDP in its *Gotha Programme* (1875).

Attempts were made to hold the major Marxist and socialist parties together by means of international organisations. The International Working Men's Association (known also as the First International, 1864–76) fell apart because of tensions between Marxists and anarchists. The Second International (1889–1914) was divided by rows between revolutionary and revisionist socialists. These attempts at unity finally collapsed when most European socialist parties chose to support their individual national governments at the outbreak of the First World War. Contrary to the socialist belief that international working-class solidarity would halt a European war by calling a universal 'general strike', the events of 1914 demonstrated the superior hold of nationalism over socialism as an ideology in the hearts and minds of the working class.

Thus Marxism entered the twentieth century divided and has remained so to the present day, the doctrinal divisions over 'true' Marxism usually being sharpened by nationalism and national rivalries.

Marxism in the twentieth century: 1914–53

By far the most successful branch of Marxism in the early twentieth century was that associated with V. I. Lenin and the Bolshevik Party. Lenin developed Marxist thought by tailoring it to specifically Russian conditions. He led the Bolshevik Party as a revolutionary movement, seized power in 1917 and ultimately set up the world's first socialist state in 1924. This state, the Union of Soviet Socialist Republics, survived until 1991.

'Marxism-Leninism', as it was later officially styled, recognised that Russia was not economically, socially and politically advanced enough for a socialist revolution on the Marxist model. Marx had assumed that such a revolution would occur in the most developed capitalist societies of Western Europe and the United States. According to Lenin, historical conditions in which a 'bourgeois' revolution would precede a 'socialist' revolution by decades or even centuries could be telescoped into one dramatic event. This, as Lenin outlined in *What is to be Done?* (1902), could be accomplished if the proletariat were organised and led by a 'vanguard' of full-time, professional revolutionaries, highly disciplined and of sufficient commitment and intellectual calibre to devise and carry out an appropriate strategy. In Lenin's view, expounded in *Imperialism: The Highest Stage of Capitalism* (1916), revolution in the West had been temporarily postponed because the leading capitalist powers had exported the most acute forms of exploitation to their colonies and 'semi-colonies', such as Russia.

The collapse of the Tsarist regime under the pressures of the First World War gave the Bolsheviks their chance. The bourgeois revolution in March 1917, led by liberals under Kerensky, overthrew the tsar but lost popular support through the new government's commitment to continue the war. Russian military collapse followed and the Bolsheviks, very much a minority party, seized their opportunity. They began to establish their regime, accepted a humiliating peace with Germany in the Treaty of Brest-Litovsk (1918), and after years of civil war founded the Soviet Union (1924). The construction of socialism could at last begin.

Marx's concept of the 'dictatorship of the proletariat' was implemented, as was Lenin's principle of strict party discipline (**democratic centralism**). Further justification of Bolshevik control was

> **democratic centralism**
> A principle of party organisation applied to the Communist Party of the Soviet Union by Lenin and later Stalin. It supposedly meant free discussion of issues until an authoritative decision was made, after which dissent was not tolerated. In practice, it was a cloak for dictatorship and the suppression of opposing points of view.

based on the claim of the party's particular status as the vanguard of the working class. Because of the very real danger of internal 'counter-revolution' a dictatorship was set up, complete with all the apparatus of tyranny: secret police, censorship, control of the media and the suppression of all possible sources of opposition.

Stalin, Lenin's successor, consolidated this system and emerged as absolute dictator. He liquidated all critics within the party, including most Old Bolsheviks, notably Leon Trotsky, in a series of purges known as the 'Great Terror'. Trotsky had argued for a vigorous export of socialism to capitalist countries. Stalin, however, stressed the importance, as his slogan stated, of 'socialism in one country', and in a series of Five-Year Plans set about a massive programme of industrialisation. Military expansion was also undertaken to protect the Soviet Union from its capitalist and fascist enemies.

The creation and apparent success of the USSR meant that, with few exceptions, Marxism was effectively the same thing as Soviet communism. This process reached its zenith by about 1950. By this time the USSR had become a military and industrial superpower, the rival of the USA. It had overcome the Nazi invasion (1941–45) and had used the Red Army and compliant local communists to impose its ideology on Eastern Europe. Marxist parties throughout the world looked to the Soviet Union for inspiration and guidance. Some, like China, had their own communist revolution, and powerful communist parties emerged in Western countries like Italy and France.

The seeming success of Soviet communism, reinforced by intense propaganda at home and abroad, stifled criticism among Marxists and presented other socialist parties with a major problem. To what extent was the Soviet Union an exemplar for socialists everywhere? Some, such as the British socialist George Orwell, would have none of it. He denounced Soviet tyranny in uncompromising language in articles and novels. Others, notably the Communist Party of Great Britain (CPGB), were far less condemnatory until the 1950s. The more pro-Soviet elements on the left and outside the CPGB became known as 'fellow travellers'.

Marxism in the twentieth century: 1953–2000

Cracks appeared in the Soviet hegemony after the death of Stalin (1953). His successor, Nikita Khrushchev, denounced Stalin's 'cult of personality' and other excesses, to the Twentieth Party Congress (1956), raising the hope of a more 'liberal' communism in Eastern Europe. A wave of disillusion swept through Western communist parties, exacerbated by the violent Soviet repression of the Hungarian Revolution (November 1956). Later Soviet actions in Czechoslovakia (1968), Poland (1979–80) and Afghanistan (1979) drove many Western communist parties to distance themselves from Russia and to modify their own ideologies in a more 'Eurocommunist' direction. The Italian, Spanish and French communist parties particularly stressed an ideological distancing from the Soviet party, emphasising individual as well as class rights and accepting parliamentary 'roads to communism'.

The People's Republic of China under Mao Zedong, meanwhile, had gone its own way after the death of Stalin. In Mao's view revolutionary movements need not come from the industrial working class. They could be initiated by the peasants in non-industrial societies and create socialism in line with their class needs. This was an analysis particularly attractive to Marxist and revolutionary movements in developing countries, fighting colonialism and imperialism. By the early 1960s there was an open split between the Soviet and the Chinese communists over ideology and strategy.

Marxist groups elsewhere progressively withdrew from the Soviet model. Paradoxically, some of these groups became more significant the further they moved away from Soviet Communism, as exemplified in the multiplicity of Marxist groups involved in the revolutionary upheavals in Paris in 1968. In the Third World, orthodox communist parties were either crushed by the state, as in Indonesia in the 1960s, or evolved along lines of their own, as in Yugoslavia, North Korea and Albania.

During the 1980s, change had begun in the USSR itself when Mikhail Gorbachev became leader. He attempted to reform the system by 'glasnost' ('openness') and 'perestroika' ('modernisation'). This sent shock waves through the communist world, leading rapidly to the demise of pro-Soviet communist regimes in Eastern Europe. Communism then collapsed in the Soviet Union itself and the USSR fell apart under the pressure of long-suppressed nationalisms. It was dissolved in December 1991, giving birth to fifteen independent states.

At present only Cuba and North Korea can be regarded as old-style communist states. China purports to remain true to the faith but it is very definitely 'communism with Chinese business characteristics'. One wonders how long the booming capitalist nature of the Chinese economy, and the new social groups it has generated, can be squared with the democratic centralism of the Chinese party.

Marxism in the twenty-first century

The collapse of Soviet communism caused many people to believe that Marxism itself would shortly be extinct: it had obviously failed. On the other hand, some Marxists rejoiced. Marxism was now liberated from its association with totalitarian regimes, both in theory and in practice, as well as in the popular mind. Already in the 1960s and 1970s some continental theorists, like

Georg Lukács and Louis Althusser, had attempted to reform Marxist theory. They softened the harsh features of the later Marx by stressing his pre-1848 writings which were less 'scientific' and more humanistic.

Of particular interest was Herbert Marcuse, who had considerable influence on the radical student movements of the 1960s. According to Marcuse, the capitalist class maintained its grip by absorbing into the system any opposition it could not crush: a strategy Marcuse called **repressive tolerance**. The working class was thus rendered impotent by means of material prosperity and trashy popular culture, which were orchestrated by the capitalist mass media. Indeed, most social insti-tutions conspired in this invisible oppression, including schools, universities, churches, trade unions and the family. Only those excluded from the system could be expected even to dream of challenging it. Such elements included students, ethnic minorities and others on the fringes of society. Marcuse's analysis held a particular attraction for young people, since he associated economic and political liber-ation with cultural and sexual freedom. By the 1990s, however, his influence had waned as economic crises within the capitalist system and the triumph of consumer capitalism undermined the revolutionary potential of the very groups he had identified as the new revolutionaries.

> **repressive tolerance**
> A term coined by Herbert Marcuse in the 1960s to describe the way in which Western democracies contained and manipulated dissent, thus preserving the power of the privileged.

More conventional leftist politics, at least in Britain, was conducted by a new plethora of small, quarrelsome groups such as the Socialist Party of Great Britain, the Socialist Workers' Party, the Workers' Revolutionary Party, the Socialist Labour League, the Communist Party of Great Britain and the Communist Party of Great Britain (Marxist-Leninist). Few of these had much impact. Most of their energies were consumed in constant splits, regroupings, purges and reorganisations. Some of them contested 'bourgeois' elections but gained derisory support.

An exception to this was Militant Tendency, a group that infiltrated the Labour Party in the 1970s and early 1980s under the guise of promoting a newspaper, the *Militant*. They gained control of Liverpool City Council and a number of Westminster MPs were said to be Militants. After bitter struggles in the early 1980s the Labour Party eventually proscribed Militant and its membership, purging them from the party and paving the way for the decidedly reformist 'New' Labour Party of the late 1990s.

Initial hopes that the fall of the USSR would liberate Marxism from Stalinism do not appear to have been realised, as global capitalism and liberal democracy seemed to carry all before them. This very triumph has aroused radical challenges, however, as exemplified in recent years by vigorous demonstrations against globalisation at European summits and meetings of the International Monetary Fund, the World Bank and the G8 (the group of eight leading industrial economies). How far such challenges can be accurately described as 'Marxist' is questionable. One anti-capitalist demonstrator in London (May 2001) wanted to 'smash capitalism and replace it with something nicer'.

> **liberation theology**
>
> An approach to Christianity that arose in the Catholic Church, particularly in Latin America. It emphasises the political and social implications of the teachings of Jesus and often uses Marxist theory to argue for radical social reforms to improve the lot of the poor.

Marxism can be regarded as having, to some extent, escaped the narrow confines of party and state politics and as now being free to rethink its role. It influences the women's movement, social and artistic analysis, environmentalism and, in the guise of **liberation theology** in the Third World, the Christian churches.

Encouraging though this may be to some, it leaves Marxist socialism without a clear ideological programme for revolutionary change in the modern world economy, which is characterised by growing social and economic inequalities at home and abroad.

Anarchism

In popular parlance today 'anarchy' is associated with terrorist violence, disorder and naive extremism. Historically, this understanding of the term has some validity. In fact, the word is Greek in origin and means 'without a ruler'; it does not mean 'chaos'. There has been a certain ambiguity in the term as it applies to politics. One interpretation is 'without government' (or, as modern anarchists say, 'without the state'). Another interpretation, though, implies 'without laws or rules'. It is, of course, possible to envisage societies without instruments of state coercion; religious communities or Israeli *kibbutzim* offer models of these. Anarchists have been inclined to attack authority of any kind as an intolerable oppression. This applies particularly to religious authority but may even extend to science, medicine, education and the family.

Although anarchists concur in their detestation of the state they present no generally agreed definition of that term, as one might expect from anarchists. A clear grasp of their thought is further complicated by the wide disagreement among anarchists themselves on even fundamental points, conflicts that they rather relish. It is, however, customary to divide anarchists, at least for the purposes of analysis, into those whose starting point is the *individual*, such as William Godwin and Max Stirner, and those whose starting point is the *community*, such as Peter Kropotkin. Another important difference is between those anarchists who advocate violence as a crucial tactic in advancing the cause, such as Georges Sorel, and those who absolutely reject it, such as Leo Tolstoy.

Marx attacked his critics in the First International (an early attempt to create a united international revolutionary organisation), notably Michael Bakunin, as 'anarchists' for their opposition to organisation in the socialist movement. The French revolutionary Pierre-Joseph Proudhon described himself as an 'anarchist' when he proclaimed a coherent set of recognisably anarchist ideas in *What is Property?* (1840) and *The Federal Principle* (1863).

Unlike most political ideologies, anarchism has never really been put to the test of achieving power in the modern state. In the late nineteenth and early twentieth centuries, however, anarchism had some influence in Russia, France, Italy, the USA and Latin America. During the Spanish Civil War (1936–39) interesting social experiments were attempted in Catalonia and Andalusia by a strong anarchist movement. Anarchist movements, writers and communes still exist today and have some influence as profoundly radical challenges to the existing Western social and political order. Increasingly, though, anarchism is a rather marginal movement within socialism and is often associated with radical individualism rather than with socialism.

Main themes

There are a number of themes that most anarchists share, although with considerable differences in emphasis:
- human nature;
- the state;
- liberty and equality;
- economic life.

Human nature

Generally speaking anarchists have taken a highly optimistic view of human nature, seeing it as capable of almost unlimited development. However, they regard it as having been radically warped by systems of economic, political and intellectual control.

The central objective of anarchist movements, therefore, is to destroy these obstacles to human fulfilment. Exactly how this is to be done varies according to different thinkers' perspectives. William Godwin, in *An Enquiry Concerning Political Justice* (1793), observed human nature as determined by the environment but perceived human existence as the product not of nature but of reason. Rational beings were capable of individuality, but this could flourish only in conditions of freedom. Taken to its logical conclusion, this meant that almost any form of joint endeavour, even a theatrical performance, since it involved authority, direction and rules on the part of those involved, constituted an infringement of the individual's liberty.

Peter Kropotkin, in *Mutual Aid* (1897), believed that the development of human liberty and co-operation was a biological imperative. From his studies of animal and primitive human behaviour in Siberia he concluded that the Darwinian account of endless competition and conflict among species required drastic modification. In Kropotkin's view, animal species survived and developed through a process of spontaneous, natural co-operation without the equivalent of government. This idea re-emerged in late twentieth-century ecological theories and powerfully influenced the Green movement.

The state

While most ideologies have taken a positive attitude to the state, or regarded it as a necessary evil, to anarchists it is anathema since it is, by its very nature, coercive. State power is in principle, and frequently in practice, absolute. Potentially no area of life is free from the state's interference. To anarchists its taxes rob the citizen and its agents and laws oppress him.

Basically, then, the state is 'anti-human'. Its ultimate expression is war. This is not merely a critique of totalitarian states: even liberal democracies constitute a systematic oppression of individuals. Indeed, liberal and representative democracy is especially reviled as fraudulent. Democratic majorities are likely to be as tyrannical as dictatorships. Majorities can be easily manipulated by elites, who use them to impose a subtle form of social control (Marcuse's 'repressive tolerance'). From the anarchist perspective the individual has inalienable rights which cannot be transferred to a democratically elected assembly, or even infringed by the decisions of a direct democracy, which includes the active participation of all citizens.

Such radical rejection of the state raises acute problems. First, there is the practical question of how anarchists can be tolerated by a political system from which they are so deeply alienated and which they seek to overthrow. Moreover, anarchists eschew the option of political action within a democratic state – except perhaps as a means of propaganda. Anarchists do not usually participate in the democratic process to change government since their object is to destroy government altogether. The logical anarchist alternative, therefore, is the overthrow of the state by revolution. Some, like Godwin, have argued this could be by peaceful means through rational argument, while others have advocated various forms of illegal, if non-violent, direct action. Yet others, such as Georges Sorel, in *Reflections on Violence* (1905), asserted that the general strike, in which organised labour would demolish the economic and political system by refusing to work, would be an effective form of such action. Still others, following the ideas of Sergei Nechaev, go the whole way in urging outright revolutionary violence, utterly unrestrained by moral or humanitarian considerations.

Not surprisingly, this hostile attitude to the state is counter-productive since even the most liberal of regimes, when faced with a serious revolutionary threat, would take firm steps to suppress it. Even apparently innocuous inter-action with the authorities could be construed as collaboration with the detested state. On these grounds, demonstrators against capitalism in London (May Day 2001) refused to negotiate arrangements with police for an orderly march; predictably, the demonstration ended in turmoil.

Given their intense dislike of organisation, authority and discipline it is not surprising that anarchists have, with few exceptions, been unable to mobilise themselves effectively.

A further difficulty with anarchism is that although its advocates are very clear about the need to abolish the state, they are far less clear about its replacement. Anarchists of a liberal or individualist perspective argue that a system of 'market forces' would emerge in which even law enforcement would be, in effect, revenge carried out by the victims of criminals or by agents hired for that purpose. Those of a 'collectivist' inclination try to devise federations of small self-governing communities or, like Proudhon, place their faith in the emergence of a constellation of voluntary organisations, which they envisage springing up spontaneously.

Liberty and equality

Anarchism has been described as an attempt to fuse together the two main values of post-French Revolutionary thought: liberty and equality.

Both the individualist and the collectivist wings of anarchism are agreed that the state is the main enemy of liberty and its abolition is, therefore, axiomatic. The individualist wing emphasises this *negative* liberty, in other words freedom *from* state or other social coercion. The collectivist outlook stresses *positive* freedom, freedom *to* pursue positive purposes through full human development. This, it is claimed, can only occur in a social context, since our authentic goals are derived from our communal nature.

As for equality, individualist anarchists argue that this is implicit in the belief that every human being is a rational creature, capable of deciding his own best interests. Collectivist anarchists argue that all human beings have needs – physical, mental and cultural – which society ought to be constituted to fulfil, recognising equality of entitlement.

There is clearly tension between the two schools of thought, since individualist anarchists regard any attempt to determine and supply these needs by the collective action of institutions as, in itself, a threat to freedom.

Some anarchists of Christian inspiration, such as Tolstoy, argue from the premise of the equality of man before God.

Economic life

One point on which all shades of anarchist thought are united is the rejection of 'state socialism', or the **command economy**, on the old Soviet model. Beyond this point, agreement breaks down. 'Individualist anarchists', a notable American anarchist strain, emphasise the merits of a totally unregulated market economy, to supply such usually collectivised services as policing, law enforcement, defence and fire protection. Each individual can do whatever he likes with his own property and freely exchange goods and services with others. Property in this context is taken to include his life and person. In this regard individualist anarchism resembles classical liberalism pushed to an extreme position.

> **command economy**
> A system in which all economic decisions, such as wages, prices and output, are made by the state. It was a particular feature of Eastern European communist regimes.

Collectivist anarchists view this form of anarchism with utter horror. They denounce the injustice of a society in which the rich and powerful would flourish and the rest be trampled underfoot. Moreover, market transactions affect others with, for example, devastating effects on the environment and on the poor.

Collectivist anarchists begin with two assumptions: first, all wealth production is essentially social, rather than individual, involving collective effort; second, if they are to enjoy a free and full life, all individuals have needs which should be met by society.

For the achievement of these goals various models have been proposed, such as communes, co-operatives and mutual societies of all kinds, some modelled on the medieval guild system. Most of these models, however, remain at the level of vague aspirations. Nor is it clear how such a dramatic shift from existing economic arrangements could be made without catastrophic disruption to the economic system, with all that would imply for the poor – the supposed principal beneficiaries of an anarchist society.

Sub-species of anarchism

Just like other ideologies, anarchism has fragmented into numerous different and conflicting sub-groups.

One of the most important was 'mutualism'. This assumed that groups can emerge from within society to conduct trade without exploitation and thus can form the nuclei of a new society. These ideas, articulated by Proudhon, were fashionable before the First World War and spilled over into socialist, co-operative, friendly society and similar movements. Harsh reality, however, caused mutualism to lose ground to the 'anarcho-syndicalists' who later merged their ideas with a type of revolutionary trade unionism known as 'syndicalism'. Syndicalism was powerful in Britain before 1914 and in France, where it dominated the largest trade union, the CGT (Confédération Général du Travail). The key intention was to challenge and ultimately overthrow the existing order through militant trade unionism. Trade unions would channel the revolutionary aspirations of the working class into a general strike in which there would be a total withdrawal of labour by a united working class. The economies of the advanced capitalist states and their associated governmental apparatus would thereby be subverted. A new society would emerge on the basis of these syndicates, or 'workers' unions'. Notably, anarcho-syndicalism played a significant role in Spain during the Civil War (1936–39).

'Anarcho-communism' was a critique of the state capitalism that emerged in post-Revolutionary Russia among Bolshevik and non-Bolshevik socialists alike. A significant force in the period 1917–21, it was eliminated by Lenin and Stalin, though it survived as a hostile commentary on the Soviet Union in the West.

Critiques of anarchism

Many commentators have dismissed anarchism as peripheral to worthwhile political debate. Self-proclaimed anarchists manifesting their beliefs in street demonstrations are seen more as a public nuisance than a serious challenge to the status quo.

Anarchism has for many people seemed contrary to human experience. Anarchists have been unconvincing in their proposals as to how, in any society established on their principles, criminals, deviants and social misfits would be dealt with. Similarly, they have been strikingly weak in their concrete proposals for the construction of a just and efficient economic system. With doctrines that militate against any realistic application, anarchism has not only failed to change society but has never been tried.

There is, moreover, a deep-seated contradiction in that anarchism fails to reconcile the twin values of individual liberty and the common good. Even if the state were eliminated completely, experience of societies where the state has collapsed suggests that this would be followed not by utopia but by a period of chaos, swiftly succeeded by renewed tyranny. Those parts of the world where organised government has failed, such as parts of Africa and the former Yugoslavia, are scarcely evidence to support anarchist optimism for the end of the state.

There is further evidence to challenge the rosy view many anarchists have of the world of nature and primitive peoples. Kropotkin's ideas of a co-operative animal commonwealth have not been upheld by studies of animal behaviour, particularly of primates. Anthropological investigation into 'primitive' societies shows them to be riddled with superstition, cruelty, hierarchy and arbitrary power, rather than tranquil oases of 'noble savages'.

The basic premises of anarchism, it can be argued, are logically inconsistent. How, for example, could such an evil as the state have arisen in the first place if early man had, in fact, lived in a condition of innocent communistic bliss? There are ethical difficulties as well. Most people find the justifications of revolutionary violence advanced by some anarchists morally repugnant. Even advocacy of direct action by more moderate elements can be opposed as being an indefensible challenge to authority, at least in a liberal democracy. In any case, the practical outcome is always far short of an anarchist society and often enough the prelude to violence and a reaction by the authorities that erodes such liberty as already exists.

These criticisms suggest that anarchism is an ideological dead end, especially if narrowly defined. From a wider perspective, though, anarchist thought has spilled over into a whole range of political movements such as feminism, environmentalism, civil rights and challenges to globalisation. If anarchism does not provide answers, perhaps it raises some good questions, and if anarchism is but a dream, dreams are not without their value.

Summary

Marxism is rightly identified with one man, Karl Marx. Marx modified his ideas over time and other Marxist writers have contributed to the development of Marxist thought. Marx borrowed his philosophical methodology from Hegel, developing a theory of history in which the dynamic of progress was class conflict, a conflict that would ultimately result in the end of class altogether. Marx incorporated the concept of inherent conflict ('contradictions') into his theories of economics and politics. Whether or not 'socialism' could be achieved only by revolutionary means divided Marxists and democratic socialists during the late nineteenth century. The twentieth century appeared to vindicate aspects of Marxist theory. By the 1960s over one third of humanity lived under regimes that claimed to be 'Marxist'. By the early twenty-first century, however, Marxist states had almost disappeared or had drastically modified their policies. Some might question whether Marxism has much to offer today. Marxists believe it still offers a valid critique of capitalist society in the modern globalised economy. Others believe it is a failed ideology associated with failed political experiments in the USSR and elsewhere.

Anarchism is associated in popular opinion with terrorism and chaos, or with unrealistic 'utopian' politics. This perception is largely inaccurate. Most anarchists have a very optimistic view of human nature; all detest the state; some reject all authority. Anarchists have proposed alternative ways of overthrowing the state, ranging from rational persuasion to a general strike, or even violent revolution. Liberty and equality are highly esteemed by all varieties of anarchist, and all reject the Soviet model of the 'command economy' in which all economic activity is controlled by the state. About the future structure of society anarchists are vague. They favour small-scale, co-operative social and economic units. Anarchist attitudes and ideas have influenced such movements as the ecologists and still provide a critique of Western society.

REFERENCES AND FURTHER READING

1 Lewis S. Feuer, *Marx and Engles: Basic Writings on Politics and Philosophy* (Fontana, 1976), p. 286; italics in original.

Berki, R. N. *Modern Ideology: SOCIALISM* (J. M. Dent, 1975).

Bottomore T. B. and Rubel, M. *Karl Marx, Selected Writings in Sociology and Social Philosophy* (Penguin, 1974).

Femia, J. V. 'Marxism and Communism', in R. Eatwell and A. Wright (eds.), *Contemporary Political Ideologies* (Pinter, 1993), pp. 100–26.

Goodwin, B. 'Marxism' and 'Anarchism', in B. Goodwin, *Using Political Ideas* (John Wiley and Sons, 2001), pp. 65–96 and pp. 121–45.

Jennings, J. 'Anarchism', in R. Eatwell and A. Wright (eds.), *Contemporary Political Ideologies* (Pinter, 1993), pp. 127–46.

Lichtheim, G. *A Short History of Socialism* (Fontana/Collins, 1977).

MacIntyre, A. *Marxism and Christianity* (Penguin, 1971).

Vincent, A. 'Anarchism', in A. Vincent, *Modern Political Ideologies* (Blackwell, 1996), pp. 114–40.

Woodcock, G. *Anarchism* (Penguin, 1983).

Wright Mills, C. *The Marxists* (Penguin, 1975).

SAMPLE QUESTIONS

1 Write a critical appraisal of the Marxist analysis of society and politics.

2 Is Marxism an inherently revolutionary creed?

3 'A discredited and obsolete ideology.' Examine this view of Marxism.

4 How might anarchism be seen as part of the socialist tradition of politics? Is anarchism merely an extreme form of liberalism?

5 Does adherence to anarchist ideology render anarchist movements politically impotent?

6 'Anarchism is a political indulgence by the privileged, it has no relevance to the real issues involved in governing a society.' To what extent would you agree with this condemnation of anarchism?

Fascism

13

Events have made 'fascism' a term of political abuse rather than one of serious ideological analysis. Moreover, self-proclaimed fascists have claimed that fascism is beyond intellectual analysis and have despised those who favour rational examination of their beliefs. However, we take fascism seriously as an ideology by examining fascist values and the concrete actions of some of the regimes that have declared themselves fascist, notably Hitler's Germany and Mussolini's Italy. We also consider movements often described as fascist in modern Britain and elsewhere and consider whether facism is still a viable political creed.

POINTS TO CONSIDER

➤ How far do explanations of the rise of fascism cast light on its nature?

➤ What does it mean to say that fascism was essentially non-materialistic?

➤ How useful is it to distinguish Italian Fascism from German Nazism?

➤ Was fascism as hostile to international capitalism as it was to Bolshevism?

➤ Why did fascism have such little impact on Britain compared with its effect on continental European countries?

➤ Is fascism a realistic threat to modern democracies?

We have created our myth. The myth is a faith, a passion. It is not necessary for it to be a reality. It is a reality in the sense that it is a stimulus, is hope, is faith, is courage. Our myth is the nation, our myth is the greatness of the nation! And to this myth, this greatness, which we want to translate into a total reality, we subordinate everything else. (Benito Mussolini, *The Naples Speech*, 24th October 1922)

Blood mixture and the resultant drop in the racial level is the sole cause of the dying out of old cultures; for men do not perish as a result of lost wars, but by the loss of that force of resistance which is continued only in pure blood. All who are not of good race in this world are chaff. (Adolf Hitler, *Mein Kampf*, 1925)

Fascists were originally revolutionary socialists of the 1890s. By the era following the First World War fascism had acquired its modern links with radical right-wing politics. The term 'fascist' originated in the early 1920s as a self-description of the political movement in Italy led by Benito Mussolini. The word itself is generally thought to derive from the bundle of wooden rods (*fasces*) carried before Roman consuls as a sign of authority, symbolising strength in unity. The movement was initially based on the nationalist groups (*facsi*) which emerged during and after the First World War and which were largely composed of ex-servicemen and claimed to be a new political force to rejuvenate tired nations made decadent by liberalism and democracy. Indeed, it might be claimed that fascism is the only genuine twentieth-century ideology.

As an analytical term, 'fascism' has its limitations. It has become used, especially by the left, as a blanket expression of political abuse of their opponents. Moreover, the label 'fascist' has been applied to a wide variety of regimes from Pinochet's Chile to Saddam Hussain's Iraq, to the point where it becomes almost meaningless. Even before 1945 there were wide divergences in theory and practice among states generally described as fascist, such as Franco's Spain, Hitler's Germany and Mussolini's Italy. It is possible to argue that Nazism's extreme racism, for example, makes it an ideology in its own right and not merely an extreme form of fascism.

Fascists themselves have compounded the problem by emphasising, and even glorying in, its non-rational essence. A clear, authoritative, internally consistent exposition of fascist ideology simply does not exist. Besides, historical manifestations of fascism have been so tied up with the extraordinary personalities of its leaders that some critics have simply dismissed it as a vehicle for political power. Such articulation as exists was later fudged to provide a spurious intellectual justification for illegitimate power, such as Franco's fascist regime in Spain.

There is a problem caused by fascism's ambiguous relationship with both past and future. German Nazism and Italian Fascism both sought justification and inspiration in a glorious, if largely mythical, past. They challenged many of the modern world's values and assumptions, especially those proceeding from the eighteenth-century Enlightenment. At the same time they emphasised youth, energy and dynamism and made full use of available twentieth-century technology for propaganda purposes. Hitler, for example, proclaimed the excellence of traditional, rural, peasant Germany but his election campaigns made imaginative use of the then novel instruments of cinema, microphone and aircraft.

Fascism cannot be regarded as belonging to a particular historical period, even though it reached its greatest force as a movement during the 1920s and 1930s and its greatest political power in the early 1940s. Many aspects of fascist thought are alive and well in the modern world and not just in formally 'fascist' political parties.

Explanations of fascism

Faced with the difficulty of clearly articulating a comprehensive account of fascist ideology, some critics have tried to provide explanations for the emergence of fascist regimes in the inter-War period derived from cultural, historical and even psychological interpretations.

Anti-Semitism had been a feature of European culture and thought for many centuries before the Nazis adopted it as a major element of their philosophy. Fascism's roots may be found in pre-Christian German mythology, early nineteenth-century Romantic literature, and even traditional fairy tales. Italian Fascism, in particular, has been identified with artistic movements like **futurism**.

> **futurism**
> A movement in art in the early twentieth century, especially in Italy, which delighted in machines, speed, aircraft, cars and all aspects of the new century.

The nineteenth-century roots of much of what became fascist thought can be more clearly identified. G. W. F. Hegel, the great German philosopher and nationalist, was one important thinker who stressed the organic nature of the state and society. Some have drawn attention to the importance of racist theorists in the nineteenth century, such as Arthur Gobineau with his *Essay on the Inequality of Human Races* (1855) and Houston Stewart Chamberlain with his *The Foundations of the Nineteenth Century* (1899). Friedrich Nietzsche was also especially influential. He identified the importance of inequality between individuals, sexes, nations and races, the will to power of *Übermenschen* ('Supermen') who create their own morality. Fascists, especially Nazis, seized on Nietzsche's ideas of society as made up of the leader, the elite and the masses – the 'true' democracy'. The Nazis added a fourth group, the *Untermensch* ('sub-human'), parasitic on society and doomed to eradication.

Psychological explanations have also been presented, such as the interpretation of fascism as a 'mass psychosis' or the political manifestation of the 'authoritarian personality'. A particularly influential explanation has been that of Erich Fromm, in *The Fear of Freedom* (1942), that fascism proceeds from the isolation, loneliness and insecurity created in a liberal society and people's desire to end this situation by relinquishing their freedom to others.

After 1945 a fashionable explanation provided by Karl Popper and Hannah Arendt was that fascism was very similar to communism in that it also was a form of totalitarianism. This was essentially a system in which all distinctions between the state and society were obliterated and in which the state was the supreme authority, having absolute control of all forms of intellectual, cultural, economic and social activity and to which the citizen owed absolute obedience.

Although much historical analysis has concentrated on detailed biographical study of key figures such as Hitler and Mussolini, one of the most widely accepted approaches has been the Marxist view that fascism was a last-ditch stand by monopoly capitalism against its inevitable collapse. Other analysts have pointed to the extraordinary impact of the First World War on European society – the militarisation of society, the overheated patriotism and the stress on such values as self-sacrifice, obedience and dramatic action.

While these approaches all have some value they are open to challenge. Excessive reliance on psychological explanation removes the essential historical dimension. Moreover, if fascism were to be related to certain individual person-ality characteristics, it would imply particularly high concentrations of such personality types at particular times and places, which would seem absurd. Marxist explanations omit matters of race, which are surely fundamental, at least to Nazism, and provide no real explanation for the mass support enjoyed by Hitler and Mussolini. Nor is it obvious that fascist regimes in fact serve the interests of capitalism. On the contrary, both Hitler and Mussolini at various times expressed strong anti-capitalist sentiments and, of course, the 'Nazi' Party was an abbreviation for the National *Socialist* German *Workers* Party.

The most serious objection to these explanations is that they do not take fascist *ideas* seriously enough. They may tell us something of the nature of the regimes but not of the beliefs which shaped them.

Fascist ideas

We must state at the outset that, although it is difficult to present a structured account of fascist ideology there are a number of fascist *values* that inter-relate more or less logically. (Though there were marked differences between Italian Fascism and German Nazism.) It is to these factors that we now turn. They can be grouped under the following:
  • conflict, struggle and war;
  • non-materialism;

- irrationalism and anti-intellectualism;
- nation and race;
- the leader and the elite;
- the state and government;
- fascist economic and social theory.

Conflict, struggle and war

Fascism attached an astonishingly positive value to war. War was regarded as the ultimate conflict in a world in which struggle was the essence of existence. Permanent peace was not only nonsense, it was dangerous nonsense, as humans grow strong in permanent struggle and decadent in an era of peace. Modifying (or distorting) Charles Darwin's theories on the struggle for survival as the motor of the biological evolution of species, fascists claimed that human societies, like other organisms, were similarly engaged in what Herbert Spencer described as 'the survival of the fittest'. In some interpretations this *Social Darwinism* was regarded as an endorsement of untrammelled market economics. Fascists rejected such conclusions. For them the basic unit was, in the Italian Fascist case, the *nation* and, for the German Nazis, the *race*. Inequality between the peoples of the earth was an unquestioned presumption.

On these premises of inequality and the necessity and desirability of conflict, a whole moral system was erected in which the victory of the nation or race was the ultimate 'good'. In Germany this led to racial laws governing marriage, and allowing systematic racial persecution. Ultimately, the attempted **genocide** of Europe's Jews and Gypsies, and the enslavement of 'inferior' races, such as Russians and Poles, grew out of these ideological assumptions of racial struggle. In attempts to purify the German nation and return it to its original 'Aryan' purity, selective breeding and adoption programmes were inaugurated. Persons with physical or mental disabilities were sterilised or even systematically murdered.

genocide
The extermination of all members of an ethnic group, usually on the grounds of racial 'inferiority'. Usually associated with the Nazi attempt to rid Europe of Jews, Gypsies and other peoples by a process of mass murders during the Second World War.

Italian Fascism did not go to these extremes, but under German influence racial laws were introduced in the late 1930s and some collaboration with the elimination of European Jewry occurred in the latter stages of the war. Other fascist and semi-fascist regimes in Rumania, Hungary and elsewhere in Eastern Europe followed suit.

The myth of racial superiority was also used to justify German and Italian external expansion. In the case of Nazi Germany it was justified by the desire to acquire *Lebensraum* ('living space') for the German people at the expense of the 'racially inferior' Slavs. Italy sought to create a new Roman empire in Africa,

Germany sought expansion in Eastern Europe in the late 1930s, while Italy invaded Ethiopia in 1935. This, with the all-pervasive culture of militarism, aggression and conflict, was to lead directly to the Second World War.

Fascism was anti-internationalist in regard to national identity, but promoted a form of internationalism with other fascist movements involved in their own struggle against liberalism, communism and bourgeois democracy. A kind of 'fascist international' was created by Mussolini and Hitler to advance the movement against its enemies in struggles such as the Spanish Civil War (1936–39). Fascist movements gained control in several countries prior to the Second World War, most notably in Hungary, Rumania and Finland. Modern technology enables contemporary fascist movements to exchange ideas and tactics via the internet.

Non-materialism

A very important source for fascist values was 'non-materialism', the belief that materialistic values of modern 'bourgeois' society – of material comfort, security and easy living – were utterly destructive of 'traditional' society and 'higher' civilisation. For fascists, the values of war were far superior to the values of peace. These values included daring, courage, comradeship, obedience, patriotism and unswerving loyalty to leaders. Fascist doctrine can be summed up as a combining of radical nationalism, revolutionary action, authoritarianism and aggressive violent purposes.

Much of this was derived from the military experience of many fascists during the First World War, though there were important sources in cultural and artistic movements of the late nineteenth and early twentieth centuries. Another inspiration was the spiritual qualities of the countryside, nature and peasant life – the embodiment of 'true' national values – as a healthy alternative to the harsh economic and social realities of the city.

Irrationalism and anti-intellectualism

One of the difficulties of analysing fascism on an intellectual plane is the fact that fascists vigorously rejected rational analysis as the basis of a political philosophy. In this, they rejected the entire intellectual project of the European Enlightenment of the previous two hundred years. However, fascist beliefs are not beyond rational examination.

Fascists preferred, in a famous phrase, to 'think with the blood'. This meant relying on experience, intuition, emotion and action rather than reflection, faith rather than reason, trust rather than doubt, aggression rather than debate. Within this culture, in marked contrast to the liberal tradition, there was no room for dissent or debate, only conformity. Nor was conformity to be merely external. Fascism wanted minds and hearts as well. Here, it has been presciently observed, fascism was closer to a religion than to a conventional, secular political movement. This similarity was not merely confined to external trappings, such as official 'feast days', rites of passage, ceremonies of initiation, quasi-religious songs, images, rallies, and styles of art and architecture. The established churches, especially the Catholic, were uneasily aware that beneath such symbols was a value and belief system that rivalled their own. Both Mussolini and Hitler were raised as Catholics, but both rejected their church and Christianity. Mussolini was atheistic; Hitler sought to create a new religion based on pagan Germanic values. For both, Christianity was a threat both because it competed for the belief of the people and, more seriously, because it preached a doctrine of peace, humanity and fellowship clearly at odds with the core of fascist doctrines of conquest and struggle.

Nation and race

The central position of race and nation in fascist thought has already been mentioned. It is important to distinguish between the two. Race is in theory a biological fact with distinguishing features that are genetically inherited. It is thus a 'given' set of physical characteristics that cannot be changed. It does not automatically follow that a sense of racial hierarchy should lead to eugenics, euthanasia or genocide (after all, racism was a key ideological feature of the British Empire), but racial hatred was a major feature of Nazism and most modern fascist movements.

Nationality, however, is in principle a legal status. States have procedures by which one can change one's nationality. 'Nation' can also imply a sense of identification with, and belonging to, a group of people shaped by a common culture, history, language and other factors. In both cases national identity is not a permanent characteristic of a human being. It can be changed, admittedly with difficulty, but changed none the less.

Italian Fascism tended to emphasise the 'nation' as the ultimate political source of all legitimacy and an object of absolute allegiance. German Nazism, by contrast, emphasised both the *Volk* and the 'race'.

The term *Volk* means more than just 'people'. It has elements of the special spiritual and cultural qualities of a nation that should, must, be defended against all forces that would weaken and undermine its vitality. Each nation, each *Volk*, has its own special qualities, but the German *Volk* carries the seeds of a higher spiritual and cultural order, a special role in human history.

An elaborate theory of race was made the basis of state policy. According to this, humanity was sub-divided into different races, which had different and identifiable characteristics and could be placed in a hierarchical order. The highest race was the 'Aryan', of which the Germans were the nearest contemporary example (though their Aryan purity had been somewhat compromised by the admission of inferior races into their bloodline). Aryan superiority was partly physical and intellectual, but also cultural. Aryans alone were capable of originality and progress. Other races could be placed in a hierarchy, with negroes, Gypsies and aboriginal peoples at the bottom. Jews were in a special position as they could mimic Aryan qualities, but were ultimately parasitic and utterly destructive of the Aryan race. As the *First Programme of the Nazi Party* (1920) made clear: 'None but those of German blood, whatever their creed, may be members of the nation. No Jew, therefore, may be a member of the nation.' Nazi rhetoric often compared Jews to vermin or a dangerous virus. This belief was used to 'justify' the introduction of racial laws in 1933, discrimination and persecution on racial grounds, and, ultimately, the racial extermination of such enemies as an act of 'self-defence' by Aryans.

In practice, Nazi theories on race were perhaps that creed's most significant doctrine. Hitler was obsessed with it and German state policy was dominated by it before and during the Second World War, regardless of the military, practical and economic consequences. It is important to realise that in Nazi thinking their racial theories were scientifically established facts. They devoted much effort to identifying and classifying various racial groups and sub-groups according to pseudo-scientific criteria.

Italian Fascism was far less racist, acquiring a racist dimension only in 1938 when there was a need to strengthen the alliance with Nazi Germany, and racism was seen by most Italian Fascists as irrelevant and was not strictly enforced. Much greater emphasis was placed on the nation, which was identified both with the existing Italian people and the Italy of the Renaissance and Imperial Rome.

Emphasis on nation and race made the creation of any form of international political movements particularly abhorrent to fascists. International fascist movements were rather difficult to create, but were attempted nevertheless. However, had fascism triumphed in war against its enemies the tensions between such extreme nationalist movements would have come to the fore. Communism and liberalism were obvious candidates for fascist detestation, but so also was global capitalism, all on grounds of their internationalism. In Hitler's case the fact that Jewish identity transcended national boundaries, and that Jews were prominent in both communism and capitalism, was another reason to fear and hate them.

The leader and the elite

All versions of fascism despise democracy and communism for their emphasis on equality. Fascists believe that inequality of individuals, as well as of peoples, is a plain fact of nature. Political systems should take account of this – hence their belief in a ruling elite and a powerful and authoritative ruler, the 'Superman', who embodied the General Will of the people and would lead the nation to renewal and glory.

Fascist Italy and, especially, Nazi Germany rejected the former governing classes, which they blamed for their nation's misfortunes. In Italy the Fascist Party would constitute the new elite, comprised of those who had the requisite moral values. In Nazi Germany, an explicitly racial elite was to emerge in the form of the **SS**. Originally a bodyguard for Hitler, the SS was developed by its leader, Heinrich Himmler, into a military and political elite, chosen according to criteria of racial purity, to form guardians for the new Germany.

> **SS (*Schutzstaffel*)**
> Originally Hitler's bodyguard, it evolved under Heinrich Himmler into a racially elite organisation which was intended to be the ruling caste when Germany achieved victory.

Even more important than the elite was the concept of the leader. The leader would relate to the nation in an almost mystical way, personi-fying and articulating its aspirations beyond any mere constitutional status, untrammelled by legal restraint or the 'unnecessary' intermediaries of elections, parliament and the media to hold him to account.

So significant was the role of the leader, in both theory and practice, that subsequently almost any regime with a dictatorial and charismatic leader has been liable to be labelled 'fascist'. Indeed, fascist movements are so identified with their leaders that they rarely outlast in power the death of their leader. In Germany this '*Führer* principle' was applied generally to society with major concentrations of power being vested in individuals in industry, regional government, universities and central government ministries.

The state and government

Fascism is an anti-democratic and anti-individualist doctrine. Individuals are subordinate to the needs of the state and nation. It is believed in fascist theory and practice that the state should be absolute and totalitarian as the embod-iment of the nation. This entails using state terror against its opponents, a single party dictatorship and a monopoly of ideology and communication to create a perfectly co-ordinated national community and solve society's ills. Certainly, in both Germany and Italy the state acquired immense legal and practical powers, intruding into all areas of life and tolerating no opposition. However, there were differences between the two countries.

For Mussolini the state was superior to all else, even the nation itself. In fact, the Italian nation, in Italian Fascist theory (and arguably in historical reality) was the creation of the state. In Hitler's scheme of things, the state was certainly very powerful but was ultimately an instrument of the race, which preceded it in importance. The German race was by no means confined to the geographical area known as 'Germany'. Many Germans lived outside the boundaries of the German state of the 1930s. It was, therefore, Hitler's aim to bring them within the rule of the *Reich*.

Both Hitler and Mussolini assumed that the individual had meaning and value only as part of these larger and superior entities, and that true freedom was found only in the total submission of the individual to them.

Neither Nazism nor fascism had a well-developed theory of government beyond the dictatorial powers of the *Führer* or *Duce* (respectively the German and Italian for 'leader'). Technically, Germany was ruled under emergency powers granted to Hitler in March 1933 by the constitutional procedures of the Weimar Republic. Indeed, the *Führer*'s powers were assumed to transcend the normal boundaries associated with government. The ultimate law of Germany thus became the 'will of the *Führer*'. In practice, and in spite of its reputation for ruthless efficiency, historical research on the Third Reich shows it to have been disorganised, arbitrary and chaotic, riddled with disputes, ambition and petty jealousies. In fact, Hitler was a 'lazy dictator' who often stood aside from internal Nazi Party conflicts, was indecisive and delegated much authority to subordinates.

Mussolini's powers were, in reality, more constrained that Hitler's. In 1943 his party's supreme body, the 'Fascist Grand Council', overthrew him. Mussolini did, however, give some thought to a political structure to rival the discredited parliamentary system. This resulted in the 'Corporate State', an attempt to reconcile the conflicts of various groups in society (especially labour and capital) by organising 'corporations', largely based on professional or economic groups (such as doctors or vine growers), and having these represented in a deliberative body under the firm control of the state. In 1939 it replaced the Chamber of Deputies. Fascist movements elsewhere in Europe were impressed by the apparent success of Germany and Italy in conquering unemployment. How far this was a genuine attempt to create an alternative to political democracy and how far simply a cloak for Mussolini's personal power is debated. However, one must note here that the fascist principle of the supremacy of the group over the individual was clearly apparent, as *groups* rather than *individuals* were represented.

Fascist economic and social theory

For a movement that owed its popularity in large measure to the economic stresses of the inter-War period, fascism developed no very organised economic theory. Such as it was, fascist economic theory inclined towards a socialist approach, with a suspicion of and hostility to capitalism – notwithstanding the Marxist understanding of fascism as 'the ugliest face of capitalism'. The Italian Fascist Party manifesto of 1919 was emphatically socialist in context. It called for the confiscation of large landholdings, extensive public ownership and minimum wages. In part this was tactical, an attempt to wean the newly enfranchised working class away from international socialists. There is, however, more to fascist economic approaches than political opportunism.

While claiming to represent the interests of both workers and employers in the national socialist society that was being created, both Nazism and fascism eventually turned to policies which strengthened the power of employers and weakened the rights of employees. This was especially true as fascist parties sought more extensive support among the middle classes after they had largely failed to create high levels of working-class support. At the same time the power of the state to represent the whole nation and not simply factions or groups was strengthened.

Under both Hitler and Mussolini the state played a major role in the economy. Though Hitler personally had little interest in economics, his finance minister, Schacht, applied, without acknowledging it, Keynesian methods of state spending to stimulate the economy. Mussolini tried, with some degree of seriousness, to create a 'corporate state' in which specific industries were organised under state direction, so as to eliminate any potential conflict between them and the national interest, or between competing groups, especially capital and labour. In 1930 a National Council of Corporations was set up, placing workers in categories and designed to protect their interests. This was to lead Oswald Mosley, a former British cabinet minister, to abandon the Labour Party and set up the British Union of Fascists in 1932, with the goal of establishing a similar structure in Britain.

Fascist economic goals were strictly subordinated to the policy of national self-assertion. Industrialisation in Italy was encouraged to strengthen the military base. Within this general approach, the policy of 'autarchy', or self-sufficiency, played an important role. The policy, pursued with only limited success, was intended to strengthen the nation by reducing its dependence on imports and external economic forces in general.

Social policy had much the same goal. In Germany, the basic community was held to be the *Volk*, which was perceived as transcending all classes or sectional interests. The word has a racial rather than a political or socio-logical meaning. The *Volk*'s cultural, physical and moral health was of crucial importance. It was here that fascist regimes played a strong part, from material benefits to entertainment facilities, from youth movements to subsidised opera. The goal, however, was the well-being not of the *individual* but of the *nation*. Nazi social policy, for example, involved both the banning of abortion in order to expand the population and euthanasia of the mentally and some physically handicapped people in order to improve the genetic stock of the nation.

Women were to be confined to the private sphere of the home. They were subordinate to men, their proper role being to provide support for their menfolk and to produce lots of healthy workers and warriors. In that sphere they were to be honoured – and patronised – as heroines of the new fascist society.

Modern European fascism

Fascist movements in Europe were strongest from the 1920s to the early 1940s. They appeared to have been discredited and defeated by 1945. Fascist governments in Spain and Portugal survived until the 1970s, ending only with the death of General Franco (1975) in the former and a military coup in the latter (1974). But fascist movements never entirely went away; they distanced themselves from the excesses of the past, reformed and repackaged their programmes, sought respectability and new opportunities and power. Fascism in Europe today is confined strictly to the political fringe. However, elements of the above are certainly apparent in many political groupings in modern Europe and elsewhere.

A case can be made that full-blooded fascism was a temporary aberration in European history, very much of its time and place (between 1919 and 1945) and finally annihilated for ever by total defeat in the Second World War. However, one can envisage that as the memories of 1939–45 recede into the mists of time, a new and substantially modified form of fascism may yet prove a powerful political force. Primo Levi, an Italian Jewish writer and Auschwitz survivor, killed himself in 1987 partly because he observed that fascism was on the march among a new generation, a generation that did not understand the nature of a fascist regime and who were highly susceptible to the blandishments of revisionist historians who denied the **Holocaust**.

> **Holocaust**
> The systematic murder of Jews in Europe by the Nazis during the Second World War.

Many of the ingredients of fascism are demonstrable today. The collapse of communism has left a gaping economic, political and even spiritual hole in Eastern Europe. Many countries, such as France and Britain, now have sizeable ethnic minorities with evident possibilities of friction with the majority community. Dramatic economic, social and cultural change, partly the product of globalisation, has shattered old certainties, weakened traditional institutions and left many social groups uneasy and bewildered. Anti-cosmopolitanism is a major feature of modern fascist parties as it was of their inter-war predecessors, generating a rejection of the multi-cultural, multi-racial and multi-religious nature of modern Western societies.

Growing assertion of national awareness, regional identity and the development of 'minor' nationalisms in Scotland, Northern Ireland and Spain's Basque country have accompanied the evolution of the European Union. Terrorist violence and disturbing echoes of fascist style and atmosphere have been characteristic features. Virulent nationalism has exploded in former Yugoslavia and elsewhere with terrible consequences. The flood of migrants into Western Europe from Africa, Asia and Eastern Europe has provided fertile grounds for fascist-style propaganda. In many countries there seems to be growing disillusionment with liberal democracy itself as voters demonstrate low turn-out and opinion polls register deep cynicism about politicians.

The expansion of the European Union to the poorer nations of Eastern Europe may fuel fascist movements in both Western *and* Eastern Europe. Economic restructuring and job losses in inefficient agriculture and industry in the East will create poverty while stimulating population flows into the West and competition for jobs.

One interesting, and perhaps alarming, phenomenon has been the emergence of new movements with a strong emphasis on the nation, authority and discipline. The uniforms, parades and mass rallies have receded and a much slicker, television-friendly, 'reasonable' and 'unthreatening' image is presented to the electorate. Democratic processes are accepted and elections contested. Leaders wear business suits rather than military-style uniforms. Links with violent and illegal behaviour are publicly repudiated. Such movements have had some success. One example is the National Front in France.

The National Front appeals to the working classes and lower middle classes threatened by globalisation, job losses, insecurity, immigration, big business and the far left. The 1986 National Assembly elections, using proportional representation for the first and only time during the Fifth Republic, resulted in the National Front winning thirty-five seats for its 10 per cent share of the vote. By the 1997 elections the National Front's share of the vote rose to 15 per cent but won only one seat in the National Assembly, a seat from which it was later disqualified for financial irregularities. In the first round of the presidential election in April 2002 Jean-Marie Le Pen, the National Front's charismatic (if somewhat eccentric) leader, slightly increased his shared of the vote to almost 17 per cent, pushing Lionel Jospin, the Socialist candidate, out of the race altogether. Le Pen's subsequent defeat in the final vote (gaining only 18 per cent share of the vote) did not remove the impression that fascism had become a major political force in France, giving encouragement to far-right political parties across Europe. This impression was not entirely removed by the failure of the National Front to win a single seat in the 2002 elections to the National Assembly.

The Northern League and the National Alliance in Italy, and also Austria's Freedom Party, have received significant electoral support, the latter even joining Austria's coalition government in 2000. German extreme-right parties have tended to be most successful in the former communist parts of Eastern Germany, at the expense of the Christian Democrats. Finally, the anti-immigrant Lijst Fortuyn party became the second party in the Dutch parliament in the May 2002 election, following the assassination of its leader.

In the newer democracies of Eastern Europe, more blatantly fascist movements have sprung up, such as Vladimir Zhirinovsky's avowedly anti-Semitic (and curiously named) Liberal-Democratic Party in Russia. The regimes of Tudjman in Croatia and Slobodan Milosovich in Serbia during the 1990s displayed many of fascism's most appalling features, including 'ethnic cleansing'.

These developments raise the question whether fascism is in reality under-going a revival, or whether these movements, at least in Western Europe, are no more than hard-right conservative parties still fully compatible with the democratic tradition.

Overall, the prospects for revived fascism still look poor. Democratic government has been the norm in Western Europe for over half a century. Political and economic stability, rising living standards, welfare measures and full employment have dulled the edge of political controversy. Travel, television and education have produced, according to some liberals, a more tolerant and sophisticated populace. Only a very serious crisis, such as a world economic slump or a long and unsuccessful war, seems likely radically to disturb this relative domestic political tranquillity, although one might point to the 'social **apartheid**' existing in some northern English cities between white and Asian populations that erupted into violence in the summer of 2001 as evidence of a

> **apartheid**
> The system of 'separate development' of the different races of South Africa which allocated legal rights and status on the basis of race. It lasted from the late 1940s until the accession to power of Nelson Mandela in 1994.

less optimistic situation. In such a grave crisis the far right in Europe would be forced to reveal whether it is genuinely committed to the democratic process and liberal institutions or fundamentally rejects them.

Fascism in modern Britain

Prior to the 1930s, fascism in Britain was confined to a handful of tiny groupings of admirers of Mussolini's Italy. But with the formation of the British Union of Fascists (BUF) in 1932, under the leadership of Oswald Mosley, it became a significant movement. Mosley fitted the role of charismatic leader nicely. He was strikingly handsome, with an impressive military record. He had been a Conservative MP and, later, a Labour minister. Mosley was disillusioned over the failures of parliamentary democracy to tackle the severe unemployment of the 1920s and 1930s, which he attributed to a failure of free-market economics and international finance. His solution was a mixture of Keynesian spending by government on public works, a 'common market' composed of the British Empire, and a corporate state on the Italian model, with economic self-sufficiency as a major goal. Government would be dynamic and vigorously involved in society and the economy.

While Mosley assumed that the BUF would gain a parliamentary majority by constitutional and conventional means, once in power it would take extraordinary powers radically to reconstruct the political system on fascist lines. Initially, Mosley's movement was not overtly anti-Semitic, but with Hitler's successes after 1933 the BUF increasingly imitated the Nazi Party. Mosley's movement was seriously discredited (notably at a party rally at Olympia in 1934) by its violence, its attacks on Jews, communists and other opponents, and its general image of aping alien, un-English ideologies. The outbreak of war with Germany and Italy, Mosley's internment and the later revelations of Nazi bestiality finally demolished it.

After the war and a spell in prison, Mosley tried to revive his political fortunes by launching the Union Movement, which aimed at a united Europe and the expulsion of Afro-Caribbean and other immigrants. This achieved very little and Mosley became wholly marginalised.

Fascism in Britain seemed extinct. At its height it never returned even one MP (partly, of course, due to the British electoral system, but mainly because of its unpalatable political views). In 1967, however, the National Front (NF) was formed. It purveyed a strongly anti-immigrant policy, rather than the anti-Semitism of the BUF. Itself an amalgam of a complex grouping of tiny racist parties, the National Front was riven by dissension and splits, and although it caused something of a stir in the 1970s it failed disastrously in the 1979 general election. Right-wing sentiment favoured the Conservatives under Margaret Thatcher. The NF lost much support in 1979 and subsequently splintered into the NF and the British National Party in 1982.

The BNP's ideology is avowedly neo-Nazi, adapted to the British outlook. In recent years it has cloaked itself with the mantle of democracy and has enjoyed some electoral success at local level, as when it won a council seat in the Isle of Dogs in London in 1993. In reality it wants to dismantle the liberal British state and replace it with a corporatist one under an authoritarian leader. Other far-right groups indulged in some low-level terrorist activity directed against non-white Britons, leftists and gays. Groups like Combat 18 and the League of St. George have been associated with football violence and 'white' rock music and have formed links with continental far-right groups and Loyalist paramilitaries in Northern Ireland.

In 1997 the BNP put up fifty-six candidates and in ten constituencies won over one thousand votes. While it never came near winning a seat it acquired the right to a television election broadcast, received much-needed publicity in a media that largely ignores the politically extreme BNP, and won some new members to its cause.

By 2001 there were disturbing signs of a far-right revival in Britain. In the general election the BNP took 16 per cent of the vote in Oldham. This was followed by violent disturbances in Oldham, Burnley and Bradford, in part stimulated by the activities of the BNP and other far-right organisations. Liberal opinion was bewildered, alarmed and uncomprehending. While it is too early to assess these developments fully, some factors appear salient, and were identified as such in a series of reports on the riots published in December 2001. The economic stagnation of much of urban England, especially in the former textile towns of northern England, was identified as a major cause of racial and other social problems. In the 2002 local government elections the BNP won three council seats in Burnley, a small but significant number of the seats they contested. These BNP results can either be seen as a crushing defeat, as their opponents averred, or, as they themselves claimed, a significant electoral breakthrough in the face of universal hostility from the liberal media.

There has been a failure of the white working class and the deeply traditional Muslim Asian community to integrate with or even understand each other. Both white and Asian youths are alienated from society in general and (especially among Asian Muslims) their elders in particular. There is in addition general economic, social and cultural deprivation and a widely held perception by poor whites that 'the immigrants get everything' from the local authorities.

More generally, the BNP has also been able to capitalise on popular dislike of the European Union and the Euro, on a general impression of crime and moral decay, and on fears of an uncontrolled flood of 'bogus' asylum seekers. Moreover, many traditional, white, working-class Labour voters plainly believe New Labour is no longer their party and has become middle-class, liberal and overly concerned with the rights of minorities more than with the interests of the working class and the poor.

In these circumstances the far right has been able to peddle easy solutions to complex problems. It is too early to decide whether the rise of the far right is a temporary aberration or a significant development. Past experience suggests that they are unlikely to gain 20 per cent of the vote in any constituency and the electoral system effectively disbars them from parliament. Only a massive economic or political crisis is likely to change this. None the less, the far right have a considerable capacity to provoke conflict and disturbance.

As has been noted, categorising states, regimes or movements as 'fascist' is not always easy. It has proved convenient for the left to label a wide range of unpalatable views and regimes as 'fascist'. Many modern historians have been anxious to stress the differences between various 'fascist' regimes, rather than their similarities, but some salient characteristics are recognisable.

Fascist values are rejected as morally alien to the Judeo-Christian and Enlightenment-liberal tradition. Fascists themselves would not find this a problem, as they are opposed to these traditions as a key element of their philosophy (for want of a better word). Claims that fascism 'had its good points', such as tackling crime, creating political stability and ending unemployment, should be dismissed as ephemeral, superficial and far out-weighed by its enormous crimes against humanity. Fascism was and is not a coherent ideology.

All fascist movements may be said to have all or most of these characteristics: racism, opposition to democracy, to liberalism and to equality, aggressive assertion of the nation-state, dictatorial government under a strong leader and an emphasis on military or quasi-military values. These values involve obedience, loyalty, order, hierarchy and a cult of violence, physical strength and all the paraphernalia of flags, drums, marching, ceremonies, uniforms, emotionally roused crowds and general political theatricality.

It is easy to get carried away by the threat fascism poses to modern democracies. The possibility of a fascist party coming to power in Britain or any other democracy today is so remote as to be hardly worth worrying about. Democratic culture in the EU is very strong and deep. However, the fascist right does threaten the rights of ethnic, racial and religious minorities and other groups to live their lives free from abuse and from the threat of violence or of vandalism to their homes and businesses. Complacency is hardly possible in a continent that produced so much racism, xenophobia and violence during its long and turbulent history – a continent from which fascism sprang as one of its less admirable accomplishments.

Summary

Fascism is particularly resistant to rational enquiry, partly because fascists themselves scorn the intellect and partly because it has become a portmanteau term of political abuse. However, even if fascist ideas are difficult to present in structured form, fascist values can be fairly easily identified. These include a positive view of conflict, struggle and war; a stress on non-material values, irrationalism and anti-intellectualism; and a glorification of the nation or race. Obedience to the leader and state are ultimate values, and society and mankind in general are seen very much in hierarchical terms. Fascist economic theory is subordinate to the foregoing. The European experience of fascism of course culminated in a disastrous war and terrible atrocities, and some have argued that fascism ended in 1945. However, many of the factors that engendered fascism, such as racism, alienation and moral confusion, are around today, so reports of its demise were perhaps greatly exaggerated.

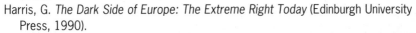

FURTHER READING

Eatwell, R. 'Fascism', in R. Eatwell and A. Wright (eds.), *Contemporary Political Ideologies* (Pinter, 1993), pp. 169–91.

Eatwell, R. *Fascism: A History* (Vintage, 1996).

Griffin, R. *The Nature of Fascism* (Routledge, 1993).

Griffin, R. (ed.) *Oxford Readers: Fascism* (Oxford University Press, 1995).

Harris, G. *The Dark Side of Europe: The Extreme Right Today* (Edinburgh University Press, 1990).

Harris, G. 'The Extreme Right in contemporary Europe', *Politics Review*, 8:3 (1999), pp. 8–10.

Hayes, P. *Fascism* (Allen and Unwin, 1973).

Heywood, A. 'Fascism', in A. Heywood, *Political Ideas: An Introduction* (Macmillan, 1998), pp. 212–37.

Leach, R. *British Political Ideologies* (Prentice Hall, 1996).

Merkl, P. H. and Weinberg, L. (eds.) *The Revival of Right-Wing Extremism in the Nineties* (Frank Cass, 1997).

Spiller, J. 'A Future for British Fascism?' *Politics Review*, 9:2 (1999), pp. 10–12.

Thurlow, R. *Fascism in Britain* (Blackwell, 1987).

Vincent, A. 'Fascism', in A. Vincent, *Modern Political Ideologies* (Blackwell, 1996), pp. 141–71.

Wilford, R. 'Fascism', in R. Eccleshall *et al.*, *Political Ideas: An Introduction* (Routledge, 1996), pp. 185–217.

SAMPLE QUESTIONS

1 Is fascism anything more than an 'emotional spasm'?

2 How crucial to fascism is racism?

3 Has the tragic experience of Europe with fascism disqualified it from serious intellectual consideration?

4 'Fascism was an aberration, a product of particular circumstances; it has no future in the twenty-first century.' Do you agree?

5 Does fascism offer serious solutions to the problems of industrial society?

6 Are all fascist movements innately totalitarian?

Environmentalism and ecologism

14

Environmentalism and ecologism constitute one of the most recent ideological movements. Though the terms are often used interchangeably, it is more useful to regard ecologism as a philosophy that believes in a thorough-going root and branch transformation of society, whereas environmentalism believes that dangers to the environment can be tackled within the existing political, economic and cultural order. We examine here the genesis of the movement in the explosion of concern at the apparent threat to the planet in the 1960s, and its subsequent evolution as an ideological force and political movement. The various elements, spiritual and scientific, which have influenced the 'green' movement are presented and subjected to critical analysis. Finally, we consider whether the movement is little more than a current fad, or whether we are all 'green' now.

POINTS TO CONSIDER

➤ Can the origins of the ecological movement be realistically traced back to the eighteenth or nineteenth century?

➤ How far is ecologism a political ideology and how far a quasi-religious faith?

➤ How far is the green view of man's place in nature a valid one?

➤ Are the greens correct to adopt such negative views of industrialism?

➤ How far is green ideology intellectually coherent and based on empirical evidence?

➤ Are green politics practical politics?

After ten thousand years of settled societies, and only two hundred years of substantial industrialisation, human activities and the pollution they generate threaten irreversible changes on an unprecedented scale to the world's climate. (Clive Ponting, A Green History of the World, 1991)

When viewing some of the dumpier parts of the earth, it is hard to imagine that there might be arguments in favour of pollution. And yet there are. By any standard of measurement the majority of people on earth are now richer, healthier, and longer-lived than they have ever been ... These improvements in the human condition came with the industrial revolution, which created most of our pollution.

... The countries that are most industrialised and hence, one would think, most polluted have the best morbidity, mortality and income statistics. National well-being might also be said to be a by-product of pollution. (P. J. O'Rourke, All the Trouble in the World, 1994)

> What would the world be, once bereft
> Of wet and of wildness? Let them be left,
> O let them be left, wildness and wet;
> Long live the weeds and the wildness yet.
> (Gerard Manley Hopkins, Inversnaid, 1881)

Environmentalism and ecologism are two strains of what has come to be labelled the 'green movement' or the 'greens' (with or without a capital 'G'). Though the terms 'environmentalism' and 'ecologism' were once used interchangeably, most people would now discern a distinction between them. Environmentalists believe that green issues, however important they are, can be addressed within the existing political and economic structures. To succeed, this would require wise government, appropriate legislation and the voluntary adoption of environmentally sound practices by consumers. Ecologists deny that this is possible. The environmental crisis is so great, they believe, that only a thorough-going reorganisation of the political, social and economic system would achieve a solution. This would necessitate a massive change in human values.

The green movement, like all ideological and political movements, is driven by people with a complex mix of ideas, often in conflict and usually involved in controversy with their fellow greens and with their ideological opponents. This is to be expected of a movement that is so new and is still working out its fundamental beliefs and a political strategy to garner support and win influence and power in the conventional political world. It is not an easy task for a movement that challenges many of the fundamental assumptions of the modern industrialised world.

For most of this chapter we will concentrate on the more ideologically distinct views of ecologism, but the ways in which other movements have been influenced by environmentalism will also be discussed. For convenience we shall use the term 'green' when referring to any position with an ecological slant to it, and 'Green' when referring to a political party.

The rise of environmentalism and ecologism

The term 'environmentalism' defines concern for the natural world and its protection from excessive human depredation. It constitutes no clear political or ideological agenda. The term is derived from the Ancient Greek words *oikos* ('household', 'habitat') and *logos* ('science', 'argument'). Precursors of ecologism can be found in the writings of Greek and Roman poets and their love of the bucolic life on their country estates (although they might be more properly viewed as, at most, 'environmentalist' in their view of nature). Medieval and Renaissance poets and artists celebrated the natural world and its spiritual values. But it was during the eighteenth and nineteenth centuries that there arose a strong reaction to the world view derived from Judeo-Christian religious and moral values, the mechanistic ideas of Cartesian philosophy and Newtonian physics, and, most of all, the industrial revolution.

Rousseau's writings were highly critical of the 'corrupting' nature of 'civilisation' and contrasted the modern world unfavourably with the peaceful, agrarian world of the American 'noble savage'.

> **Romanticism**
>
> A style of arts and thought of the late eighteenth century concerned with expressing feeling and emotion. It involved a revolution in thinking about the basic values of art, morals, politics and religion. It sought to create a world view infinitely larger and more varied than the one it set out to supplant.

Nineteenth-century **Romanticism** and a love of wild places as displayed in the poems of William Wordsworth and the Lakeland poets were also part of the reaction to industrialism. The twentieth century saw the growth of the 'countryside' as a place of recreation and leisure pursuits, a place for the urbanised to live out **Arcadian** fantasies (especially if they earned their living in the towns). Perhaps most significant are such critics of industrialisation as William Morris and Leo Tolstoy, both of whom exposed industrialisation as taking the human value, satisfaction and skill out of work, as well as destroying what was beautiful in the natural world. Nor are the origins of ecologism always to be found among the libertarian left – rather embarrassingly for modern greens. The Nazis, for example, were influenced by some green concerns, such as alternative energy sources and soil conservation.

> **Arcadia**
>
> A word used to describe an idealised landscape of rural simplicity. Arcadia is something of a fantasy-land of happy, contented peasants enjoying the fruits of their labour, conjured up by those who have never had to earn a living from the land.

The experience of most people in the industrial cities of the nineteenth century was one of breaking human ties with nature and the natural world. Britain has the oldest industrial-urban population in the world. Most Britons are now five generations from the land and from working the natural environment. Indeed, for most of the last century the British rural environment has itself been subject to the processes of industrialised agriculture to meet the demand for food and raw materials.

While environmentalism is manifestly of long standing, the modern ecological movement can be dated from the 1960s and 1970s when a number of books, studies and reports appeared which argued that humanity, even the living world – the **biosphere** – was under unique threat from a combination of over-population, intensive agricultural methods and chemical pollution. The greatest single threat was the profligacy of the industrial process itself, a process based on false

> **biosphere**
> The area of the earth in which life in its many and varied forms exists; the film of life that covers the surface of the earth both on land and in the seas. Environmentalists argue that the biosphere is threatened by modern industrial and farming activities.

assumptions. Economic resources (most notably fossil fuels) were not infinite. The external costs of economic development, such as the destruction of the rain forests, the poisoning of the oceans and the rapid extinction of many living species, could not be simply dismissed.

Other anxieties were to follow as the century drew to a close. These included the harmful consequences of the erosion of the ozone layer, global warming, the proliferation of nuclear power generation (and with it nuclear weapons), and the impact of motor vehicles and road building on the environment, human health and wildlife. Spectacular environmental disasters, such as the Seveso dioxin chemical plant disaster in Italy (1976), the Bhopal chemical plant explosion in India (1984) and the Chernobyl nuclear power explosion in the USSR (1986), intensified environmental worries.

The crucial point is that these portents of deep gloom were based on an allegedly *scientific* analysis of the situation, which gave them an apparently solid intellectual basis and greatly enhanced their persuasiveness. Rachel Carson, in *Silent Spring* (1962), exposed the damaging impact of pesticides on the human food chain. Paul Ehrlich, in *The Population Bomb* (1968), raised concerns about rapid population growth and its impact on the environment. Scientific reports, such as the Club of Rome's *Limits to Growth* (1972), Barbara Ward and Rene Dubos's *Only One Earth* (1972), and United Nations conferences highlighted the environmental threats. A drumbeat of articles, books and television programmes throughout the 1980s and 1990s produced growing evidence of ozone damage, rising rates of species extinction, resource depletion, and the dangers to the biosphere of new forms of pollution.

The emergence of these concerns coincided neatly with a wide range of *spiritual* and *cultural* developments that gave a powerful ethical, almost religious, dimension to the issue. These ranged from criticisms of the dehumanising effects of society and large-scale industrial enterprises, such as Fritz Schumacher's *Small is Beautiful: Economics as if People Mattered* (1973), to alternative 'New Age' religiosity, and a widespread scepticism, especially among the young, towards the value system of capitalist society.

These scientific and spiritual dimensions influenced the creation of a *political* response, which constituted the development of an ideology and the belief that something radical could and should be done about the headlong rush to destruction. This belief emerged from the political upheavals from the 1960s onwards. Political parties with a commitment to an ecologist ideology appeared in the 1980s, and became known as – and even officially called themselves – 'greens'. In the 1990s the collapse of communism, and the apparent intellectual and practical bankruptcy of socialism, have subsequently bolstered the political dimension of the ecological movement. If you *still* want to be radical, there is nowhere else to go.

The importance of the formation of green political parties lay in their underlying belief that it was necessary and possible to preserve the world. This involved political action. Support for green issues has steadily grown over the last four decades, although it ebbs and flows with the expansion or contraction of the economy. Usually, concern rises with economic growth and full employment and declines when the economy moves into recession and jobs are at risk.

Green is different

At this juncture it is perhaps useful to point out that ecologism is different from other ideologies in several ways, besides its comparative youth. First, though, a caveat. In practice there is often a marked gap between the policies of parties which profess a particular ideology and the principles of the ideology itself. Differences arise from the exigencies of functioning as a political party in a given constitutional, social and cultural context, such as the simple need to win as many votes as possible. As we shall see later, that certainly applies to Green parties in Britain and continental Europe. Moreover, greens themselves tend to confuse issues by implying that they are somehow beyond ideology: for instance, 'neither right nor left but forward' is the slogan of the German Green Party. This is true in the sense that, unlike other ideologies, ecologism puts the animate and inanimate world centre stage, rather than regarding it simply as a resource for human exploitation. Indeed, some thinkers have attempted to construct complete ethical systems in which humankind is *not* the central concern. Instead, 'Life' itself is.

One can pursue this theme further. Green political allegiance tends to impose certain lifestyle obligations, ranging from utilising bottle banks for recycling to vegetarianism. Ecologism can thus resemble a *religious*, rather than *political* creed. There is nothing new in that. All political movements have strong elements of faith and 'pseudo-religious' beliefs in them.

Both the British and the German Green parties have been racked by conflict between 'dark' (or 'deep') 'greens', who favour the most radical approach, and 'light' (or 'shallow') 'greens' who are much more moderate, pragmatic and, above all, prepared to operate within the existing systems. Dark greens believe that humans should interfere in nature as little as possible, that all species – and not just humans – have moral value (and, potentially, moral *values*). Most dark greens would encourage direct action against polluters and environmental destroyers, and support a move away from the consumerist, industrialist values of modern society. Light greens think that change must come from within the present system, through regulations, tax changes and slower, more sensitive economic growth.

Underlying these differences is a question of fundamental importance: for whom or what is the environment being preserved? The obvious answer is 'for humankind'; we cannot live on 'spaceship earth' without taking into account the well-being of all non-human passengers. The dark green answer, however, is '*not* for the benefit of humans, but for the benefit of *all* creatures'. If one takes this stance man is dethroned from his position at the centre of all things and drastically new ethical structures must be generated.

Green themes

We will now explore a number of themes that are fundamental to the ecological perspective:
- human nature and nature;
- green views on politics;
- green economics.

Human nature and nature

Like all ideologies, ecologism incorporates a view of human nature. Unusually, though, *human* nature is firmly situated in the context of nature in general. Other ideologies, notably liberalism, tend to present the natural world as simply a backdrop for human activities or, as in Marxism, a resource to be exploited for the fulfilment of human aspirations, aspirations assumed to be unlimited. For ecologists, human beings are merely part of a much wider natural order. This order is characterised by interdependence: the well-being of one living species depending on that of others and, in turn, contributing to the well-being of the whole biosphere.

'Spaceship earth'

It is imperative that humans individually and as societies live in harmony with the rest of creation and according to principles implicit in the natural order. An analogy is sometimes made with a 'spaceship' – 'spaceship earth' – a beautiful but fragile craft and, crucially, all we have got. This fact, plus the inherent limitations on resources in the closed system of the 'spaceship', implies definite limits to human activity, especially limits to material consumption. Moreover, the spaceship and the natural world are useful models for human societies, being based on co-operation, diversity, equality of value, balance and self-regulatory stability. Neither the spaceship nor the natural world would survive without these values.

> Alone in space, alone in its life-supporting systems, powered by inconceivable energies, mediating them to us through the most delicate adjustments, wayward, unlikely, unpredictable, but nourishing, enlivening, and enriching in the largest degree – is this not a precious home for all of us earthlings?[1]

Population control

If spaceship earth is to survive, there must be a reduction in the number of passengers it is expected to carry. Greatly influenced by the ideas of Thomas Malthus, *Essay on the Principle of Population* (1798), an economist who realised that human population growth would inevitably outstrip food supply and create disaster, ecologists have argued for population control and reduction. The twentieth century experienced massive population growth, reaching over 6 billion by its end. By the middle of the twenty-first century world population may stabilise at 8 to 10 billion. Greens fear there are already too many people and that present levels of material wealth (and pollution) cannot be sustained, let alone universal aspirations to (Western) affluence. Excess population has detrimental consequences for bio-diversity, food supplies, environmental preservation, quality of life and the ability of the eco-system to sustain life – certainly advanced life. Policies should be designed to encourage smaller families, to reduce world population over the long term to perhaps one billion, the estimated population of the world in 1800.

Such theories are in conflict with many religious and cultural beliefs. Greens apparently have an up-hill struggle in persuading poor folk to reduce their family size when the logic of their societies is that children are assets to help bring in an income and sustain one in old age. Some greens have cheered China's 'one child' policy and even the compulsory sterilisation that occurred in India under a state of emergency during the 1970s, and have advocated even more authoritarian measures. Other greens, alongside politicians in the developing world, point out that one Westerner uses – and wastes – far more of the earth's resources than many dozens of the poorest people. Some discern racist tinges in concern over population growth in Africa and Asia.

Science, mysticism and nature

In part, green beliefs are based on a scientific analysis of the natural world, an analysis that is generally accepted within the scientific community and lends ecologism much of its legitimacy. However, science is often identified by greens as contributing to the problem by creating the technologies that have driven industrialisation and consumerism. Environmentalists believe that science and technology are major elements in the solution to environmental problems. Many ecologists, however, reject science and believe that only major changes in the religious and moral bases of mankind can restore the world and bring humans into a new balance with nature.

Ecologists' mystical appreciation of the natural world is derived from a number of sources, including Eastern religions. The 'oneness' of the human and natural world (especially in Buddhism); the alleged beliefs and natural lifestyles of 'primitive' peoples; and a (largely imaginary) understanding of pre-civilised and pre-Christian societies of the West are enlisted in the green cause.

The quasi-religious understanding of the Gaia hypothesis and the supposed speech of a nineteenth-century American, Chief Seattle, provide an illustration of this strand of green thinking.

The conjunction of scientific theory with a quasi-religious perception of the biosphere is most clearly seen in the 'Gaia hypothesis' of James Lovelock, in *Gaia: A New Look at Life on Earth* (1979) and *The Ages of Gaia: A Biography of Our Living Earth* (1989). Put simply, Lovelock argued that the earth was kept habitable for living things by the interaction of innumerable biological systems. Life itself made life possible by a built-in, self-correcting mechanism which automatically took account of changes in the environment and made appropriate adjustments. Thus, although the temperature of the earth has varied considerably over time, the atmosphere has been kept breathable by compensating processes among living creatures.

This apparently objective, scientific description, which has been widely accepted, was translated into a powerful ideological underpinning of green politics by the cultural resonances created by the fact that 'Gaia' was a Greek goddess, 'Mother Earth'. The Gaia thesis was interpreted by some as implying that all life on earth constituted a sort of single living organism, possibly endowed with consciousness and will. It also claimed that the present economic, political and social system was wrecking the subtle interactions that preserved life on planet earth, with potentially catastrophic consequences.

Although actually a forgery, Chief Seattle's speech neatly summarises the ecologists' attitude to the modern world, on which has been conferred the imprimatur of Rousseau's 'noble savage':

> If we do not own the freshness of the air and the sparkle of the water, how can you buy them?
>
> We are part of the Earth, and it is part of us. The rocky crests, the juices of the meadows, the body heat of the pony, and man – all belong to the same family.

> The shining water that moves in the streams is not just water, but the blood of our ancestors. If we sell you land, you must teach your children that it is sacred – that each ghostly reflection in the clear water of the lakes tells of memories in the lives of my people. The water's murmur is the voice of my father's father.[2]

Such a perception is, of course, in marked contrast to the idea of the natural world and man's relationship to it, as presented in the Judeo-Christian tradition in *Genesis*. Here God's creation is inherently good but it is emphatically placed under the authority of Man. Indeed, man dominates the rest of creation:

> ... God said unto man, Be fruitful and multiply, and replenish the Earth and subdue it: and have dominion over the fish of the sea and over the fowl of the air and over every living thing that moveth upon the Earth.[3]

In contrast to humankind's 'domination', modern Christian thinking has redefined man's role as 'steward' over nature, with authority counter-balanced by responsibility for its proper use. Nature is the creation of God and should be treated with respect as His handiwork.

The Christian perception jars with the scientific view of the universe which emerged in the seventeenth century, and which subsequently underpinned the 'Enlightenment' of the eighteenth century. Here the assumption was that the universe could be rationally understood and manipulated to human advantage by breaking it down into its component parts, rather like a machine, to 'see how it worked'. The ecological perspective emphasises a *holistic* understanding in which the whole is not simply the sum of its parts but transcends them in a developing system, of which mankind is but a part.

It is evident, then, that there is a tension within ecologism, between its 'scientific' and its 'mystical' bases, which has never been wholly resolved.

Critics have denounced as improper the greens' inclination to extract eternal moral principles from scientific studies. For example, although humans are said to be simply part of nature, even the most rigorous advocates of this position imply that humans are somehow *outside* the system as well. Humans have, uniquely, a moral responsibility to proceed in particular ways, but the question arises why shouldn't humans simply exploit the environment like any other animal? If human actions destroy a species, so what? Millions of species have been eliminated throughout the history of the planet, which would get along well enough without humans, as it did for aeons before humans evolved. Nor is it evident that there is a *moral* imperative to preserve life on earth; it might be *prudent* to do so for humankind's survival, but that is not the same thing.

Green views on politics

It is not easy to fit green political views into the conventional left–right spectrum, nor is it evident that green ideology can be subsumed under the general headings of liberal, conservative and socialist. Greens tend to be rather proud of this exclusivity, though in fact most subscribe to the liberal-democratic ideal of much of the Western world. (Eastern religions and primitive tribes seem to be little esteemed as useful models in this regard.) The other major political movements and ideologies all, in the view of greens, tend to assume industrialisation and the consumer society to be a 'good' thing. All believe politics to be heavily involved in the creation of conditions for economic growth, at whatever cost to the planet and its other inhabitants. Traditional ideologies remain overwhelmingly 'human-centric', or *anthropocentric*, in their beliefs and policies, a bias that green politics sets out to change.

However, this position is not obviously derived from green theories of nature. Indeed, one could argue that conservative thought, with its emphasis on links across the generations, its cautious approach to technological quick-fixes, its precautionary attitude to change, and the value it accords to the agricultural sector, natural harmony and awe in the face of the universe, is closely related to ecologism. More alarmingly, it might be argued that the full implementation of a green agenda would be possible only under a highly authoritarian political system. So far, greens have had only modest success in persuading the masses that they should voluntarily reduce their standard of living. Besides, proposals for reducing population size evoke disturbing comparisons with forced sterilisation in India, the 'one child' policy in China and even **eugenics** and 'ethnic cleansing'.

There is some sense in which 'democracy' as an ideal can be generated from basic green principles. All living beings can be regarded as 'stakeholders' in the health of the planet. For many greens, this has important implications for the treatment of

> **eugenics**
> The 'science' of selective breeding by promoting the reproduction of 'desirable humans' and preventing the creation of the 'less desirable'. Eugenics was widely supported by people of all political persuasions, left and right, prior to the Second World War and Nazi eugenics which discredited its precepts.

animals. Greens also champion a very inclusive concept of democracy which includes generations yet unborn who are also 'stakeholders' in the well-being of the planet. Furthermore, nature itself appears to show the value of harmony in diversity – a model therefore for tolerance and a pluralistic society.

Critics have pointed out that 'nature' is a very ambiguous guide for the reconstruction of human society. Nature contains many models, some resembling the most mechanical of totalitarianisms, others a 'Hobbesian' 'war of all against all'. Natural selection, for example, is, as Charles Darwin discovered, a major engine of biological evolution. However, Social Darwinism, an attempt to apply evolutionary ideas to human society, was an important underpinning of racism, fascism, eugenics and mass extermination of assorted people defined as 'sub-human' – hardly a model of natural balance, let alone a basis for human morality.

As a new ideology, ecologism is still vague about how to move from this wasteful society to a green one. In that sense it is like nineteenth-century Marxism or late eighteenth-century liberalism in presenting a strong critical analysis of society but a weak theory of transformation to another society. This is certainly an area that has to be addressed by green politicians if they wish to make headway in electoral politics.

Green economics

The starting point of green economics is a critique of the all-pervasive system of 'industrialisation', which constitutes a sort of 'super-ideology', of greater significance than whether society is organised on free-market capitalist or state socialist principles.

Industrialism

This applies to more than the factory system, more than capitalism, even more than what would be regarded as 'conventional' economics. The main features have been succinctly itemised by Ian Adams:

- a devotion to economic growth and industrial expansion and continuous technical innovation;
- a belief in the overriding importance of satisfying people's material needs;
- large-scale centralised bureaucratic control;
- scientific rationality being the only kind of reasoning that matters;
- large scale units – in industry, administration, etc – are most efficient;
- a predominance of patriarchy and an emphasis on 'masculine' values of competition, aggression and assertiveness;
- an anthropocentric view that sees the earth and all that lives on it as simply there to be exploited for any human purpose;
- a hierarchical social structure where power and wealth is concentrated at the top;
- economic considerations predominate in society and moral, social and artistic values are of lesser importance.[4]

From the green perspective, a society built around the above value system is utterly pernicious. It not only debases human beliefs, it also squanders irreplaceable physical and biological resources and degrades the environment, ultimately to the point of ecological collapse. Nor does such a system provide for genuine human needs: material and spiritual poverty are everywhere apparent, even in the so-called 'developed' world.

Though this system is powerfully entrenched it is based on several demonstrable fallacies. First it assumes, against all reason, that the resources of the earth are infinite, as is its capacity to absorb the detritus of rampant consumerism. Furthermore, against all evidence, the general method of measuring well-being, especially in terms of Gross National Product (GNP), is utterly inadequate and misleading, mostly for what it leaves out of the reckoning. GNP does not measure 'externalities', for example, such as the costs to the community of atmospheric pollution, noise, accidents, stress, and so on caused by the constant increase in motor transport. Nor does it measure the distribution of 'wealth' so produced. Even more seriously, the future viability of the economic developments it purports to measure is ignored. Whole swathes of the 'real' economy, such as goods and services provided by informal family and community systems (of crucial significance in any society, but especially in the Third World) are dismissed as insignificant because they are not measurable in monetary terms.

Anti-materialism

The modern economic system has created vast material wealth, but has done little to increase the sum of human happiness over the last few decades. Material comfort in itself cannot significantly improve the quality of life once most basic material needs have been met (as they have been in the West). Environmentalism, along with justice and equality, is an issue that becomes more important in what many greens call 'post-materialist societies' where *quality* of life rather than the *quantity* of material goods becomes increasingly meaningful.

The problem is that most people on earth are poor. They struggle to get the basics of life, let alone comfort. Economic development has progressively dislocated their contact with the natural world but has not established new foundations of social harmony. Greens believe these problems can be solved by the better distribution of existing wealth rather than by greater production. Many in the developing world regard this view as essentially a Western indulgence, even a new form of Western imperialism – 'ecological imperialism' – to keep them subservient.

There are growing numbers of ecologists who realise that there must be close links between environmental programmes and developmental programmes if humans and nature are to have the natural ecological balance restored.

Growth

Above all, the industrialised system is based on the principle of 'growth'. Greens argue that this growth can and should be halted, or at the very least, dramatically reduced. This would involve a range of radical measures, among them a redefinition of the concept of 'work'. The term 'work' should no longer be confined to paid employment, but should include just about any activity with a beneficial (according to green criteria) outcome. Growing one's own vegetables, helping elderly neighbours, playing the guitar or teaching one's own children at home could all be included. One of the practical consequences is the notion of a guaranteed basic income, in which all citizens would receive as of right a minimum income whether they 'worked' in the conventional sense or not.

For greens, economic activity should satisfy need, rather than greed. Moreover, it should be so organised as to provide for the social and emotional needs of producers and consumers. To achieve this, greens favour small-scale and co-operative enterprises.

Sustainability

The application of green criteria to the economy in general would also focus on reducing the consumption of energy and non-renewable resources with the goal of establishing a sustainable system. Greens declare interest in such energy sources as solar, wind, wave and geo-thermal power, rather than non-renewable fossil fuels like coal or oil, or potentially highly dangerous and costly nuclear power. Greens are also inclined to favour, as part of this 'sustainable' system, reducing trade (so often rigged against the interests of the poor) and encouraging localised production (so as to reduce the drastic environmental costs of transport). New social and political values built around the reduction of pollution and consumption and a more just distribution of wealth within and between societies will be required.

Attractive though this might sound, 'sustainability' is nowhere very clearly defined. Does it mean modest and strictly directed growth, no growth at all, or a reduction in growth?

In fact, green economics poses a number of serious problems, which will be examined further under a critique of the ecologist position.

Critique of the ecologist position

At first sight ecologism is a persuasive blend of incontrovertible scientific evidence, ethical purity, spiritual insight and humane sensibility. It has an immediate appeal to many, especially the young. Moreover, a green political position implies an almost religious commitment to a lifestyle consonant with its principles. Furthermore, although Green political parties, with an agenda avowedly based on these principles, seem to make as many compromises with mundane reality as any other ideological movement, green thinking has percolated into all the mainstream parties and movements.

Nonetheless, the green position is open to challenge in several key areas. These are:
 • Intellectual incoherence;
 • scientific implausibility;
 • practical difficulties.

Intellectual incoherence

Critics have not been slow to point to some fundamental weaknesses. An obvious difficulty is the green argument that because nature exhibits certain features of inter-species co-operation which maintains the biosphere indefinitely, human beings *should* act in harmony with this fact. This is strikingly evident in the way greens tend to interpret Lovelock's Gaia theory. Philosophers, however, sternly reject the notion that one can make such an ethical link, a logical leap from what *is* to what *ought* to be.

Greens are not always consistent about how they understand man's position *vis-à-vis* the rest of nature. Sometimes it is implied that mankind is simply a part of nature, with no claims to superiority or special treatment, in which case mankind has no more obligations to nature than a slug has to a cabbage leaf. Sometimes, though, they rather shamefacedly admit humans have unique awareness and moral responsibility – mankind is *in* nature, but not wholly *of* it.

This confusion is related to another question. Are greens bio-centric or anthropocentric? In other words, is the environment to be preserved for its own sake and its own values, or simply because it suits humanity and human values? For example, it is often argued that the enormous diversity of species in the rain forests should be nurtured because of their possible medicinal value, or that wilderness should be preserved for aesthetic reasons. Deep or dark greens often specifically reject such human-centred values. To them, nature has its own values independent of human concerns.

Again, a number of highly contentious issues lurk along the borderlands of the green world view. Many greens espouse the cause of animal rights, in itself contentious, because such ethical positions appear to be in harmony with the broader green outlook, which might suggest that mosquitoes and flu viruses have as much right to live as humans. But the full interpretation of animal rights could be electorally unpopular; and, even though animal species are in ferocious competition for resources, the concession of full citizenship rights to disease and vermin would amount to mass human suicide. Some fringe groups advocate just that. Critics have been quick to point out an eccentric, even downright crank, element in some green organisations that, for all their claims of scientific probity, give houseroom to 'alternative' medicine, 'pagan' mysticism and general irrationalism.

This brings us to a central conflict within the green outlook, which is its attitude to reason and rationality. Although greens claim to uphold a uniquely science-based ideology, they harbour a deep and abiding suspicion of the scientific tradition and its rational and mechanistic understanding of the universe as a universe that can be analysed and understood rather than mystically apprehended.

Hard-nosed critics argue that myth, rather than science, dominates the whole green outlook, and the myth in question is the most potent one of all, that of the 'Fall of Man'. This myth presents itself in manifold guises. Sometimes it is suggested that prehistoric man lived in blissful harmony with nature and that all went awry with the invention of agriculture. Sometimes the fall is postponed to the emergence of modern science during the seventeenth century; sometimes the Enlightenment is to blame. But generally the villain is held to be the industrial revolution of the late eighteenth century and after.

Scientific implausibility

Green writers in the 1960s and 1970s made much of scientific evidence that forecast impending doom. Predictions were made, and given quite detailed statistical support, that raw materials and fuel resources were running out. This would lead to price rises, economic turmoil and ultimately the collapse of the whole economic system. Similarly, population growth would outstrip food production, causing calamitous famines. Pollution would render the atmosphere unbreathable. All these apocalyptic disasters were confidently forecast to occur by the year 2000 at the latest. But they didn't. As a result, critics have dismissed the green outlook as a modern version of the 'end of the world' terrors which have gripped the West at various times over the last millennium.

Of course, in a real sense, all things will come to an end, but this is no basis for a serious political philosophy. In fact, the world has abundant resources. The known reserves of fossil fuels and most metals have risen since the doom-laded predictions of the early 1970s. Indeed, the price of most raw materials has tended to decline over the long term as new sources become available. Oil price rises in the 1970s, for example, had much to do with Middle Eastern politics, and the existence of a strong oil-producing cartel, but little to do with the availability of a fossil fuel supply. The high price encouraged fuel conservation and the search for new, more secure deposits of oil in Alaska and the North Sea. Technology has reduced the need for copper in telecommunications and electricity supplies. Most manufactured goods require fewer raw materials in their construction than previously.

Food production has continued to outstrip population growth, reducing the incidence of famine among the world's poor. Malthusian predictions appear to have been confounded (though not, perhaps, proved wrong for all time) as science and technology have dramatically improved the yield of most crops.

Deforestation and diminishing bio-diversity are concerns, but they do not constitute the disaster that most greens would claim. Greens have a record of exaggerating the scale of the crisis, using sloppy scientific methodology, manipulating statistics and making downright dishonest use of many scientific reports to create a false impression of environmental disaster. Indeed, whatever claims they make of holding the moral high ground, greens are yet another body of self-interested pressure groups seeking special treatment by government.

Of course there are difficulties, but these can be managed by wise government decisions. The free market can help reduce wasteful consumption of irreplaceable resources, as is the case with oil, and stimulate new pollution-reducing technologies. Alternative energy sources will be developed when the time and prices indicate.

Green preoccupation with planet earth may be parochial; there are effectively unlimited resources of energy and raw materials in outer space which humans will eventually access. The overcoming of adversity by intelligence and ingenuity is the story of human history. Scare stories have always abounded. There was once a fear that the scarcity of oak trees for shipbuilding would render Britain defenceless at sea. Similarly, a shortage of charcoal was supposed to lead to the end of the iron industry in the eighteenth century, except that coal came along as a viable alternative.

Critics regard much green concern about the environment as reactionary. To greens the past is better than the present or any likely future. Greens lack a serious understanding of human history and the social, technological and scientific improvements that have created healthier, wealthier and, in some ways, environmentally more friendly societies. Third World poverty and early death are not, critics point out, very green. Primitive people do not have some superior wisdom, only a shorter life expectancy. Pre-industrial societies also reduce bio-diversity by poor environmental management. (**Easter Island** is a fine example of 'primitive wisdom' to be avoided.) Much modern environmental degradation, so the anti-greens argue, arises from the desperation of poor people to keep themselves and their families alive. Much Western green thinking can be seen as the indulgence of the scientifically illiterate and the comfortably off.

> **Easter Island**
> An isolated Pacific Ocean island which when visited by Europeans in the eighteenth century appeared to have reached a high level of civilisation that subsequently collapsed. Recent studies suggest this was a consequence of poor husbanding of the island's resources.

Practical difficulties

A 'common-sense' view of the green version of society is that it is impractical and utopian. It is all very well to urge the abolition of capitalism and its replacement by 'something nice', but more details are urgently required. Green supporters are often criticised for being typically Western, white, middle-class people with no direct experience of industry or business – teachers, lecturers and the like. Almost by definition these are impractical people, dreamers with little understanding that a green society is a luxury that the poor, especially in the Third World, simply cannot afford.

Such criticism is not wholly fair. Greens can argue, with some justification, that theirs is a relatively new and dramatically different ideology that is exploring as yet largely uncharted waters.

More serious is the accusation that greens simply have no strategy for moving on from where we are now to where greens want us to be. Sometimes it appears that simply appealing to reason and evidence will in itself transform society. Sometimes the adoption of green lifestyles, ranging from vegetarianism and cycling to various forms of communal living, is presented as the road forward.

There seems little awareness that immensely powerful structures, interest groups and value systems have created the present order, and will be fiercely resistant to any attempts to change it. Moreover, any transformation is likely to be, in the short run and probably in the long run, highly distasteful to large numbers of people. Greens are rather deficient in revolutionary theory, and, unlike Marxists, do not pinpoint any particular social groups who will develop into engines of social change. The assumption that 'everyone' or 'all living things' will be the beneficiaries and thus the instruments of change leaves greens wide open to accusations of naivety and living in a fantasy-world, particularly from the more tough-minded political left who see them as distracting attention from the class struggle.

Green political parties, certainly in the West (and ecologism is very distinctly an ideology of the West), operate within the liberal-democratic political system, but so far not very successfully. Indeed, deep greens tend to regard democratic politics as a form of collaboration with the system that, far from being part of the solution, is in fact part of the problem. Meanwhile, conventional political parties appropriate just enough of the green analysis to give a 'greenish' tinge to some of their own policies, thus neutralising the more radical demands of the movement. The electorate is, in effect, inoculated against a genuine green revolution by mild doses of environmentalism.

However, the deep green programme is no more effective. Demonstrations and media stunts get some publicity but do not drastically challenge the existing order. Some deep greens have sought to remedy this deficiency by constructing some sort of coalition among those most adversely affected by the present arrangements – the unemployed, the marginalised, hill farmers for instance – but with little success. It is uncertain whether such groups are particularly politically aware or open to green persuasion. In fact, most groups appear anxious to get a foothold in the world as it is, rather than to transform it into something different, even if it is 'something nicer'.

The greening of politics

Many European countries have green political parties. Some, notably in Germany, where Green Party politicians have served in coalition governments, have enjoyed modest success. In Britain the Green Party (formed in 1985 out of the Ecology Party, which was founded in 1975) has been far less successful if measured in the conventional terms of votes, elected representatives and levels of opinion-poll support. Votes peaked in the 1989 European Parliament elections but declined rapidly in subsequent Westminster elections, although greens have won a few council seats in local government and the occasional Euro-Parliament seat (on the basis of very low voter turnouts).

Although this might appear to suggest that ecologism is a fringe movement, such an inference would be mistaken. Ecologist, or at least *environmental* influence, has spread far beyond the Green Party to become a significant feature in mainstream politics. All political parties and movements are anxious to advertise their green credentials.

Conservative environmentalism

An important element in conservatism is 'conservation' and slow, incremental change in society. Conservatives stress the importance of the generational links between those who have gone before, those who are alive today, and those yet to be born. Conservatism is often linked to anti-industrialisation, anti-urbanism and pro-hunting, the countryside and hunting being vital elements in environmental protection. Environmentalism is very much a countryside and small town or 'historic' city concern. Care about the urban environment tends to centre on the preservation of ancient buildings and townscapes. Somehow, Bath seems more worthy of preservation than Manchester, even though both are Roman towns and both are of considerable 'historical' importance.

Socialist environmentalism

Socialists argue that capitalism exploits both humans and the natural world. Environmental objectives will be met only by a move towards a post-capitalist society. Many Marxists look on environmentalism as a diversion from the class struggle, while some socialists see it as even more important than the class struggle. Environmental socialists think that class struggle unjustifiably postpones the need to reform society along environmental lines. Planning, tax, regulations and other reforms are needed now to encourage a green lifestyle, including recycling, greater use of public transport and energy efficiency.

Liberal environmentalism

Liberals argue that the 'market' can help solve most environmental problems. The key issue is that 'public goods', such as fresh air, fish and water, an aesthetically pleasing environment and wild animal species, are 'free'. There is an incentive for people to use up a declining free resource before it is gone. If, however, one places a price on everything in the natural world then the market will ensure that valued goods, such as animals, plants, air and water, will survive. The failure of the market adequately to protect the environment derives from interference by government regulations – which distort markets – and from the lack of value placed on the environment by people and businesses. Indeed, the latter exploit the environment with the polluting and damaging side effects of their activities (known as *externalities*) and leave society to clean up, thus keeping their own costs down. Create a properly functioning market, where people carry the full costs of their activities, and you produce a better way of protecting the environment.

Feminist environmentalism

This term applies to the belief that a link exists between the male oppression of women and male oppression of Mother Earth as a consequence of male power and male ideologies of domination of the human and natural world. Women have a special role in green politics because of their crucial role as mothers and carers.

Fascist environmentalism

Environmental concerns are seen as important elements in fascist movements. Earth, forests and mountains are of special significance to the 'soul' of a nation or race. Both Italian Fascism and German Nazism invoked rural and peasant values as the backbone of their movements, even though their militarism involved an expansion of industrialisation to provide the materiel for war. In recent years the French National Front and the British National Party have also sought to stress their green credentials as another way of garnering support from elements of the electorate who are disillusioned at the failures of mainstream parties to treat green issues with great urgency.

Anarchist environmentalism

Nature left to its own devices exhibits a degree of self-government, harmony, balance and diversity – 'anarchy' – attractive to anarchists, who believe the world's problems spring mainly from formal structures of government. Small communities and self-sufficiency are the goals of this element in the environmental movement.

Several other social and political movements are highly consonant with green attitudes, such as animal rights, vegetarianism, nature conservation and even folk music, canal restoration and real ale.

Radical green politics may be on the wane. In part this is because of insoluble contradictions within the movement. For example, if 'traditional' parties and governments do adopt and implement some effective green proposals, the need for revolutionary change is reduced. Again, some green policies are, however much this is denied, essentially technological fixes – such as the development of wind and tidal power, and the introduction of the catalytic converter for motor car exhaust fumes. These, if they work (or at least appear to be working), undermine the deep green case for root and branch social revolution.

However, the evidence still mounts that there are major problems. Global warming and radical climate change continue to be proved by scientific and personal observation of the weather. Reports increasingly identify the scale of the problem. The 2002 Environmental Sustainability Index, for example, placed the UK ninety-eighth out of 142 countries, noting its poor record on reducing air pollution, protecting habitats and reducing greenhouse gases. The UK has one of the worst records for reducing household waste and increasing recycling.

Whether in fact the shift in global consciousness in a green direction leads to a total political change remains to be seen. As things stand, the jury is out. At most it appears to be painfully slow, while the environmental challenges appear to grow. If change does occur it may well be by means outside the conventional constitutional or even revolutionary political traditions by an as yet unidentified process.

Summary

As ideologies go, environmentalism and ecologism are very recent creations. Environmentalism has come to mean a concern with threats to the environment, threats which can be effectively dealt with within the status quo, while ecologism radically challenges the entire economic and social structure and even proposes a new value system and morality. Both are traceable to a reaction to the Enlightenment, Newtonian physics and industrialisation, but the concerns grew with a widespread realisation in the 1960s that economic expansion and the social structure and value system underlying it could not go on indefinitely without making the planet unfit for life. Greens therefore proposed alternatives ranging from technological solutions to a reordered society and a new value system. Attractive though green ideas appear, they have been attacked as unscientific, impractical and even immoral. Politically the greens have received little electoral support, especially in Britain, but green assumptions and values are increasingly becoming part of the wider political culture.

REFERENCES AND FURTHER READING

1 B. Ward and R. Dubos, *Only One Earth* (André Deutsch, 1972).
2 Chief Seattle, supposedly spoken by him in 1854.
3 Genesis 1:28.
4 I. Adams, *Ideology and Politics in Britain Today* (Manchester University Press, 1998), p. 177.

Adams, I. *Ideology and Politics in Britain Today* (Manchester University Press, 1998).

Bramwell, A. *Ecology in the 20th Century: A History* (Yale University Press, 1989).

Connelly, J. and Norris, P. 'Making Green Policy: A Guide to the Politics of the Environment', *Talking Politics*, 4:2 (1991/2), pp. 96–100.

Dobson, A. *The Green Reader* (Andre Deutsch, 1991).

Dobson, A. *Green Political Thought: An Introduction* (Routledge, 1992).

Dobson, A. 'Ecologism', in R. Eatwell and A. Wright (eds.) *Contemporary Political Ideologies* (Pinter, 1993), pp. 216–38.

Goodwin, B. 'Green Ideologies', in B. Goodwin, *Using Political Ideas* (John Wiley and Sons, 2001), pp. 223–48.

Heywood, A. 'Ecologism', in A. Heywood, *Political Ideologies: An Introduction* (Macmillan, 1998), pp. 264–90.

Kenny, M. 'Ecologism', in R. Eccleshall *et al.*, *Political Ideologies: An Introduction* (Routledge, 1996), pp. 218–51.

McCormick, J. 'Environmental Politics', in Patrick Dunleavy *et al.*, *Developments in British Politics 4* (Macmillan, 1990), pp. 267–84.

Myers, N. (ed.) *The Gaia Book of Planet Management* (Pan, 1985).

O'Rourke, P. J. *All the Trouble in the World* (Picador, 1994).

Ponting, C. *A Green History of the World* (Sinclair-Stevenson, 1991).

Porritt, J. *Seeing Green: The Politics of Ecology Explained* (Blackwell, 1984).

Vincent, A. 'Ecologism', in A. Vincent, *Modern Political Ideologies* (Blackwell, 1996), pp. 208–37.

Ward, H. 'Environmental Politics and Policy', in Patrick Dunleavy *et al.*, *Developments in British Politics 3* (Macmillan, 1990), pp. 221–45.

SAMPLE QUESTIONS

1 On what grounds do ecologists attack industrialism?

2 Is the green analysis simply nostalgia for a non-existent past?

3 How fundamental are the differences between environmentalists and ecologists?

4 How scientific is the ecologist position?

5 Is it true to say 'we are all green now'?

Feminism

15

Feminism is one of the most recent ideologies to emerge, although its origins can be traced far back into history. We examine its historical roots and identify and discuss the different forms of feminism that have developed over the last two centuries. We then link feminism with other ideologies and conclude with a critique and assessment of feminism in the modern world.

POINTS TO CONSIDER

➤ Since feminism is ignored in so many areas of key importance in other ideologies, is the term 'ideology' really appropriate for it?

➤ Why is feminism very new, very middle class and very Western? Or is it?

➤ How susceptible to rational analysis is radical feminism?

➤ Have the main elements of the feminist critique of Western society been answered and reformed over the last three decades?

➤ Why have so many feminist perspectives been absorbed into mainstream culture and political parties?

➤ Are men the new 'oppressed' gender in Western society?

Women must keep quiet at gatherings of the church. They are not allowed to speak; they must take a subordinate place, as the Law enjoins. If they want any information let them ask their husbands at home; it is disgraceful for a woman to speak in church. (St Paul, *First Letter to the Corinthians*, 14:34–5)

St. Paul enjoined self-effacement and discretion upon women; he based the subordination of woman to man upon both the Old and the New Dispensations. . . . In a religion that holds the flesh accursed woman becomes the devil's most fearful temptation. (Simone de Beauvoir, *The Second Sex*, 1949)

While women represent 50 per cent of the world population, they perform nearly two thirds of all working hours, receive one-tenth of world income and own less than 1 per cent of world property. (UN Report, 1980)

It is an obvious point that half of humanity has always been women, obvious, that is, until one considers how few women appear on lists of 'great people' who have shaped the course of human history. History – or '*His*-story' as some feminists describe it – is that of men and their doings. Women, if they appear at all, do so as a support for men, or as suffering the consequences of war and disaster. Rarely, they appear as rulers in their own right, often characterised by male historians as endowed with particular viciousness and ruthlessness, qualities common in men but 'unseemly' in women. Either women lack the potential to make noteworthy contributions to society, which is unlikely, or something else is at work here.

Feminism, one of the most recent ideologies to emerge, attempts to analyse the social position of women, explain their apparent subsidiary role in history and offer the basis for reform and the advancement of women in all areas of society. Feminists believe that there is a fundamental power struggle between men and women. This, like the struggles around class and race, is potentially revolutionary. Indeed, it is the oldest power struggle, the least public in its manifestations of conflict, the most fundamental in its implications for society.

Although concerns about the condition of women have been traced to medieval times, or even classical antiquity, it makes more sense to begin our survey with the end of the eighteenth century and the French Revolution. The Enlightenment and the revolution influenced women in France and elsewhere in Europe with the prospect of liberty and equality. Mary Wollstonecraft, in *A Vindication of the Rights of Woman* (1792), is an important early 'feminist' writer. She argued that women should have the same legal rights as men on the grounds of equal humanity, moral worth, rationality and freedom. It was wrong that women should be defined by their sex so as to be denied educational, legal, economic and political rights. Once equality was established there would be a beneficial revolution in the relationship between men and women.

Sensible as such ideas appear today, they challenged the male-dominated power structures that held sway at all levels of society during the nineteenth century. Men who recognised the case for universal male suffrage, who fought for rights for the industrial working classes, usually resisted their extension to women. As men were steadily enfranchised women hoped that their interests could be advanced by means of vote and parliament. The campaign for female suffrage became the major feature of what is called 'first-wave feminism'.

'First-wave' feminism

The 'first wave' of feminism (roughly 1830–1930) was similar to other nineteenth-century political campaigns, such as Catholic emancipation or anti-slavery, in which women had been active. These early feminist philosophical arguments were translated into political movements that focused on property and divorce rights, and equality in voting rights.

J. S. Mill's *The Subjection of Women* (1869) supported those rights. Greatly influenced by his wife, Harriet Taylor, Mill argued that women should have equal rights with men, based on equal reason and education, an equal right to work and to vote. There was no rational reason why the uniqueness of women in having children should lead to their being denied equal rights with men. Indeed, in 1867 Mill, as an MP, made a failed attempt to add female suffrage to the Reform Bill.

In the USA the rights of *man*, spelt out in the Declaration of Independence, were an obvious starting point to argue for the rights of *woman*. A 'National Women's Suffrage Association' was set up in 1869 to advance these rights. Political campaigns by women began later in Britain, but in 1903 the 'Women's Social and Political Union' was formed to fight for female suffrage. So was born the *Suffragette* movement.

As the male franchise grew, the arguments for denying women the same rights as acquired by working-class men steadily lost their force. New Zealand was the first country to give women the vote on the same basis as men in 1893. The USA followed in 1920. The First World War had raised the profile of women in employment and so political recognition had to be made of their contribution to the war effort. In 1918 women were allowed to vote on reaching the age of 30. By 1928 women in Britain had the vote on the same basis as men, though in much of continental Europe the vote came much later – in France not until after the Second World War and in Switzerland in the 1980s. By then women in the democracies had acquired legal and political equality.

The results, however, were not entirely satisfactory. The extension of the franchise did not dramatically increase female participation in political life. Women also remained worse off than men, especially in wages and job opportunities.

Suffrage alone clearly was, and is, not enough to transform the position of women. Feminists of the 'second wave' sought to analyse why this should be so and what was to be done.

'Second-wave' feminism

A radically new development occurred in the 1960s and 1970s, the so-called 'second wave' of feminism, inspired by such writers as Simone de Beauvoir, *The Second Sex* (1953), Betty Friedan, *The Feminine Mystique* (1963), Kate Millet, *Sexual Politics* (1970) and, most famously, Germaine Greer, *The Female Eunuch* (1970). It shifted the entire debate from what might be generally considered *political* to the psychological, cultural and anthropological fields. These explorations extended the women's movement far outside the conventional bounds of political discourse and posed a formidable challenge to most basic assumptions of culture and civilisation.

Women needed radical social change *and* political emancipation if they were to be 'liberated' from thousands of years of male **oppression**. *Liberal* and *radical* feminism agreed in their demand for both elements to improve women's lot. Both equal

> **oppression**
> The social process whereby one group or individual holds back other groups or individuals from having the power to pursue their own interests and keeps them in a position of subservience by coercion. Women, social classes, the disabled, racial and religious groups, homosexuals are all groups that see themselves oppressed by the power and values of 'majority' society.

rights legislation and considerable social change, especially in popular attitudes on gender issues, are needed to improve the lot of women and redress the power balance between men and women.

In Britain, a great deal of legislation has been introduced to advance the cause of greater gender equality: Abortion Law Reform (1967), Divorce Law Reform (1969), Equal Pay Act (1970), Sex Discrimination Act (1975), Employment Protection Act (1975) and Domestic Violence Act (1977). However, there has been very limited progress in dealing with the forces of structural gender inequality in society and enforcement of legislation is weak.

Some second-wave feminists argued for greater inclusion of women on the grounds of female moral superiority. Women were especially endowed with sympathy, emotion and a culture of co-operation as a consequence of their experience of motherhood. Men were seen as being tough, competitive and emotionally limited. Human history was a struggle between these conflicting male and female virtues between and within people. Feminists involved in the peace movement, for example, argued that the potential for destruction is now so great that it is vital that the female side of humanity gains more influence in politics and society to avoid nuclear war and environmental destruction.

'Third-wave' feminism

By the 1990s some feminists argued that second-wave feminism was becoming rather dated. Major civil liberties and legal advances for women had occurred. Technological developments, such as the contraceptive pill and household labour-saving devices, had liberated women from the burdens of unplanned childbearing and the grind of housework that had held back earlier generations. Some of the major writers of second-wave feminism, such as Germaine Greer in *Sex and Destiny* (1985), became sympathetic to the importance of family life and child rearing for women, while Camille Paglia, in *Sex, Art and American Culture* (1990), questioned the 'victim' status of women in much feminist writing.

The 1990s, it was claimed by feminists of what might be called 'third wave' or 'new' feminism, was the time to consolidate what had been achieved. Women are still disadvantaged in many areas of life in modern societies, but the principle of female equality, now largely accepted and backed by legislation, needed to be made a stronger reality in *practical* rather than just *theoretical* terms. A number of issues of gender discrimination remain to be addressed: female pay in Britain remains, on average, around 75 per cent of male wages; women are more likely to be found in low-paid, part-time, low-status, insecure, low-skilled and temporary work than men are; few women are at the top of the major professions of law, medicine, academia, the media and the senior civil service. In addition, in 2001 40 per cent of the FTSE Index companies were identified as having no women on their board and the proportion of leading businesses with women on the board fell from 69 per cent in 1999 to 57 per cent in 2001.

Unlike second-wave feminism, contemporary feminism doubts the importance of conventional political activity in changing structures of inequality in society. Natasha Walter, in *The New Feminism* (1998) and *On the Move: Feminism for a New Generation* (1999), is an important contemporary feminist writer. She addresses some of the issues raised by the position of women in contemporary society and argues that, while a great deal of gender inequality still exists in modern societies, there are a number of changes to be considered. Women's lives cannot be seen just in terms of 'oppression', or inequalities addressed by politics. Women have new forms of power in work, politics and the media available to them to redress gender inequalities. Besides, women do not need a 'feminist' movement as such to advance their interests. They can use the existing power structures in work and the many other organisations in which women participate to forward the feminist cause while advancing their own individual interests. Finally, these changes in feminist thinking amount to a new form of feminism, one much more in tune with the **individualistic** and **apolitical** world in Western societies.

New feminism can be criticised on similar grounds to its second-wave predecessor. It concentrates on privileged women – white, middle-class, well-educated, Western, Christian, employed, heterosexual – and does little for the vast majority of women in the world. Women in developing countries face far worse forms of gender inequality than those in the West, with far fewer resources than their sisters in industrialised nations, and receive little help in their struggle.

> **apolitical**
> Put simply, this term means 'lacking in political content'. One might see apolitical views as having no ideological perspective, no underpinning political beliefs. 'Apolitical' is often used as a term of criticism for those who have no interest in politics.

Today, any self-respecting Western woman would see herself as a 'feminist', with considerable choice in lifestyle and career, and not automatically dependent on a male. Feminism is not associated only with the radical or political left of politics. Women of all political persuasions argue for female equality in principle. Neither is it only a movement confined to the developed world. Women in developing countries increasingly see a

> **individualistic**
> Ideas and actions that centre on the individual and his/her needs and interests. By contrast, 'collectivist' ideas and policies that see social progress and individual advancement as occurring only by the action of a group, such as a nation, class, religion or race.

crucial role for themselves in social and economic progress, in population control and environmental protection. They look to both the traditions of their own society and the major elements of Western feminist thinking for inspiration.

Main elements of feminist thought

Feminist thinkers do not adhere to a simple 'left-right' view of politics (politics being based on fundamental class and economic conflicts in modern democracies). Neither do they see politics in terms of the state, as most 'traditional' ideologies and movements do. Female emancipation, and the achievement of female equality with men, requires a broader front than party politics or the achievement of power within the state. It requires an analysis of the power relations between men and women in all areas of society. One can see this in a number of areas:

- sex, gender and 'sexism';
- public and private spheres of life;
- patriarchy.

Sex, gender and 'sexism'

Another crucial principle is the distinction between 'sex' and 'gender'. Sex is a biological fact; the key difference between men and women is women's ability to have children. Men have physical power and aggressive tendencies, the biological function of which is to protect their women and children. Most societies have placed a major emphasis on male *physical* power. Industrial societies still place great stress on these gender divisions, even when their importance is clearly in decline with falling birth rates and growth of work dependent on educational and intellectual abilities.

For most feminists (but not all) these biological distinctions were of very minor significance. What *was* significant was *gender*. This is a social construct; a cultural phenomenon that assigned different roles to women and a whole apparatus of imposed behaviour patterns, expectations, thoughts, aspirations and even dreams. It is not 'biological' or 'natural' that women should take the bulk of childcare responsibilities; this has occurred as a result of social and cultural developments that should be changed to the benefit of women and, most feminists believe, men.

Sexism is an ideology of oppression of one gender over another that promotes the idea that 'genderised', socialised relations between men and women are natural and biological, and unable to be changed. There are sexist women but most sexism in society is male and directed towards the subjugation and exploitation (sexual or economic) of women. It is an ideology of 'imperialism' of men over women and reflects the power relations between men and women in society, with men having control over most forms of power.

Public and private spheres

The first challenge was the conventional distinction between *public* and *private spheres* of social life. Most, but not all, political writers had focused almost exclusively on the public realm of government, law, economics, the state, and had more or less assumed that the relationship between men and women (especially the married relationship) was essentially a private matter, outside the scope of politics.

Feminists boldly asserted that there was no such public–private distinction and that the most intimate dimensions of such relationships had profound political consequences. Moreover, the politically powerful public sphere, dominated by men, impacted on the politically weak private sphere, still dominated by men but within which the lives of women were confined.

If women were to be truly equal with men then there would need to be female emancipation within both the private sphere and the public sphere. Perhaps men or the state should have a greater role in child-rearing, releasing women for a greater role in the public sphere. Perhaps there should be a 'wage' for the work done by women in the private sphere. Whatever the answer, there is agreement among feminists that such divisions are not 'natural' or 'biological' in origin, but social, and as such can be reformed by social and political change.

Patriarchy

This can be perceived as the mainspring of feminism. Men and women have gender roles in society, but women have their role imposed on them by men. Consciously and unconsciously, in virtually all cultures and all times, women have been imprisoned within this imposed world. This *patriarchy* ('rule by men') permeates all aspects of society, public and private, as well as language and intellectual discourse. It thus remains the most profound of all tyrannies, the most ancient of all hierarchies. The root of oppression rests in men's superior strength and greater brutality, together with the female terror of being raped and the patriarchal ideologies that enslave minds.

One of the most important ideological props of patriarchy is religion. Most religions allot a predominant role to male gods. Most known societies are *matriarchal* ('ruled by women') in neither their social structures nor their theology. Nevertheless, Judaism, Christianity and Islam are particularly singled out for opprobrium by feminists as being religions that place women in a role subordinate to men in both theology and society. Patriarchy is thus a social construct, not a natural condition.

Women's movements therefore seek liberation from patriarchy by various means ranging from specific political campaigns, such as demand for liberal abortion laws, to 'consciousness-raising' by debate, discussion and publications, or simply 'living the future' – adopting a 'liberated' lifestyle and related values and sharing these with the 'sisterhood'.

Schools of feminism

'Feminism' is an ideology with a difference. This makes it peculiarly difficult to analyse and criticise in the terms usually applied to ideologies. Firstly, it *includes* a great deal that other ideologies skim over or take for granted, especially the distinct experience of women in society. Secondly, it *leaves out* much of the territory usually dealt with by ideology, such as law, the state, government, legitimacy, economic systems and historical explanation. Much of its language, ideas and evidence are drawn from such disparate disciplines as psychology, socio-biology, literary studies, sociology and anthropology.

Some critics have even challenged the notion that feminism can properly be called an 'ideology' at all, preferring to see it as a cultural or even a literary movement. Others have argued that it is an incomplete ideology, and really makes sense only if incorporated into more orthodox schools of thought such as liberalism, socialism or conservatism. However, it can hardly be denied that feminism has made a substantial impact and, whatever one's reservations in according it the title of 'ideology', it is like most ideologies in at least one respect: there are sharp, even bitter, divisions within feminism on its aims, goals, methods, theories and inspirations. Four major strands of feminist thinking can be identified:

- liberal feminism;
- socialist feminism;
- conservative feminism;
- radical feminism.

Liberal feminism

Liberal feminism dominated the 'first wave' of feminism during the nineteenth and early twentieth centuries, with intellectuals such as Mary Wollstonecraft, Harriet Taylor and J. S. Mill all making contributions. Liberal feminism focuses on the full extension of civil and legal rights to women by legislation. This form of feminism is essentially liberalism, stressing the importance of the individual, with the emphatic assertion of female equality. It demands a 'level playing field', secured by law, so that women earn the same as men and can aspire to the same jobs as men. It accepts the competition of the marketplace and assumes that women can, and should, compete equally with men.

In the second wave Betty Friedan, among others, argued that women were directed by a cultural myth that made them look to the family, the private sphere, as their proper role in life. Equal rights would enable women to become educated and have a greater role in public life. British feminists took up this cause, and later, so did politicians. A series of acts assigned greater rights to women, among which were the Abortion Act (1967), the Equal Pay Act (1970) and the Sex Discrimination Act (1975). Such legislation gives women rights that enable them as individuals to have greater choice about their lives.

Liberal feminism may be criticised as little more than Western liberalism with a female dimension, and most of its goals are already achieved or within striking distance. Less moderate critics regard it as merely a prop to sustain the status quo. Others see it as essentially the preserve of middle-class women who ignore the plight of their counterparts in the working-class.

Liberal feminism remains a very important element in the West today. Most women in developed societies have individual choices and freedoms that are now almost taken for granted, but they owe much to the liberal feminist struggles for equal civil and political rights over the last two centuries.

Socialist feminism

Some of the 'utopian socialists' of the nineteenth century, such as Fourier, Saint-Simon and Robert Owen, believed that their ideas had important implications for women. For example, Fourier envisaged a highly permissive sexual environment, with women liberated from the burdens of childcare and housework by transferring most of these family functions to the community. Owen, in particular, thought of religion as enslaving women through marriage.

Marx, however, was much less interested specifically in the liberation of women, and was conservative in his own family life. A socialist revolution, he believed, would liberate women as a desirable side effect. Subsequent communist regimes have paid lip service to women's equality but in practice have tended to take a conservative position, especially on the political role of women. Male left-wing leaders in many movements, especially in the 1960s, had attitudes that led some women to lose faith in traditional socialist politics and drove them towards a more radical agenda. Some groups, like 'Militant' in the 1980s, were scornful of the women's movement, seeing it as irrelevant, a middle-class intellectual indulgence and a diversion (like anti-racism) from the central revolutionary task of overthrowing capitalism.

Engels, on the other hand, showed considerable interest in the situation of women. In *The Origin of the Family, Private Property and the State* (1884) he stated that the family was the root of women's oppression, but that it had its origin in an economic system, capitalism, based on private property. It is dominated by men; property is owned by men and passed on mainly to men. The whole ideology of the system was designed to reinforce this control of women by men, which reduces women to the status of men's property.

Socialist feminists, therefore, see that only the ending of capitalism and the liberation of women from its shackles, both ideological and institutional, can end the oppression of women. Feminism is part of the class struggle and can only be achieved as part of that general struggle. Some socialist feminists believe that class is so important in forming attitudes that it cuts women off from their fellow women in other, opposing classes. Middle-class women have more in common with each other and their fellow middle-class men than they have with their working-class sisters.

Women play a key role in capitalism, serving its interests in several ways. Women in the labour force increase productivity, weaken the wage bargaining powers of male labour, and enter or leave the labour market in times of capitalist 'boom' or 'bust'. They are vital in producing, raising and socialising the next generation of workers into the values of the system. The family ensures that men at work will remain disciplined in order to keep an income. Finally, women reduce the domestic burden of child rearing, allowing men to concentrate on meeting the demands of the capitalist system.

Marxist feminist Juliet Mitchell, in *Woman's Estate* (1971) and *Psychoanalysis and Feminism* (1974), argues that female oppression in capitalist society is not just economic, but involves many aspects of psychology and culture that can and must be changed.

Socialist feminism is open to criticism from a variety of angles; for example, the destruction of the family as the cement of the private property system is as likely to produce an atomised and irresponsible society (perhaps modified by despotism) as a co-operative one. Such experiments in collective living as have been tried have not been a great success. Marxists of a more traditional hue have taken the view that the pursuit of such goals as pay for housework diverts attention from the central goal of abolishing capitalism. Non-Marxist socialists dismiss the image of the working man cosseted and indulged by his house-keeping, child-raising and domesticated wife as hopelessly outdated.

Conservative feminism

This may at first sight appear something of a contradiction in terms. There have been, however, some attempts to construct a theory of female liberation based on the belief in 'equal but different' roles and the natural division between the public and private areas of social life. Attempts to be equal on men's terms, according to men's values and in men's interests are doomed to failure and create a new form of female exploitation and manipulation, with grave social consequences for the upbringing of children and the relationship between the sexes. Conservative feminists take the view that women should have 'sover-eignty' within their *own* sphere of life. Cultural manifestations of this approach, such as the strict dress code of many Islamic countries, may appear repressive but in reality they strengthen respect for women and their freedom.

Thus family life is a very important and respected sphere of female activity and fulfilment. Many conservative feminists argue that too much feminist theory attacks the vital role of women in child rearing and home making. Indeed, many women actually want to be family centred, and find deep fulfilment there, rather than in careers and salaried work in the public sphere. Some feminist writers, such as Jean Bethke Elshtain in *Public Man, Private Woman* (1981), have evolved a variation of these views and claim that women's life experience, for example of motherhood, has nourished values such as co-operation, tenderness and sensitivity that have universal application.

Radical feminism

The most recent and most interesting form of feminism, if the most difficult to fit into the conventional definitions of ideology, is radical feminism. It is a very important element in the second wave of feminism.

Radical feminism holds that the suppression of women is a fundamental feature of almost all societies, past and present, and is the most profound of all the tyrannies. This oppression, this *patriarchal* oppression, is all-pervasive and takes many forms – political, cultural, economic, religious and social. It functions by a socially defined role for women, *gender*, which has little to do with genuine social differences and everything to do with the exploitation of women *as a group* by men. This exploitation permeates the whole culture and must therefore be challenged by an attack on all fronts – political, economic, cultural, artistic, philosophical and scientific.

Within this broad coalition there are a number of competing standpoints. One of the most extreme of these claims that everything, including science, philosophy and even language itself, is the product of a given social order, an order totally dominated by men. This male hegemony must be challenged by a rejection of all that it entails, even to the point of creating a new language for 'women to speak unto woman'. A rather less extreme, but nonetheless challenging, view is that women are essentially different from men, more attuned to the maternal virtues of tenderness, caring and intuition, and are more in harmony with life, nature and the ecological nature of the planet itself. Feminist critics, however, feel this is a retreat to the comfort of a romanticised version of woman's nature favoured by men. This, of course, raises the fundamental, and as yet unresolved, issue of whether women are actually substantially different from men.

The implications of feminism for men raise interesting points. Some feminists believe that to liberate women is simultaneously to liberate men: the two sexes will be able to negotiate a new and healthier relationship. To others, men seem redundant: women simply do not need them (hence the famous remark, 'a woman needs a man as a fish needs a bicycle'). This easily leads to the more extreme manifestations of feminism; for example, Andrea Dworkin, in *Pornography: Men Possessing Women* (1974), comes close to defining 'maleness' as essentially violent, negative, destructive. Male sexual redundancy might even be approaching, thanks to modern scientific advances, to the point of men being unnecessary even for breeding. For some feminists this has led to 'political lesbianism' in which women relate only to each other at every level, not just sexual, in modes determined by themselves without reference to the male world.

Critics argue that these several strands of feminism are mutually incompatible. The widest gap is between those who argue that there is very little fundamental difference between men and women, and those who identify profound biological, even spiritual, differences. Some critics of feminism condemn it as essentially elitist, ethnocentric, racist and even sexist. Feminism's strongest supporters are to be found in the wealthy industrialised societies of the West, among women who have largely achieved legal and political equality. Women in the developing world, whom Western feminists are accused of neglecting, suffer oppression on a scale unimaginable in the developed world. Indeed, within developed countries feminism is criticised by black women as being concerned with emancipation that essentially benefits white women and does little for their black and brown sisters.

Changes in the economy have reduced the role of large-scale, male-dominated industries that placed a premium on physical strength. The 'new economy' of 'high-tech' industries and services is almost designed to enhance the employment opportunities of women, reliant as they are on education and social skills, brain rather than brawn. Women do not require men for economic support. Increasingly, many women do not need a man for his role in child rearing. The economic value of men to women as providers declines with rising male unemployment – and unemployability – rates. There are growing concerns about the 'redundant' male in modern society. Seeking solace in drink, violence and crime, as his 'proper', traditional social roles decline, the 'redundant' male falls behind women in education and the world of well-paid jobs that are associated with the new knowledge-based economy. Time will tell if there will be a need for a 'men's movement' to enhance the role of men in society.

Summary

Feminism is a relatively new ideology, dating, for all practical purposes, from the late eighteenth century. Three 'waves' of feminism can be detected. The first, of about 1830–1930, was concerned chiefly with legal and political rights. The second, in the 1960s and 1970s, focused on much more fundamental personal and relationship issues. The 'third wave' in the last decade or so has been essentially a reflection on and reappraisal of what has been achieved. Feminism is different from other ideologies in that it largely ignores or takes for granted much of what other ideologies are concerned with. Even more significantly it denies the boundaries between the 'private' and 'public' spheres. The key target of feminism is 'patriarchy' – male domination in all its myriad forms. Feminism can, however, be divided into several different 'schools' each with a distinctive focus – liberal, socialist, conservative and radical – that sit uneasily with each other. Critics of feminism have denied that it is really a distinctive ideology at all; the most sceptical have dismissed it as an indulgence of middle-class Westerners. Finally, unlike almost all other ideologies which eventually give birth to political parties, feminism has not done so. Its influence, at least in the West, has been enormous.

FURTHER READING

Bryson, V. *Feminist Political Theory: An Introduction* (Macmillan, 1984).

Bryson, V. 'Feminism', in R. Eatwell and A. Wright (eds.) *Contemporary Political Ideologies* (Pinter, 1993), pp. 192–215.

Bryson, V. *Women in British Politics* (Huddersfield Pamphlets in History and Politics, 1994).

Goodwin, B. 'Feminism', in B. Goodwin, *Using Political Ideas* (John Wiley and Sons, 2001), pp. 189–221.

Heywood, A. 'Feminism', in A. Heywood, *Political Ideologies: An Introduction* (Macmillan, 1998), pp. 238–63.

Jowett, M. 'New Feminism in Contemporary Britain', *Politics Review*, 9:3 (2000), pp. 12–14.

Kemp, S. and Squires, J. *Oxford Readers: Feminism* (Oxford University Press, 1995).

Lovenduski, J. and Randall, V. 'Feminist Perspectives on Thatchersim', *Talking Politics*, 3:3 (1991).

Purvis, J. 'Equal Opportunities for Women', *Talking Politics*, 2:1 (1989), pp. 20–3.

Vincent, A. 'Feminism', in A. Vincent, *Modern Political Ideologies* (Blackwell, 1996), pp. 172–207.

Walter, N. *The New Feminism* (Little, Brown, 1998).

Wilford, R. 'Feminism', in R. Eccleshall *et al. Political Ideologies: An Introduction* (Routledge, 1996), pp. 252–83.

SAMPLE QUESTIONS

1 'The central concept of feminism is patriarchy.' Do you agree with this statement?

2 'Feminism is unique in that it makes no distinction between the public and private areas of life.' Discuss.

3 'Feminism ignores almost everything that other ideologies regard as crucial; that is its fundamental weakness.' Do you agree?

4 Is feminism obsolete?

5 Are the divisions between feminists more important than the beliefs they have in common?

Concluding remarks

It was the best of times, it was the worst of times, it was the age of wisdom, it was the age of foolishness, it was the epoch of belief, it was the epoch of incredulity, it was the season of Light, it was the season of Darkness, it was the spring of hope, it was the winter of despair, we had everything before us, we were all going direct to Heaven, we were all going direct the other way – in short, the period was so far like the present period, that some of its noisiest authorities insisted on it being received, for good or for evil, in the superlative degree of comparison only. (Charles Dickens, *A Tale of Two Cities*, 1859)

Politics takes place within a framework of ideas and concepts, ideological and religious beliefs, and social and political institutions moulded by the struggles arising from their interplay. Ideas greatly influence the practical politics of any society and are always closely associated with the complex interactions between principle (what an individual feels is morally right) and how it affects their self-interest (however defined). One might strongly argue, with justification, that much of relevance to the study of key concepts and movements has been missed out of this book, things that are of greater concern and impact on society than the 'tired, old' ideas and movements discussed above. We believe that these ideas and movements are not out-dated, that they are still the main influences on modern politics, particularly in the Western world, as well as in other societies.

This book concentrates on the Western Enlightenment tradition of political concepts and ideas. Elements of the tradition can be found in modern political movements, as we have already discussed, and also in some new ones as yet on the political fringes. Some have had a marked effect on mainstream political debate; some have sought an influence on the main political parties; but it is as interest or pressure groups that such movements have had most effect on political parties and state institutions.

As space precludes a discussion of all of them, we will briefly examine:
- religion and politics;
- disabled rights movements;
- gay rights movements;
- animal rights movements.

Religion and politics

Religion has always played a major part in politics. Marxists have been especially strong on recognising the crucial role of religion as a means of social control, of reinforcing the status quo in society. Indeed, many conservatives have claimed that religion is a vital and positive social 'cement', holding society together.

Religious identity plays a very important role in the creation of the national identity of most countries. Judaism and Christianity, via the Bible, have had a great influence on the development of concepts of human rights in Western countries. British socialism has been deeply influenced by the nonconformist Christian tradition. Conservatism in Britain and the Christian Democratic parties of Germany and Italy have been closely identified with particular forms of the Christian tradition (Anglicanism in Britain and Catholicism in Germany and Italy).

However, the Christian tradition in Western Europe is declining in importance as a form of moral and political reference. Church attendances are down to a tiny proportion of the population (although they do tend to rise during periods of political and economic crisis). Religion is believed by many to be at best a marginal influence on modern politics and at worst a dangerous purveyor of intolerance, bigotry and hatred. When one considers the 'Troubles' in Northern Ireland, the Israeli–Palestinian struggle, the conflict between India and Pakistan, religion plays a crucial part as an irritant. The term 'religious fundamentalist' conjures up the image of the religious bigot, but we shall argue that this is often an unjust verdict.

The nature of religious fundamentalism

'Fundamentalism' was a term originally applied to an approach to religion in which it was assumed that the original purity of the faith had been compromised and that purification by means of a return to the well springs was required. For religions with a strong basis in scriptures, notably Protestant Christianity, Islam and Judaism, this involves going back to what is taken to be the original meaning of the texts, texts whose ultimate validity is their divine inspiration. Fundamentalism is, however, not confined to these faiths. There are versions of it in Roman Catholicism, with some Catholics hoping for a return to pre-Vatican II (1962–65) doctrines and practices.

One might even speak of 'secular fundamentalism' on the far left, appealing to the original (or what is claimed to be the original) doctrines of socialism and a rejection of various compromises or 'revisionism'. 'Secular fundamentalists' are so called because they are vehemently opposed to any religious contribution to politics and society, and condemn religion outright as having nothing of value to give to the human experience.

However, the word 'fundamentalism' has recently acquired a specific political sense, especially in the USA, where there has been an attempt to apply moral absolutes, derived from Christianity, to a wide spectrum of political, social and economic issues. Islamic fundamentalism, as evinced in Iran and, until 2002, Afghanistan, is similarly an attempt to apply a strict interpretation of religious beliefs, in this case based on the Koran, to a restructuring of those countries.

Historically, organised religion has always attempted to influence the political process, partly to promote its own moral values and partly to strengthen its own institutional position within society. Fundamentalism is somewhat different.

First, it denies the convention, implicit in Western liberalism, of distinct private and public spheres of belief and activity. The concept of a secular society assumes that religion will be confined to an individual's private life, that church and state will be separate and each will stick firmly to its own business. Fundamentalism flatly denies this distinction. Moreover, it claims that certain moral principles readily translate into a political programme and are founded on divine authority. In America, these tend towards extreme rigidity, justified as being based on the unchangeable word of God as revealed in the Bible. In Europe the Catholic Church has certainly sought and achieved political influence, for example, through Christian Democrat parties. Catholic social teaching, promulgated in a number of papal and conciliar documents over the last two centuries, has plainly developed substantially and has, in practice, shown considerable flexibility.

A second striking feature is that, while fundamentalists of all varieties tend to reject modern *culture*, they are adept at using modern *technology* and the processes of manipulation associated with it. This was vividly illustrated in the use, among other things, of television, the internet and electronic data by evangelical Christians and fundamentalist Muslims to promote their religious beliefs and support candidates for public office who share their political programmes.

Many commentators have described fundamentalism as a characteristic of profoundly disturbed societies. Much of its strength comes from its simplifications, its claim to ultimate authority, its confidence in explaining crises and providing solutions and in the case of Islamic fundamentalism its validation of indigenous culture, values, tradition and history against the powerful and secular West.

Fundamentalism today

It would be unwise to under-estimate the power of fundamentalism in many societies. Perhaps most significantly, the sense of participation in a cosmic struggle between good and evil gives a sense of deep inner commitment to its followers. With the collapse of communism and, arguably, the decline of nationalism, perhaps only fundamentalism can give beliefs this inner assurance. Religious fundamentalism has been on the rise in the USA (Christianity and Islam), Israel (Judaism), India (Hinduism), and throughout the Islamic world of the Middle and Far East and Northern Africa.

However, in Europe and particularly in Britain, fundamentalism seems to have virtually no mainstream political impact. There are occasional flurries of moral reaction, as with John Major's 'back to basics' proposals in the early 1990s, but there is no substantial organised political campaign. The Protestant Unionist parties of Northern Ireland are sometimes perceived as 'fundamentalist', but their political goal of Protestant domination, or at least independence from the Irish Republic, is closer to the political goal of the tribe than to a moral crusade. Islamic fundamentalism is a small but significant element among British Muslims, a community characterised by being both highly law-abiding but also poorly integrated into British society.

Critiques of fundamentalism

Fundamentalism has come under ferocious attack on a number of counts from the liberal, socialist and even conservative traditions (with which it is often confused).

The first count is that many people do not accept the claim that moral imperatives have divine sanction at all. Even for those who do, the problem is how to accommodate such claims within a modern pluralist society. Vigorous pursuit of fundamentalist goals will inevitably cause intolerably divisive pressures in society. Civilised and rational discourse becomes impossible with those who regard all opposition as diabolical, all criticism as immoral and all compromise as treason.

In practice, fundamentalism, it is alleged, drives people to extremes by justifying acts which reasonable people would see as outrageous – suicide bombings in Israel, attacks on abortion clinics in America, anti-Western terrorist attacks in the USA and elsewhere. Within America, fundamentalists have been strongly criticised by mainstream Christian churches such as the Catholics, Episcopalians and Quakers, for promoting a narrow, intolerant, over-literal reading of the Bible and for taking positions on nuclear weapons, capital punishment, economic liberalism and environmental issues which have only the most tenuous biblical authority. Fundamentalists, their detractors argue, confuse early American principles with Christian values. Similar criticisms are made of the Islamic world where, for example, Arab or Iranian nationalism is sometimes confused with Islamic orthodoxy.

Finally, according to its critics, fundamentalism does not work. It provides no real solutions to the problems in the modern world. In those countries where it is a powerful influence it has been characterised by a puritan minority imposing their fanatical will on the majority with little tangible benefit to society.

One must not blame religion or religious fundamentalism for the ills of the world. Radical secularism and the political pseudo-religions of fascism and communism have created as much misery and death as has religion during the twentieth century. In fact, it has often been religion that has inspired people to enormous sacrifices in resisting such tyrannies: Protestants in Nazi Germany, Catholics in Communist Poland and Orthodox Christians in the USSR all contributed to the resistance to their respective totalitarian regimes.

Disabled rights movements

The term 'disability' is a controversial one. It has a number of negative connotations: a disabled person is physically or mentally 'unfit' or 'incapable', or somehow 'inferior' to one who is 'able', and is 'separated' from the 'able-bodied' population. Campaigners for 'disabled rights' often prefer to use 'differently abled' as a more positive description of people who do not have the same physical or mental capacities as others but who are still capable of making positive contributions to society. In law, 'disability' is defined as 'a physical or mental impairment which has a substantial and long-term adverse effect on the person's ability to carry out normal day-to-day activities'.[1]

Most disabled rights campaigners seek to change public attitudes towards the disabled by challenging the use of words that are claimed to be derogatory. For example, referring to a 'hearing impairment' is preferable to saying 'deaf'; 'visually impaired' is a more accurate description of most of those described as 'blind'; and 'cripple' is a now unacceptable word to describe people with mobility problems. Words *are* important and influence how disabled people are treated by the able-bodied. Carefully thought-out descriptive terms are part of a process, disabled campaigners hope, of creating a more positive image of people with disabilities and their potential contribution to the common good.

The growth of the disabled rights movement (although 'movements' is a probably a more accurate description of the wide range of organisations involved) comes from a number of social trends. Three factors have multiplied the numbers of disabled voters in society: insurance companies estimate that people are five times more likely by the age of 65 to become disabled and unable to work than to die; advances in medical technology have amplified the likelihood that congenitally disabled people will survive into adulthood; rising life expectancy ensures that more people will live long enough to become disabled in old age. When one adds to the steadily growing constituency for disabled rights the increasing unwillingness of disabled people, like other disadvantaged groups, to tolerate discrimination and a 'second-class' status in life one can see that the potential for political action is strong and rising.

Disabled people have a moral right as human beings to equal opportunity and equal treatment in society. Disabled rights activists argue that it is not enough to be sympathetic to disabled people; more needs to be done to enable them to play a full part in society, including the world of work.

A person's particular disability may preclude them from certain types of work but not *all* types of employment. Relatively few people are so disabled that they cannot work and are forced to be totally dependent on welfare benefits. In practice, discrimination in the labour market ensures that disabled people are less likely to be appointed to a job, are less likely to be promoted once in an occupation, and are far more likely to be unemployed than able-bodied people, trapping them in poverty. The Disability Discrimination Act (1995) makes it unlawful for an employer to discriminate against disabled people but, say disability campaigners, the legislation lacks effective enforcement powers.

Public attitudes towards the disabled need reform. Too often the disabled are ignored, patronised, treated with distaste by the able-bodied. Only when there is a more positive image of the disabled will public attitudes change and opportunities for the disabled in society improve. Some disabled activists are not prepared to play the 'noble victim', suffering in silence and gratefully receiving society's charity – a role that flatters the feelings of the able-bodied and does nothing for the disabled.

Disabled activists are also deeply worried about the implications for the disabled of modern medicine and genetics. At one level, science offers the possibility of identifying inherited genetic disabilities and alleviating or even eliminating them. At another level, however, medical and genetic science raises the potential for identifying 'defective' foetuses and offering parents the choice of abortion. A whole class of people is created, a disabled 'second class' that can be eliminated from society before they are born, removing their potential contribution to society as well as their right to life. Disabled rights activists would want to know who has the right to determine what is 'normality' and to set the standards by which human life will be determined.

Disabled rights campaigners try to influence government in ways similar to other pressure groups. Some are *insider* groups, such as the Royal National Institute for the Blind (RNIB), quietly at work behind the scenes to influence government policies and legislation. Other disabled rights campaigners point out that Acts of Parliament give rights and protection to disabled people but that there is no effective enforcement by bodies such as the Disability Rights Commission. Radical campaigners believe direct action and protests are the only way to bring the discrimination faced by disabled people onto the political agenda, to empower the disabled and encourage them to be socially integrated. They want to make it clear to government and the public that disabled people are not to be ignored, patronised and given a few 'crumbs' for which they are supposed to be grateful.

Gay rights movements

One might assume that sexual preference is a matter for individual choice and is of little concern to government and society at large so long as individuals consent to their involvement in particular sexual activities which take place in private and 'don't scare the horses'. Perhaps only 4 per cent of the population are exclusively homosexual, but possibly over 20 per cent have had some form of homosexual experience. The 'gay' population in society, whether great or small in number, is a significant one in politics (if only because of the higher percentage of gay people found in elite political and, especially, cultural groups).

Sexual activity has always been subject to social (or 'normative') sanctions and legal constraints. Society and the state always assume that private sexual activity has a public dimension that comes within the political sphere. Gay activists agree. They have involved themselves in political campaigning to change the law, especially on the age of consent for male homosexual activity and opposition to 'Clause 28' of the Local Government Act (which made teaching children about homosexuality, or 'promoting' it, a criminal offence), and to change public attitudes towards homosexuality.

Unlike lesbianism, which is not affected by the criminal law and forms a separate feminist issue, male homosexuality, has been a criminal offence in most Western countries until quite recently. Until the Sexual Offences Reform Act (1967) gay men faced prosecution for homosexual sex, even between consenting adults in a private place. This provided a 'blackmailer's charter' and posed a threat to the careers and reputations of gay men if their sexual orientation were exposed.

The 1967 Act removed the criminal nature of homosexuality. However, a number of legal discriminations remained. Anal sex remained illegal (whether gay or straight), gay men were still committing an offence if they indulged in group sex, gay couples had no joint property and pension rights comparable to heterosexuals and the age of consent for gay men remained at 21 years. Gay activists challenged these and other legal discriminations.

The age of consent for gay men remained at 21 after the 1967 Act, while heterosexual sex was legal at 16. Gay rights activists attacked the different age limits as discriminatory, unfair and against equal rights principles. They argued that gay people knew their sexuality at the same age as straight people.

If this was the case, the age of consent created undue suffering for gay teenagers and unfair criminalising of adult males having sex with young men (whereas it was not a crime to have sex with women over 16). After many years of campaigning the age of consent was reduced to 18 in 1994 and then further to 16 in 2001, but only after the Parliament Act had been invoked to overturn the opposition of the House of Lords to the proposed legislation.

The law recognises only heterosexual couples as having the right to marry. According to gay rights activists, gay couples suffer legal discrimination in pension, social security and property rights because they are not allowed to marry. The law needs to be changed to give long-term gay couples the right to some form of legally recognised 'marriage' (for want of a better word) with its concomitant rights and obligations.

Immigration legislation is also believed to discriminate against gay people. British citizens can bring into the country their alien wives and husbands, but not their non-British gay partners. This is another area of gay rights campaigning.

Whatever legal improvements occur in society gay men and women face considerable discrimination in work and social situations that damages their receipt of equal rights and equal opportunities and amounts to 'oppression' of a group of people on the grounds of sexual orientation. Gay activists assert that the majority heterosexual society (the one that generates most sexual criminality) has established a dominant ideology that asserts their sexual activities as 'normal' and gay sex as 'perverted', 'deviant' and 'abnormal'. This sanctions discrimination and also verbal and physical assaults on gay people and their property. It also creates a culture of intimidation that makes straight politicians and other holders of power in society unwilling to address gay concerns for fear of damaging their own careers and personal standing.

It is believed that there are far more gay MPs than have openly declared their sexuality and that gay people are less likely than straight to be chosen by political parties as candidates for parliament, especially the Conservative Party and the Labour Party in some of the old industrial constituencies. This belief may owe more to perceptions of popular prejudice than to reality. There is little evidence that voters are unwilling in large numbers to vote against a gay candidate. Indeed, anti-gay votes are likely to be countered by the votes attracted to candidates who openly state their gay sexuality. 'Outing', the publicising of the gay sexuality of reticent public figures, is a controversial tactic used by some gay rights campaigners – a strategy that their opponents within the gay community say does more harm than good to the cause of equal rights opportunities for gay people. Gay activists in groups such as 'Stonewall' and 'Outrage' have been willing to 'out' MPs and other public figures who support anti-gay legislation or make anti-gay statements in public.

Another target of gay rights campaigners is the insurance industry, which discriminates against gay males, in particular in policy acceptance, premiums and payouts, because of AIDS. Gay men in Western societies are more likely to suffer with HIV and AIDS than are heterosexuals. Some insurance companies refuse to offer policies to gay men, others charge significantly higher premiums for gay men than straight and all offer lower rewards on completion of policies if the policyholder is a gay man.

Some gay activists target the major religions, especially Christianity, Judaism and Islam, for homophobic beliefs which legitimise anti-gay beliefs in society and contribute to the social oppression of gays.

Sexual orientation does not easily equate with formal political ideologies and gay activists attack all the major political parties for their homophobic policies. Much gay rights political activity has strong elements of counter-culture to it. 'Outing', 'gay pride' marches and the provocatively outrageous activities of some gay activists in pursuit of gay rights might, in the minds of moderate gays and their supporters, cause more harm than good. Unhelpful stereotypes of gay people are reinforced in some campaigns even when these campaigns are themselves attacking the stereotyping of gays by heterosexual culture as consisting of butch women, effeminate men and 'screaming queens'.

However, perhaps such high-profile campaigning by gay rights activists is important. There are still widespread assumptions in society that homosexuality, especially male homosexuality, is deeply 'wrong'. Improving the treatment of gay people in society is a matter not just of changing legal discrimination, but also of changing the attitudes of the majority of the population. There is still a long way to go.

Animal rights movements

Animal rights campaigners are concerned with many aspects of humanity's relationship with the animal world. Fundamentally, activists object to the exploitation of animals by humans in whatever area: for food, as an industrial resource, as objects of scientific testing, or for sport. Upholders of animal rights, even from ancient times, have a concern that the abuse and exploitation of animals somehow weakens the moral restraints placed on humans not to abuse and exploit other people. They often identify a close link between the denial of rights for animals, especially the higher primates such as chimps and gorillas, and the denial of full and equal rights to some classifications of humans on the spurious bases of race, gender, sexual orientation and disability.

Many philosophers of the Enlightenment in the seventeenth and eighteenth centuries argued strongly that animals did not have any rational basis for rights as compared to humans. Animals were not rational, did not have a consciousness, and were merely resources placed on earth for human convenience. Any attempt to give them rights was not only nonsense but would weaken the claims human beings had to a moral autonomy superior to the rest of creation.

However, by the late eighteenth century some thinkers were attempting to place restraints on human cruelty to animals. Jeremy Bentham, in *Introduction to the Principles of Morals and Legislation* (1789), declared that humans were wrong in seeing rationality as the basis for treating animals with care: 'The question is not, Can they *reason*? Nor Can they *talk*? But Can they *suffer*?' It is the perceived *suffering* of animals that led to bans on badger , bull and bear baiting, and cock fighting over the century after Bentham and may eventually lead to the banning of fox, deer and hare hunting with dogs in the twenty-first.

Concern over cruelty, exploitation and suffering led many in Britain during the nineteenth century to establish the major principles of vegetarianism. The growth of vegetarianism closely paralleled the rise of a wide range of radical and socialist movements which have campaigned for human rights and better animal welfare legislation over the last two centuries.

Strictly speaking, one should distinguish between animal *rights* movements, which emphasise the moral status of non-human creatures, and animal *welfare* movements, which seek to improve the conditions under which animals are reared for food or used as pets. Animal rights activists often dislike animal welfare campaigners as the latter accept the subordinate position of animals in relation to humans but desire to improve the conditions under which they are kept. Some animal rights campaigners assert that exploitation, not welfare, is the issue.

We shall cast a very cursory glance at a number of areas in which animal rights campaigners are active.

Modern writers, such as Tom Regan in *The Case for Animal Rights* (1983) and Peter Singer in *Animal Liberation: A New Ethics for our Treatment of Animals* (1965), have argued that animals possess rights, rights that are oppressed and abused by humans. Animals can feel suffering, have some understanding of their environment and are thus entitled to proper treatment from humans. In recent years, genetic science has reinforced the case for human rights to be recognised as appertaining to chimpanzees and gorillas and other higher primates who share almost all the genetic make-up of *homo sapiens sapiens*.

Many animal rights campaigners attack vivisection and animal experimentation on the grounds that they are part of the structure of exploitation of animals by men. The British Union for the Abolition of Vivisection, for example, rejects the claim made by scientists that animal experimentation is necessary for scientific and medical research. Computer technology and other means of research have made vivisection redundant, according to the Humane Research Trust (another anti-vivisection group). The government is condemned for being more concerned with the needs of business than with animal welfare. Particularly objectionable are farms that breed animals for experimentation.

Factory farming methods are also a target of animal rights campaigners. The conditions under which animals are raised for intensive food production disregard animal welfare and are primarily concerned with protecting business interests and the supply of cheap food.

Hunting is a special target of animal rights campaigners as it is simply exploiting animals for sport. Particularly subject to condemnation is fox hunting (especially as it is perceived as combining cruelty and high-class status). If some cruel sports such as badger baiting are banned, why should other animal cruelty sports still be legal? Cruel sports exploit animals, involve inflicting pain and fear and degrade the people who take part in them. Some success in the campaign against fox hunting was achieved in 2002 when the Scottish Parliament voted to introduce a ban on hunting with dogs. The Scottish decision will have an impact on the anti-hunting campaign in England and Wales.

Animal rights campaigning uses every form of political action, from protesting and attempting to lobby government to terrorism. Some animal rights campaigners have sought to work within organisations such as the National Trust and the RSPCA to bring about change. They have had very limited success. The Animal Liberation Front appeals to a higher moral law than legislation when it campaigns against the exploitation of animals by businesses, whose interests are protected by the same oppressive legal system that allows animal exploitation and cruelty. Other direct-action campaigners are not interested in having a dialogue with hunters or animal experimenters, or even in influencing public opinion. They see traditional political methods as having failed to protect animal rights and the level of animal suffering as too great to wait for a change in public opinion or for eform through government action.

The competitive nature of ideologies and movements

Some of the movements we have discussed are, by the standards of the 'dominant' ideologies of the Western world, 'extreme' or 'fundamentalist'. This is not surprising. Most ideologies and movements in their early stages are in competition with and in opposition to the prevailing beliefs and opinions of their age. With the exception of conservatism, all the other movements we have looked at underwent long periods of apprenticeship as 'new' movements, challenging the established social values and social and political order of their day. One can identify a number of 'stages' through which they pass to become, sometimes, part of mainstream ideas.

1 They have to establish clear parameters to their own ideological distinctiveness. What are they trying to say? What does someone have to believe as a set of core values in order to be part of this movement? This often creates an impression of extremism and radicalism, generating bitter resistance to the ideas of the new movement in mainstream society.

2 The political and ideological struggle of the new movement will have no access to power in its early stages of development. It lacks the need to compromise, to adjust to other views, and to face the realities of power. Thus a level of ideological purity can be maintained that is never possible once in government. Governments that attempt to pursue ideologically pure programmes usually result in terror for millions. A regime that is built on an immature ideology tries to make or reform society in its own image, to force reality into conformity with its theoretical straitjacket.

3 If such a movement fails to achieve power quickly, as is usually the case, the compromises required to attain power will mean that, over time, it becomes less 'radical', more 'pragmatic', more 'respectable', its ideas becoming part of the 'common-sense' ideological baggage of society. It will have made the transition from being primarily a 'restrictive' ideological movement to being a 'relaxed' one: from a movement less concerned with detailed understanding of the ideas of the key thinkers associated with it to one that attempts to bring into play policy programmes broadly in sympathy with basic – but flexible – principles.

4 Eventually, the movement may become part of the 'establishment', the 'dominant' ideology of its society, the 'respectable consensus'. As such, while it may make references to its past and present 'radicalism', it will, in practice, have no desire to reform society significantly along the lines envisaged by its early idealists. It is thus likely to provoke new critiques of society, new plans for reform, new movements and new ideological debate.

These stages, for want of a better word, will not take place in a vacuum. They are usually 'archaeological' records of social and economic, intellectual and moral changes and the struggles connected with them. Ideologies and movements that fail to adapt to social change, that do not reflect its direction and impetus, will not only have a declining influence on society but will cease to be politically relevant and will eventually fade from the political scene.

One recent intellectual movement – 'fashion' might be a more accurate term – that has attempted to recreate a vacuum at the heart of political analysis is 'post-modernism'. Post-modernism asserts that there is no objective truth and no ultimate reality. It challenges the assumption of the Enlightenment that it is possible to use reason to understand reality as a unified and integrated theoretical construct and so be able to impose intellectual order and understanding on the world. Post-modernists claim that social reality is too complex to be subject to the tenets of the major ideological traditions.

Some might find this a reasonable response to the modern world. But one needs to *understand* the world, to make sense of it in order to act. There is the great danger that post-modernism simply leads to a nihilistic world view, an intellectual atomisation and an inability to act to make the world a better place, or at least to stop it getting worse. Post-modernism might be an interesting academic debate, but it may not be one that citizens and politicians facing real and pressing problems are willing to join.

The importance of rationality

Western society over the last three centuries or so has been greatly influenced by the Enlightenment. The Enlightenment took many forms in different European countries during the late seventeenth and through the eighteenth centuries. It presupposed the importance of rational thought, enquiry, belief in progress, investigation of evidence, a rejection of superstition, a dislike of irrational thought, and a scepticism about all religious, moral and scientific thinking.

Concurrent with this intellectual movement there has been the continuing presence of atavistic and irrational beliefs, destructive, fatalistic and always waiting, patiently, for the tiring rigours of rationality and experimentation, assessment and rejection of failure to overwhelm their supporters. Out of these dark crannies of the minds of millions come irrational and radical movements and ideas trying to change society in their image. The members of such movements regard their goals as so important that they devalue and degrade constitutional structures and promote simple solutions to complex problems, solutions often associated with a romanticised view of violence as a political tool. They also appeal to the supreme 'truth' of their belief that those who resist or do not share their views are 'legitimate' targets for terror, death and the infliction of pain.

Such elemental ideological forces can be easily identified in fascism, extreme nationalism, far left-wing politics, and religious fundamentalism of all kinds. But ideological flight from reality into irrationality can also be observed in some parts of the environmental and animal rights movements, *and* in feminism, liberalism, conservatism and socialism. The demands of 'political correctness' in many American universities have played a valuable role in challenging many of the assumptions of an ideological world of 'dead, white, European males'. All too often, political correctness has become a means by which those who do not share the same ideological and political agenda are subject to abuse rather than debate, threats rather than arguments, and in some cases disciplinary procedures and loss of jobs, all in the cause of advancing 'disadvantaged' groups in liberal societies.

The values of an open society will not be defended if its enemies are only to be identified by their wearing of swastika armbands, red berets or the accoutrements of religion. Ideological oppressions associated with political movements and ideas one supports must also be subject to the same level of critical analysis one applies to the opinions one dislikes if a free society worth the name is to be sustained.

Glossary of major figures

The following individuals are among the most important of those mentioned in the text. Space precludes going into detail, but we hope by means of three or four short sentences at least to place them in the context of their time and work.

Louis ALTHUSSER (1918–90)   French Marxist philosopher. Stressed scientific nature of Marxism. Knowledge was a 'production process' involving theoretical raw materials related to the society of the day and its particular circumstances. The economy determined knowledge only 'in the last resort'. Major works: *For Marx* (1969), *Lenin and Philosophy, and Other Essays* (1971).

St Thomas AQUINAS (c.1224–74)   Italian Dominican friar and Aristotelian scholar. Major theologian and writer. Produced rational basis for arguing the existence of God. Very influential in the development of the concept of the just war. Strong believer in the moral basis of political activity. Major work: *Summa Theologica* (1266–73) (60 volumes).

Hannah ARENDT (1906–75)   German-Jewish philosopher and political theorist. Fled Nazi Germany to the USA and became citizen. Particularly concerned with justice and order in society. Saw modern political thinking as having abandoned political values for social ones. Major works: *The Origins of Totalitarianism* (1951), *On Revolution* (1963), *Eichmann in Jerusalem* (1963).

ARISTOTLE (384–322BC)   Athenian scientist, educator and philosopher. Student of Plato and teacher of Alexander the Great of Macedon. Major figure in the study of politics. Classifier of political systems. Founded a university in Athens known as the *Lyceum*. Critical of radical democracy, preferring government by the educated and competent few. Major influence on the development of science until the Renaissance and on political science until the present. Major work: *The Politics*.

Clement ATTLEE, First Earl (1883–1967)   Leader of the British Labour Party (1935–55), deputy prime minister during World War (1942–45), and prime minister (1945–51). As PM he led a government that established the welfare state, nationalised many key industries, began dismantling the British Empire, and authorised the British A-bomb project.

St AUGUSTINE of Hippo (354–430)   Roman bishop, writer, rhetorician and theologian from North Africa. Defended the newly established state religion of Christianity against its critics. Only earthly state can protect men as God can. Politics and government seeks peace but can never replace Christianity as the true object of life. Evil in the world is the conscious decision to misuse free will. Major work: *City of God* (413–25).

Caius Octavianus AUGUSTUS (63BC–AD14) Roman politician and statesman. Adopted son of Julius Caesar. Destroyed Caesar's assassins in civil war. Defeated Mark Antony and Cleopatra in another civil war. Became first Roman emperor. Restorer of the Roman world after a century of wars. One of the Western world's greatest – and most ruthless – political geniuses.

Michael BAKUNIN (1814–76) Russian anarchist, revolutionary and atheist. Opposed Marx in the First International. Saw state and religion as working together to oppress mankind. Identified need for free communities of people working together with communal property rights. Not a systematic thinker and writer. Never completed his major books.

Stanley BALDWIN, First Earl of Bewdley (1867–1947) British Conservative PM (1923–24, 1924–29, 1935–7). Dominated inter-war British politics. Symbol of political stability in the turmoil of the inter-war years. Chief figure in the abdication crisis of Edward VIII in 1936.

John BALL (d.1381) English priest and leader of the Peasants' Revolt (1381).

Simone de BEAUVOIR (1908–86) French feminist writer and philosopher. Author, among many other things, of *The Second Sex* (1949), which was a major influence on 'second-wave' feminism. Its key argument is that 'a woman is not born, but made'.

Samuel BEER (b.1911) Contemporary American political scientist. Specialist in British politics.

Daniel BELL (b.1919) American political scientist and sociologist. Neo-conservative polemicist. Argues that politics is not longer ideological, but is dominated by practical problems of economic growth and social reform. Suspicious of big government. Author of *The End of Ideology* (1960) and *The Coming of Post-Industrial Society* (1973).

Tony BENN (b.1925) British Labour politician, diarist, broadcaster. Minister in Labour governments in the 1960s and 1970s. On left of the party. Supporter of constitutional reform. Campaigned to become Labour leader in 1980s. Author of *Arguments for Socialism* (1980) and *Arguments for Democracy* (1981).

Jeremy BENTHAM (1748–1832) British Utilitarian philosopher and legal writer. Humans are motivated by self-interest and the pursuit of happiness. These are basis for democratic government, law and social policy. Great influence on nineteenth-century liberalism. Main works: *Fragments on Government* (1776) and *Principles of Morals and Legislation* (1789).

Sir Isaiah BERLIN (1909–97) British university teacher and writer. Great influence on liberal thought, especially his *Two Concepts of Liberty* (1957). Other major works: *Karl Marx* (1939), *The Lion and the Fox* (1953), *Four Essays on Liberty* (1969).

Eduard BERNSTEIN (1850–1932) German Social Democrat politician, journalist and leading thinker on revisionist socialism. Saw himself as modernising Marxism in light of modern developments. Sought a peaceful transition to socialism. Major work: *Evolutionary Socialism* (1898).

Sir William BEVERIDGE, First Baron Beveridge (1879–1963) British civil servant and economist. Chair of the Beveridge Committee that produced the 1942 White Paper on the establishment of the social security element of the welfare state.

Otto von BISMARCK, Prince Bismarck, Duke of Lauenburg (1815–98)   Prussian-German statesman and creator of the Second German Empire (1871–1918).

Robert BLACHFORD (1851–1943)   British leading figure in the early Independent Labour Party (ILP).

Tony BLAIR (b.1953)   British Labour leader (1994–) and prime minister (1997–). Moderniser of Labour Party under banner of New Labour. Replaced Clause IV and the 'socialist' commitment to public ownership. Moved party to the right. Led party to landslide election victories in 1997 and 2001.

John BRIGHT (1811–89)   British radical Quaker orator and politician. Along with Richard Cobden he was a leading figure in the Anti-Corn Law League that campaigned for free trade in the 1830s and 1840s.

John BRUCE-GLASIER (1859–1920)   British Independent Labour Party figure.

Charles BUKOWSKI (1920–94)   American poet and author.

Edmund BURKE (1729–97)   British-Irish politician, thinker and writer. Usually identified as inspiring conservatism and its values. Great believer in social stability, limited government and gradual change, tradition. Supported many of the demands of the American colonists but was highly critical of the French Revolution. Major work: *Reflections on the Revolution in France* (1790).

George W. BUSH (b.1946)   Republican president of the USA (2001–). Former governor of Texas. Seen as a right-wing conservative. Strong advocate of unilateralist American foreign policy initiatives such as National Missile Defense and withdrawal from some arms control and environmental treaties.

R. A. BUTLER, Richard Austin ('RAB'), and Baron Butler of Saffron Walden (1902–82)   Senior British Conservative politician. On the liberal-left of the party. Responsible for Education Act (1944) and aided Conservative acceptance of the welfare state. With Labour's Hugh Gaitskell he gave his name to *Butskellism* to describe Conservative and Labour economic policies of the 1950s.

Rachel CARSON (1907–64)   American scientist, biologist and writer. Major work: *Silent Spring* (1962).

Houston Stewart CHAMBERLAIN (1855–1927)   British, later German, writer on racist structuring of human society. Saw Germanic peoples as superior. Major work: *The Foundations of the Nineteenth Century* (1899). Much admired in Nazi Germany as an influential thinker on racial theory.

Joseph CHAMBERLAIN (1836–1914)   British Radical and, later, Conservative politician. Made his reputation as a social reformer in Birmingham politics. A leading political figure of his time. Campaigned against Irish Home Rule and for partial trade protection measures.

CHARLEMAGNE, Charles the Great (742–814)   King of the Franks. Created an empire that covered most of modern France, Belgium, the Netherlands, Germany and parts of Spain and Italy. Holy Roman Emperor (800–814). Seen as an early advocate of a united Europe.

Winston Spencer CHURCHILL (1874–1965)   Conservative, Liberal and again Conservative politician and statesman. Major twentieth-century British political figure. Nobel Prize winner. Soldier, historian, orator, writer. Held several government posts over a long political career: home secretary, first lord of the Admiralty, minister of munitions, lord chancellor and several others. Prime minister (1940–45 and 1951–55). Crucial role as war leader in the Second World War. Wrote *A History of the English Speaking Peoples*, memoirs of both world wars, a biography of Marlborough and many other articles and books.

Marcus Tullius CICERO (106–43BC)   Roman writer, orator, lawyer, statesman and philosopher. Major figure during the last century of the Roman Republic. Held many senior government posts. Put down the Cateline Conspiracy to overthrow the state. Opponent of Julius Caesar and later Mark Antony and Octavian. Executed by Mark Antony. Surviving writings include *Letters*, *Speeches*.

Richard COBDEN (1804–65)   British manufacturer and politician. With John Bright, the leading advocate of free trade and the Anti-Corn Law League. His campaign, resulting in the repeal of the Corn Laws in 1846, ruined him financially.

G. D. H. COLE, George Douglas Howard (1889–1959)   British economist, journalist and academic. Leading social-democratic thinker. Advocated 'Guild Socialism', a co-operative system co-ordinated by the state. Wrote *A History of Socialist Thought* (1953) and many studies of Fabian and Marxist socialism, as well as contributing to practical ideas for social improvement.

Bernard CRICK (b.1929)   Former British professor of politics. Major works: *In Defence of Politics* (1962), *Essay on Citizenship* (2000).

Anthony CROSLAND (1918–77)   British Labour politician, economist and writer. Social-democratic thinker and writer. Held many government posts: foreign secretary, education secretary, local government minister. Wrote *The Future of Socialism* (1956).

Charles DARWIN (1808–82)   British naturalist. Theorist on evolution, based on researches conducted on world voyage in the *Beagle*. Major work was *The Origin of Species* (1859). Ideas on 'natural selection' as the engine of evolution were distorted by late nineteenth-century political thinkers into the concept of 'Social Darwinism' to advocate racism, imperialism and class domination.

Jacques DELORS (b.1925)   French politician and civil servant. President of the European Commission (1985–95). Strong advocate of European Union. Formulated 'Delors Plan' for the creation of a single European currency.

Jacques DERRIDA (b.1930)   French linguistic philosopher, literary critic and psycho-analyst. Major work: *Margins of Philosophy* (1972).

René DESCARTES (1596–1650)   French mathematician and philosopher. Challenged the scholarly tradition and dogmas of his day. Sought to understand the basis for truth. Cartesian philosophy can be summed up in his phrase, 'I think, therefore I am'.

Charles DICKENS (1812–70)   British novelist. Massive number of novels and letters. Supporter of social reform and social justice. Best-known writings: *Oliver Twist* (1837), *A*

Christmas Carol (1843), *Great Expectations* (1860-1), *A Tale of Two Cities* (1859, *David Copperfield* (1849–50).

Benjamin DISRAELI, First Earl of Beaconsfield (1804–81)   British Conservative politician. Novelist: *Coningsby* (1844) and *Sybil* (1845). Coined notion of 'two nations' in Britain that modern Conservatism should strive to bring together. Hence, creator of 'one-nation conservatism'. Prime minister (1868 and 1874–80). Popular imperialist and advocate of a greater role for skilled working-class people in the democratic process (under Conservative leadership).

Iain DUNCAN SMITH (b.1954)   British Conservative politician. Party leader (2001–).

Ronald DWORKIN (b.1931)   Lawyer and jurist. Major work: *Taking Rights Seriously* (1978).

Paul EHRLICH (b.1932)   American population biologist. Author of many works on environmental and population matters, most notably *The Population Bomb* (1968).

T. S. ELIOT, Thomas Stearns (1888–1965)   American, later British, writer and poet. Politically, on the right: 'a classicist in literature, a royalist in politics and an Anglo-Catholic in religion'. Chief works include: *Prufrock* (1917), *Murder in the Cathedral* (1935), *The Waste Land* (1922), *Four Quartets* (1935–42).

Friedrich ENGELS (1820–95)   German socialist. Part of the 'Manchester circle' of German industrialists. Major work: *The Condition of the Working Class in England* (1845). Collaborated with – and financially supported – Karl Marx. Many joint works on socialism and revolution. Major collaborative effort: *The Communist Manifesto* (1848). Worked to create a revolutionary workers' movement. Major role in establishing Marx's reputation after his death in 1883.

Q. FABIUS MAXIMUS, CUNCATOR ('Delayer') (275?–203BC)   Roman general during Second Punic War (218–201BC). Sought to defeat Carthaginians by delaying battle until such a time as would be most favourable to victory.

Louis FARRAKHAN, Louis Eugene Wolcott (Louis X) (b.1933)   Black American leader of radical 'Nation of Islam'.

Johann Gottlieb FICHTE (1762–1814)   German philosopher and nationalist. Seen as one of the intellectual ancestors of German nationalism in the nineteenth century and German totalitarianism in the twentieth.

Sir Robert FILMER (d.1653)   English royalist. Defender of hereditary monarchy. Major work: *Patriarcha: or the Natural Power of Kings* (1680). John Locke's *First Treatise on Government* is a refutation of Filmer.

Michael FOOT (b.1913)   British Labour politician and journalist. On left of the party. Leader of the Labour Party 1980–83.

Michel FOUCAULT (1926–84)   French philosopher. Saw power as widely spread in society. Exercised within and outside formal political institutions in a manner that severely limits real choice. Actions become self-evident truths that ensure compliance by most people in being controlled. Major works: *Power/Knowledge: Selected Interviews and other writings 1972–1977* (1980).

Charles FOURIER (1772–1837)   French utopian socialist, social reformer. Advocate of a system of associated enterprises as an alternative to capitalism.

Anatole FRANCE, Jacques Anatole François Thibault (1844–1924)   French novelist, poet, critic. Nobel Prize winner (1921).

General Francisco FRANCO (1892–1975)   Spanish general and Fascist dictator (1939–75).

Betty FRIEDAN (b.1921)   American feminist writer and activist in 'second-wave' feminism. Founded National Organisation of Women (NOW). Author of *The Feminine Mystique* (1963).

Milton FRIEDMAN (b.1912)   American economist. Leading member of 'Chicago School' of economics. Major theorist of tight monetary control by government ('monetarism'). Very influential on neo-liberal and New Right politics. Strong critic of Keynesianism. Chief works: *Capitalism and Freedom* (1962), and, with wife Rose, *Free to Choose* (1980).

Erich FROMM (1900–80)   German psychoanalyst and social philosopher. His *To Have and To Be* (1979) discusses the drive to ownership and consumerism in a materialist society.

Francis FUKUYAMA (b.1952)   American political writer on the right. Very influential in the US Republican Party and the New Right. Analyst for both US government and private business. Major work: *The End of History and the Last Man* (1992). Controversially claimed that liberal democracy was the end product of human political development – especially in the wake of the end of the Cold War.

Hugh GAITSKELL (1906–63)   British Labour politician and economist, on right of the party. Labour leader 1955–63. Advocated reform of the Labour Party to make it more electable.

William Lloyd GARRISON (1805–79)   American campaigner for the abolition of slavery.

José ORTEGA Y GASSET (1883–1955)   Spanish philosopher and writer. Author of *The Revolt of the Masses* (1930), a critical account of mass society.

Charles de GAULLE (1890–1970)   French general and statesman. Leader of Free French forces after fall of France (1940). First president of the Fifth Republic (1959–69). Suspicious of American domination of Western Europe. Rejected British applications to join the EEC in 1963 and 1967.

Ernest GELLNER (b.1925)   Cambridge academic and social anthropologist. Major work: *Nations and Nationalism* (1983).

Sir Ian GILMOUR, Lord Gilmour of Craigmillor (b.1926)   British historian and Conservative politician on left of the party.

William Ewart GLADSTONE (1809–98)   British Liberal politician and statesman, classical scholar. Chancellor of the exchequer, prime minister (1868–74, 1880–5, 1886, 1892–4). Dominated British politics throughout most of the nineteenth century. Strong supporter of liberal causes at home and abroad. Supported Irish Home Rule, failed to implement it in the face of opposition both within and outside the Liberal Party.

Arthur GOBINEAU, Count Joseph Arthur de (1816–82) French aristocrat and racial theorist. His *Essay on the Inequality of Human Races* (1859) was highly influential on development of theories of racial hierarchy, and, later, on Nazi theories of racial superiority.

William GODWIN (1756–1836) British philosopher and political writer. Strong influence on anarchist and socialist thinking. Married Mary Wollstonecraft. Father of Mary Shelley, author of *Frankenstein*. Major work: *An Enquiry Concerning Political Justice* (1793).

Mikhail GORBACHEV (b.1931) Soviet politician and statesman. Last leader of the USSR (1985–91). Sought to reform the communist system and end the Cold War with the West. Began end of Soviet domination of Eastern Europe.

T. H. GREEN, Thomas Hill (1836–82) British philosopher and social reformer. Major influence on the development of New Liberalism. Critical of *laissez-faire* liberalism. Saw a limited role for the state in improving individual and social conditions. Major works: *Prolegomena on Ethics* (1883) and *Lectures on the Principles of Political Obligation* (1879–80).

Germaine GREER (b.1939) Australian feminist writer. Major works: *The Female Eunuch* (1970) and *Sex and Destiny* (1985).

William HAGUE (b.1961) British Conservative politician. Leader of the Conservative Party (1997–2001).

Lord HAILSHAM, Quintin HOGG (1907–2001) British Conservative politician and lawyer. Lord chancellor under Edward Heath and Margaret Thatcher. Supporter of constitutional reform. Wrote a number of books on British politics, notably *Elective Dictatorship* (1976) and *Dilemma of Democracy* (1977).

Keir HARDIE (1856–1915) British Labour politician. One of the founders of the Labour Party. First Labour MP.

Roy HATTERSLEY (b.1932) British Labour politician, journalist and commentator. Holder of several senior Cabinet posts.

Friedrich von HAYEK (1899–1992) British political philosopher and economist of Austrian descent. Strong believer in liberty. Major influence on neo-liberalism and New Right ideas of the 1980s and 1990s. Major works: *The Road to Serfdom* (1948), *The Constitution of Liberty* (1960) and *Law, Legislation and Liberty* (1979).

Denis HEALEY (b.1917) British Labour politician on right of the party. Has held many senior posts in government, notably defence minister, chancellor of the exchequer.

Sir Edward HEATH (b.1916) Senior Conservative politician and statesman. Tory Party leader 1965–75). Prime minister (1970–74). Deeply committed to British membership of the EU.

G. W. F. HEGEL, Georg Wilhelm Friedrich (1770–1831) German philosopher and university teacher. Very influential on nineteenth century thought, especially Marx. Developed model of dialectical thinking (hypothesis–antithesis–synthesis–hypothesis) as the way knowledge develops. Saw the state as an ethical ideal: 'The Divine Idea as it exists on earth'. Major works: *Phenomenology of Spirit* (1807) and *Philosophy of Right* (1821).

Johann Gottfried HERDER (1744–1803)   German poet, philosopher and theorist of nationalism. Major Romantic and anti-Enlightenment thinker. Saw nations as having a distinct cultural 'spirit', natural units into which humans are divided. Strongly anti-state as it crushes national spirit.

Heinrich HIMMLER (1900–45)   German Nazi leader of the SS. Played a key role in the organisation of the state terror and extermination of Jews and others as part of Hitler's New Order in Europe. Condemned to death at Nuremburg war crimes trials. Committed suicide.

Adolf HITLER (1889–1945)   German leader of the Nazi Party. Created it as powerful political force. Chancellor of Germany (1933–45). Instituted totalitarian dictatorship and the suppression of opposition parties and organisations. Persecutions and attempted extermination of Jews and others identified as 'sub-humans'. Ideas clearly laid out in *My Struggle* (1925). Committed suicide.

Thomas HOBBES (1588–1679)   English political philosopher, mathematician and classical scholar. Lived through the Civil Wars, Cromwell's rule and the Restoration. Argued for a strong state to ensure order in society. Suspicious of democracy as leading to strife and civil war. Major work: *Leviathan* (1651).

L. T. HOBHOUSE, Leonard Trelawney (1864–1929)   British sociologist, academic and journalist. Leading influence on development of New Liberalism. Strong role for the state in promoting individual liberty and social good. Major works: *The Theory of Knowledge* (1896), *Morals in Education* (1906), *Development and Purpose* (1913).

J. A. HOBSON, John Atkinson (1858–1940)   British economist and writer of economics and sociology. Made significant contribution to New Liberalism. Major works: *The Evolution of Modern Capitalism: a Study of Machine Production* (1894), *Imperialism* (1902).

Quintin HOGG, *see* Lord Hailsham

Saddam HUSSEIN (b.1937)   President of Iraq (1969–2003).

H. M. HYNDMAN, Henry Mayers (1841–1931)   British socialist leader. Helped found (Social) Democratic Federation (1881). Left to form National Socialists (1916). Defender of Marxism in several books.

Thomas JEFFERSON (1743–1826)   Third American president (1801–9). Major figure in the American Revolution and War of Independence (1776–83). Helped draft *Declaration of Independence* (1776).

Peter JENKINS (b.1934)   British journalist, political commentator and broadcaster.

Sir Keith JOSEPH (1918–95)   British Conservative politician. Held senior Cabinet posts under PMs Heath and Thatcher. Major influence on development of New Right and neo-liberal opinions in the Conservative Party during the 1980s.

Karl KAUTSKY (1854–1938)   German Social Democratic journalist, theorist and politician. Strong Marxist element to his thought when he was young. Became less of a Marxist in later life.

Alesander KERENSKY (1881–1970)   Russian socialist. Led Russian government after the overthrow of the tsar from May to November 1917. Fled Russia when Bolsheviks seized power. Settled in USA.

John Maynard KEYNES, First Baron (1883–1946)   British economist of New Liberal views. Major influence on the social-democratic consensus and on mid-twentieth-century economic thought by his *Treatise on Money* (1930) and *The General Theory of Employment, Interest and Money* (1936). Stressed the importance of using state economic levers to ensure full employment.

Nikita S. KHRUSHCHEV (1894–1971)   Soviet politician and statesman. Became Soviet leader soon after the death of Stalin (1953). Began de-Stalinisation process at home and improvement of relations with the West abroad. Built Berlin Wall (1961). Overthrown in 1964 after perceived failures, including the Cuban Missile Crisis (1962).

Neil KINNOCK (b.1942)   British Labour politician. Leader (1983–92). European commissioner.

Peter KROPOTKIN (1842–1921)   Russian aristocrat, explorer, geographer and anarchist thinker and writer. Argued for the creation of a society of self-sufficient communities. Major works: *The Conquest of Bread* (1906), *Fields, Factories and Workshops* (1901) and *Mutual Aid* (1902).

Harold J. LASKI (1883–1950)   British socialist writer, academic and Labour politician on the left of the party. Major work: *Democracy in Crisis* (1933).

V. I. LENIN (Vladimir Ilyich ULYANOV) (1870–1924)   Russian revolutionary leader of the Bolsheviks (1893–1917) and Soviet leader (1917–24). Major reviser of Marxism in voluminous writings. Created concept of a revolutionary elite to lead the working classes in revolution. Major works: *The Development of Capitalism in Russia* (1899), *What Is To Be Done?* (1902), *Imperialism: The Highest Stage of Capitalism* (1916).

Jean-Marie LE PEN (b.1928)   French politician. Leader of the French National Front, a party of the far right.

Primo LEVI (1919–87)   Italian writer, chemist and commentator. Survivor of Auschwitz. Wrote accounts of his experiences in books such as *If This Is A Man* (1947) and *If Not Now, When?* (1982).

David LLOYD GEORGE, First Earl of Dwyfor (1863–1945)   British Liberal politician and statesman. As chancellor of the exchequer in 1909 introduced National Insurance as part of the 'People's Budget'. Prime minister (1916–22). One of main figures at the Versailles Peace Conference (1919).

John LOCKE (1632–1704)   English liberal political philosopher, epistemologist, medical and psychological researcher. His political writings stressed tolerance, the existence of natural rights, the importance of property, the need for representative government, justification for revolt. Very influential in British and American political thought. Major works: *Essay Concerning Human Understanding* (1690), *A Letter Concerning Toleration* (1689), *Two Treatises on Government* (1690).

LOUIS XIV (1638–1715)   French monarch. Established the principle of 'absolutism' after many years of domestic conflict. Dominated Europe.

James LOVELOCK (b.1919)   British scientist and writer. Developed the 'Gaia Hypothesis' that sees the planet as a living, self-regulating system.

Georg LUKÁCS (1885–1971)   Hungarian philosopher and critic. Marxist theorist. Stalinist and supporter of the infallibility of the Communist Party. Major work: *History and Class Consciousness* (1923).

James Ramsay MACDONALD (1866–1937)   British Labour politician. A founder of the Labour Party. Prime minister (1924, 1929–31 and 1931–5). His forming and leadership of a Conservative-dominated coalition government in 1931 split the Labour Party.

Niccolo MACHIAVELLI (1469–1527)   Italian/Florentine writer, public official, diplomat and playwright. Advocate of Italian unity. Established many of the major theoretical principles of modern political science. Developed a theory on state power and how to get and keep it. In his major works, *The Prince* and *The Discourses on Livy*, was seen to advocate an immoral and wicked approach to practical politics. The church placed his works on the Index of banned books after his death.

Alistair MACINTYRE (b.1929)   British academic and philosopher. Major works: *Short History of Ethics* (1963), *Secularism and Moral Change* (1967).

Iain MACLEOD (1913–70)   British Conservative politician on 'one nation' wing of the party.

Harold MACMILLAN, First Earl of Stockton (1894–1986)   British Conservative politician. Held many senior posts in government. Prime minister (1957–63). In retirement was very critical of Mrs Thatcher's social and economic policies.

John MAJOR (b.1943)   British Conservative politician. Held several senior government posts before becoming Prime minister (1990–7).

Rev. Thomas R. MALTHUS (1766–1834)   British economist. Supporter of liberal economic principles. His rather gloomy *Essay on the Principles of Population* (1798) argued that population would tend to outstrip food supply unless kept under control.

MAO ZEDONG (1893–1976)   Chinese nationalist and communist leader. Leader of China (1949–76). Revised Marxist-Leninist thinking to claim that revolution can occur in a peasant as well as an industrial society. Believed in continuous revolution of the masses. Stirred up the disastrous 'Cultural Revolution' in China during the 1960s.

Herbert MARCUSE (1898–1979)   German neo-Marxist political philosopher. Strong critic of industrial capitalism and its oppression. Stressed revolutionary potential of groups other than the working classes. Major works: *Reason and Revolution* (1941), *Eros and Civilisation* (1958) and *One Dimensional Man: Studies in the Ideology of Advanced Capitalist Society* (1964).

Karl MARX (1818–83)   German revolutionary socialist. Highly methodical and original thinker. Major sociologist, historian and economist. Journalist and political activist. Collaborated with Friedrich Engels on development of socialist theory and critical analysis of capitalism. Voluminous writer. The greatest single influence on the development of socialist thought in the nineteenth and twentieth centuries. Major works: *German Ideology* (1846), *Communist Manifesto* (1848), *Capital* (1867, 1885, 1894).

Giuseppe MAZZINI (1805–72)   Italian nationalist leader, revolutionary, republican and fighter for Italian unity and independence. Believed that world peace would follow when all peoples lived under their own national governments.

Friedrich MEINECKE (1862–1954)   German historian. Distinguished between 'cultural nations' and ' political nations'. The former tend to have strong cultural unity, the latter are more open. Major work: *Cosmopolitanism and the National State* (1907).

Robert MICHELS (1876–1936)   German sociologist. In *Political Parties* (1911) Michels developed his 'iron law of oligarchy': all organisations, however democratic or socialist, are essentially run by specialised oligarchies, dominating apathetic and subordinate members.

James MILL (1773–1836)   British philosopher, radical and economist. Closely associated with Utilitarianism and classical liberalism. Supporter of the values of middle classes. Father of J. S. Mill.

J. S. MILL, John Stuart (1806–73)   British Utilitarian and liberal philosopher, sometime MP. Great defender of individual freedom against tyrannical government and tyrannical public opinion. Supported votes for women and working-class rights. A considerable influence in development of liberal theory. Major works: *On Liberty* (1859), *Considerations in Representative Government* (1861), *The Subjection of Women* (1869).

Kate MILLET (b.1934)   American feminist writer of 'second-wave' feminism. Major work: *Sexual Politics* (1970).

John MILTON (1608–74)   English poet and political figure of the Civil Wars and Interregnum. Justified the trial and execution of Charles I in *The Tenure of Kings and Magistrates* (1649). Defended the principle of press freedom in *Areopagitica* (1644). Major poetical work: *Paradise Lost* (1667).

Juliet MITCHELL (b.1940)   British Marxist socialist and feminist. Strong on interplay of economic, social and cultural elements in position of women in society. Major work: *Women's Estate* (1971).

Charles de Secondat, Baron de la Brede et de MONTESQUIEU (1689–1755) French philosopher. His *Spirit of the Laws* (1748) identified and discussed the concept of the 'Separation of Powers' of legislature, executive and judiciary. Great influence on American Constitution.

Thomas MORE (1478–1535)   English statesman and writer. Chancellor under Henry VIII. Refused to recognise Henry as head of the Church of England. Executed. Major work: *Utopia* (1516).

William MORRIS (1834–96)   British utopian socialist, poet and craftsman. Saw industrialisation as undermining the pleasure of craftsmanship. Founded Socialist League and Works and Crafts Movement.

Herbert MORRISON, Baron Morrison of Lambeth (1888–1965)   Senior Labour politician of the 1930s and 1940s. Architect of nationalisation policies of the 1940s.

Gaetano MOSCA (1857–1941)   Italian political sociologist and legal academic. Theorist of elitism. In *The Ruling Class* (1896) he saw elite rule a fact of history. Elites exploit the ruled and seek to turn themselves into permanent elites.

Oswald MOSLEY (1896–1980)   British politician. Once a leading Labour figure. Founder and leader of British Union of Fascists. Imprisoned during the Second World War.

Charles MURRAY (b.1943)   American conservative writer and thinker. Attempts to explain poverty and the creation of the 'underclass' in terms of welfare dependency and individual inadequacy. Major works: *Losing Ground: American Social Policy (1950–1980)* (1984), *The Bell Curve* (1995).

Benito MUSSOLINI (1883–1945)   Italian Fascist leader and dictator (1922–43). Initially sceptical of Hitler, he allied Italy with Nazi Germany.

NAPOLEON I (Bonaparte) (1769–1821)   French general and emperor (1804–14). Brought order to France after the Revolution. Conqueror of much of Europe. Supported expanding frontiers of human knowledge. Innovator in government and law. Major influence on nineteenth-century politics, even after his defeat, exile and death.

NAPOLEON III (Bonaparte) (1808–73)   French emperor (1852–71). Nephew of Napoleon I. Overthrew the Second French Republic. Pursued expansionist foreign policy. Defeated by Germany in Franco-Prussian War (1870–71).

Sergei NECHAEV (1847–82)   Russian revolutionary and apostle of terrorist violence. Major work: *Revolutionary Catechism* (1869).

Sir Isaac NEWTON (1642–1727)   English scientist and mathematician. Discoverer of the laws of gravity.

Friedrich NIETZSCHE (1844–1900)   German philosopher, writer and essayist. Major European thinker. Great believer in the importance of 'Will' in history and society, and the role of strong individuals. Ideas picked up and misused by Nazis. Major works: *Thus Spoke Zarathustra* (1883–4), *Beyond Good and Evil* (1886), *Ecce Homo* (1908), *The Will to Power* (1901).

Steven NORRIS (b.1945)   British Conservative politician of liberal views. MP (1983–97).

Robert NOZICK (1938–2002)   American philosopher and politics academic. Great influence on New Right politics. Supporter of minimal state and minimal intervention. Strong defence of property rights should be the basis of government and society. Major work: *Anarchy, State and Utopia* (1974).

Michael OAKESHOTT (1901–90)   British conservative political philosopher. Very influential thinker on modern New Right. Stressed important role of civil associations to underline his support for a limited role for the state. Major works: *Rationalism in Politics and Other Essays* (1962), *On Human Conduct* (1975).

George ORWELL, Eric Blair (1903–50)   British socialist, journalist and novelist. Major political novels were *Animal Farm* (1945) and *Nineteen Eighty-Four* (1949).

Mosei OSTROGORSKI (1854–1919)   Russian political scientist. Argued that modern political parties were controlled by senior figures who undermined democratic influence of individual members. Major work: *Democracy and the Organisation of Political Parties* (1902).

Robert OWEN (1771–1858)   British utopian socialist, philanthropist and wealthy self-made manufacturer. Challenged *laissez-faire* economic doctrines. Influential on development of co-operative movement and British socialism. Experimented in new forms of economic and social life at New Lanark (Scotland) and New Harmony (USA).

Thomas PAINE (1737–1809)   British political writer and radical. Supported and was personally involved in American Revolution and French Revolution. Personally involved in both. Stressed egalitarianism and individual freedom. Influential on both socialism and liberalism. Major works: *The Rights of Man* (1791/2), *The Age of Reason* (1794).

Matthew PARRIS (b.1949)   British broadcaster and journalist. Once a Conservative MP.

Sir Robert PEEL, Second Baron (1788–1850)   British Conservative politician and statesman. Held several Cabinet posts, including home secretary where he established the police force. Repealed Corn Laws (1846). Supported Catholic Emancipation (1829). Prime minister (1834–35, 1841–46).

PERICLES (*c.*490–429BC)   Athenian statesman.

Philippe PÉTAIN (1856–1951)   French general and politician. Hero in the First World War. President of the Vichy regime which collaborated with Nazi Germany (1940–44). Imprisoned after the Second World War.

General Augusto PINOCHET (b.1915)   Chilean general and politician. Overthrew elected government of Salvador Allende (1973). President of Chile (1973–98).

PLATO (427–347BC)   Athenian philosopher. Pupil of Socrates and teacher of Aristotle. Founded a university in Athens, the *Academy*. Writings are one of the most influential collections in history. Often seen as founding philosophy. His major works are *Republic* and *Laws*. The former advocates a structured society with trained specialists as political leaders. Major influence on the early development of Christianity and on Western culture.

Georgii V. PLEKHANOV (1856–1918)   Russian Marxist thinker. Invented term 'dialectical materialism'. Introduced Marxism into Russian revolutionary movements.

Sir Karl R. POPPER (1902–94)   British philosopher of Austrian descent. Defender of liberal values and scientific thought. Opponent of Nazism and communism. Very influential on neo-liberalism in the 1970s and 1980s. Major works: *The Open society and Its Enemies* (1945), *The Poverty of Historicism* (1957), *The Logic of Scientific Discovery* (1959).

Michael PORTILLO (b.1953)   British Conservative politician.

Enoch POWELL (1912–98)   British Conservative and, later, Unionist politician on the right of the party. Strongly opposed non-white immigration into Britain. Opposed Britain's membership of the European Union. Suspicious of US power in the world.

Pierre-Joseph PROUDHON (1809–65)   French socialist and anarchist thinker. Early writings stress a strong opposition to the state. Later writings see role for a very minimal state. Major works: *System of Alternative Economics* (1846), *What is Property?* (1840), *The Federal Principle* (1863).

Samuel von PUFENDORFF (1632–94)   German writer on law. Major work: *Of the Law and Nature of Nations* (1672).

Thomas RAINSBOROUGH (d.1648)   English soldier and republican advocate during the Civil War.

John RAWLS (1921–2002)   American political philosopher. Very influential thinker on liberalism and social democracy. Major works: *A Theory of Justice* (1970), *Political Liberalism* (1993).

Ronald REAGAN (b.1911)   Thirty-ninth president of the USA (1981–89). Presided over massive US military build-up and record federal budget deficit. But instrumental in helping to bring Cold War to an end in the 1980s.

David RICARDO (1772–1823)   British economist, politician and stockbroker. Political radical. Founder of classical school of political economy. Major work: *Principles of Political Economy and Taxation* (1817).

Oscar ROMERO (1917–80)   Salvadorean Roman Catholic bishop and Nobel Prize winner (1979). Murdered after speaking out in favour of the poor.

Jean-Jacques ROUSSEAU (1712–78)   French political philosopher and educational theorist. Offended French government. Major intellectual influence on French Revolutionary thought. Belief in natural human goodness and the corrupting influence of civilisation on human nature. Wide impact on socialist, liberal, anarchist and fascist ideas. Concept of the 'General Will' a basis for democracy and totalitarianism. Major works: *The Social Contract* (1762), *Emile* (1762), *Confessions* (1770).

Salman RUSHDIE (b.1947)   British novelist and journalist. Offended orthodox Muslims by his *The Satanic Verses* (1988) and subsequently went into hiding after death threats.

John RUSKIN (1819–1900)   British author, social philosopher and art critic; established the Pre-Raphaelites. Founded Ruskin College, Oxford, for working people. Highly critical of capitalist industrialism and its damaging impact on beauty, sound social relationships and misuse of wealth.

Claude, Comte de SAINT-SIMON (1760–1835)   French aristocrat and socialist. With Robert Owen and Charles Fourier, Saint-Simon is seen as one of the founding fathers of socialism. Stressed importance of application of knowledge to solution of social problems.

Lord SALISBURY, Robert Arthur Salisbury, Third Marquess (1830–1903)   British Conservative politician and statesman. Held numerous senior government posts. Prime minister (1885–86, 1886–92, 1895–1902).

Michael SANDEL (b.1953) Contemporary American professor of government. Communitarian thinker, one of several who have stressed the failings of liberal individualism. Has written many books on politics and democracy. Major work: *Liberalism and the Limits of Justice* (1982).

Hjalmar SCHACHT (1877–1970)   Nazi German finance minister.

Fritz SCHUMACHER (1911–77)   British-German environmental theorist, conservationist and economist. Stress on importance of self-help technology for developing nations. Major work: *Small is Beautiful: Economics As If People Mattered* (1973).

Joseph Alois SCHUMPETER (1883–1950) Austrian-American sociologist and economist. Stress on the role of the innovative capitalist in economic change. 'Creative destruction' is at heart of capitalism. Major works: *Theory of Economic Development* (1912), *Business Cycles* (1939), *Capitalism, Socialism and Democracy* (1942).

Roger SCRUTON (b.1944) British Conservative philosopher and historian of philosophy.

Claude de SEYSSEL (c.1510) Councillor to King Louis XII of France.

George Bernard SHAW (1856–1950) Irish playwright, commentator and wit. Member of Fabian society.

Samuel SMILES (1812–1904) British doctor and writer. Advocate of individual effort and initiative as outlined in biographies of great engineers and, chiefly, *Self Help* (1859).

Adam SMITH (1723–90) British economist. In *The Wealth of Nations* (1776) he outlined the basic theory of free-market economics. Of considerable influence on the development of nineteenth-century liberalism and modern neo-liberalism.

John SMITH (1938–94) British Labour politician and leader 1992–1994.

Georges SOREL (1847–1922) French supporter of revolutionary violence. Very influential on fascist thinking. Major work: *Reflections on Violence* (1905).

Herbert SPENCER (1820–1903) British philosopher and journalist. Supporter of evolutionary concepts. Major work: *Principles of Psychology* (1855) and *Man Versus the State* (1884).

Baruch SPINOZA (1632–77) Dutch philosopher. Major writings are on religion and ethics.

Joseph STALIN, Joseph Djugeshvili (1879–1953) Soviet leader (1924–53) and dictator. Developed concept of 'Socialism in One Country' and shaped Marxist theory to suit his own grip on power. Industrialised USSR in 1930s. Massive purges of real and imagined opponents in 1930s under 'The Terror'. Deal with Nazi Germany in August 1939 did not prevent the USSR being attacked in 1941. War leader in Second World War. Spread communist control over a number of states in Eastern Europe.

Max STIRNER, real name Johann Casper Schmidt (1806–56) German philosopher. Influential on Marx and individualist anarchism. Major work: *The Ego and His Own* (1845).

R. H. TAWNEY, Richard Henry (1880–1962) British socialist, educator and economic historian. Active in trade union and Labour movement. One of first critics of an affluent society. Believed that capitalism created moral disorder. Major works: *Religion and the Rise of Capitalism* (1926), *The Acquisitive Society* (1921), *Equality* (1931).

Harriet TAYLOR (1807–58) British feminist. Wife of J. S. Mill. Influenced his views on female suffrage.

Margaret H. THATCHER (b.1925) British politician. Leader of Conservative Party (1975–90). Supporter of neo-liberal and New Right policies for social reform.

Alexis de TOCQUEVILLE (1805–59)   French aristocrat, liberal historian, sociologist and politician. Very influential thinker on the problems of democracy. Author of *Democracy in America* (1835 and 1840).

Leo TOLSTOY (1828–1910)   Russian aristocrat, novelist and pacifist. Writer of considerable eminence. Chief works: *War and Peace* (1863–9), *Anna Karenina* (1873–7).

Destutt de TRACEY (1754–1836)   French philosopher. Invented term 'ideology' as the science of ideas.

Leon TROTSKY, Lev Davidovich Bronstein (1879–1940)   Russian revolutionary and opponent of Stalin. Supporter of concept of global revolutionary movement for socialism. Murdered by Stalin's agent in 1940.

Franjo TUDJMAN (1922–99)   Croatian president (1990–99). Academic historian and Croatian nationalist. Declared Republic of Croatia independent of Yugoslavia (1992).

Graham WALLAS (1858–1932)   British socialist and political psychologist. Stressed the irrational forces that influence politics. Major works: *Human Nature and Politics* (1908), *The Great Society* (1914).

Michael WALZER (b.1935)   American academic in politics, history, moral philosophy, concepts of the just war and the welfare state.

Barbara WARD (1914–81) and Rene DUBOS (1901–82)   Ward was a British economist, journalist and conservationist, Dubos an American-French genetic scientist. Authors of *Spaceship Earth* (1966) and *Only One Earth: The Care and Maintenance of a Small Planet* (1972).

Beatrice WEBB (1858–1943) and Sidney WEBB, Baron Passfield (1859–1947) Leading British members of the Fabian Society, researchers in economic and social history, and campaigners for social reform.

Max WEBER (1864–1920)   German sociologist. Major theorist of social class, bureaucracy and development of capitalism. Believed that he was modernising Marxism – although usually seen as challenging it. Major work: *The Protestant Ethic and the Spirit of Capitalism* (1904–5).

Ann WIDDECOMBE (b.1947)   British Conservative politician and novelist.

Harold WILSON, Baron Wilson of Rievaulx (1916–95)   British Labour politician, academic and writer. Cabinet minister in post-war Labour Government. Labour leader (1963–75). Prime minister (1964–70 and 1974–76). Author of a number of books on British politics and Cabinet government.

Thomas Woodrow WILSON (1856–1924)   27th US President (1913–21). Liberal and idealist politician. Took USA into the First World War. At Versailles Peace Conference pressed for national self-determination and the League of Nations. Introduced women's suffrage.

Gerrard WINSTANLEY (1609–after 1660)   English radical pamphleteer. Leader of the Diggers movement for land reform. Influential on socialist ideas. Major work: *The Laws of Freedom in a Platform* (1652).

Mary WOLLSTONECRAFT (1759–97)   British early feminist and campaigner for women's rights. Major work: *A Vindication of the Rights of Woman* (1792).

William WORDSWORTH (1770–1850)   British poet. Particularly associated with Lakeland and the Romantic movement. Major works: *Lyrical Ballads* (1798), *The Prelude* (1850), 'Intimations of Immortality from Recollections of Early Childhood' (1807).

Suggested further reading

Below is a portion of the vast literature available for further reading in this subject and which has been consulted during the preparation of this book. Key texts by major authors are cited in individual chapters and so are not included here. You should also keep up to date with *Talking Politics* and *Politics Review*, magazines that often publish articles about political ideas and movements. Ultimately, even the best textbooks cannot keep you abreast of how key ideas relate to the world of politics. Regular reading of good-quality newspapers and newsmagazines is vital to developing a fully rounded grasp of the subject. We particularly recommend the *Guardian Weekly* and *The Economist*. Similarly, television and radio (especially BBC2 and Radio 4) broadcast many valuable and interesting programmes that relate to the issues raised by this book.

Adams, A., *The Logic of Political Belief* (Harvester Wheatsheaf, 1989).

Adams, I., *Ideology and Politics in Britain Today* (Manchester University Press, 1998).

Alter, P., *Nationalism* (Edward Arnold, 1989).

Anderson, B., *Imagined Communities: Reflections on the Origins and Spread of Nationalism* (NLB/Verso, 1983).

Arblaster, A., *The Rise and Decline of Western Liberalism* (Blackwell, 1984).

Bacherach, P., and M. Baratz, 'The Two Faces of Power', in F. G. Castles, D. J. Murray and D. C. Potter (eds.), *Decisions, Organisations and Society* (Penguin, 1981).

Barbalet, J. M., *Citizenship* (Open University Press, 1988).

Barker, E., *Principles of Social and Political Theory* (Oxford University Press, 1961).

Barker, J., *Arguing for Equality* (Verso, 1987).

Bartleson, J., *A Genealogy of Sovereignty* (Cambridge University Press, 1995).

Bauman, Z., *Freedom* (Open University press, 1988).

Beauvoir, S. de, *The Second Sex* (Penguin, 1953).

Bedau, H. A. (ed.), *Justice and Equality* (Prentice-Hall, 1971).

Beer, S., 'The Roots of New Labour: Liberalism Rediscovered', *The Economist* (7 February 1998), pp. 23–5.

Bellamy, R., *Liberalism and Modern Society: An Historical Argument* (Polity Press, 1992).

Berki, R. N., *Modern Ideology: SOCIALISM* (J. M. Dent, 1975).

Berlin, I., 'Two Concepts of Liberty', in *Four Essays on Liberty* (Oxford University Press, 1958).

Birch, A. H., *The Concepts and Theories of Modern Democracy* (Routledge, 1993).

Bosenquet, B., *The Philosophical Theory of the State* (Macmillan, 1923).

Bottomore, T. B. and M. Rubel, *Karl Marx, Selected Writings in Sociology and Social Philosophy* (Penguin, 1974).

Bramwell, A., *Ecology in the 20th Century: A History* (Yale University Press, 1989).

Bryson, V., *Feminist Political Theory: An Introduction* (Macmillan, 1992).

Bryson, V., *Women in British Politics* (Huddersfield Pamphlets in History and Politics, 1994).

Burleigh, M., *The Third Reich: A New History* (Macmillan, 2000).

Callaghan, J., *Socialism in Britain since 1884* (Blackwell, 1990).

Connelly, J. and P. Norris, 'Making Green Policy: A Guide to the Politics of the Environment', *Talking Politics* 4:2 (1991/92,), pp. 96–100.

Cooper, R., 'Dawn Chorus for the New Age of Empire', *Sunday Times* (28 October 2001).

Coxall, B. and L. Robins, *Contemporary British Politics*, 2nd edn, (Macmillan, 1994).

Cranston, M., *Freedom: A New Analysis* (Longmans, 1954).

Cranston, M., *What are Human Rights?* (The Bodley Head, 1963).

Crespigny, A. de and K. Minogue, *Contemporary Political Philosophers* (Methuen, 1976).

Crichley, T. A., *The Conquest of Violence* (Constable, 1970).

Crick, B., *Socialism* (Open University, 1987).

Crick, B. (ed.), *National Identities: The Constitution of the United Kingdom* (Blackwell, 1991).

Crick, B., *In Defence of Politics* (Penguin, 1994).

Dahl, R., *Democracy and its Critics* (Yale University Press, 1989).

Deutsch, K., *Nationalism and Social Communication* (Massachusetts Institute of Technology, 1953).

Dobson, A., *The Green Reader* (Andre Deutsch, 1991).

Dobson, A., *Green Political Thought: An Introduction* (Routledge, 1992).

Drucker, H., P. Dunleavy, A. Gamble and G. Peele (eds.), *Developments in British Politics* (Macmillan, 1984).

Drucker, H., P. Dunleavy, A. Gamble and G. Peele (eds.), *Developments in British Politics 2* (Macmillan, 1988).

Dunleavy, P., A. Gamble and G. Peele, *Developments in British Politics 3* (Macmillan, 1990).

Dunleavy, P., A. Gamble, I. Holliday and G. Peele (eds.), *Developments in British Politics 4* (Macmillan, 1993).

Dunn, J. (ed.), *Democracy: The Unfinished Journey 508BC to AD1993* (Oxford University Press, 1992).

Duprat, G., N. Parker and A.-M. Rieu (eds.), *WHAT IS EUROPE? Book 3: European Democratic Culture* (The Open University and European Association of Distance Teaching Universities, 1993).

Dutton, D., *British Politics Since 1945: The Rise and Fall of Consensus* (Blackwell, 1991).

Dworkin, R., *Taking Rights Seriously* (Duckworth, 1979).

Eagleton, T., *Ideology: An Introduction* (Verso, 1991).

Eatwell, R., *Fascism: A History* (Vintage, 1996).

Eatwell, R. and A. Wright (eds.), *Contemporary Political Ideologies* (Pinter, 1993).

Eccleshall, R., *British Liberalism: Liberal Thought from the 1640s to 1980* (Longman, 1986).

Eccleshall, R., V. Geoghegan, R. Jay, M. Kenny, I. MacKenzie and R. Wilford, *Political Ideas: An Introduction* (Routledge, 1996).

'Liberalism Defined: The Perils of Complacency', *The Economist* (21 December 1996), pp. 19–21.

'Survey: FULL DEMOCRACY: Happy 21st century, voters!', *The Economist* (21 December 1996).

'Nations and their Past: The Uses and Abuses of History', *The Economist* (21 December 1996), pp. 53–6.

Etzioni, A., *The Spirit of Community* (Fontana, 1995).

Femia, J., *Gramsci's Political Thought* (Oxford University Press, 1981).

Finer, S. E., *Comparative Government* (Penguin Books, 1974).

Finnis, J., *Natural Law and Natural Rights* (Clarendon Press, 1980).

Flathman, R., *Political Obligation* (Atheneum, 1972).

Friedman, D., *The Machinery of Freedom* (Harper & Row, 1973).

Gellner, E., *Nations and Nationalism* (Blackwell, 1983).

Goodwin, B., *Using Political Ideas* (John Wiley and Sons, 2001).

Goodwin, G. L., 'The Erosion of External Sovereignty?' *Government and Opposition*, 9:1 (1974), pp. 61–78.

Goodwin, R. E., *Green Political Theory* (Polity Press, 1992).

Gray, J., *Liberalism* (Open University Press, 1995).

Gray, T., *Freedom* (Macmillan, 1990).

Green, D. G., *The New Right* (Wheatsheaf Books, 1987).

Griffin, R., *The Nature of Fascism* (Routledge, 1993).

Griffin, R. (ed.), *Oxford Readers: Fascism* (Oxford University Press, 1995).

Hampsher-Monk, I., *A History of Modern Political Thought: Major Political Thinkers from Hobbes to Marx* (Blackwell, 1995).

Harris, G., *The Dark Side of Europe: The Extreme Right Today* (Edinburgh University Press, 1990).

Harris, G., 'The Extreme Right in Contemporary Europe', *Politics Review*, 8:3 (1999), pp. 8–10.

Hastings, A., *The Construction of Nationhood: Ethnicity, Religion and Nationalism* (Cambridge University Press, 1997).

Hattersley, R., *Choose Freedom* (Michael Joseph, 1987).

Hayes, P., *Fascism* (Allen and Unwin, 1973).

Heater, D., *Citizenship: The Civil Ideal in World History, Politics and Education* (Longman, 1990).

Held, D. (ed.), *Models of Democracy* (Polity, 1987).

Held, D., *Political Theory Today* (Polity, 1991).

Held, D., 'Democracy: From City-states to a Cosmopolitan Order', *Political Studies*, 11 (1992), pp. 10–39.

Held, D., *Prospects for Democracy* (Polity, 1996).

Heywood, A., *Political Ideas and Concepts: An Introduction* (Macmillan, 1994).

Heywood, A., *POLITICS* (Macmillan, 1997).

Heywood, A., *Political Ideologies: An Introduction* (Macmillan, 1998).

Hinsley, F. H., *Sovereignty* (Cambridge University Press, 1986).

Hobsbawm, E., *Nations and Nationalism since 1780* (Cambridge University Press, 1990).

James, A., *Sovereign Statehood* (Allen and Unwin, 1986).

Jowett, M., 'New Feminism in Contemporary Britain', *Politics Review*, 9:3 (2000), pp. 12–14.

Kedourie, E., *Nationalism* (Hutchinson, 1985).

Kennedy, P., *Preparing for the Twenty-First Century* (HarperCollins, 1993).

Kemp, S. and J. Squires, *Oxford Readers: Feminism* (Oxford University Press, 1995).

Laslett, P. and W. G. Runciman, *Philosophy, Politics and Society* (Blackwell, 1972).

Leach, R. *Contemporary Political Studies: BRITISH POLITICAL IDEOLOGIES* (Philip Allen, 1991).

Lichtheim, G., *A Short History of Socialism* (Fontana/Collins, 1977).

Lovenduski, J. and V. Randall, 'Feminist Perspectives on Thatcherism', *Talking Politics*, 3:3 (1991).

MacIntyre, A., *Marxism and Christianity* (Penguin, 1971).

Macpherson, C. B., *The Life and Times of Liberal Democracy* (Oxford University Press, 1977).

Manning, D. J., *Modern Ideologies: LIBERALISM* (J. M. Dent, 1976).

Matthews, R. I., *International Conflict and Conflict Management* (Prentice Hall, 1984).

McLellan, D., *Ideology* (Open University, 1995).

Meldon, A. (ed.), *Human Rights* (Wadsworth, 1970).

Merkl, P. H. and L. Weinberg (eds.), *The Revival of Right-Wing Extremism in the Nineties* (Frank Cass, 1997).

Millar, J. D. B., *The World of States* (Croom Helm, 1981).

Morgenthau, H. J. and K. W. Thompson, *Politics Among Nations* (Alfred A. Knopf, 1985).

Myers, N. (ed.), *The Gaia Book of Planet Management* (Pan, 1985).

Nolte, E., *Three Faces of Fascism* (Mentor, 1969).

Oakeshott, M., *Rationalism in Politics* (Methuen, 1962).

O'Rourke, P. J., *All the Trouble in the World* (Picador, 1994).

O' Sullivan, N., *Modern Ideologies: CONSERVATISM* (J. M. Dent, 1976).

Pateman, C., *The Problem of Political Obligation* (Wiley, 1979).

Plamenatz, J., *Ideology* (Macmillan, 1972).

Plamenatz, J., *Man and Society, Volume One* (Longman, 1976).

Plamenatz, J., *Man and Society, Volume Two* (Longman, 1976).

Plant, R., *Modern Political Thought* (Blackwell, 1991).

Ponting, C., *A Green History of the World* (Sinclair-Stevenson, 1991).

Porritt, J., *Seeing Green: The Politics of Ecology Explained* (Blackwell, 1984).

Purnell, R., *The Society of States: An Introduction to International Politics* (Weidenfeld and Nicolson, 1973).

Purvis, J., 'Equal Opportunities for Women', *Talking Politics*, 2:1 (1989), pp. 20–3.

Rae, D., *Equalities* (Harvard University Press, 1981).

Raphael, D. D. (ed.), *Political Theory and the Rights of Man* (Macmillan, 1967).

Raphael, D. D., *Problems of Political Philosophy* (Macmillan, 1976).

Rees, J. C., *Equality* (Macmillan, 1972).

Renwick, A. and I. Swinburn, *Basic Political Concepts* (Stanley Thornes, 1990).

Ryan, A. (ed.), *The Idea of Freedom* (Oxford University Press, 1979).

Sabine, G. H. and T. L. Thorson, *A History of Political Theory* (Dryden Press, 1973).

Sandel, M. (ed.), *Liberalism and its Critics* (Blackwell, 1984).

Sassoon, D., *One Hundred Years of Socialism* (Fontana, 1997).

Scruton, R., The *Meaning of Conservatism* (Macmillan, 1984).

Seliger, M., *Ideology and Politics* (Allen and Unwin, 1976).

Shaw, R., *The Labour Party Since 1945* (Blackwell, 1997).

Smith, A., *The Ethnic Origins of Nations* (Blackwell, 1986).

Smith, A., *National Identity* (Penguin, 1991).

Spiller, J., 'A Future for British Fascism?' *Politics Review*, 9:2 (1999), pp. 10–12.

Tawney, R. H., *Equality* (Allen and Unwin, 1931).

Thomas, G. P., 'British Politics 1945 to Date: The Postwar Consensus', *Taking Politics*, 7:2 (1995), pp. 117–24.

Thomson, D. (ed.), *Political Ideas* (Penguin, 1966).

Thurlow, R., *Fascism in Britain* (Blackwell, 1987).

Vincent, A., *Modern Political Ideologies* (Blackwell, 1996).

Waldren, J., *The Problems of Rights* (Oxford University Press, 1984).

Walter, N., *The New Feminism* (Little, Brown, 1998).

Watts, D., 'The Growing Attractions of Direct Democracy', *Talking Politics*, 10:1 (1997), pp. 44–9.

White, R. J., *The Conservative Tradition* (Adam and Unwin, 1964).

Wilding, P., 'Equality in British Social Policy Since the War', *Talking Politics*, 2:2 (1989/90), pp. 54–8.

Woodcock, G., *Anarchism* (Penguin, 1983).

Wright, A., *British Socialism* (Longman, 1983).

Wright, A., *Socialisms: Theories and Practices* (Oxford University Press, 1987).

Wright, A., 'Social Democracy and Democratic Socialism', in R. Eatwell and A. Wright (eds.), *Contemporary Political Ideologies* (Pinter, 1993), pp. 78–99.

Wright Mills, C., *The Marxists* (Penguin, 1975).

Index